MURDERER
WITH A
BADGE

Also by Edward Humes:

BURIED SECRETS

MURDERER
WITH A
BADGE

THE SECRET LIFE OF A ROGUE COP

EDWARD HUMES

A DUTTON BOOK

DUTTON
Published by the Penguin Group
Penguin Books USA Inc., 375 Hudson Street,
New York, New York 10014, U.S.A.
Penguin Books Ltd, 27 Wrights Lane,
London W8 5TZ, England
Penguin Books Australia Ltd, Ringwood,
Victoria, Australia
Penguin Books Canada Ltd, 10 Alcorn Avenue,
Toronto, Ontario, Canada M4V 3B2
Penguin Books (N.Z.) Ltd, 182–190 Wairau Road,
Auckland 10, New Zealand

Penguin Books Ltd, Registered Offices:
Harmondsworth, Middlesex, England

First published by Dutton, an imprint of New American Library,
a division of Penguin Books USA Inc.
Distributed in Canada by McClelland & Stewart Inc.

First Printing, November, 1992
10 9 8 7 6 5 4 3 2 1

 REGISTERED TRADEMARK—MARCA REGISTRADA

LIBRARY OF CONGRESS CATALOGING IN PUBLICATION DATA:

Humes, Edward.
    Murderer with a badge : the secret life of a rogue cop / Edward
Humes.
        p. cm.
    Includes bibliographical references.
    ISBN 0-525-93498-7
    1. Leasure, William Ernest. 2. Criminals—California—Los
Angeles—Biography. 3. Police—California—Los Angeles—Biography.
4. Police corruption—California—Los Angeles—Case studies.
5. Murder—California—Los Angeles—Case studies. I. Title.
HV6248.L344H86 1992
364.1'09794'93—dc20   92–52878
                                                                CIP

Printed in the United States of America
Set in Plantin
Designed by Leonard Telesca

Author's Note:
In the interest of protecting the privacy of individuals whose identities are not central to
the true story told here, certain names and other descriptive details have been altered in
several instances.

CONTENTS

ACKNOWLEDGMENTS

In researching *Murderer with a Badge,* I was extremely fortunate to receive the assistance and cooperation of numerous and opposing sources—those who investigated and charged William Leasure; those who supported him and sought to prove his innocence; his friends and alleged accomplices; the long-suffering but painfully open families and friends of the victims; and Leasure himself. The diverse points of view and interpretations these sources represented enabled me to make some sense of the complex facts, events, and voluminous records in the Leasure case. I owe all of them deep thanks.

I would like to acknowledge a special debt of gratitude to Detective Addison "Bud" Arce and retired Detective Henry "Hank" Petroski of the Los Angeles Police Department; Deputy District Attorney James Koller of the Los Angeles District Attorney's Office; Richard Lasting and Michael White, attorneys-at-law; and Sheryl Duvall and Casey Cohen, criminal justice consultants. Their time, patience, and cooperation were invaluable, and deeply appreciated.

As always, my heartfelt thanks go to my editor, Laurie Bernstein; my literary agent, Susan Ginsburg; and my partner, Donna Wares.

MURDERER
WITH A
BADGE

■ PROLOGUE

San Gabriel, California
Sunday, March 20, 1977
6:30 A.M.

IN LATER YEARS, SAN GABRIEL would lose its innocence to drug wars and drive-by shootings, a numbing tide of violence that would settle like smog over this small suburb on the cusp of Los Angeles's parched foothills. In time, the gang-bangers and coke dealers would take over even the legendary stripper bar and police hangout, The Other Ball, where San Gabriel cops once drank beer, played cards, swapped stories, and, they say, provided seamy inspiration for a soon-to-be-famous ex-cop by the name of Joseph Wambaugh. If the fatal events of March 20, 1977, had happened a decade later in this new City of San Gabriel, they would have seemed like business as usual, just another statistic for the files.

But San Gabriel was a very different place on that chilly Sunday morning in 1977, as Gilberto Cervantes drove home from early-morning Mass for the last time. The city remained a drab and sleepy bedroom community in the shadow of Los Angeles, three exits and four square miles off the San Bernardino Freeway, a place where suburban homes on wide, grassy lots could still be bought on a workingman's wage, and where the afternoon smog that steamed off the freeway in hot brown waves still seemed a small price to pay for a slice of the California dream. Most of all, at least in the minds of its citizens, San Gabriel remained a refuge, a place where murder was a curiosity, something that might happen down the road in the big city. But not here, the neighbors would later say. Not on our streets.

Certainly Gilberto Cervantes never saw it coming. He had gotten up before dawn that Sunday, as he did every Sabbath, dressing in his battered suit, bidding his bedridden wife good-bye, then driving the half mile to San Gabriel Mission Church for sunrise Mass. He endured the ritual, silent and grim as always. Then he left his customary offering of two dollars, unchanged after a decade, and departed at quarter past six.

Gilberto drove home in his hulking green Cadillac, one of the few outward signs of prosperity the crusty seventy-six-year-old allowed himself. His house and sprawling grounds were an unkempt mess. He wore secondhand clothes and hoarded boxes of yellowed newspapers and broken appliances in his home—stacked next to the other cardboard boxes filled with cash. Impoverished appearances aside, Cervantes owned twenty-nine houses, apartment buildings, and commercial properties throughout Los Angeles. Add to that the family's thriving tortilla factory and delivery business, and he was worth at least six hundred thousand dollars. The approaching California real estate boom was about to make him a multimillionaire in a few years more. Not bad for a Mexican peasant who grew up barefoot and dirt poor on a barren tenant farm, immigrated to the States in the early twenties, then parlayed a ten-cent-an-hour job frying tortillas into a fortune.

Fifty years later, though, his good fortune made him a target.

As he turned into the driveway of his home at 1527 South Palm Avenue, a light blue pickup truck with a camper shell and two men inside eased to a stop at the curb. One of the men climbed out and padded up the driveway after Gilberto, the dull blue metal of a Smith and Wesson .357 Magnum protruding from his belt, a gardener's gray cloth gloves on his hands. Balding and a trifle heavyset, he spoke in a thick Oklahoma drawl as he leaned in the truck window and told his companion to drive a few houses up the street. The stubby fireplug of a man at the wheel did as he was told, then began to toy nervously with his metal watchband as he waited, engine idling.

The man with the accent raised his gun and took aim as Gilberto pulled into his two-car garage, shut off the Cadillac, and opened the door to get out.

Seven neighbors awakened at the sound of a single gunshot, looked groggily at their bedside clocks, noted the time as around 6:30, then fell back to sleep, certain they had been disturbed by a car's backfire. Later, they would all tell police the same story: It had never occurred to them to investigate the sound or to dial 911. This was, after all, peaceful and safe San Gabriel.

Shot through the heart, Gilberto staggered and slumped

against his open car door, his keys jangling as they fell to the concrete. The gunman walked to his truck and told his companion, "Drive." The pickup drifted slowly, inconspicuously away. As they left, Gilberto pulled himself to his feet and staggered fifty-four feet up the long driveway—an agonizing and amazing journey for a man mortally wounded and left for dead. He was trying to reach the front of the house, and was only a few feet away when he finally collapsed. Nearly two hours passed before passersby spotted him lying dead, frozen in a face-down crouch.

Police investigating the killing found little evidence and no witnesses, other than an elderly woman who had seen a blue pickup with two men inside as she walked her dog that morning. She could not describe either of the men—she had just smiled at them and moved on. The lack of evidence did not surprise investigators. Clearly the motive was not robbery—nothing had been taken, as far as anyone could say. Rather, it looked to be a professional hit, and hit men didn't leave witnesses. Various relatives fell under suspicion, and rumors circulated that a Los Angeles policeman somehow was involved. But there was no proof, no leads, really, and the case quickly made its way to the unsolved homicides file—a thin collection in 1977, but one destined to fill several file cabinets at San Gabriel P.D. in later years. Soon enough, the small department had its hands full with fresher cases. And the Cervantes homicide was forgotten—until ten years had passed, and a stubby man who played nervously with his watchband came forward with a strange, violent story of contract murder and his good friend, an LAPD officer by the name of Bill Leasure.

Los Angeles
April 1991

"What would make a man like you kill?"

William Ernest Leasure shakes his head, then leans forward on the cold metal of the visiting room counter. The handcuffs that bolt him to the leg of his iron stool rattle with the movement. "Nothing," he tells his private investigator. "Absolutely nothing. Seventeen years on the force, and I never even fired my gun."

Leasure pauses. He has the inoffensive expression of a favorite uncle, kindly and bland, although after a time, something seems not quite right about it. Perhaps his manner is just too wildly out of place within the harsh, clanging environment of the jail visiting room, with its chorus line of vacant stares and desultory mutters. Or perhaps it's the penetrating way he looks at you after completing a thought, gauging your reactions, taking note of each facial twitch and posture change. It's something good cops always do . . . and good liars, too.

"I'm the nicest, quietest, mildest guy you'll ever want to meet," Leasure says. "I've never killed anyone. I'd never hurt a fly."

And there lay private investigator Sheryl Duvall's puzzle: He is right. Everything she has uncovered about the man's background and personality screams that he could never be a murderer.

Yet, in a few short weeks, this oddly pleasant man, this police- man accused of thefts, frauds, and murders for hire, will stand trial, and could well begin a lifetime behind bars . . . or be sentenced to inhale boiling cyanide vapor at San Quentin Prison.

Sheryl Duvall is Leasure's last line of defense from that deadly solution, to be brought into court only if he is found guilty of mur- der. If that happens—a very real possibility in everyone's view ex- cept Leasure's—her job is not to prove him innocent, but to prove he deserves to live.

A detective of motivations rather than actions, Duvall is charged with finding in Leasure's past a sympathetic, comprehensi- ble reason why he might kill—and why Leasure might then deserve mercy, rather than retribution, from his jury. Yet, alone amid the long string of capital cases Duvall has examined, an explanation for Bill Leasure has eluded her.

"Because I'm innocent," he says in his sincere, dogged way, and even Duvall, hardened by the broken lives of dozens of other murder cases, has to wonder if this one time, the claim of inno- cence just might be true.

"You can't explain something I didn't do," Leasure insists, eyes locked on hers, his face so pale from long years in jail that he almost seems to glow. "You'll never find a reason for it. Because there isn't any."[1]

PART I

1986

SILENT WATERS

A policeman's lot is not a happy one.
—W. S. GILBERT
The Pirates of Penzance

CHAPTER 1

As the yacht *LA VITA* eased into its slip and the Skipper throttled the twin engines down to a quiet rumble, Bill Leasure leapt lightly from the deck and stooped to tie the mooring lines. He was an average man of average build, his balding scalp a fiery red from the California sun, a man who resembled, more than anything else, a kindly accountant, with his wispy brown mustache and owlish features. He was the sort of person you might look full in the face one moment, then be unable to describe a few minutes later—unless you happened to notice the watchful hazel eyes behind his metal-rimmed glasses, eyes that quietly, dispassionately dissected and observed. Cop's eyes.

Leasure finished securing the lines and climbed back on board the cabin cruiser, where he began stowing gear and packing his bags. They would be leaving the *La Vita* for good that afternoon, another successful trip up the California coast, another blending of profit and pleasure. This trip to sell a yacht made an even dozen, and Leasure felt well satisfied. Calling in sick to his LAPD sergeant, who had heard enough about Leasure's chronically troublesome stomach to last a lifetime, had paid off handsomely once again. Or so it seemed.

The day was Thursday, May 29, 1986, and the *La Vita* had just sailed into a trap. Bill Leasure didn't know it yet, but after this day, he would not see the sun again for more than five years.

Both he and the Skipper had felt uneasy on this journey, though neither could say why. They originally had planned to take the boat to Seattle, but the weather of the Pacific Northwest still churned with the change of seasons—too rough a ride that time of year, even for a stout forty-two-foot vessel like the *La Vita*. They discussed canceling the voyage, but then said no, that would be silly. Instead, they had returned once again to the milder waters of San Francisco's Bay Area, setting aside their vague misgivings.

Now, as he packed, Leasure calmly studied the somnolent harbor. Nothing seemed amiss. This was a weekday, early afternoon, and the marina was deserted, all the boats tied down, their sails furled and covered, outboards lifted from the corrosive salt water.

Even on weekends, the Marina Bay Yacht Harbor remained sleepy, a doggedly upscale enclave carved out of an industrial slum in Richmond, California, part of the coastal sprawl stretching north from San Francisco. Huge cranes, derricks, and towering stacks of rust-speckled shipping containers the size of semi-trailers were visible at the heavily commercial Port of Richmond across a half-mile stretch of water, an image that the gay blue paint and ersatz Cape Cod architecture of the yacht harbor couldn't quite overcome. The oily scum of freighter bilge still migrated from the port, staining the brackish waters of the marina and the glossy white fiberglass of the pleasure boats moored inside. Still, there were plenty of motor yachts and sailboats moored at Marina Bay, and the sound of riggings clanging against metal masts filled the air around Leasure, a chorus of anvils.

As he gathered his things, the Skipper, a short and wiry dock rat by the name of Robert Denzil Kuns, left the *La Vita*'s bridge and headed for the marina clubhouse. "We'll wash up, then go get something to eat," he called to Leasure. "I'm starving."

Leasure nodded and watched his friend make the long walk from their slip—the farthest from the pier gate, carefully chosen for its privacy and its ease of entry and exit. The sun glinted off Kuns's hairless head as he wound through the rows of sailboats and yachts, and Leasure had to chuckle: He always told Kuns he cut quite a figure, with his shining, shaven scalp, Lincolnesque whiskers, and calloused bare feet. As unobtrusive as Leasure might be, Kuns always stood out.

They looked to be an odd pair, but in truth, they had much in common: Both were quiet, even shy at times, able to spend long hours at sea together in a comfortable, close silence. When they did talk, it was usually at night, sitting above deck, their ship and their skin silvered by starlight, their boat hissing through black waters on a cushion of ghostly foam. In wistful voices, they would dream aloud of making their fortune together, then moving to a Caribbean island—preferably one they could buy for themselves. Then they could spend their days chartering boats, basking on the beach, sipping margaritas like a couple of retired buccaneers. This was not idle talk; this was The Plan. And if you were to ask either of them what they thought of the other, they would say, without hesitation, that each trusted the other as a brother. Not bad, considering one wore the midnight blue uniform of the Los Angeles Police Department, while the other sported a rap sheet for armed bank robbery.

"I'm the kind of guy who always sees the best in a person," Leasure would say when some friend on the force would pull him aside and question the propriety of this friendship. "He's a good guy who made a mistake. He deserves the benefit of the doubt."[1] Leasure's LAPD colleagues trusted his judgment, so they shrugged off their concerns. They were certain Bill was a good cop, and good cops didn't hang out with assholes: It was that simple. And when Leasure would bring the other guys from LAPD's Central Traffic Division out on his yacht, with the cooler full of beer and the fish biting, well, any lingering doubts about the Skipper vanished in the spray.

A novice on the water when he first met Kuns, Leasure had become an accomplished seaman under the Skipper's tutelage, capable of navigating treacherous seas and, in the end, becoming a more daring yachtsman than his teacher. Leasure loved nothing better than throttling the engines to the red line, then blasting off into a rough chop, sending the boat lunging and leaping through the waves. Kuns, who tended to imbue boats with human feelings and personality while Leasure considered them mere machines, would wince at such pounding treatment. "You've got to have a feel for what you're putting this poor boat through," he would admonish Leasure time and again. But his normally restrained and unemotional friend would just laugh into the wind, then continue banging ahead at full speed, ocean spray making him squint, a mischievous grin splitting his face. Kuns would end up laughing, too—these trips turned them both into kids.[2]

They had set sail three days before from Southern California, intent on selling the *La Vita* to a Bay Area yacht broker Kuns had dealt with in the past. The broker, Mervin Gray, possessed Kuns's favorite quality: He asked few questions. Leasure had never met the man before, but a short while after Kuns left for the men's room, a smallish, middle-aged fellow approached the *La Vita* and hollered hello. Leasure knew it had to be Gray.

"Come on aboard, I'll show you around," Leasure offered.

With quiet pride, he showed Gray the staterooms, salon, and galley, a mixture of rich dark woods and smooth fiberglass. "I'm getting to know a lot about boats," Leasure said as he conducted the tour. "This one, we brought up from charter service in Mexico. It's really fast. It'll do fifteen knots."

But when Gray asked him the simplest of questions—what make of boat the *La Vita* was—Leasure stammered. "I don't know," he said. "I'm just helping Rob out, crewing for him. He's the expert." Then he changed the subject, offering to show Gray the twin turbocharged diesels that gave the *La Vita* its speed and power.

"I bought a yacht a lot like this one," Leasure remarked a few minutes later, as he dropped the hatch on the engine room. "Only bigger."

"Oh really?" Gray asked. "What kind is that?"

Again Leasure hesitated, looking a trifle embarrassed. "You know, it's a funny thing, but I can never remember that. It's some Taiwan make. They're all the same."

Gray was surprised, but he dropped the subject, biting back the next logical question: How could you possibly buy something as expensive as a yacht and not know what kind it was? Leasure just smiled at him and went about his packing.

By then, Kuns had returned to the boat. He and Gray had settled on a price of forty-five thousand dollars for the *La Vita,* a boat worth at least two and a half times that much, despite its age and weathered condition. "I need a quick sale," the Skipper explained when they shook hands to close the deal. "We want to get on the first plane out of here." The Skipper still was feeling uneasy— something about Gray seemed odd, strained. Again, Kuns chalked up the feeling to an overactive imagination, suppressing the urge to flee. Instead, he and Leasure accepted Gray's offer to take them to lunch in Berkeley, at their favorite Italian restaurant.

Leasure, Kuns, and a third man who had crewed on the *La Vita,* Gino, headed to the yacht broker's motor home in the marina's windswept parking lot. Leasure had started to take their duffel bags off the boat, but Gray suggested they leave them behind. They could come back for the bags after lunch, then head to the airport from the marina. When they agreed to his plan, Gray covered his sigh of relief with a cough.

Now, he knew, there would be ample time to bait the trap.[3]

While the men dined on marinara and pasta, Gray's wife, Gloria, called the Oakland Police Department. Investigators there had been waiting the past week for her call, ever since they learned, quite by chance, that the last yacht Kuns had sold the Grays was stolen. This yacht, the *Coruba,* also was supposed to have been a retired charter vessel out of Mexico. In truth, the Oakland police had discovered, it was really the *Wildcat,* a yacht stolen from the Southern California city of Long Beach.

At the time, the police were not sure who the real thief might be—the Grays, Kuns, or someone using them both as fronts or dupes. The police knew only that the thief was a master. Whoever had stolen the *Wildcat* had skillfully concealed its true identity by rechristening it with a new name, modifying its hull serial numbers, adding new canvas, slapping on a fresh paint job, and, most important, by obtaining genuine registration papers in the name of the *Coruba.* Because the papers were legitimate—the nautical equivalent of obtaining a dead man's birth certificate and claiming it as your own—the transformation and theft were perfect, virtually untraceable. Discovery came only through the unlikeliest of flukes: The sole West Coast distributor for that make and model of boat just happened to drive across the Oakland Estuary at the very moment the *Coruba* was temporarily docked below the bridge for some repairs. The dealer recognized the boat from a wanted poster he had received in his Southern California office a few days earlier. He quickly called the police—and Mervin Gray had a lot of explaining to do.[4]

Cornered in a dismal gray police interrogation room near downtown Oakland, things might have gone badly for the little yacht broker, especially when police investigators hunted down three other boats Kuns had sold Gray in the past year. Those yachts also had been altered with fresh paint and phony hull numbers, then resold by Gray to unwitting yachtsmen throughout the Bay Area. The police knew then that Kuns had to be the thief, and they would have charged Gray as an accomplice as well, except for one thing: He mentioned that Kuns had telephoned just a few days earlier and promised him another yacht within a week or so.

"Maybe I can help you catch him?" Gray suggested, a strained hope making his voice hoarse. "He trusts me, you know."

And, that simple, the trap was laid. Four yachts recovered so far—a half million dollars worth of boats, with more on the way. They didn't know exactly who would be ensnared with Robert Denzil Kuns, but the Oakland Police investigators sensed they were on to something big.[5]

Once Gloria Gray's call came in, the police engineered an elaborate stakeout at the marina. A police helicopter, a Coast

Guard cutter, and a SWAT team were deployed, enough firepower to keep a platoon of Marines at bay. The Grays had warned detectives that Kuns often boasted of keeping machine guns on board for security on the high seas. The police decided to take no chances.

Oakland Police Detective Sergeant William Godwin drew the assignment of searching the *La Vita*, checking for evidence that it was stolen while the stakeout team awaited the crew's return from lunch. Burly and ruddy, with thinning gray hair, Godwin crossed the weathered boardwalk leading to Kuns's slip, a good ten-minute walk from the locked marina gate. From the dock, he checked the engraved hull serial numbers on the transom. Sure enough, he could see they had been altered and replaced with a phony code, just like the *Coruba* and the other boats Kuns had brought to the Bay Area. There was fresh paint on the transom as well. Godwin knew the *La Vita* was another hot yacht.

He clambered on board, peering into the cabin and staterooms to make certain no one was hiding below deck. Then he began a leisurely search of the boat. For the most part, he saw a typical jumble of charts, fishing gear, and cooking utensils—the necessities of daily life aboard any seagoing vessel. There were no machine guns, no obvious contraband. But when he picked up a green canvas athletic bag from the floor of one of the staterooms, he felt a familiar heaviness inside. Godwin unzipped the bag and found a loaded .45-caliber semi-automatic Detonics pistol, two extra clips of ammunition, and a shoulder holster. A quick check of the gun's serial number by police radio gave him the name of the owner: William E. Leasure, address, care of the Los Angeles Police Department.

"Uh-oh," Godwin said to his companion officers. "Whoever stole this boat stole a cop's gun along with it."

He had his dispatcher patch him through to LAPD in an attempt to reach Leasure. He wanted to ask his fellow officer when he had last seen the pistol. Godwin eventually got routed to LAPD's Central Traffic Division, where, he learned, Leasure worked traffic patrol and investigated auto accidents. After several telephone transfers and holds, he was connected to Leasure's watch commander.

"Officer Leasure's not in today," the sergeant told Godwin. "He's home on sick leave for a hiatal hernia."

"Can you call him at home?" Godwin asked, a new suspicion dawning, one he hated to consider, but which suddenly seemed a distinct possibility—that this cop might not be a victim of a theft, but a thief himself.

After a long pause, the sergeant reported that Leasure wasn't answering at home.

"Uh-oh," Godwin said. "We might have a situation up here . . ."[6]

• • •

Rob Kuns is a unique individual. We were friends. He's very likable. He knew a lot about boats, and what he didn't know, he made up. How would I know any different? We had fun. I admit that. It was fun. But I was Kuns's dupe.

Sure I helped him crew five boats. He offered me airfare, expenses, and a sailing trip on a boat. I said sure. Why not? But I never stole a boat in my life. I never knew he was stealing boats. He used me. I can't believe someone who was my friend would use me like that.

And, clearly, I acted like an innocent man. I told people about the trips. I used my own name. I kept records of my expenses and profits— the things the police are using against me now, to say I'm a crook. But if I was a crook, I wouldn't have done those things, I wouldn't have been so open about it. I took other police officers on the boats. That's not the way a guilty man acts. I think people will see that.[7]

• • •

The arrest did not go as planned.

As the police questioned Mrs. Gray, she grew confused about where Kuns and Leasure might be headed after lunch. She thought they might be departing for L.A. right after eating. The SWAT team, the helicopter, and most of the policemen who initially set up an ambush at the marina then raced off to the Oakland Airport, incorrectly assuming that the crew of the *La Vita* was about to elude arrest by taking to the air. By the time Sergeant Godwin found the gun and duffel bags on board the yacht—sure evidence that the crew would return to the *La Vita*—it was too late to recall the troops in time.

When the hulking motor home returned to the marina a short time later, only Godwin and a skeleton crew of policemen were on hand. There was no time for any elaborate takedowns or ambushes. As Kuns, Leasure, and the third crewman, Gino, left Gray's motor home and walked to the marina gate, the five plainclothes policemen still on hand simply converged on the group with shotguns and pistols drawn, yelling for them to freeze. The arrest was so disorganized that Godwin, pounding down the boardwalk from the yacht, found himself trapped on the wrong side of the locked gate to the docks, with no key to open it. He had to point his service revolver through the gate's metal bars.

Confronted with the sudden appearance of five strange, heavily armed men, Leasure's first instinct was to lunge forward, nearly leaping into the water. Then he realized they were policemen and he stopped himself, raised his arms, mustered an expression that combined indignation with genuine bewilderment, and stood perfectly still.

Godwin's partner, Detective Art Roth, breathless from running in from the parking lot, searched the men one at a time as the other policemen kept their weapons trained. Godwin, meanwhile, started yelling at a bystander working on his yacht a few yards away, trying to keep his eye on Leasure, Kuns, and Gino, while asking the goggle-eyed yachtsman to come over and unlock the goddamn marina gate. The other policemen were shouting, too, and in this general confusion, Kuns was able to lean over and hiss a desperate request to Leasure: "The gun. You got to say it's yours. I can't take a gun rap on top of this."

Although the Oakland police couldn't have known it, the .45 Godwin had found on board the *La Vita* and assumed was Leasure's actually belonged to Kuns. Leasure had bought it from a gun dealer years before, then resold it to Kuns, though it was still registered to the LAPD traffic officer. As a paroled bank robber, Kuns could not legally own a handgun—Leasure had to buy it for his friend, who felt too vulnerable at sea without weapons on board. "When you're at sea, you can't call a cop," Kuns had often reminded Leasure. "You have to defend yourself." But now Kuns could face hard prison time for being a felon in possession of a firearm. So when he asked Leasure to claim ownership, Leasure nodded yes. He didn't know what sort of investigation had led the Oakland detectives to the *La Vita,* but whatever it was, Leasure felt certain he would be released as soon as he told them he was a fellow officer. The least he could do was relieve his friend of a possible gun rap.[8]

"What's going on, officers? What's the problem?" Leasure asked the Oakland policemen, as Roth began handcuffing each of his captives.

By this time, Godwin had gotten the key to the marina gate and wrestled it open. "You're being arrested for grand theft of a yacht."

"Wait, I'm a police officer. My name's Bill Leasure, I'm with LAPD." He glanced at Kuns, who stood impassively, his hands manacled from behind. Then Leasure turned back and stared levelly at Godwin. "If this boat is stolen, I had no idea. I was just crewing for my friend. I can't believe this. It must be a mistake."

"I know you're a cop," Godwin said, almost glumly. He didn't like the idea of arresting a policeman. "And it's no mistake."

The tentative smile on Leasure's face vanished. "How did you know I was a police officer?"

"I ran the serial number on the weapon in your bag. It came back registered to you, care of LAPD."

"Oh," Leasure said quietly.

"Isn't it your weapon?"

"Well, yes, it is.[9] But I haven't done anything wrong."

Godwin looked him over. The soft-spoken, obviously distressed man before him seemed genuinely perplexed. Maybe he really was all right. "I certainly hope that's true," Godwin finally said. "But we're going to have to bring you downtown."

"I can't wait to tell you my side of the story," Leasure said.

Godwin nodded. "I can't wait to hear it."

Detective Roth would later recall Leasure saying something else: "I guess I'm in a lot of trouble, huh?"[10]

"I never crewed for Robert before and know nothing of his dealings," Leasure said later, talking to Godwin cop to cop, hoping for a quick and easy release through the courtesy of a fellow officer. "I am willing to take a polygraph if asked to. My wife and I make a good living and I don't need to deal in stolen property to support myself, and I don't."[11]

Later, Leasure was so sure he could badge his way out of trouble, he even whispered to Kuns in a holding cell, "I'll think of you when I get out of here."[12]

But there were inconsistencies in Leasure's account of the trip north aboard the *La Vita*. And when it became clear Leasure had lied—that there had been other trips and other deals between Bill and the Skipper—Leasure had to change his story, although he never wavered in his adamant insistence that he was innocent. Too late, though: As every policeman should know, including Leasure, once you lie to a cop and get caught at it, he'll never believe you again. There would be no early release for Bill Leasure now, no matter what he said. Godwin was sure the soft-spoken LAPD officer had something dirty to hide.

While Leasure was talking and digging himself a hole, Kuns had resolutely invoked his right to remain silent. A seasoned con, he knew a suspect's own words most often became the strongest evidence against him. It's the guys who think they're smart enough to explain their way out of anything who end up doing hard time, Kuns knew—from bitter experience. When he heard what Leasure had said in his initial statement to the Oakland Police, all Kuns could do was shake his head sadly and whisper, "The fool. The fool."[13]

CHAPTER 2

WHEN ONE OF LEASURE'S LAPD sergeants, Jim Berg, heard of the arrest in Oakland, he turned to another cop and confided, "No way Bill's dirty. I'll bet anything it's a cover story. They're sending Leasure into the jail to do some undercover work."

"Yeah," the other cop agreed. "He's perfect for under-cover—no one would ever believe he could pull it off."

The story of Leasure's arrest aboard a stolen boat flashed through Central Traffic Division the next day like a hot tip at the racetrack, whispered over and over with that same open-mouthed mixture of awe, doubt, and eagerness. Here was a police depart-ment where officers were confronted daily by the big-city realities of brutality, graft, and drugs. They know the toll temptation can take on even a good cop. Yet these hardened LAPD officers could not conceive of Bill Leasure as crooked. Not a single cop who knew him leaned back and said, I knew it—I always suspected he was up to no good. Other officers in the division might have drawn such comments, but not Bill. They just could not believe it.[1]

Of course, to say otherwise would be to acknowledge that, all these years, a chameleon had been in their midst, fooling them, mocking them, enforcing the law by day, crossing the line by night. Most cops fancy themselves keen judges of human nature; few are willing to believe they can be fooled, at least, not that badly. "If all this is true about Leasure," Berg vowed, "I'm putting in my papers. It's time to get the hell out."

It wasn't that Leasure would win any popularity contests at LAPD. He was well liked, certainly, but he was not particularly close to many of the other guys. He kept to himself. For a police-man, he was unusually shy, nonconfrontational—the last person, Berg kept telling everyone who would listen, that you would expect to be involved in a crime.

The squad room at any police department is a rough, often profane place. Swearing is a principle means of communication; ethnic and sexist jokes abound. A vocal minority at LAPD was known to talk openly of playing "Gorillas in the Mist" when arrest-ing blacks, or "watering the fruits" when rousting gay hustlers, or of wanting to "slip 'em the old baton" when dealing with attractive women. Such talk was so ingrained into L.A. cop culture that the comments were passed freely back and forth via computer termi-nals built into patrol cars. All the street cops knew this communi-cations system was screened by their superiors, yet they felt free to voice their bigotry uncensored. They knew the LAPD brass rarely, if ever, chastised subordinates for their sexism, racism, or profanity. It was considered a harmless "outlet" for men and women who risked their lives daily—no matter how uncomfortable it might make many police officers feel, prejudice had deep roots at the department.[2]

Leasure, though, never quite seemed to fit into this environ-ment. He didn't like to cuss or make racist comments. His com-puter messages were as bland as strained carrots. He was amiable enough—supportive, helpful, nearly always willing to do a favor for a fellow cop—and he'd laugh at the sophomoric humor, though un-comfortably. Mostly, though, he was either hunkered down at a desk, painstakingly filling in reports, or he was out sick, or on va-cation, or he was simply nowhere to be found, out in the field someplace, visiting friends and killing time when he should have been chasing speeders. His good friend and sometime partner, Of-ficer John Balicki, would try to hunt him down for lunch or coffee breaks, but Leasure couldn't be found where he had told dispatch he'd be working. Balicki would shrug it off—a lot of cops sneaked away for a little personal business after finishing a call, though Leasure did seem to elevate the practice to an art form. One time Leasure suggested he and Balicki spend a few hours of work time repairing Balicki's car. "It'll only take a couple hours," Leasure told his incredulous friend. The police have a special radio code for such officers. In a system where you go "Code 7" for a lunch break or "Code 3" when requesting backup in an emergency, Bill Leasure was "Code 1": whereabouts, unknown.

"How do you get so much time off?" Leasure's friend Barbara Sanchez often asked. Sanchez, an ex-cop and fellow native of suburban Detroit, was a security guard at the Arrowhead bottled water plant in Central L.A. and the ex-wife of one of Leasure's childhood friends. Leasure would spend as long as two hours a day, one or two days a week, visiting with her when he was supposed to be out on patrol. "Shouldn't you be out writing tickets, Bill?"

Leasure would just laugh and ignore her half-joking, half-serious digs, then tell her about his yachts, or his latest trip to Europe, or the alligators he had bought and installed in his swimming pool. For some reason, the silent Bill Leasure became positively chatty around Sanchez, who liked the guy, but always resisted his gentle attempts to pick her up. "I just need someone to talk to," Leasure told her. "Someone who won't judge me."[3]

Judging Bill was no easy task. You'd ask him if he wanted to go to lunch, and he'd say yes; then, if you asked what he felt like eating, he'd say he didn't care. Chinese okay, Bill? Sure, fine. Then if you changed your mind and said, let's make it Italian instead, he would say, fine, okay. He often seemed devoid of opinions. Driving with him on patrol was like sitting next to a television set switched off. If he liked you enough, maybe you'd get twenty words out of him over the course of an eight-hour shift, and that would consist of small talk on his favorite subjects—Corvettes, scuba diving, yachts, money-making schemes. If he really liked you, maybe he'd invite you and the wife to go cruising on his sailing yacht—a fifty-foot behemoth called *Santine*. But when you told him, Bill, this is fantastic, he'd just shrug, saying nothing. And when you asked him how he could swing an expensive boat like this on a traffic cop's pay, you generally got the same answer: a shrug and a smile, or perhaps a two- or three-word explanation, "We've got partners."

"Knowing Bill Leasure as long as I have, he cannot—I won't say lie—but he cannot give a full answer," another of his sergeants and a longtime friend, Richard Litsinger, would later tell LAPD Internal Affairs investigators. "It would be completely consistent with his personality. Just say, yeah, I'm not giving an answer. That's just Bill Leasure."[4]

Habitually secretive, Leasure kept whole aspects of his life hidden, even from close friends. Officer Balicki, a man with whom he socialized, flew private planes, and gambled in Las Vegas, never knew Leasure owned a yacht, or an expensive waterside condo, or a secret bank account abroad. He was stunned to learn of these things from news stories after Leasure's arrest. As far as Balicki had known, Leasure, though always scheming to acquire property and wealth, never actually went beyond the planning stages—like the times he'd sit down at the blackjack table in Vegas and begin to fantasize about the private island he could buy, or the fast jet planes he could own, if only he could get lucky with the cards. But when Balicki asked what kind of money his friend was bringing to the table, it turned out that Leasure's willingness to take risks did not equal his desire for profit: He went to Las Vegas for a weekend of gambling with forty dollars cash in his pocket. "It'll last," he told Balicki, who could only laugh at a man who so badly wanted to be rich, but who seemed unwilling to sweat a drop for it. "You've got to understand, Bill's a dreamer," Balicki would tell friends when they looked askance at the contradictions between Leasure's talk and actions. "He's always dreaming."[5]

The same contradictory attitude came through on the job. At a department known for its aggressive, physical style, Leasure was, by far, the most unaggressive cop on his shift at Central Traffic, if not in the entire division. One former partner remembers coming across a derelict lying in the street while walking a beat with Leasure in their early days at the department. The partner wanted to arrest the man and book him into jail. Leasure insisted they call an ambulance to make sure the man wasn't sick or injured before they moved him. "That's the kind of guy Bill was. He was always concerned about people, no matter who they were."[6]

"All right you guys, go out and kick some ass tonight," one of Leasure's sergeants routinely said after each roll call. "Except for you, Bill."

"It was as though Bill was some CPA who had wandered into the police station," the same sergeant, Daryl Dement, would later observe, saying he was "floored" by the allegations against Leasure.[7]

Just about every cop has a nickname, chosen by his colleagues. Leasure's was Mild Bill.

Certainly there was nothing in his unremarkable seventeen-year record as a traffic cop to suggest he was anything more than his nickname suggested. His "package," as police personnel files are called, reveals no misconduct, no brutality complaints, no serious disciplinary problems. The file reads like a grade school report card for a kid who always did well in "citizenship," where praise for his "clean and neat uniform appearance" and carefully penned paperwork were highlights. He was continually described as average and lacking in initiative during his tenure at LAPD, though more kindhearted sergeants noted that his "easy-going personality" had a "calming effect in stressful situations."

Leasure was never brusque with the citizenry, much less abusive, though he'd be the first to admit that the class of citizen traffic cops get to deal with tended to make that easy, compared to the high percentage of criminals and crazies cops encounter on regular patrol. Leasure always made a point of expressing concern and sympathy at accident scenes or for car-theft victims. His package contains numerous laudatory letters from members of the public, most of them women, who had encountered Officer Leasure on the job and just couldn't say enough about him.

He ended up dating two or three of them in the process, more than willing to use his uniform for a little pleasant manipulation. That was not unusual for policemen—everyone on the force knows the badge can get you access to places, things and people. But most of the guys at Central Traffic were surprised to learn Leasure had the gumption to try it, and had been quite successful—another revelation that came with his arrest. And it also raised the question of whether Bill Leasure's legendary niceness might be less a matter of genuine empathy and more of a disguise: Most of those same women he started out helping ended up deciding Bill Leasure was not a very nice man at all.

Reluctant to write tickets, Leasure preferred instead to let wayward drivers go with a warning and a good talking to. As a result, his public popularity soared. Within the department, however, some officers and sergeants pegged him as a slacker. Writing tickets was, after all, his main task. Most traffic officers view ticket writing as a means of promoting safe driving and saving lives—to them, Leasure's self-righteousness about giving violators a break made a mockery of their daily occupation. And, of course, writing fewer tickets meant his daily "recap" suffered, averaging one or two traffic citations a week, compared to the six or seven his LAPD sergeants considered appropriate—the recap being analogous to a ticket quota. Some of Leasure's supervisors believed he was guilty of dodging patrol duties and radio calls, and accused him of being a "drone"—an unaggressive cop who puts in his time, and little more. "You've got no initiative," one sergeant told him. "All you care about is your next day off."

No amount of drubbing from his sergeants would light a fire beneath the laid-back Officer Leasure, however. He would take the criticism without protest, although he blushed hotly at the accusations at times. Once, when he took flak for repeatedly failing to show up for a scheduled firearms qualification at the department shooting range, he offered no excuses, but a different side of Officer Leasure peeped out with his murmured reply: "Yeah, well, I'm one of the few officers in the department who can shoot a perfect score."

His ambivalence about police work went back to his first days on the job. He had been discharged from the Marine Corps in 1969 at Camp Pendleton north of San Diego, with no marketable skills in a country weary of the war in Vietnam and hostile toward its veterans. A military career program called Project Transition had just begun at the base, and the first class offered happened to be law enforcement. It could just as easily have been firefighting or bus driving, for that matter. Leasure took the course, and an instructor from LAPD ended up recruiting him. He liked the Southern California weather and couldn't think of anything better to do—his native Detroit and the car assembly-line job awaiting him there didn't seem particularly alluring after the exotic lushness of Southeast Asia. So he said, why not? He applied to the police academy and was accepted, becoming a policeman by default later that year. He was assigned to Central Traffic in 1970 and spent most of his career there.

He did a temporary year-long stint in the department's auto repair fraud unit, where he specialized in pretending to need repairs for his car, then busting mechanics for padding bills and faking part replacements. Shy, nonthreatening, and something of a mechanical genius, Leasure was a natural for this sort of undercover work. It was as if the job description had been created with him in mind—someone service stations inevitably would try to victimize, and who had the mechanical skills to spot the deception immediately. He loved the work, excelling and, for the first time, impressing his LAPD bosses. But he lost the position when the department bureaucracy decided that someone with the rank of investigator should hold the job. Leasure decided not to seek the promotion. He went back to traffic accidents and speeding tickets, where he resumed his usual lackluster but consistent profile.

So long as he was dependable on the street, Leasure's fellow officers didn't mind if he put in minimal effort. Comfortably average, he was a role model for the lazy, a nonthreat for the ambitious. If you wanted to advance to sergeant or detective rank, to work homicide or narcotics, Leasure wouldn't get in your way. He liked working night shifts, he liked writing reports on traffic accidents— slowly, painstakingly. "He was slow, slow," Sergeant Litsinger recalled. "That totally irritated some of the sergeants." He even told one friend that he deliberately flunked a sergeant's exam, so he would not be promoted, and would have fewer responsibilities and more free time.

Traffic was a stepping-stone for most officers, but for Leasure, it was a career. He would never be the kind of cop who spent his working life on the edge. Quite the opposite: He preferred to channel his energies into outside interests.

He regularly volunteered for the most boring scut work at the Central Traffic division—working the front desk or, worse, manning the kit room, checking out police "Rover" radios, rifles, flares, and other equipment stored there. Everyone else hated the kit room, but Leasure reveled in it—it required little effort, kept him off the streets, and left him time to do some work on the side. One day, while working the kit room, he passed the time by calculating how much he could make importing several dozen used military planes from Saudi Arabia: a quarter of a million dollars pure profit, he figured. His friend Sergeant Berg saw the scribbling and asked him what he was doing.

"This could net a forty percent profit, Jim," Leasure said, turning the page around for him to see. "All I need are some investors to come up with $500,000. You interested? I can let you in for forty thousand."

The sergeant couldn't tell at first if Leasure was serious or not. Berg considered himself a wheeler-dealer in his own right—always making a few extra bucks at the swaps, opening up his own woodcutting business—but Leasure was talking about international trade and military liaisons, as if he had been moving through such waters all his life. It was totally over Berg's head, not to mention the fact that forty grand was a lot more than he took home in a year of police work.

"Where the hell would I get money like that, Bill?" Berg asked, laughing. "You're kidding, right?"

Leasure looked at him for a moment, then smiled and shrugged. "Well, it was just an idea," he said quietly. "I think it would work." He went back to his figures.

Berg walked off smiling, too, but later, after Leasure's arrest, he would remember the sure way this lowly traffic cop had described how to go about purchasing planes from the Saudi military, and he had to wonder if he might be wrong about Leasure after all. "I've worked with this man for thirteen years, had dinner with him at least three hundred times," he would later muse. "And you know, I don't know a damn thing about him."[8]

Well, that wasn't quite true. There was one thing Leasure often liked to talk about—brag about, really—and Berg and the others at Central Traffic always thought it oddly out of character for an otherwise obsessively private man. If he got to feel comfortable enough with you, his normal silence would give way and some kind of interior dam would seem to burst. Quietly, in that low voice that always provoked choruses of "Pardon me," and "What was that, Bill?"—as if he was telling a particularly juicy secret—Leasure would share a piece of himself, or at least his favorite image of himself. And it became clear that he liked people to know how rich he was.

The same fellow who frequented weekend swap meets, selling old junk and car parts for spare pocket money, also made sure Sergeant Berg and a select few of the other cops at Central Traffic knew about his home with tennis courts and swimming pool in Northridge, his marina condo and boat slip in Long Beach, his rental home in Sun Valley, his ownership of two yachts. Most of all, Leasure was renowned throughout LAPD as a collector of and authority on Corvettes. He had anywhere between twelve and seventeen of the sleek, expensive sports cars at any one time—some of them pristine, others in pieces, scattered through his yard. Still others were salted away in garages and at friends' houses—odd, some thought, but they guessed he had to put them somewhere. Leasure restored wrecks and resold them, he would explain, which, his friends figured, was why he could afford so many of the pricey sports cars. But he did occasionally buy Corvettes that were pristine collector's items, including a rare vintage model with outsized engine, built exclusively by Chevrolet for the racetrack—one of four like it in the world. Another time—and, to his friends, this again seemed oddly out of character—he had to travel out of town to attend a car auction for a Corvette he desperately wanted. Arriving late at the airport, he ran to the boarding area, where his gate was closed and the plane was about to push out. In plain clothes—jeans and a T-shirt—he nevertheless flashed his LAPD badge. "Police business," he exclaimed, cooking up a lie that prompted the airline to reopen the gate and the plane, something it will usually do only in emergencies. And he got his Corvette.

Leasure also bought himself a $30,000 airplane, a souped-up North American T-6 military trainer, once used by the Air Force to train its fighter pilots. It was a temperamental, powerful aircraft, decked out in camouflage colors and capable of outflying some small jets. Leasure reveled in it—again, revealing a side of himself that seemed at odds with the Mild Bill persona. He was part-owner of two other airplanes, though those were in pieces, awaiting restoration.

Finally, for those at the department who cared to listen, Leasure spoke of secret bank accounts in the Cayman Islands, his well-stocked gun room complete with machine guns and the deadly black tubes of silencers, and his claim to own an island in Belize.

Sure, Bill, sure, his friends would say at times, blowing off his more outrageous claims as big talk from a lazy dreamer. Only crooks have accounts in the Caymans, Bill. You know that. But still, the guy had bucks—no doubt about that. He was always happy to loan a needy friend on the force a few thousand, on generous terms. And, though widely known as unrelentingly frugal, he always kept five or six hundred dollars in his locker at work, "just in case I see something I want to buy."[9]

When Leasure spoke of such things, it never sounded like bragging—even though, in the final analysis, it was clear that Leasure was, in his low-key, detached way, puffing up for his comrades. They would boast about their latest busts, some scumbag they ground into the dirt for talking back. Leasure, who would fret about having to treat a suspect roughly (and rarely did), would compensate by showing everyone else what a classy life he led compared to most other cops. If he was an outsider at times from the ribald banter and easy camaraderie of other cops, he quietly tried to show them just what they were missing by leaving him out, a slight note of condescension behind those pale hazel eyes.

And yet few, if any, of Leasure's colleagues thought it odd that a traffic cop could afford such a seemingly lavish life-style. Laughing and shrugging off the question whenever it arose, Leasure always had a ready explanation—his wealth came from family money, wise investments, or his wife, Betsy Mogul, a supervising city prosecutor. Besides, his frugality was legendary. His preferred cuisine was fast food, his clothes off-duty were largely limited to jeans and T-shirts, his favorite shopping place was the swap meet. "I save everything," he often said, and it was true. Anyone who saw his jammed and littered house and yard knew that, a weird contradiction to the wealthy image he wanted to cultivate.

Besides, Leasure had engendered a certain degree of goodwill among his fellow officers. Not only was he generally game for a quick loan, but he was the guy you could call at 3:00 in the morning when your car broke down. He'd get dressed, show up, and squirm around under the car until he got it going, no questions asked (and little conversation offered, either, but that was Bill, take him or leave him). He enjoyed playing the man people relied upon, the indispensable fixer who was up to any challenge and who, as a result, no longer felt left out—the same way he craved, almost like an adolescent, the fast cars, planes, and pounding boat trips that were so much at odds with his otherwise detached, cold, monosyllabic daily life.

The prying eyes from Internal Affairs who came by Central

Traffic to question his co-workers after the arrest up north suggested he was a classic underachiever with a secret life—a Walter Mitty type, silently toiling in anonymity while hatching grandiose plots and complex crimes. They said good ol' Bill's image was an act, that they had searched his eight-car garage and found hot Corvettes and stolen property from a half dozen pirated yachts. They said his motor yacht moored in Long Beach, the *Thunderbolt,* along with the sailing vessel *Santine* in San Pedro, were stolen. The same vessels on which several of Leasure's fellow officers had spent weekends cruising or fishing were pirated, the Internal Affairs investigators said—the *Thunderbolt* from a Fullerton dentist, and the *Santine* from a Los Angeles developer. "He was thumbing his nose at the department every time he took a boat out," one of the investigators concluded. Greed and an insatiable appetite for thrills were his motivations, they suggested: His entire life was a lie, a cover for a bitter, small man who had no honor, no empathy, and no goal other than to prove he was better than anyone else.

Leasure, they said, was turning out to be the dirtiest cop in L.A.

But none of the people who knew and worked beside Bill Leasure really bought the theory. If he had been an undercover drug agent or some other hard-driving cop exposed daily to dirty money and overwhelming temptation, perhaps eyebrows would have been raised long ago, maybe someone would have whispered behind his back. But Mild Bill? If he had a garage full of hot goods, then he must have been duped by one of his weirdo friends—that Kuns character, or that sleazy welder who was always messing with his watchband, who traded guns with Leasure and took unauthorized ride-alongs in his squad car. Sure Leasure was an underachiever, everyone agreed. But a secret life as a master thief? They'd sooner believe he'd been dating Madonna.

Which is why Jerry France's story sounded doubly unbelievable.

• • •

I took the sergeant's tests, but I'm the kind of guy who was really never motivated to be a sergeant. I liked being a traffic officer. I really was pretty unique. Most officers hate it, but I like working traffic. . . . I guess that blows the theory that I was some kind of thrill-seeker, out for money, out for blood. I didn't even like writing traffic tickets—that was their biggest complaint. I'd rather let people off with a warning.

• • •

Even the hardened cynics at Internal Affairs found Jerry France hard to take. If they had heard his story in a vacuum, without the arrest up in Oakland to back it up, they would have booted him out without another word.

But in what would become the first of many strange coincidences in the case, Jerry France found himself in a police interrogation room on May 29, 1986—the same day police in Oakland descended on the *La Vita*. France wanted to beat some hot check and theft charges, and to do it, he was ready to inform on someone. That someone was Officer William Leasure.

Jerry France had not yet graduated to robbing banks for a living at this time in his life, as he would in later years—although his knobby thinness and red-rimmed eyes were already making tellers nervous throughout Los Angeles. Instead, in the summer of 1986, France continued to do what he did best: He made a living at what policemen derisively call "paper hanging."

And he was quite successful at it, a minor legend among his peers, despite his shaggy, disreputable looks. Jerry France had a certain easy way about him, he talked a good game, skillfully mixing untruths with a small kernel of fact—the technique of a talented liar, and the one vital skill a paper hanger must possess. His system was foolproof in its simplicity: He would use phony identification to open a checking account with the minimum required deposit—say, ten dollars—then he would drive immediately to the nearest mall. Once there, he would write his checkbook empty buying televisions, VCRs, compact disc players, and other pricey electronics, as much as he could cram into his car's trunk and backseat. Weekend shopping was best, because the banks were closed. By the time his checks began bouncing the following Wednesday or so, Jerry had already burned his old checkbook, opened a new account under a different name, and started hanging more worthless paper across town.

Using this method, France had hung worthless checks all over Southern California; the policemen who occasionally caught up with him would clap him on the shoulder and say his rap sheet was the stuff of Guinness. He'd sell his purchases for fifty cents on the dollar or less, usually through his brother Dennis, a welder and gun nut with a whole coterie of Los Angeles policemen for friends and willing customers. Jerry couldn't imagine a safer way to fence his goods. Who'd suspect a cop?

It wasn't a bad living, and he probably could have kept it going for quite a few years, but Jerry France was his own worst enemy. A junkie and a speedballer, he'd shoot up a volatile mixture of

cocaine and heroin several times a day, giving him the constant sen-
sation that his skull was packed with gunpowder and match heads.
His eyes glowed like brake lights whenever he was high; long-
sleeved shirts concealed snaking lines of needle scars even on the
hottest of summer days. After a while, he could no longer steal fast
enough to support his habit. He got sloppy.

Even stoned, though, Jerry France could always talk. So every
time his carelessness got him busted, he did the natural thing for a
career criminal anxious to avoid prison: He became an informant.

They knew him well at the downtown precinct in Long Beach,
the gritty former Navy town south of L.A. that served as his home
turf. He had helped the police in Long Beach clear six cases in four
weeks in April 1986, ratting out several fellow thieves and his own
drug dealers—and in the process, skating to freedom on several
thousand dollars' worth of bad paper that detectives were ready to
pin on him.

A month later, Jerry France found himself in trouble again in
Long Beach on hot check charges. This time, though, France had
no dealers or thieves to offer up in exchange for a break. He had
used them all up. But after a few sweaty hours in lockup, he said
he had something else to offer. "I've got something really heavy for
you this time," he told his interrogators. "It involves an LAPD
cop."

The story that next unfolded was so outrageous that the Long
Beach investigators who handled France weren't sure what to make
of it. They knew he was a pathological liar—he bragged about
working for the CIA, for one thing, and now and then claimed to
be privy to a variety of global conspiracies. Very imaginative for a
junkie, but not exactly the sort of information that inspires faith in
a snitch's credibility. Basically, the police in Long Beach had a policy of believing about every other sentence Jerry uttered—and only
after corroborating every bit they could.

Still, the story he spun about boat thefts, murders, and other
crimes involving his brother Dennis and a traffic cop named Bill,
incredible as it sounded, probably needed checking out. The Long
Beach cops decided to pass the story—and Jerry France—on to
LAPD's Internal Affairs Division. Investigators there could do
whatever they wanted with the information.

On May 29, when Jerry France repeated the story for LAPD
investigators—*before* Leasure was arrested up north—very little was
done, primarily because the story sounded so unbelievable, but also
because it was rife with inconsistencies.

First of all, Jerry claimed Leasure not only stole boats, but

that he seized them at sea like a latter-day Bluebeard, killing the oc-
cupants, dumping the bodies overboard, then selling the yachts. He
claimed Leasure and his brother had made millions of dollars in the
process, and that they operated a "Murder Incorporated" together.
And not only did France implicate Leasure and his own brother in
murderous yacht thefts, but he also accused the policeman of buying his hot check televisions, then re-selling the stolen property a
few blocks from the station—while on duty, right out of his black
and white. Once, Jerry said, Bill had scored some heroin for him as
a favor, then let him shoot it up in the backseat of his patrol car.
Finally, Jerry claimed several other officers were involved in trafficking stolen property and weapons with Leasure, including the
department's nationally famous ballistics expert, a man most cops
considered above reproach.[10]

At Internal Affairs, investigators have a profile of the sort of
policeman who is likely to cross the line. Mild Bill Leasure did not
fit that profile, did not even come close. And Jerry was unable to
provide a single time, date, or place for any of the yacht thefts or
alleged murders he described. In the world of snitches and police
interrogation, such vagueness is the hallmark of an experienced
liar—if you avoid giving details, you can't be accused of getting it
wrong. Later, you can look up old newspapers or make inferences
from the questions police ask, and, gradually, you can fill in the
blanks. It was obvious what France was doing. And it meant that,
at best, his story might contain a nugget of truth buried amid the
embellishments; at worst, it was pure fantasy. Jerry France had described Bill Leasure as five-eight or five-nine, 280 pounds, 45 to 50
years old, with gray hair—a description requested as a kind of veracity test. Since Leasure was at the time 2 inches taller, 110
pounds lighter, and a lot younger and balder than Jerry France had
suggested, it seemed pretty clear that this particular junkie snitch
didn't know Bill Leasure from Hulk Hogan.

When Jerry France finished talking, the investigator interviewing the bloodshot Mr. France basically told him thanks, but no
thanks. Even at I.A.D., where investigators see police misconduct
on a daily basis and are inclined to think the worst of their fellow
officers, they know scumbags try to smear good cops all the time.

Then everything changed. Leasure was arrested—aboard a
stolen boat. Someone might as well have tossed a grenade into
police headquarters, for all the ducking and covering that followed. The investigator who had been ready to dismiss Jerry
France with an unenthused "We'll get back to you" frantically
started working the phones to get him back to the station. No

matter that he was proven to be a liar almost immediately, when the Oakland police reported finding the original owners of the stolen yachts, alive and kicking. No one had been shot, no one had been dumped overboard. The yachts all had been stolen from the docks, late at night or early in the morning, with no one around, and certainly no one hurt. The most sensational portion of France's story—the murder allegations—had fallen apart within hours of his interrogation.

But it was too late by then. Based on Leasure's arrest and the statements by Jerry France—identified over-optimistically in early police reports as a "confidential reliable informant"—search warrants were sworn out, Leasure's alleged accomplices at LAPD were hauled in for bewildering interrogations, and a twelve-man investigative task force was formed. Word of a potentially explosive scandal in the making had sped up the chain of command in a matter of minutes. An assistant chief would supervise the task force and report directly to Police Chief Daryl Gates.

There was a cancer in the department, the chief announced. He planned to slice it out.

• • •

I've never met Jerry France in my life. He's a liar. I've never stolen anything. I've never stolen a boat. I've never shot anyone on—or off— duty. I never shot at anyone. I've never desired to shoot anyone.

I've had opportunities on the job. I've been in situations where other policemen might have killed somebody. One time we captured two suspects in the robbery of a pharmacy, it was my partner and another policeman at the door of their car, I'm at the rear, covering. Then I hear this click, click, click, click. What's that, I wonder. Then I look around this wall, and there's a third suspect, pointing his gun at the other policemen, trying to cock it. It's stuck. His job is to shoot the cops, but there's an old casing jammed in the chamber. It won't fire. So I pulled out my gun and told him to drop it. A lot of other officers would have just shot him. I know they would have shot him. But you've got to use judgment. I knew his gun was jammed. I didn't have to shoot him. I could have, and no one would ever have questioned it. But I didn't. That's the kind of "killer" I am. That's what a "thrill-seeker" I am. They used to call me Mild Bill at work. Now all my friends have turned against me. They believe all this stuff, all these lies.

That's what hurts the most.

• • •

The shock wave generated by Bill Leasure's arrest extended far beyond the police department. In her small Glendale apartment, Irene Wong[11] gripped that day's *Los Angeles Herald-Examiner* and saw the plans she had laid for the rest of her life crumble with each line of newsprint she read. She stared at the grainy black and white picture of Bill and wondered at his foolishness. And hers.

They had met seven years before, in 1979. "There. Over there," the tiny Chinese woman had shouted that day, pointing wildly at a row of cars parked on Commercial Street downtown. "That's my father's car!"

She had jumped off her bus twelve stops early, having spotted the car through a smeary bus window and a gap in the afternoon swirl of traffic and pedestrians outside. Her father's car had been stolen the week before, given up for lost—until she saw it sitting there, displayed as baldly as a billboard, parked in front of an expired meter. Irene had been so blinded by excitement at her discovery, she nearly was run over by an LAPD patrol car when she burst from the crowded sidewalk, waving and shouting, heedless of passing cars.

"Please help me, officer! He'll get away."

The policeman she had flagged down stepped slowly from his black and white cruiser, leather belt and holster creaking. His dark blue uniform was immaculate, surgically creased. Though not particularly tall, he towered over Irene—she was barely over five feet, a thin waif often mistaken for a child.

"What's the trouble, Miss?" he asked. "How can I help you?"

Something about him startled Irene into silence. It was his voice, both sympathetic and deferential—qualities a shy and fearful teenager, brought up in a strict and traditional home, expected from no one, least of all a policeman. When she failed to speak, he stooped low enough to look her in the eye, then repeated his question slowly, gently, his manner more like a doctor at a patient's bedside than a cop working the Los Angeles streets.

"You said something about a car?" he urged. "Why don't you show me?"

Irene nodded, the eighteen-year-old's shyness making her whisper. She walked with him to her father's car, explaining who she was and what had happened. Another officer in the police cruiser talked into a radio, then called out that the license number on the car had indeed been reported stolen.

"Looks like we solved a crime here, Miss Wong," the officer said. "We'll be able to recover it for you right now." He began jotting information down in his notebook, asking questions as he wrote. She told him she was a student at the downtown campus of Cal State, that she lived at home with her parents, that she worked part-time in a restaurant. He seemed very interested, asking her about her major and her plans for the future. Irene was surprised— and flattered. She gave him her phone number and address, all the while studying the policeman.

Irene wouldn't have called him handsome, but there was something very attractive about the man. Later, when asked if she could define what had drawn her to him, all she could say was that he had a very nice way about him: gentle and sweet, fatherly and comfortable. She tried to picture his features later, after they parted, and had trouble doing it. But she remembered his smile beneath his thin mustache. It had made her want to smile back.

After he had filled out a report, he popped the car's hood and hot-wired the ignition—a peculiar skill for a cop to possess, but one that came naturally to a fellow who had worked with cars since before puberty. No need for a tow truck with me around, he told her, then drove her home in her father's car, his partner tailing behind in the patrol car. He carefully explained what had to be done with the police reports and insurance claim forms. When he was through, Irene leaned over to read his name tag. "Thank you so much, Officer Leasure," she said, too shy to look him in the eye. "You've been wonderful."

"Don't mention it, Irene," he said. "And call me Bill."[12]

They began dating soon after. He impressed her—shocked her, really—on their first date. Leasure rented an airplane and took her flying high above the Los Angeles basin, climbing out of the smog. She never would have pegged the soft-spoken policeman for a pilot. It seemed too daring a pursuit for someone who acted, for the most part, like a kindly old man. She decided then that she had found the man of her dreams—the first man she ever dated. Their age difference didn't matter to her—he was thirty-three at the time they met, fifteen years her senior—although she was concerned about what her parents would say. Fervently racist when it came to their daughter's relationships, they wouldn't be happy about her dating an Anglo, particularly an older one. Bill had suggested they keep their romance a secret, and she readily agreed.

Irene, as Leasure saw it, had been both sheltered and abused by her parents, but with Bill, a whole new world opened up for her. He shuttled her around the city in his patrol car. Off duty, in a sleek silver Corvette, he drove her to the mountains for the first time in her life, showed her waterfalls and evergreens—things she had only seen in pictures before. She had spent her whole life in Southern California, and she had hardly spent a day at the beach. Bill changed all that. He gave her a first taste of boating. In time, he talked her into moving out of her parents' home and into an apartment he paid for, gently prodding her toward freedom and a life of her own. He helped her study and took her on trips abroad, to the Caribbean and Mexico. Most important of all, he treated her like a person, at least at first, with respect and gentleness, considerations her parents had rarely shown her. Sure, he was a little cheap— their meals tended toward McDonald's or, on a special occasion, a Sizzler chain restaurant that served cops and their guests for free. It was an odd, poor man's counterpoint to the dreamer's boasts about cars and bank accounts and yachts, Irene thought. Still, how could she not fall in love with this kind older man?[13] Within a year, they began to plan a life together.

But then the years began to pile up, and the plans still remained plans. He became distant and cold once he had won her over, given to leaving her alone for weeks on end, then showing up late one night, unannounced, for a few muttered sentences, some perfunctory sex, and a see you later. Yet she continued to pin her future on the relationship, even though engagement never led to marriage, and Bill would never set a date. Oh, he always had plausible excuses. He complained he was too far in debt to get married. His former live-in girlfriend was possessive and vindictive and, worst of all, a lawyer. If they got married, she would file a palimony suit against him and claim half of all his possessions, he said. "We've got to wait. Be patient," he told Irene over and over. "I'll work it out."[14]

Certainly Bill was perfectly willing to introduce Irene to all his friends, police and civilian alike. He was open about their relationship, hugging and kissing her around some of his friends, allaying her suspicions further—and displaying his youthful trophy for the others to see at the same time.

From the beginning of their relationship, he seldom brought her to his home in Northridge. On one of the few times he did, Irene spotted another woman's clothes in his closets. She screamed that she knew he was with someone else, that she had suspected all along, that she was going to leave him. But Bill calmly explained that the clothing belonged to his by-then-notorious ex-girlfriend. "She refuses to take them," he told her. "What can I do?"

Usually he preferred to go to her apartment in the city of Glendale, north of L.A., or to one of his yachts, or to a trailer he kept at his friend Art's house, or to Art's sailboat, which Bill claimed to own in part. Wherever they ended up after a date, they almost never spent the night together—he had to get up early for work, he'd say, and preferred to leave from home. "Why should you have to get up early just because I do," he'd say. "I'm just thinking of you."

When she became pregnant after six years with Leasure, Bill initially said he wanted to marry her, that he wanted to start a family with her. Irene was ecstatic. But a few weeks later, he said he had been thinking about it, and that the time just wasn't right for them to have children. He needed more money, he needed more time, he needed to extricate himself from his volatile ex-girlfriend. Later, he said. Soon.

When she tried to insist, to say it was time for them to make a firm and final commitment, Leasure turned stony. "If you want the baby, you're on your own."

Reluctantly, she agreed to have an abortion—at her own expense. The perennial cheapskate, Leasure never offered to pay, Irene complained to friends later. She felt humiliated and betrayed, and told Leasure they were through. But after a brief separation, he came around again to her tiny apartment, tearful and repentant. He had a way of turning Irene's grievances back on her, and this was no exception. He cried and complained that no one understood him, that he risked his life daily in the streets (a traffic cop's exaggeration, if not an outright lie), that he needed compassion, not abuse. Pretty soon, the tables had turned and Irene was asking herself if she had been too hard on him. In the end, she was the one comforting the weepy policeman, her anger displaced by guilt. These were the only times Irene ever saw Leasure display any emotion, brief outbursts calculated to gain her sympathy, which faded just as quickly as she acquiesced. Part of her knew what he was doing, saw the manipulation for what it was. But still, she took him back. Like always.[15]

Now, a year later, sitting at home reading about Leasure's arrest, she once again appeared to be pregnant—again carrying his baby. She was consumed with worry. What would she do with Bill in jail? How could she help him? She slowly read through the newspaper article, refusing to believe in his guilt, certain there had to be a mistake.

Then Irene reached the part that shattered her. It was toward the bottom of the article, and she had to read it several times over before its meaning sank in. But there it was. No matter how many times she reread the passage, the words stayed the same: the part about Betsy Mogul, the city prosecutor. Bill's wife.

Seven years together, and Irene never knew Bill was married, so skilled had he been at dissembling and excusing.[16] At times she had accused and suspected him of a double life, but always he had a plausible explanation. Always he would use coldness to bully her, or tears to manipulate her. Now she saw their entire time together had been a lie. Leasure and Mogul had been married in 1976—three years before Irene and Bill ever met.

The paper slid from between her fingers. Her mind was numbed. In a fog, she answered the telephone: A friend was calling to say he had seen the news about Bill. Maybe she should phone the FBI, the friend suggested. Maybe he would call himself. Irene mumbled that she'd think about it.

What she thought about, though, was her time with Bill, and how, despite the long years together, she really knew very little about him. He had always deflected her questions about his job and his finances. He had always gotten up from their bed at 1:00 or 2:00 in the morning, then left her, every night. And still, she had refused to see. How could she have been such a fool?

Then there was her job at the bank, the job Irene no doubt would lose because of Bill, she suddenly realized. He had asked her so many times to make deposits for him—in her account, in her name, cashing checks from Robert Kuns and his other business partners. "I've got money problems," he had explained. "It'll help to use your name."[17]

She had done it for him gladly, without question. She was his love—why shouldn't she? But now she saw darker motives. The checks had been written to and from the same people the newspaper had linked to stolen yachts. He had been using her, she decided. He had involved her.

When Bill called her from jail a few days later, she shrieked at him. He begged her not to tell his wife about their relationship, a plea that earned him stony silence. He said everything would work out, that he was innocent, that he never meant to hurt her, that he loved her. But please, he asked, one thing: destroy all the bank records. "Flush them down the toilet," he said. "We don't want anyone to get the wrong idea." Irene hung up on him.[18]

After a while, she gathered all her records together in one neat pile—canceled checks and bank statements, along with the postcards and letters he had sent her describing his many yachting expeditions and trips to the Cayman Islands. But she didn't flush them. She just put them on the table and waited for the FBI to call.

• • •

[Irene Wong] was a brilliant, sweet girl. She really filled a void in my life. But she has multiple personalities. She hates me one minute, loves me the next. She says she didn't know I was married, but that's not true. She knew. She used to get mad when she saw Betsy on TV running for city attorney. I know she knew.

The truth is, I was basically her protector. I saved her life a couple times. I helped her develop. She had never even walked around barefoot before, if you can believe that. She probably would never have been normal if not for me.

But now they want to use that against me. Sure, I had a girlfriend. It was wrong, I regret it. But what does it have to do with my case? They're just trying to slime me. What business is it of anyone's that she had an abortion? What does it prove? I helped Irene Wong, not hurt her. What does that prove?

CHAPTER 3

THE DOWNTOWN LOS ANGELES Denny's is shoehorned next to the sooty concrete barriers of a freeway interchange, an unlikely splash of color and cooking grease at the end of a lumpy, ill-traveled street perpetually torn by the jackhammers of urban renewal. The restaurant stands just a few blocks from the mismatched pair of structures that form the heart of L.A.'s justice system—the drably modern nineteen-story box that is the Criminal Courts Building, and the blackened granite and ancient pigeon droppings of the archly named Hall of Justice, home to the county sheriff's department and its maze of holding cells and hearing rooms. Closer still is the windowless fortress of the Los Angeles County Jail, a stark black rectangle set against the smog-blurred, gray-green outlines of the Santa Monica Mountains, a stern reminder of the wages of crime readily visible from the restaurant parking lot.

With such neighbors, the downtown Denny's has become an inevitable pit stop for the criminal justice system—a Formica oasis where the clatter of dishes can drive away the memory of barred doors slamming home, and where the aroma of strong, steaming coffee in clean white cups can help you forget, finally, the rat-warren smell of urine and sweat that permeates all places where humans are caged. Policemen and guards seek refuge from the streets and the cellblocks and the witness stand here, as do the just-released inmates with their brown paper bags of personal property. Usually this makes for an odd and uneasy assemblage of antagonists. Sometimes, though, the mingling is deliberate, and Denny's becomes a quiet meeting place for furtive alliances, as cops and their informants share whispers over Danish.

This was the place Officer Bill Leasure chose to meet his friend and fellow gun enthusiast, Dennis France, for coffee and conversation. They were regulars. Leasure would arrive in uniform and patrol car. France would appear in his soiled coveralls, fresh from the welding shop. Surrounded by other cops, they would speak quietly of their mutual business.

But on this humid and smoggy day in August, Dennis France had called another policeman—Detective Tom King, an investigator at LAPD's Internal Affairs Division. Leasure had been in jail more than two months, and France was getting edgy. After months of stonewalling the policemen who wished to question him about Leasure, France had called to say he was ready to talk.

"Let's meet at 'the restaurant,' " the investigator told France—letting him know that even their old secret rendezvous was no longer a secret. But make it another restaurant in the same Denny's chain, King said. He named a different Denny's south of downtown, more convenient to his home. France said fine.

"Bill and I always came to Denny's," the stubby little man told the pair of Internal Affairs investigators who came to meet him. "That's where we'd meet."

He grew quiet when the waitress came to fill their cups. The policemen stared and the man slouched in the booth, unimposing and nervous, playing with the clasp on his stainless-steel watchband, snapping it open, then closed, then open once again. When the waitress was gone, he moved his stare from his cup of coffee, glanced with narrowed eyes at nearby patrons, then said in a conspirational whisper: "I know a lot about Bill Leasure. I done lots of things with him. Lots."

The policemen nodded, waiting. This could be the break they had been looking for in their investigation of stolen yachts and hot cars. Leasure was still in custody up north, still claiming he was guiltless after more than two months in jail, and still sounding like the last guy in the world likely to cross the line. I was just crewing for Kuns, he told his interrogators in Oakland. I didn't know the boat was stolen. I'm innocent, can't you see? But the I.A.D. men who checked Leasure's boats and searched his jam-packed garage were convinced he was dirty. That it took cops up in the Bay Area to nail one of LAPD's finest only added to their anger and embarrassment. Which is why they were sitting at breakfast with Dennis France, a semiliterate welder and close friend of Leasure's—who, they believed, had helped him steal a couple of yachts as well.

Dennis France was brother to the liar Jerry France. Jerry, the police had come to realize, had been merely parroting tidbits he had picked up from Dennis, then filling in the holes with his own fabrications, hoping to earn himself a deal on his hot check charges. Some of his information had checked out, but most of it was garbage, particularly, it seemed, the wild allegations of murder at sea. Now he was tainted as a witness—too many lies, too little credibility. You could never convict a Bill Leasure with Jerry France on the stand.

But Dennis France seemed to be the real thing. The police were convinced he was in on the yacht thefts—his name had surfaced in Bill Leasure's personal notebooks too many times in reference to yachts and trips to the Bay Area. The notebooks showed Leasure acted as France's personal banker, holding his money, among other things. They couldn't prove anything concrete against him yet, but France didn't know that. If they could get him to roll over on his friend—to give information and testimony in exchange for some kind of deal—they could nail shut the case against Leasure, take it away from the outsiders up north, and make an example of a rogue cop in the process.

"Tell us more," Detective Tom King urged. He was an imposing man with salt-and-pepper hair and a quiet, poker-faced authority that made him a devastating bluffer. He had a clipped way of talking, as if the words were being sliced out of a paper cutter. More often than not, it got to people, made them nervous. Now he was trying to persuade France to cooperate by suggesting his arrest was imminent. "This would be a good time for you to come clean, Dennis. Before we go forward—without your help. Then it'll be too late."

But France shook his head with mulish patience. "You got to protect me before I'll talk—I'm afraid something might happen to me. I know too much."

He was a short, stout man, pale and balding and harmless looking, his round face creased with worry lines. The watchband relentlessly snapped open and shut in his thick, blunt fingers. "I got a family, kids, bills. So I ain't gonna go to jail, no way. I want, what d'ya call it, uh—" He looked at the stone-faced cops for help. They weren't going to help, but the word finally came to him. "I want *immunity*." He pronounced it carefully, gravely.

"Immunity?" King's companion, Detective Gilbert Hetrick, an auto theft expert, asked. "Why's that?"

"No jail," France said.

Sure, sure, anything was possible, King and Hetrick suggested, but first they had to know what he knew. They would make no promises without hearing the story he had to tell. They waited and played the staring game.

But France stubbornly refused to speak in anything but vaguely disturbing generalities. Their coffee cups were refilled, drained, refilled again, and still he would only hint at what he knew. He surprised King by saying he was well aware that only a district attorney, not a cop, could make an official offer of immunity—a point of law few people know anything about. "My preacher used to be a police officer," France eventually murmured. "He told me things."

Finally, Dennis handed them a strange hypothetical. What if he robbed a bank? And what if Bill Leasure made him do it? Could France make the deal and roll over on Leasure, even if Leasure played just a behind-the-scenes role? The detectives remained non-committal. "We'd have to know more," King said. France continued with the hypotheticals: What if he told me to waste everyone in the bank, and I was to do it? Shoot eight people, on his order. Could we make a deal then? The detectives paused, taken aback. King finally suggested it would be pretty hard to make a deal with someone who had killed eight people. Undeterred, Dennis France changed the hypothetical: What if it was two people?

"Now I'm not sayin' anything like that happened," France said, talking fast now, moving his eyes from one cop to the other, trying to read them, a salesman making his pitch. "Just that I did things for Bill. I know about the boats—and a whole lot more. And I ain't sayin' nothin else until we make a deal with the D.A."[1]

The Internal Affairs investigators looked at one another, shrugged, and excused themselves for a short discussion on the phone with their boss. The truth was, they had nothing on France—at least, nothing to justify an arrest, other than Jerry France's questionable word—so there was no way to pressure him into talking. King thought Dennis France was sounding disturbingly like Jerry France with his talk of hypothetical killings. Maybe there were some bodies floating around in this case after all, he said. But King's boss, Sergeant David Wiltrout, an I.A.D. administrator with no criminal investigation experience, said it sounded like another load of bullshit. Jerry had been full of it when he talked about murders, and so was his brother Dennis. King should focus on the boat thefts, the sergeant said, and see if the D.A. would give France what he wanted. Immunity.

"Shouldn't we at least take him down to headquarters, try and sweat something out of him?" King asked. "Before we give him a walk?"

No, Wiltrout instructed. Take him to the D.A. Let's move before he changes his mind.[2]

• • •

Dennis France is a liar. He just wanted to stay off death row, and he knew he could do that by implicating me. He's sleazy and illiterate, but he's not stupid. He's street smart. He got a deal, all by himself, that the best lawyers in L.A. couldn't get, that they'd kill for . . .

He's no better than a jailhouse snitch. No difference. Wiltrout knew he was a liar. They all know it. But they're willing to do anything to get me. They're not interested in finding the truth. They just want to win the case. Can you imagine, my life depends on the word of that man? It's terrifying. Unbelievable.

Hopefully, the jury won't believe it either.

• • •

King and his partner took Dennis France to the Criminal Courts Building, to the office of a deputy district attorney assigned to the Special Investigations Division, which prosecutes corrupt government officials and dirty cops. When the white plastic foam cups of coffee had been distributed and the chairs were pulled up, the D.A. told France he would be immune from prosecution if he told them the truth about Leasure.

"Whatever I tell you, you can't use against me?" he asked. "Not anything?"

"That's right," the D.A. said. "Not anything."

"I can live with that," the little man replied. He took a deep breath and the policemen flipped open their notebooks, anxious to hear the inside story on the boat thefts and frauds, and whatever else France would spill. They felt an eager pride at cracking the case wide open. King felt a certain uneasiness as well. That hypothetical bank robbery still bothered him, as did Jerry France's tale of murders at sea—but even he couldn't have envisioned what was about to follow.

Their mistake became instantly, sickeningly clear.

"I killed two people for Bill Leasure," France calmly announced. "And I drove the car on a third hit.

"I did the shooting, but Bill paid me. It had nothing to do with boats, but it was all for Bill. He does contract murders."

The policemen and the D.A. sat in stunned silence for a moment. They had expected a tale of rich men's yachts pirated at sea and sold for obscene profit. Instead, they had just given immunity to a hired killer, and there wasn't a damn thing they could do about it.[3]

Except, of course, to go after Bill Leasure.

Now they had to pray France was telling the truth, rather than merely shifting blame for his own crimes. That latter possibility was unthinkable—it would mean they had allowed a murderer to walk free with nothing to show for it. No matter how unlikely a murder suspect Leasure might be, they had no choice now but to turn their folly into a whole new case—one that, in the end, could shake the entire Los Angeles Police Department from top to bottom.

Finally, the D.A. pulled a battered tape recorder from his desk, then a stack of cassette tapes. "Let's get started," he sighed. "It's going to be a long day."

The case of the dirtiest cop in L.A. had just begun.

PART II
1946–1986

MILD BILL

Of the good, we think always of wisdom, tolerance, kindliness, generosity, humility; and the qualities of cruelty, greed, self-interest, graspingness and rapacity are universally considered undesirable. And yet in our structure of society, the so-called and considered good qualities are invariable concomitants of failure, while the bad ones are the cornerstones of success.

—JOHN STEINBECK
The Log from the Sea of Cortez

CHAPTER 4

"**B**ILL, COME HERE!" BETSY Mogul called. "There's somebody out by one of the Corvettes!"

Bill Leasure walked slowly to the kitchen window where his wife stood. He peered outside. Sure enough, a strange man, asleep and, by the expression on his face, snoring lustily, lay curled up in a bedroll next to one of Leasure's Stingrays. "Can you believe that?" Betsy was angrily complaining as Leasure quietly studied the situation.

The sports cars were sitting on an asphalt basketball court in back of the house. The year was 1979, before Leasure had built an eight-car garage on the asphalt to house his assorted treasures. The existing two-car garage was too packed with tools, car parts, and cartons stacked to the ceiling to leave room for even an additional shoebox, much less indoor parking, so the Corvettes stood outside with the rest of Leasure's automotive paraphernalia scattered about the blighted yard. The gate to the back yard was locked, but the fence was low, easy to scale, which was not unusual for their quiet neighborhood. But it left the Corvettes vulnerable.

"I guess some transient let himself in the yard last night to get some sleep," Bill observed quietly, almost with amusement. Then he looked uneasily at Betsy, who was not amused at all—she had experienced a threatening run-in with another transient-type character not long before. Leasure added, "I'm sure he's harmless."

He shifted his gaze uncertainly to his two houseguests, Dan Fitzpatrick and Dan's girlfriend, Barbara Sanchez, who were still working on their first cups of coffee of the morning. Dan was staying at the Leasure home temporarily. He had quit the Detroit police force and moved to California, emulating his friend Leasure—he had grown up with Bill in suburban Wayne, Michigan. Barbara, still a Detroit cop, was visiting Fitzpatrick for two weeks that summer. Except for Bill's and Dan's long-standing friendship, the foursome did not know one another very well, which, along with the overall oddities of the cluttered Leasure-Mogul household, had made for a strained week. Now this. The guests glanced politely out the window, wishing whoever was out there would go away and defuse the situation. But the man slept on, his head thrown back. As Barbara Sanchez would later recall it, Betsy was boiling.

"I'm sure he's just some old drunk," Barbara finally said.

"Well, do something," Betsy demanded of her husband.

Leasure looked uncomfortable, his voice barely audible. "Well, I'll call the department, get someone to ask him to move along."

"Ask him? You'll do more than that. Get your gun," Barbara Sanchez recalls Betsy saying. "He might be dangerous. He's a trespasser. Shoot him if you have to."

To Barbara, Betsy sounded as if she were overreacting. Leasure tried reasoning with her. "Don't worry, I'll get them to send a unit over," he said. "That's what they get paid for." The transient continued sleeping contentedly next to the Corvette, unaware of the drama unfolding in the kitchen twenty yards away.

Betsy was not mollified. "What about you?" Sanchez remembers her asking, turning to Barbara. "You're a cop. You get the gun."

"Hell, I'm not going to shoot him," Barbara remembers answering. "You can't just shoot somebody for trespassing. You're a city attorney, you know that."

"Two cops, and neither one of you wants to do anything!" Betsy replied, as Sanchez recalls. Then Betsy faced her husband. "What kind of policeman are you, anyway? You haven't even arrested anybody in seven years." She walked out of the kitchen before Bill could reply, leaving him red-faced and silent.[1]

Almost any other person would have shouted right back at her, Barbara thought at the time, but to her surprise, Bill Leasure never said a word. Later, she would realize that was his way: Stony silence, rather than protest, was how he dealt with anger. He just went to the phone and called LAPD. They dispatched a patrol car and, twenty minutes later, two officers sent the transient scuttling on his way. Bill carefully examined his prized Corvette for damage, found none, then came back in, again blushing furiously as he walked past his guests. Barbara felt embarrassed for him. It was the most interaction she had seen between Bill and Betsy during their entire visit. Mostly they seemed to live apart—occupying the same house, but leading separate and detached lives. Barbara found herself wondering, not for the first time, what had brought these totally opposite people together.[2]

Like most policemen, Bill Leasure met many of his friends and most of his opportunities on the job. Through a traffic investigation, he had come to know Betsy Mogul, an assistant city attorney with long, kinky, jet black hair and a diminutive stature that did little to undermine her clipped air of authority. At the time, she handled criminal misdemeanors for the city, and had been assigned to prosecute one of Leasure's arrests in 1974. They began dating while he was still in the process of divorcing his first wife. They married two years later.

Their backgrounds couldn't have been more divergent. Assertive and mercurial—exactly the opposite of the outwardly passive Bill—Betsy had grown up in Baltimore in a gregarious show business family. Her father, Albert Mogul, had been a renowned psychic in the forties and fifties, performing in London for British royalty and at the White House for Presidents Truman and Eisenhower. Though Albert Mogul was billed publicly as an illusionist, his family believed his psychic powers to be genuine. They spoke of his profitable facility for predicting stock market results, and of one memorable public performance in which he correctly predicted the following day's horse race results at a local racetrack. Several individuals of questionable background—"men with violin cases," was how the Mogul family described them—soon showed up and persuaded Albert to eliminate that particular segment of his act, which he promptly did.[3]

When he left show business, Mogul moved his family to California and opened a prosperous furniture store in central Los Angeles. Betsy, always an excellent student, a voracious reader, and a collector of books, chose to study law, graduating from USC and passing the state bar in 1972. Two years later, she joined the City Attorney's staff. In that vast government-run law office, where the weight of bureaucracy wears down many an ambitious young lawyer, Betsy Mogul soon became a standout.

As part of the usual rotation of jobs in her office, she eventually came to rule the seamy world of the city court annex at the L.A. County Jail, where the prosecutors she supervised branded her "Straight-up Betsy." The nickname owed to the fact that she seldom would cut deals that reduced charges or set criminals loose earlier than the law required. Whether she supervised the prosecution of the city's endless throng of petty criminals—thieves, addicts, robbers, purse snatchers—or, later, when she was promoted to head of Special Operations and took toxic polluters, slumlords and consumer frauds to court, she nearly always took the same simple approach. A defendant either pleaded "straight up" to the charges she filed and took his chances with the judge, or Betsy Mogul would take him to trial, convict him, and ask for the max. Period. Even the slightest violation of the law was intolerable to her, her co-workers believed. As far as they could see, a purse snatcher fit into the same moral dung heap as Charlie Manson, by Betsy's lights. "She had the ability to hate every one of them. I mean, hate every one of them," one co-worker observed. "None of us could ever match that moral outrage. And so you always felt, professionally, a little uncomfortable, that she knew you weren't as on the scene as she was. And, indeed, you weren't.

"If you asked me a year ago who wouldn't do so much as fail to return two extra pennies in change, I would point to Betsy. She just had this absolute and profound outrage about the slightest deviation from the law."[4] Her sterling reputation only added to the bewilderment years later when her husband's hidden life suddenly came into focus.

As part of a justice system that thrives on compromise and convenience rather than conviction and conscience, it came as no surprise that Straight-up Betsy was disliked long before her husband's arrest—not only by defense lawyers, but by a good number of her fellow prosecutors as well. Her personal convictions were so firm, and she expressed such confidence in their correctness, that many saw her as arrogant. Still, Betsy Mogul was respected, if not widely liked, within the City Attorney's office. She had strength and clout and, when she felt like turning it on, a certain charm and sense of humor, witty or bitingly sarcastic, depending upon her mood. It didn't hurt that she was a favorite and personal friend of the office's top officials, either. And in any case, like her or not, respect her or not, everyone in the office knew you didn't cross Betsy Mogul.

The one thing about her that puzzled the other assistant city attorneys was why she married that Milquetoast of a traffic cop, Bill Leasure. The office had buzzed for days when the marriage was announced—why would an aggressive, ambitious shark like Betsy, who made no secret of her desire to win the elected office of City Attorney, then perhaps move higher, settle on such a seem-ingly quiet nobody? Leasure showed no desire or ability to rise above the police equivalent of private first class—exactly the sort of person Betsy had always seemed to loathe. The mystery fascinated her co-workers. Not that anyone would dare ask.

Their differences were dramatic. If Betsy had enjoyed a mod-erately privileged youth, Leasure, by contrast, grew up in a blue-collar enclave on the tired western edge of Detroit. Wayne, Michigan was a homogeneous small town of modest tract homes, where two generations of Leasures had endured the numbing winds that spin off Lake Erie each winter, scraping out a modest living working the assembly lines at Ford. His family lived paycheck to paycheck, with auto industry layoffs a constant threat and an occa-sional reality. Leasure came of age with little ambition or vision of the future. Working "The Line" and scraping by was the only leg-acy he could foresee.

Painfully shy as a child, Billy Leasure had seemed a veritable cliché of young insecurities: a classic middle child—third of five—he was the last one picked when the kids were choosing up sides, the kid the rest of the gang always forgot to ask along, the sad little boy singled out in class when his mortification was mis-taken for recalcitrance. His parents were kind but stoical, the sort who endured hardships in silence, and Bill was expected to uphold the tradition. When everyone else on the block was down in the basement playing at a more popular boy's house, Billy was still knocking on the door, asking the boy's mom if he could come in and play. She'd call down, "Bill's here"; then there would be a long pause, long enough for Leasure to blush crimson right up to his hairline, before a reluctant voice would drift up the stairs say-ing, "Oh, all right. He can come down." Bill would march stiffly, quietly, to the basement stairs.[5]

Young Leasure became inceasingly withdrawn and detached as time went on and similar experiences mounted—his defense was to seal himself off, bottling resentment, disappearing into silence. He was never the sort of kid who misbehaved or tested his parents. Leasure's mother, a Sunday school teacher and practical nurse, re-calls spanking him only once—when she caught him, at age ten, standing in front of the open refrigerator, guzzling a bottle of beer. It was one of the few times in his life when Leasure even imbibed alcohol.[6]

He drifted through school, the invisible kid who always threw up in gym class, his sensitive stomach a problem even then. He had few dates—he was painfully shy, particularly around girls. He preferred having pets and nursing sick animals back to health—he seemed to prize relationships in which others become dependent on him, even if it meant embracing misfits. When a child in the neighborhood with dwarflike deformities became a target of cruel remarks and treatment by the other kids, it was Leasure who befriended him. Not surprisingly, young Billy Leasure gained a reputation in Wayne as a sweet, shy, kindly boy who could do no wrong. It was an image that would last long after he had left Michigan and his old life behind.

Decades later, he would embrace and befriend a new set of misfits—Dennis France and Robert Kuns among them—people just as dependent on Leasure. To their faces, he was their best friend. But in Kuns's absence, Leasure's cruel nickname for the Skipper was "Dummy." Dennis France was "the idiot." They would come to know a far darker side of the shy boy from Wayne.

School was not a strong suit for Leasure. Decent enough on written tests, he undid those small successes with a strangely stubborn refusal to do homework. He just wouldn't do it, saw no future in it, not for twelve years of elementary and high school. When called upon to present an oral book report in class, Leasure would refuse, horrified at the notion of speaking in public, a phobia that persisted throughout much of his life. He'd slink down in his chair and try to disappear, but then, when the implacable teacher would finally call on him, he'd hoarsely whisper that he had no report to make, accepting the failing grade silently. Anything was better than feeling those thirty pairs of eyes focused on him at the front of the class.

Long after he was out of school, he remained bitter about those years, still harboring petty grudges against his old teachers—a high school wrestling coach who mocked him, a bookkeeping teacher who flunked him unjustly, and, most of all, his eleventh-grade English teacher, who, knowing Leasure was a shy, weak kid with pale skin, cast him as a weak, shy, pale nobody character in a school production of *Great Expectations*. He never uttered a word of protest, but just stopped showing up for rehearsal in response to what he considered to be cruel typecasting. The teacher flunked him and, as he later recalled, "She put mean comments on my report card. She never tried to help me at all. She was a real creep."[7]

Twenty-five years later, the memory still plagued him, vivid and painful, and his ears still burned with the humiliation when he spoke of it in his measured, emotionless voice. Leasure was not the sort of man to forget a slight—he had an extensive library of them catalogued and remembered. And yet he would shrug and insist such insults never bothered him. Leasure's good-boy trick was to never show the anger, never feel it, never even admit to himself that it was there. Instead, he would submit to authority, then fade into the woodwork.

He was forced to go to school, but he lived for summer vacation, when he would leave Wayne to stay with his older second cousins, who owned a farm in the broad, empty flatlands east of Muncie, Indiana. He'd work with the cattle, hogs, and horses, or he'd tinker with an ancient tractor his cousins used to till the fields—preferring the mute, comfortable, and unchallenging company of animals or machines over more difficult human companionship. At night, he wouldn't talk much, but would just sit in the creaking old farmhouse curled up in a chair, reading farm magazines.

After high school, Leasure expected to go to work for Ford or G.M., just like his father, brother, and uncle before him. It never occurred to him that any other sort of life outside the assembly of engine parts and axle bearings was possible. Cars were one of his few and earliest passions—hot rods, sports cars, particularly Corvettes. He felt comfortable with the orderly world of machines and motor oil. He could build a working car out of a few junked heaps with a deft mechanic's hand. Working the assembly line in Motor City would be a logical extension—his career by default, and after high school, he hired on at General Motors for a year.

But then the draft board beckoned, and with the war in Vietnam sucking up many of his young friends as Army inductees, he decided to enlist in the Marine Corps in 1966, hoping to get a choice assignment rather than awaiting the luck of the draw. The following year, overcoming his shyness long enough for a brief courtship, he married Joan,[8] a young woman he had met while he was stationed in California. A short time later, he shipped out overseas, his new wife still a virtual stranger.

Just as he felt misused by the public school system and, later, by the LAPD, Leasure came to feel the Marine Corps mistreated him as well. He didn't get the job in heavy equipment operation his recruiter had promised, spoiling the lucrative postmilitary future he had envisioned in the civilian construction industry. Instead, he received an infantry assignment—he became a ground pounder, potentially the toughest, ugliest, deadliest job in the war.

But, because of a paperwork glitch that sent ninety Marines to fill nine vacant positions, he was spared a combat role, drawing instead an unusual last-minute assignment, roughly akin to the duties of a military policeman. He was shipped out to a newly formed unit called a Combined Action Company, stationed at a place known to servicemen as China Beach. More recent, romanticized television portrayals aside, the China Beach Leasure knew consisted of an old French bunker amid a clump of sand dunes, a few volleyballs, no hospital, no nurses or any other nonlocal women to speak of, and three Vietnamese fishing villages. Leasure's job was to patrol these villages as a kind of constable, keeping the peace, guarding against North Vietnamese infiltration, occasionally helping Navy corpsmen inoculate the village children, and generally spreading goodwill. After receiving a few weeks of "orientation" in Da Nang—where he saw dead Marines in zippered black bags stacked by the planeload—the China Beach duty was a stunning surprise. Riotously green, Tolkienesque landscapes surrounded him, inhabited by an incredible array of giant butterflies, monkeys, jaguars, and apes. Shallow, warm waters offered majestic snorkeling and diving. And the local villagers were friendly. The war seemed remote and unreal from this vantage point. Leasure loved the duty so much, he signed up for a second tour. He never had to fire a shot.

Instead of enduring combat, young Corporal Leasure met a woman named Lon in one of the villages, and he soon began sneaking out of his barracks to meet her after lights-out. They spent countless nights talking together at the kitchen table in her small dirt-floored hut, as her parents, sisters, and brothers slept in the next room. The family was pitiably poor. Leasure sneaked a hot plate, a wristwatch, and some other military supplies to them, but, invariably, the family sold the items for food, then continued to cook on a fire in the middle of the hut and to tell time by the sun and the stars.

Lon taught Leasure rudimentary Vietnamese, and he taught her English, amazing her with tales of life in America. Lon couldn't conceive that a person could own more than one car or more than one house. Leasure told her he planned to own many of both once he returned to the States, making Lon laugh with his serious guarantees. Impossible, she would say. She was lithe and beautiful and had lost her right hand in a bomb blast, always keeping it hidden in a fold of her blouse. She couldn't say which side, North or South, was responsible for the injury, a distinction that Leasure felt was important, but which Lon considered irrelevant. She was fifteen years old when Leasure knew her, but war and poverty had aged her an extra ten years. He had never seen a fifteen-year-old with eyes so old.

Only after he was shipped back to the States did he realize he cared enough about Lon and her family to miss them, to wish he could do something to help his adopted family abroad. Had he thought of it before he left Vietnam, as some of his fellow Marines had done, he could have set up a bank account for them in the nearest city, then wired a little money now and then to help Lon survive the stifling poverty war had brought them. Ten dollars a month would have been a fortune to Lon, but it had never occurred to Leasure until he was home. And then there was no way to reach her—no mail delivery to her village, no way to help her or speak to her. It was too late.[9]

He was discharged from active-duty service in 1969 at Camp Pendleton north of San Diego, and was hired by a recruit-hungry LAPD within a few months. His Marine record was unblemished if unremarkable—his superiors felt he lacked initiative and esprit de corps, but that was about it. Nothing to keep the police department from snapping him up. This was an era of ghetto riots, radical politics, and heavy-handed police tactics. Ex-Marines were highly prized by an LAPD at war with much of its city.

But whatever enthusiasm Leasure carried with him to the job soon soured during a patrol with a training officer during his first year on the job. As Leasure would later tell it, his supervisor roughed up a suspect, an unfortunately large and powerful man who put up a fight and ended up escaping in the ensuing melee. Back at the station, the training officer ordered Leasure to falsify a report on the incident, covering up the excessive force and botched arrest. Then, behind Leasure's back, the supervisor told the other cops in the division that it was all Leasure's fault for not providing adequate backup, the cardinal sin of policing. It took months for him to overcome the bad reputation that followed. That bitter experience, combined with LAPD's decision a year or two later to yank him from the auto repair fraud investigations he loved, destroyed any loyalty Leasure might have felt for LAPD—and his profession in general.[10]

Arriving back in the States and assuming a new civilian job had been a jolt for Leasure in more ways than one: He found he hardly recognized the woman waiting for him, could not even pictured his wife Joan's face after eighteen months in Vietnam. He would later say he was no longer sure why they had gotten married in the first place. Still, they made a home together in Anaheim, California, a few miles from Disneyland, and a daughter was born a year later. As in all other things, Leasure said nothing to his wife about his unhappiness with their marriage. He simply endured his dissatisfaction in silence, and sought his comforts elsewhere.

Using his badge, uniform, and presence at the scene of tragedies as an entree, Leasure began a series of affairs, choosing the youngest, most defenseless women he could find. It was the wounded animals, the dwarfish boy, Lon, all over again—people who wouldn't challenge him, who would look up to him, who would let him fix things. One friend recalls that Leasure became involved with a sixteen-year-old named Karen a few years after becoming a policeman. Leasure was in his late twenties at the time, and, theoretically, could have ruined his career by having sex with a minor. He did it anyway, telling his friend, machine shop owner John Wieland, that he'd never get caught. Karen's parents eventually put an end to the relationship, but Leasure, as he had predicted, was never found out at LAPD. He just went on to new girlfriends.

Wieland was simultaneously amazed to see his mild friend find such success with women, and disgusted at the way Leasure was always "conning" his wife Joan, whom Wieland liked. It left the machine shop owner resenting being put in the middle, something Leasure did often, without a thought and fully expecting his friend to lie for him if need be.[11]

Leasure did, finally, get a comeuppance of sorts. A mysterious informant—a cop who worked at Central Division during a brief period when Leasure worked there on foot patrol—began calling wives of policemen and telling them of their husbands' adulterous affairs. Typically, the caller would tell a wife that Officer X was being unfaithful. "But don't take my word for it. See for yourself," the anonymous voice would say. Then he would give a time and place, typically some sleazy motel near downtown L.A., where the wayward cop could be found. At least three or four marriages of Central Division officers were ruined this way in the early seventies. The identity of the informer was never learned, though his victims sorely wanted revenge. Leasure told his patrol partner at the time that he, too, had been one of the mystery caller's victims.

One day, forlorn and depressed, Leasure pulled aside his then-partner, Phil Anninos, and told him that Joan had received the dreaded call from the LAPD's morality snitch. Joan found him in bed with another woman, Anninos recalls Leasure saying. Not only did it destroy their marriage, but it caused his then-pregnant wife to miscarry as well, Leasure told his partner.[12]

The Leasures separated in 1972. After a brief reconciliation, their divorce, filed by Joan, became final in April 1975. She kept the house, the furniture, the Datsun 240-Z, and their daughter; he got the Mustang Mach I, his Harley Davidson Sportster motorcycle, and his growing collection of tools and auto parts. The only reason stated in court papers for the end of their marriage was the legal cliché of "unhappy differences and irreconcilable disputes."[13]

Bill Leasure and Betsy Mogul married a year after the divorce became final. The union made them instantly prosperous: Their combined income, topping one hundred thousand dollars by the early eighties, allowed them to take on mortgage payments on the quarter-million-dollar waterside condo with boat slip in Long Beach, and a three-bedroom house in Sun Valley, both of which they rented out, as well as their tract home in Northridge, where they lived most of their marriage. Over time, Leasure accumulated his fleet of Corvettes and his endless piles of car bodies, chassis, and parts. Once he had a truck with a crane deliver a partially assembled vintage airplane into the yard. "Bill and his toys!" Betsy would complain to friends. "How are we going to pay for that?" But Bill always found a way.[14]

The Northridge area of Los Angeles where Bill Leasure and Betsy Mogul lived sits at the center of a vast complex of housing tracts occupying the floor of the San Fernando Valley, part of an unrelenting carpet of Spanish- and ranch-style homes with broad, flat lawns, each of which requires as much irrigation as a rice paddy to avoid turning brown and brittle in the California desert climate. Northridge was a thoroughly middle-class, white enclave, and Leasure's house sat on a pleasant side street in its midst. The house itself was of modest proportions, but it sat on a huge, pie slice of land that offered plenty of room for Leasure's personal treasures, an accumulation of possessions that never failed to shock a visitor.

There was the dismantled fuselage of a World War II training plane, its wings detached and stacked next to the cockpit. Partially cannibalized car bodies, engines, and other mechanical parts littered the yard, along with Leasure's Corvettes, his vintage Jeep, his Chevy Luv pickup truck, Betsy's Mercedes, and the other vehicles that came and went as Leasure traded, bought, sold, and rebuilt. An African pygmy goat roamed the yard, munching grass, tree bark, and anything else, edible or not, that appealed to its tastes—dangling wires from the old airplane included. Leasure had brought the goat home one day after Betsy had sent him out to buy a lawn mower. If she was chagrined, he was quite proud of the accomplishment, arguing: "I don't have to put gas in it, I never have to worry about it breaking down, and it's always outside, so I don't have to lug it out the door." She had never let him have the dog he wanted, so he named the goat Spot.

Inside the house, more car parts littered the floor and furniture. One bedroom served as Leasure's personal armory, where more than forty rifles, shotguns, handguns, automatic weapons, and silencers were stored, with tools for dismantling, cleaning, and rebuilding them. The parts of one or two weapons were usually lying spread out on an oily cloth, ready for reassembly. Leasure was a self-described "gun fiend"—off-duty, he always carried a piece strapped to his ankle. The more exotic the weapon, the better, no matter if it was legal or not.

Another bedroom doubled as a storage room, piled full with boxes, car parts, tires, and other unlikely clutter. Crammed into the living room stood several full-size commercial coin-operated pinball machines, the old-fashioned kind with buzzers and bells rather than electronic chimes for sound effects. Later, Leasure acquired a sophisticated flight simulator, a commercial type used to train and license pilots. At the same time, the living room couch was still covered with the shipping plastic months after its delivery. The kitchen table was weighted down with piles of paper. When Barbara Sanchez visited, she and her hosts had to eat out in the yard on a picnic table. Only the den appeared to be lived in with any regularity, with comfortable furniture and rich wood shelves lining the walls, heavy with books. The entire house and all the treasures within were guarded by an alarm system Leasure had installed.[15]

A former assistant city attorney who worked with Betsy, then moved north of Los Angeles, would occasionally stay over with the Leasures when she came to town on a case. She would have to sleep on the living room floor because the two extra bedrooms were too crammed with boxes and car parts and the rest of Leasure's collected possessions for even the slimmest of guests to fit inside. As fast as Betsy tried to clean, Leasure would mess up the house with even more accumulated junk. "It was a constant source of irritation to her," the friend would later recall. "I think it probably is a reflection of how much she loved Bill."[16]

Betsy Mogul had another ongoing complaint about her husband: his habitual secrecy. He would never tell her his days off, especially during a period of several years when he was assigned to the night shift. With her working days in court, they would barely see each other during the week, and by keeping his days off to himself, their contact at times was nil—they would literally pass each other in the hallway, and that would be it. She would complain to her friend, the former city attorney, about how she could never plan any outings with Bill because of her uncertainty about his work schedule. Then Leasure would suddenly come home one day and announce that he had several days off coming to him and he was going to Belize with his friend Art Smith, or someplace else with someone else. See you, bye, he'd say, and that would be it. Friends believed this drove Betsy crazy.[17]

Another secretive habit that appeared to bother Betsy was Bill's obsession with his briefcase. He kept it locked, always. Not even his wife was allowed to open it. "Why is Bill so uptight about that briefcase?" Betsy once asked Leasure's friend and sometime partner, Officer Jon Herrington. "A husband and wife shouldn't hide things from one another."

Herrington didn't know what to say. He knew all about Irene Wong, and imagined there were things in that briefcase Leasure might not want Betsy to know about. He also had heard Leasure boast of faking receipts for his car-related purchases—putting down $1250 for a $1000 transaction, for instance. By inflating the price, he'd get more cash out of his wife, who, as far as Herrington could tell, seemed to control the family wealth.[18] Leasure had told other friends about how he had to salt away money overseas so Betsy couldn't keep track of his activities—like taking girls with him on vacation. The financial chicanery seemed, in one way, a natural outgrowth of the couple's attitude about money. Both were thrifty and opposed to extravagance—even friends called them cheap. Leasure apparently felt he had to conceal some of his spending from his wife.

Bill confided in Barbara Sanchez and several other friends that he had to keep certain things hidden from Betsy—not just other women, but money he had set aside for personal use, his part-ownership in two yachts, the plans he had for the future. If Betsy found out about them, he'd say, she would make him stop. When he described this secret life of his, he sounded to Sanchez more like a naughty boy than a husband.

Much of their married life seemed to be spent pursuing sepa-rate activities. Bill had his cars and guns and boats and planes, and Betsy left him to it. They both loved to travel, but they were as likely to vacation apart as together. They often went out alone or with their separate groups of friends. They had joint checking, but they also maintained separate bank accounts. Often, Bill would have to ask Betsy for both money and permission to buy parts for his Corvette, his airplanes, or his well-equipped home workshop.

Sometimes, if he wanted to keep Betsy totally in the dark about a certain purchase, he would forego the fake receipt method and borrow the money outright from his friend Art Smith, an in-surance claims adjustor he had met in Betsy's courtroom. Smith gave him a telephone credit card in his company's name so Leasure could make calls that wouldn't show up on the Leasure-Mogul

home phone bill, avoiding possible complications when Betsy reviewed the bill each month. "Betsy would have . . . questions about
some of my calls," he told Smith. Almost in an off-handed way, he
informed many of his friends that he used offshore bank accounts
and kept his yacht registered in another police officer's name in order to conceal his assets from Betsy.[19]

He would never leave her, though, he'd say. When his friend
Flo Ong, whom he affectionately called his "second mother," asked
why not, Leasure was blunt in his answer: "She makes too much
money."

Leasure's friends were just as perplexed by the marriage as
Betsy's. The traumatic experience that capped his first marriage
didn't increase his fidelity. Leasure continued to cheat in his second
marriage. Despite this, Skipper Bob Kuns thought the Leasures
had a wonderful, affectionate relationship—Betsy, he observed,
seemed to be very affectionate, hugging and stroking her "Billy"
whenever they were all out on boating trips together. Of course,
Kuns also had shaken his head in wonder when Leasure expressed
his preference for Irene Wong. "If I had to choose, I'd pick Irene,"
he recalled Leasure saying. "No contest."

But with the exception of Kuns, few of Leasure's other friends
saw open affection displayed between Bill and Betsy. Sometimes it
looked more like Bill was suffering from outright intimidation. One
day he absently started puttering with one of his Corvettes without
changing into work clothes. Later, unannounced, he appeared in a
panic at Flo Ong's home and begged her to find some way to clean
the grease he had accidentally smeared on his dress shoes and good
"Made in the Shade" jeans. "She'll kill me, Flo. You've got to
help." Flo worked for hours scrubbing away the mess for a relieved
Leasure.

Always deferential in her presence, Leasure showed a peculiar
ambivalence when speaking about Betsy in her absence, alternately
complimenting her—he boasted once that she had given him a
Cadillac for his birthday—then later bitterly complaining that she
often mistreated him.

"Sometimes she makes me sleep on the floor," he told Flo
Ong. "I don't like it, but I do it." Once again, Flo asked him why
he stayed with her. This time, Leasure explained that they had a
"special" understanding. "She does her thing, and I do my thing."
Flo believed him at the time, but later came to view his portrait of
their marriage as a means of gaining sympathy, something she
could see he craved. He would eat a hearty homecooked meal at
Flo's, criticizing Betsy's supposedly harsh behavior between mouth-

fuls, but never once did he admit to doing anything wrong himself. Indeed, in all the time Flo Ong knew Leasure, she found he could never admit a mistake or indiscretion, and even when she caught him in a lie, he would twist it around and try to portray it as a good deed.

For two years, Bill had unsuccessfully pursued a romance with Flo's daughter, Cheryl. He had met the younger woman on duty, when he arrived at the scene of a car accident and found Cheryl injured in her irretrievably smashed one-week-old Toyota. When Flo arrived at the hospital a few hours later, her first look at Leasure was in her daughter's room, where he sat primly at her bedside with his policeman's hat on his lap, writing notes as Cheryl described how she had broadsided a Cadillac so hard it flipped over. Leasure seemed embarrassed at the young woman's naturally salty language and, at one point, covered his face with his notebook at a string of four-letter words she had uttered.

Flo, a jovial woman with a soft spot for strays of all kinds, thought him charming, and they soon became close friends. Cheryl pegged Leasure as boring and continually rebuffed his advances, mouthing the word "yuck" to her mother whenever Bill telephoned, which was often. Neither woman realized that Bill was married throughout this persistent wooing. He didn't wear a wedding ring around them or hint at the existence of another woman in his life for years. And even after they learned of Betsy's existence and called him on the point, he shrugged and blushed and said, "Well, you know," in his halting, shy way . . . and continued to call Cheryl to ask her out on dates. He never apologized to Flo or gave any hint that he thought he had done anything wrong. He said he only wanted the best for Cheryl. It was as if he truly believed that his image, not his acts, defined his character. He was bewildered when she angrily dismissed his spiel about risking his life every day as a policeman and needing understanding, not reproach. "You're not a nice man," Flo told him.

"But I am," he whispered, plaintive and hurt. "You just don't understand. I'm the nicest guy in the world. I never hurt anyone."

In any case, Betsy Mogul seemed unaware of what Bill was doing. As perceptive and discerning as she was of others, she was, apparently, blind to her husband's deceptions. She was so rigidly moralistic that she would warn friends who mentioned, for example, trying marijuana in college that "I don't want to hear that." Yet Bill could do no wrong. When Smith asked her once why she put up with him, her simple answer was, "I just love him, Art."[20]

And when Barbara Sanchez mentioned to Betsy how her

former husband's extramarital affair had ended their marriage, Betsy replied that she was glad she didn't have any such worries.

"God, if something happened like that with me and Billy," she said, "I would just die."[21]

* * *

Marital infidelity, you probably know, is not that uncommon among police officers. Opportunities present themselves more often than in other professions. Now, I'm not God's gift to women, by any means. I had my share of girlfriends—in between marriages—and the affair. But that's all. I regret it now. I was weak.

It really hurt Betsy. She was terribly humiliated by it all. I worry more about Betsy than I do my own cases. I feel terrible about what I put her through. She's really stood by me, through everything. I guess the things I thought were missing from our marriage were there all along. I'd never do anything like that again.

And now, with the last five years with AIDS and all, I don't think I'd ever mess around again, even if I wanted to.

* * *

If Bill and Betsy's marriage seemed a distant one to outsiders, there was a surprisingly large complement of other women in Leasure's life to fill the void—to become the confidante, friend, and lover he thought he was missing, with the accompanying infidelity granting him an extra bonus of adventure. If the woman was married, all the better. Shy, quiet Bill Leasure had a saying: "There's no married woman in the world you can't get—if you approach her at just the right time."

At 3:00 in the morning, when the tow truck rumbles off or the ambulance has left, it's the cop who's still there, ready to listen, ready to comfort. Like many policemen, Leasure knew that role well, and he found ample opportunities to play it. Perhaps more than anything, that willingness to manipulate others, particularly those in need, was the hallmark of Leasure's personality. There was an innate selfishness, even in his acts of charity, a strong measure of self-interest even as he told others—and himself—that he was doing *them* the favor. Whether he was the neglected, left-out schoolboy or the misfit cop, Bill Leasure was going to get his due.

Irene Wong was the perfect mistress for him—opposite in every way from Betsy Mogul. She was shy, dependent, compliant, weak, young, and beautiful—and she idolized Leasure, a man who had never been idolized before in his life. With her, Leasure could forget a lifetime of slights. With Irene, Leasure was king.

But before Irene, in the mid- to late seventies, the void in his life was filled, at least in part, by someone else: Paulette de los Reyes, a flighty, alluring woman with a troubled marriage of her own, a penchant for disasters, and a lifelong habit of using her pale, freckled good looks to bail herself out of trouble.

Paulette had two big problems when she met Bill through one of Leasure's LAPD partners, a towering cop known as Big John. First, there was the problem of her erratic musician husband, Tony Reyes, and the wild pendulum swings of their marriage. But looming even larger was the problem of their family business—the family tortilla business, and the crotchety old magnate who ran it, Gilberto Cervantes.

CHAPTER 5

"**I** WISH TONY WERE DEAD."
Paulette de los Reyes took a sip of white wine, her pallid, delicate features smooth and unconcerned, as if she had just remarked on the evening's dinner plans. She and Bill Leasure sat on her living room couch watching television together, a thriller about murders for hire. Wavy auburn hair lay spread out behind her on the cushion as Paulette leaned back and considered the possibilities. "Maybe I could put something in his food, poison him or something," she mused. "Something imaginative."

A familiar variation of an oft-repeated sentiment, Paulette's words were uttered, as always, in a light and teasing way, a slight smile crinkling her lipstick, but an unpleasant edge to her voice, a hint of steel behind the air of helpless befuddlement she normally preferred to radiate.

Bill merely laughed quietly, humorlessly, and said, "Good idea." Just as he always did.

It was their inside joke, a constant theme between them. Paulette had spoken of doing in Tony for years. Years later, though, in a secretly recorded conversation, Paulette would trace the beginning of her troubles to this conversation in the mid-seventies, a seed of events to come. But at the time, the words seemed merely wishful thinking, idle talk. Fun.

Bill had come to visit her at the duplex in Boyle Heights she shared with Tony Reyes, a two-story pseudo-Gothic hulk dubbed "The Munster House" by the neighbors. Paulette and Leasure sat inside watching a broadcast of "The Mechanic," starring a craggy and slit-eyed Charles Bronson as a professional assassin who efficiently dispatched troublesome people with silenced handguns and assorted other lethal weapons.

"I wish somebody would do that to Tony," Paulette murmured, after Bronson's third or fourth execution in the past hour.

"Piece of cake," Bill said.[1]

• • •

I was friends with Paulette. Just her, not Tony. I think I only met him once. I knew her because I was partners with Big John, and he moonlighted at the tortilla factory. He introduced us.

Paulette was good-looking but a scatterbrain. And she's getting worse. I never talked about killing people with her—not Tony, not anyone. Not even jokingly. She just made that up because she was scared, because they gave her phony police reports, they were telling her I had confessed and involved her. None of that's believable.

We never had an affair. Never. No sexual relationship whatsoever. People are just making that up. I don't know if she was involved in the murders. She says she isn't, but who knows? I only know I wasn't.

• • •

Piece of cake: that was how Paulette recalls Leasure often talking around her. Sure of himself, capable, confident, bordering on the pompous—there was nothing he couldn't do or didn't know, he seemed to be telling her. Bombings and killings in Vietnam. Sailing the high seas. International investments. He boasted of all these things to Paulette, outrageous talk, not to be taken seriously, a far cry from LAPD's Mild Bill. Except . . . Paulette was never quite sure. Somewhere, in all that out-of-kilter boasting, so unlike Bill, there was more than just talk. "He's an enigma," she would tell her friends when they asked why she spent time with him. "He surprises me."[2]

Leasure was kind to Paulette, admiring, anxious to impress, sweetly deferential and comforting during her knockdown dragouts with Tony. He continually told Paulette how he hated the way Tony treated her, beginning almost from the moment they met in 1975, when they were introduced by Leasure's police partner, Big John. Paulette found Leasure's dichotomy intriguing and his willingness to please her endearing—a welcome departure from her husband Tony. She found nothing ambiguous or endearing about Tony Reyes.

Small and thick, barely five feet seven inches tall and a trifle under 150 pounds, Tony was a tree stump of a man, unmovable and impervious. His jealous love for Paulette was never in question—even at its most violent—but there was little tenderness between them, and plenty of animosity. He had the large, strong hands of a lumberjack, big-knuckled and heavily calloused from years of fingering the steel strings of his bass. Paulette told Leasure that Tony could strangle her with one hand and no effort—and almost did, more than a few times.

Tony had scratched at the edge of the big time for more than thirty years, but that was as close as it ever got. Oh, he had plucked his bass with some big names, fill-ins with Xavier Cougat's band for one, and a few others now and then, but for the most part his ambition to excel as a jazz musician had always exceeded his talents. Tony Reyes—he preferred the shortened stage name over his birthname of Antonio de los Reyes—was a solid, journeyman bass player, but that was all. By the time he married Paulette, he had settled comfortably into late-night sets with no-name bands in dark and beery Hollywood bars, with expectations of greater things far behind him.

Even Tony knew he had a greater penchant for spending money than for earning it. His mother, Natalia, had kept him solvent over the years by slipping him regular infusions of cash from his stepfather Gilberto Cervantes's secret stockpiles—boxes of cash the old man kept salted away in his San Gabriel house. It drove Cervantes crazy. The old man wanted to cut his stepson off, to disinherit him. But everything he owned was half Natalia's, and she forbade it. She had always known she would have to protect her son from her husband.

The crisis came a year or so after Paulette met Leasure. After many false starts and reconciliations, Tony and Paulette were finally divorcing—and battling furiously over the tortilla business, the properties, the money, their young son. And on almost every score, Paulette saw herself losing.

The war had been a long time brewing. Paulette Fanchon was a Midwestern farm child transplanted from Sioux City, Iowa, to the acrid soil of a booming postwar Los Angeles. She and Tony moved in together in 1963, when she was twenty years old and on the rebound from a brief failed marriage. He was forty-five then, with two wives already behind him. They had met three years earlier in a Hollywood jazz club. Tony had stepped off the stage and befriended her newlywed husband first, then went after teenaged Paulette. They married five years after moving in together, a quickie ceremony in Las Vegas followed by a long night at the card tables.

The pattern of their relationship quickly became tidal in its regularity: a cycle of breakup and makeup, explosions and embraces. Love and hate merged into something ill-defined yet irresistible for the two of them, with habitual threats and accusations hurled at one another as often as expressions of love—and often at the same time. They would skulk into the darkness and slash each other's tires in fits of anger, then slip back into bed with one another. Paulette would wake in the middle of the night to find Tony looming over her in the dark, with neither of them certain of his intentions. She accused him of drugging her and forcing her to take part in orgies, giving her to other men as he looked on. He accused her of happily taking part in endless infidelities, of cavorting with other men when their son was watching TV in the next room, and of plotting against his business and his life.[3]

Tony Reyes had three children with three different women. The first child was put up for adoption and disinherited, her mother's identity shrouded in mystery in Los Angeles court records. The second—Antonio de los Reyes, Jr., a successful attorney who would eventually serve as a Los Angeles Police Commissioner—stayed close to his father, but disliked his young stepmother, who was almost exactly Tony Junior's age. And the hapless third child, young Aaron de los Reyes, became the wishbone in bitter custody battles as the only offspring of the ever-warring Tony and Paulette. Still in grade school, Aaron periodically was forced by one or the other of his parents to write pitiful affidavits to be filed in divorce court—alternately attesting to why he would rather live with one parent or the other, depending on who was hovering over him while he painstakingly penned his name to the legal papers.

Paulette and Tony separated in June 1976 after a particularly vicious fight, eight years of something approximating marriage behind them. Tony filed for divorce a week later, intent on convincing Paulette he meant business this time. There would be no reconciliation, he vowed.

A power struggle soon began at the tortilla factory, where Tony, long an absentee owner, belatedly tried to assert control over the business he jointly owned with his mother and stepfather. Paulette, meanwhile, sought the factory as her divorce settlement, and began systematically firing all the old employees at El Sol Tortillas, replacing them with workers loyal only to her. "You're to follow my orders, not Tony's or his stepfather's," she instructed the deliverymen who trucked out cases of tortillas every day. "I'm in charge." Then Tony would come in and deliver the same message, except he was supposed to be the boss. Gilberto Cervantes, in turn, began to assert that he would wrest the factory back from both Tony and Paulette, since he still retained sole ownership of the land and building, if not the business itself. The tortilla business, not surprisingly, began an ungraceful nose dive into penury as drivers began fighting among one another over routes, deliveries were missed, customers were lost, and tortillas sat moldering on the shelf at the factory. Occasionally, the lugubrious sight of tiny Paulette in her garish designer clothes tooling around East Los Angeles in a delivery van, peering over the steering wheel and trying to deliver tortillas, provided a measure of comic relief.

A few months later, at the height of the tortilla wars, Paulette's car was vandalized, its tires shredded, the paint scored. Tony telephoned her later, laughing. She had gotten what she deserved, he said.

Furious over the car and her increasingly desperate situation—Tony was making noises about wresting custody of Aaron from her in the divorce—Paulette turned for help to Bill Leasure and his latest LAPD partner, a beefy blond giant known as Big John, who had introduced Paulette and Leasure a year or so earlier.

Big John worked for Paulette at the tortilla factory. He drove an El Sol delivery van in his spare time, and when he wasn't doing that, he was dating Paulette, which infuriated Tony, divorce or no divorce. (Leasure's affair with Paulette would begin later.) Tony's jealousy did not end with the dissolution of his marriage or his own constant infidelities. He began making regular complaints to LAPD's Internal Affairs Division, claiming Big John had threatened him and had taken an extra job without LAPD permission, a department violation. After innumerable calls, Tony finally got his wish: Big John was reprimanded for moonlighting without first getting permission, and he had to give up his job at El Sol. Leasure and Big John were livid at Tony's antics.

"He needs a good scare," Leasure suggested to Paulette. "And I know just how to do it."[4]

On October 7, 1976, at about 4:00 in the morning, an explosion rocked the subterranean garage of the Hollywood apartment building in which Tony lived at the time. Several sticks of dynamite hooked to a battery and a simple windup kitchen timer had detonated beneath Tony's Dodge Polara station wagon, rupturing the transmission and flattening all four tires. No one was hurt—Tony was sound asleep in his apartment at the time—but he was understandably shaken at the apparent escalation in his war with Paulette. Leasure had told her he was an expert in demolition from his tour in Vietnam,[5] and she made sure Tony knew about it. She would later tell police that the bomb she claimed Leasure planted could not possibly have killed anyone—even if the car had been occupied. But Bill had guaranteed the explosion would scare the hell out of Tony. Of that they all were sure.[6]

A pair of overworked detectives from LAPD's criminal conspiracy section downtown investigated the bombing, but they found no firm suspects and made no arrests. Tony was notably uncooperative. He told them he had no idea who was behind the bombing or who would want to hurt him. But he knew. He knew the bomb was a message. Not long afterward, Tony acquiesced to Paulette's demand that she get El Sol as part of the divorce settlement. He even joked about it later with Paulette, when she told him Leasure had wired the dynamite as a threat, not a murder attempt. "If you had told me, I would have gotten better car insurance coverage," he said, and they both laughed.[7]

Still, the battle of de los Reyes versus de los Reyes might have continued to escalate if left uninterrupted. But something changed the course of their discord, uniting them, at least for a while. Suddenly they had a common enemy: Gilberto Cervantes.

Tony hated his stepfather, furious for years at the way the aging tortilla magnate had treated the dying, diabetic Natalia. The conflict between stepson and stepfather was elemental: Gilberto could never forgive Tony's profligate life-style, his free-spending ways, his parade of women, his dogged ability to spend Cervantes's money and his equally dogged determination to make none of it himself.

Gilberto was just the opposite, a hoarder and a miser. He refused to wear anything but secondhand suits long out of fashion. Every Christmas, his wife would buy him a new dress shirt; later, relatives rooting through the mess in Gilberto's home would find dozens of them piled unused in his closet, some of them decades old, dusty and still wrapped in faded tissue from the store. Over the years, Gilberto turned his home into a cluttered museum of useless possessions he refused to let go of, with piled boxes and stacks of ragged, reeking clothes everywhere. He had cases of wine in the kitchen from the thirties, never opened, long since turned to vinegar, yet there they sat, awaiting a feast Gilberto never threw.[8]

The only person who could control Gilberto was Tony's mother, Natalia Lara Cervantes. But by early 1977, she had fallen terminally ill, no longer able to intercede on Tony's behalf. Diabetes had taken a severe toll on Natalia, and Gilberto's general neglect of his wife had hastened her decline. She had been hospitalized several times for malnutrition, having remained for days untended in bed, unfed and uncleaned. Cervantes refused to hire a day nurse for her, but he also was reluctant to help his wife with her insulin injections.

Tony repeatedly accused Gilberto of deliberately trying to bring on her death. She eventually lost both her legs in the last years of her life—amputated when circulatory collapse allowed untended infections, then gangrene, to set in.[9]

At the same time Natalia's health began to fail, the tortilla business they had built together was faltering as well, thanks to Tony and Paulette's bitter divorce. When he heard of Tony's plans to settle his divorce by offering up the tortilla business to Paulette, Gilberto decided he had to do something to save his beloved El Sol. After learning that Paulette had her new lover Big John working at the factory, Cervantes made what was, for him, the ultimate threat: he'd write Tony out of his will. He didn't care what Natalia's last wishes might be. He would see to it Tony had no business, no real estate, no money—and that meant nothing for Paulette as well. Natalia would be gone soon—the doctors had said so—then no one could stop Gilberto from carrying out his threat. They'd get nothing—he vowed it.

It was the one threat neither Paulette nor Tony could live with. As it turned out, neither could Gilberto.

Paulette knew where to turn. In tears, she told her one true friend and confidant all about Gilberto's plan to change the will, and how it would destroy her, Tony, their divorce settlement, even their son Aaron's future. Bill Leasure listened sympathetically, telling her everything would be all right.

"Oh, everything's going wrong," she countered. The factory was falling apart, business was dying, she needed major repairs on the tortilla machinery. What should she do? Maybe she should just kill herself.

Bill calmed her, once again the man with the answers. Some of her problems would be easy to solve: For instance, he said, he knew a fellow—an experienced welder—who might be able to tackle the factory repairs at a reasonable price, and handle all sorts of other problems as well. Was she interested? Paulette gratefully accepted, and a few days later, Leasure brought one of his odder friends to El Sol Tortillas to meet her.

"Is this the welder?" Paulette asked, eyeing the scruffy little man with the flat, hard eyes Leasure had brought to the factory.

Dennis Winebaugh smiled brightly and drawled hello.

Paulette, hearing the thick accent, asked where he was from.

"Oklahoma, ma'am," Winebaugh replied. "Born and raised in Oklahoma."[10]

CHAPTER 6

I met Dennis Winebaugh at Wieland's Machine Shop. He was a welder there. He seemed like a nice person. He was an astute guy. I can weld, but I'm not a master. When I needed something critical done, I'd get Dennis Winebaugh. We got to be friends. Just casual friends. We didn't really socialize or anything.

We shared an interest in firearms—an interest I guess I've had since I was in the Marine Corps, where they drive it into you, you've got to take care of your weapon or you'll die. I guess I'm kind of a gun fiend. Not shooting, but collecting. I started to go with Dennis Winebaugh to gun shows. He was a gun fiend, too.

Dennis might have done some bad things, I don't know. I didn't know that then, and he never would have told me. He knew I would arrest him if he told me about anything criminal. That's why this whole thing is so ridiculous. . . . But as far as I'm concerned, he's the only one in this whole case with any integrity. He's the only one who hasn't made a deal with the prosecutor. He's the only one who won't rat on me. He says, "Bill hasn't done anything wrong, and I'm not gonna say he did."

• • •

A GOOD OL' BOY FROM OKLA-homa City, Dennis Dean Winebaugh had a down-home drawl, a bagful of stories, narrow gray eyes that twinkled with frequent and genuine amusement, and a fondness for powerfully lethal handguns so great that it earned him his distinctive CB radio handle: Forty-four Magnum. Or just plain Forty-four to his buddies around the welding shop.

There was something else about Winebaugh: Somehow, without really having to try very hard, he scared people. This quality did not derive from his appearance, which was hardly imposing. He wasn't particularly big or strong-looking—he seemed more on the short and dumpy side, especially in his favorite position of repose, lounging at the kitchen table in his boxer shorts and ratty white T-shirt, his prized Citizen's Band radio in front of him. Nor did he unnerve people with his claim of possessing a black belt in karate, although he seemed to have the moves to back up that boast. On several afternoons, he gave martial arts lessons to Leasure and some other policemen Leasure invited over. Bill watched Winebaugh toss a few hundred pounds of LAPD beef around the room with apparent ease, and realized Winebaugh's big talk had some apparent basis in fact.

Still, it wasn't Forty-four's physical prowess that intimidated. It was his way of looking up from his beer and glancing at a man with flat, button eyes, a reptile watching its supper crawl just close enough—the kind of stare that made you blink and look away no matter how hard you tried to meet it. That's what made Winebaugh scary. He simply had the look of someone who, bottom line, just didn't give a damn about anything or anyone. He had a finite gathering of people and objects he consciously decided to care about—a few friends, a wife, children, his gun collection, the CB base station he hunched over for hours every day. Anything else was fair game.

Rumors at work and around the neighborhood bars abounded about Winebaugh. He was said to dispatch beatings, shootings, and bombings for pay, sometimes just for revenge or fun. Truckers and CB radio freaks who knew him warned friends to steer a wide berth around Forty-four Magnum. They said he'd corner you in the asphalt desert behind some truck stop, diesel rigs spewing soot and carcinogens while their drivers parked and tried to ease down off a cross-country dose of speed, and he'd shoot you full of holes, just like in the Wild West. And if anyone asked how good he was with that nickel-plated .44 of his, he had a ready answer: "Best shot you'll ever see." He would deliver the line with that little twinkle and a smile and that disarming drawl, and it made you want to buy him a beer, stay on his good side. Because you believed him.

Bill Leasure met Forty-four Magnum at one of his friends' businesses, Wieland's Machine and Manufacturing in Paramount, where Winebaugh did his day work. Wieland's is gone now, but Paramount is still the same, one of a string of airless, inland suburbs stretching south from Los Angeles, bisected by freeways, hollowed out by recession and spiraling real estate prices—small cities where both sides of the tracks hold the same dreary, sagging look, commercial streets glittering with broken glass, graffiti covering corrugated fences. Vast stretches of the Los Angeles area look like this, hot ribbons of concrete winding through neighborhoods of sagging two-bedroom bungalows, a freeway view that disillusions tourists and newcomers daily, coloring even the streets around the sterile utopia of Disneyland.

Leasure moved to the Paramount area during his divorce from Joan, where he roomed briefly with a fellow policeman. He met John Wieland, Jr. one day in his apartment complex parking lot, where the two men started an animated discussion about Corvettes that ended with a high-speed, suspension-busting freeway ride in Leasure's silver and burgundy sports car. Leasure brought the car to Wieland's shop for repairs and, not long after, started bringing welding jobs for all his cars and other projects there. He became such a fixture at the place that Wieland finally gave Leasure his own key. He could come in and use the machine shop himself if he felt like grinding or welding after hours. Wieland and his father, who had founded the business, trusted him so much, they gave him the code to the electronic burglar alarm—he was a cop, after all, John Wieland figured. Who needs more security than that?

One day, though, Wieland came to believe his policeman friend had used and manipulated him. He learned that Leasure was putting together silencers in the welding shop, and that he even had Wieland himself working on the illegal assassin's devices without realizing what those perfect little black tubes were for. Furious at his friend for involving him, Wieland cooled his relationship with Leasure after that—building a silencer was a federal offense, one that could send him to prison or destroy his business. But that estrangement came many years after they met. Back in 1974, Bill was a welcome, frequent guest, and it was at this time that Leasure befriended one of the top welders who worked at Wieland's—Dennis Winebaugh.[1]

They were an unlikely match, given Leasure's line of work and Winebaugh's reputation for mayhem—just as, later on, Dennis France and Robert Kuns would seem equally strange soulmates for Mild Bill. But the relationship worked. Winebaugh liked the idea of having a cop for a friend. And Leasure liked hanging around with a dangerous borderline type of guy like Forty-four who, at heart, was a policeman "wannabe," and therefore easily influenced by Officer Leasure. It was the start of a pattern for the young cop, part of a dawning realization of the quiet impunity a badge could grant. Not so much a power to brutalize or command—Leasure disliked and distrusted the macho headbashers on the force. Leasure decided that long before videotaped beatings aroused national concern about brutality at LAPD. The training officer who used excessive force, botched the collar, then saddled Leasure with the blame years earlier had permanently soured Leasure on the use of force. Indeed, he had never used his gun on duty, and he was known to fret for days if he had to use any sort of physical force to subdue a suspect. Rather, the power Leasure sensed in his chosen occupation was far more subtle—the simple discovery that the uniform and the badge meant people would give you the benefit of the doubt. No matter who you associated with or what you did, so long as you did it quietly and pleasantly, drawing minimal attention to yourself, a policeman could do anything. Bill Leasure had discovered his badge conferred the ultimate freedom: to do as he pleased.[2]

Dennis Winebaugh was the perfect proof of the principle. By himself, Forty-four was a criminal, a totally inappropriate friend for a policeman. In cop vernacular, which divides the populace into three groups—policemen, citizens, and assholes—Winebaugh was firmly entrenched in group three. Yet, because Officer Leasure chose to associate with him, Winebaugh was redeemed. No questions were asked. Other police officers accepted Winebaugh, decided he must be "okay" once they knew Leasure vouched for him, befriending him, taking karate lessons from him, selling guns to him. The us-them world of police department culture guaranteed that Leasure's friendship would confer upon the big-talking welder an aura of respectability, trust, and clout he never could have achieved alone. Winebaugh, in turn, could give Leasure back an edge of dangerousness and risk he could never find writing tickets.[3]

The two of them shared an avid interest in cars. Leasure used most of the welders at Wieland to perform his automotive work from time to time, but he preferred to employ Winebaugh whenever he could. Leasure considered himself a journeyman with the acetylene torch, but Forty-four was a master, able to tackle the toughest jobs in a fraction of the time others might take. With critical components of a car—chassis work or motor mounts, which, if they failed on the freeway, could prove fatal—Leasure insisted on his friend Winebaugh's help.

They also shared a mutual fascination with guns, trading them, working on them together, sometimes heading out to the desert or the firing range for target shooting together. Some days they just sat around the kitchen table at Winebaugh's apartment, reloading used casings with fresh lead and powder—cheaper than buying whole, ready-to-shoot cartridges. Winebaugh did it because he made only a marginal living as a welder; Leasure was just nat-

urally cheap, and besides, it was something to do, part of being a
real gunslinger. They'd go to gun shows together, entering that curious milieu that brings together, no questions asked, the two most
avid groups of gun enthusiasts there are—crooks and cops. The
gun shows made them part of a subculture, a world apart where
certain weapons are revered like lost da Vincis, while others, less
valuable but still treasured, are passed around with the nostalgic
gleam other people reserve for long-lost family photos. Leasure and
Winebaugh would pick through boxes of gun parts, examining with
care and joy the metal cylinders and barrels gleaming beneath
sheens of light oil, pieces of killing machines. For them, guns were
adult baseball cards, things to be traded, savored and saved, then
pulled out on rare occasions for admiration.

Within a few months of their meeting, Leasure became a regular visitor to the Winebaugh apartment, often coming by for an
hour or two in his patrol car and in uniform when he was supposed
to be on duty miles away. He'd write a ticket or two or work an accident, then disappear for the rest of his shift. He'd find Forty-four
in his boxers at the kitchen table, speaking into his CB, and say,
"C'mon, Den. We have to talk." And that would be the signal for
Tammy, Winebaugh's wife, to pick up the kids and leave the room
so Leasure and Winebaugh could speak in privacy. Leasure barely
spoke above a whisper anyway, it seemed to Tammy, but he still
never would talk to her husband until she had cleared out.[4] Either
that, or, if she was busy and couldn't leave, they would step outside. Tammy didn't like it—didn't like Leasure, for that matter—
but she knew better than to protest. Winebaugh had gotten so mad
once at being interrupted, he had ripped his telephone out of the
wall and refused to get another one. "Ringin's drivin' me crazy," he
had said by way of explanation. Tammy always left when he told
her to.

Following one such visit, Tammy returned to the apartment
after seeing the patrol car depart. Inside, she found her husband at
the table, studying a mug shot of a petty criminal named Carlos
Sepulveda. The photo was stapled to a piece of yellow legal paper.
In Leasure's somewhat childish scrawl, the paper contained a physical description of Carlos, information from his rap sheet, his home
and work addresses, and detailed directions on how to drive to
both. When Tammy asked what it was about, Winebaugh said
Carlos was a crazy, that he had been harassing Leasure's wife,
Betsy. Carlos supposedly had been calling Betsy, threatening to kill
her, driving by the house, and generally making a nuisance of
himself—a series of encounters that preceded the transient incident

at Leasure's house. At one point, Carlos had vowed to burn down a furniture warehouse owned by Betsy's father and, a few weeks later, the place did go up in flames, probably through arson, although there had been no hard evidence and no witnesses against Carlos.[5]

"Bill wants me to take care of him," Winebaugh told his wife. "Bust him up."

"Why doesn't Bill do it himself? Why do you have to be involved?" Tammy didn't like this development, but Winebaugh brushed off her protests.

"He's a cop. He's got to stay out of it. That's why he wants me to take care of the guy."[6]

Whether this was to be a favor for a friend or a paying engagement remained unclear to Tammy. Winebaugh never got the chance to do anything about it, because Carlos was arrested on unrelated charges and deported to Mexico a short time later (notwithstanding the fact that he had illegally immigrated from Ecuador, not Mexico). Carlos stopped being a problem, making Leasure's request moot. Forty-four's willingness to do Leasure's bidding, however, cemented their relationship for good. Winebaugh began telling his friends that he worked for Leasure—and Leasure worked for him.

Not long after, Leasure brought Winebaugh to El Sol Tortillas and his good friend Paulette de los Reyes. Exactly what was said at that meeting remains unknown, except, of course, to those few present, and each would later have reasons to tell the story differently. Only this much seems clear: Leasure introduced a new worker to his new employer. And whatever else, if anything, happened that day in the airless confines of El Sol Tortilla Factory, as hot oil bubbled and flat circles of flour were cooked, toasted, and wrapped in plastic, that introduction would prove to be a pivotal moment for Bill Leasure. The events that flowed from it would change his life and alter the course of many other lives as well. Some people would die because of that introduction. Others would go to prison. All because someone who wanted control of the tortilla factory did indeed put Dennis Winebaugh to work—in more ways than one.

First Winebaugh took care of the welding. Then he took care of Gilberto Cervantes.[7]

Five thousand up front, five thousand after, that was the "standard contract" he offered for Gilberto's demise. Tony Reyes would later claim Gilberto's death arose from a deal between

Paulette and Forty-four. Paulette would pin the rap on Tony. Winebaugh would implicate them both. Still others would name Leasure as the guiding force behind the hit.

Motivations and catalysts aside, the events of March 20, 1977, are undisputed. Dennis Winebaugh asked his good friend, neighbor, and fellow welder, Dennis France, to give him a ride to the city of San Gabriel. "My car's not workin'," Forty-four explained. "Let's take yours, we can go out in the desert, do some target shootin'. But first I gotta take care of a job—I have to go hit an old Mexican."

France said fine. He would claim later that he was unsure of exactly what Winebaugh intended to do in San Gabriel when he used the word "hit"—beat the old man, kill the old man, who knew with a guy like Forty-four? Not that it mattered. France had a simple code: Winebaugh was his friend, the old man was not. If Winebaugh wanted to harm a stranger, it was no concern of France's. And if it was for a friend of Bill's, as Winebaugh had implied, all the better. Dennis France loved cops and everything about them—he was a police fanatic and, at that time, was anxious to get to know Leasure better.

Winebaugh told France to drive the pickup and wait behind the wheel while Forty-four did the job. France must have guessed what was about to happen—he had watched Forty-four tuck a Smith and Wesson .357 Magnum revolver into his belt as they left the apartment, and never said a word. They even discussed what kind of ammunition he had slipped into the cylinder: 160-grain hollow-point.

They made the long drive from their apartment building in Paramount to San Gabriel, the cool dampness before dawn blowing in their windows as they sipped paper cups of bitter convenience-store coffee. Traffic was as light as it ever got on a Los Angeles freeway—they could actually drive for ten to fifteen seconds without seeing another car. Not bad for Sunday morning.

Winebaugh said he had been told when the old man would be coming home from church—early, before 7:00. They would park just down the street from the house and wait until they saw the man's green Caddie. Then they would glide up behind it, Forty-four would get out, and France would pull up a few houses down the street and wait. "Keep the engine running, I won't be long," Winebaugh said.

They arrived twenty minutes early and had the wide residential stretch of South Palm Street to themselves while they waited—except for a neighbor, Mary Tritto, and her little dog, out for their daily walk. When Mary looked into the truck and smiled, France grew nervous and wanted to leave. But Forty-four told him to relax, the elderly lady hadn't seen a thing worth remembering. He gave her a little wave and she walked on.

When the big green Cadillac pulled into the driveway a few minutes later, Winebaugh got out and France waited, as he had been told. Forty-four wore gloves and a fatigue jacket. Less than a minute later, the report of a handgun sounded; then Winebaugh climbed back into the truck. "Let's go do some real shootin'," he said. France grunted, took a last look at the empty street, then drove off. "I'm not sure he's dead," Winebaugh muttered absently. "I got him on the right side, so I'm not sure. We'll check tomorrow."

Back on South Palm, Gilberto Cervantes finished staggering, then fell to the ground. His threat to disenfranchise his stepson had ended; his will would not be changed. Sickly Natalia would die soon and pass on everything to Tony Reyes. Then, after some predictably violent disagreements, Tony and Paulette would settle their differences—for a time.

The killing remained a mystery. The police knew of Gilberto's threat to disinherit Tony, they knew of the power struggle at El Sol, and the hatred the old man and Paulette had for one another. They knew exactly who stood to benefit from the death, and why. What they didn't know was the identity of the triggerman.

Tony and Paulette—prime suspects with plenty of motive in the minds of San Gabriel city detectives—had airtight alibis. No witness or physical evidence could be found to establish the identity of the killer. For a time, police thought they had a hot lead when they found a scrawled, penciled message, presumably from a dying Gilberto, etched onto the fender of the pickup truck in the garage, a splash of blood on the ground below. "John," it said. Certain Big John, who by then was openly living with Paulette, was their man, the San Gabriel detectives commandeered his service revolver. It was potentially the right caliber (.38s, like Big John's, and .357s, like Winebaugh's, use the same ammunition), but ballistics tests quickly showed it was not the murder weapon. And that was that. There were no other leads. The murder would remain unsolved for the next decade.

• • •

Winebaugh and France might have been using my name to scare people—claiming I was involved with doing bad things when I wasn't, just to keep people quiet. It was a lie, but I can see how it would scare people off. Who's going to go to the police if they think the police are the bad guys?

But all I ever did was introduce Paulette to Winebaugh. Whatever else happened after that, I had nothing to do with it. All I did was get him a job at the tortilla factory. Unfortunately.

• • •

A few weeks after Gilberto Cervantes's murder, a strange scene played itself out in Dennis Winebaugh's apartment in Paramount, thirty miles south of the musty house in San Gabriel where the old man had been gunned down. Inside the apartment, three men sat at a chipped Formica kitchen table, spending the afternoon talking and drinking instant coffee—Dennis France, Dennis Winebaugh, and their towering, heavy-set friend and neighbor, Bill Jennings. As the two Dennises sat at the table, loading lead slugs and gunpowder into used brass casings, they started bragging to Jennings about a "job" they had done recently for a family in the tortilla business. "We bumped a guy off," Winebaugh said. Then they stared at Jennings, gauging his reaction.

A long-haul truck driver and former biker, Jennings was not shocked easily. He had been involved in welfare fraud and a few other petty crimes—but not murder, not anything close. "I don't care to hear about that," he told his friends, not sure he believed them or not, and happy to keep it that way.

Jennings believed Winebaugh to be a big talker, and France to be a compulsive liar with a tendency toward cowardly acts of violence—"the kind of guy who would wait till you turned your back, then shoot," he would later say. Probably, Jennings figured, they were just trying to convince him how tough they were with their murderous talk. Pathetic, he thought. But why take chances? "If you're doing that sort of thing, I don't need to know about it," he told them as tactfully as he could.

Winebaugh wasn't ready to stop talking, though. He began telling Jennings about his good friend Bill at LAPD. He said he had this cop in his pocket, that he could get anything done with an ally like that behind him—and never worry about being caught. "I know lots of cops," he said, with France nodding solemnly and saying, "Me, too."

The conversation abruptly ended when one of the Dennises looked out the window and said, "Here comes Bill."

Outside, an LAPD black and white patrol car had pulled to a

stop. Leasure was in uniform and carrying something in his arms—a package of some sort, wrapped in a windbreaker, as if he was trying to conceal whatever it was he was holding. Jennings squinted out the window, but could not make out what Leasure carried. Then Winebaugh turned to Jennings and said, "You'd better go now. He'll want to talk to us alone."

Then he added a strange warning. "Remember," he said, his pleasant Oklahoma drawl making the words all the more ominous. "You'd better not let Bill know we told you about this."

"Yeah," France added. "If he knows you know, he'll waste ya."[8]

The visitor made a hasty exit, promising to keep his mouth shut, once again unsure whether or not to believe his friends. Talking about friends and accomplices on the police force—or lying about it—was a great way to make sure Jennings never went to the police to inform on France or Winebaugh. He could never know if it was true or not, or if the cop he might take his story to was one of the dirty ones. With Winebaugh and France, you never knew what to believe.

A few weeks later, Winebaugh introduced Jennings to Paulette de los Reyes. He had gotten laid off from his truck-driving job, and Forty-four told him Paulette would give him a job at the tortilla factory. Working there delivering tortillas to corner markets, he soon heard about the old man who once had owned El Sol, and how he had been gunned down mysteriously outside his home. Jennings remembered his talk with the two Dennises. "We killed an old Mexican," France had said, smiling blandly, as if he was discussing deer hunting or target shooting. Not long after, he saw both Forty-four and Dennis France come to the factory and meet with Paulette in her office.[9]

Bill Jennings knew then that France and Winebaugh had not been boasting idly. Whether Leasure was involved, or whether they had just invoked a cop's name to make him wary of going to the police, Jennings couldn't say.

All he knew was, he was going to keep quiet—very, very quiet.

CHAPTER 7

ON HER SIXTH ANNIVERSARY,
Anne Marie Smith asked for two things: new shoes and a divorce.

At first, Art Smith seemed unexpectedly amenable. They had even gone to a mall after dinner that same night and bought three pairs of shoes (she couldn't decide which color to get, so Art said get all three), then talked quietly of a friendly property settlement. Arthur Gayle Smith was nothing if not practical.

When he handed a credit card to the cashier at the shoe store, the young clerk appraised the purchase admiringly and said, "Gee, that's nice. I wish my husband would do that for me."

"Well, this is part of her anniversary present," Art said, setting the girl up, unable to help himself.

The clerk looked to Anne questioningly, but the dark, pretty woman buying the expensive Italian pumps wouldn't meet her eye. The clerk bit anyway. "Oh, that's really nice, sir. What's the other part of the anniversary present?"

Bill Leasure's good friend Art Smith smiled weakly as he signed the credit card slip. "She wants a divorce." Then they walked out, leaving the clerk staring.[1]

The calm of that evening dissipated quickly. Within a few weeks of the Smiths' March 3, 1980, anniversary, their supposedly tranquil divorce had lurched into courtroom terrorism. Anne's own daughter, Christine, had testified against her, taking stepfather Art's side over her own mother's, accusing Anne of insane bouts of anger and portraying Art as a fine husband and father. "You're not my daughter! I disown you!" Anne had shouted at Chris afterwards. Art, meanwhile, swore to his wife she would never get a cent from the divorce. "You came into this marriage with nothing," he growled, "and you're going out with nothing!"[2]

After that, Anne Smith began to live in fear of Art. Her whole family had heard her describe how he had hurled her against a wall one night, then ripped her credit cards from her wallet and her jewelry from her neck—all because she wouldn't sign a property settlement giving him the lion's share of their money. That was her version, anyway; Art and Christine swore Anne had started the fight. Not long after, on the night of May 28, 1980, Anne sobbed over the phone for more than an hour with her sister-in-law, Nicki Pontrelli, sputtering about the latest brutal hearing in court, and Art's ever-darkening threats.

"He told me, 'I'll break you,' " she wept to Pontrelli. "He said, 'This isn't over yet.' Nicki, I'm afraid Art will stop at nothing."

Now someone was tailing her, she said. Anne had been complaining to friends for weeks about men following her. She recognized one of them—thin, slouching, balding, a nondescript man wearing aviator sunglasses. He cut the kind of figure Anne never would have noticed if she didn't already know him.

But she did know Bill Leasure. And she was scared.[3]

• • •

Art Smith was a good friend. We met when I was working bunco-forgery. Art was a witness in one of my cases. Betsy was the prosecutor. I had to go over to his office on York Boulevard a couple times to work on the case. And we hit it off.

Art is a real generous guy. He was generous with his own daughter, and with the other two kids, who were Anne's from an earlier marriage. He was a really good father. Sometimes he bragged too much. He was full of himself, sure. You can't ever wrestle him for a tab in a restaurant. He's just a really, really nice guy.

I was not real close to Anne, but I liked her a lot, and we got along well. She invited me a few times to tennis, and we had dinner together a few times, over there, or we'd all go out. We were not unfriendly, and not close friends. But she was the wife of one of my best friends. I was sorry their marriage wasn't working out. I felt bad for Art, for both of them.

• • •

Anne and Art met in 1973. She was a thirty-four-year-old single mother, twice divorced from the same man. He had just hit his early forties, he was striking out in business for himself for the first time, and he also was on the rebound from a divorce.

Art had rented an apartment in the scruffy Highland Park section of Los Angeles, where his landlord was Delores Garofola, owner of Dee Ann's House of Beauty next door. Dee had almost told the crewcut former Marine sergeant to get lost—he spent half an hour trying to talk her down five bucks from the monthly rent of $150 she was asking—but he finally relented and leased the place. To Delores, he seemed like "a good American boy, a stout Marine," as she later told her daughter, Anne. She saw him as a good prospect for her divorced daughter, and Delores made a point of introducing them the next day when Anne came to work at the beauty shop.

They started dating a few weeks later. Delores smiled every time she saw the couple together—the tall, lanky, gregarious Anne and, on her arm, the shortish, broad, red-haired new boyfriend, who tended to be a bit dour at times, but who seemed to worship Anne. He was almost insufferably pleased that such an attractive younger woman would have him—he didn't just take her out, he displayed her, speaking about her looks to other people as if she wasn't present. When Anne complained later to her mother that Art was pleasant enough, but that she felt no chemistry between them, Delores told her to be sensible. This was 1973, and Dee's advice to her daughter matched the tenor of the times: She needed a husband. A single mother with two young children couldn't afford to be too picky. Art was substantial, a businessman on the rise. Don't let him get away.

In the years to come, that conversation would come to haunt Delores. She would know the ache of words uttered and later regretted, but which never could be recalled. "I was so wrong," she'd say, and then stare at her daughter's picture.

Anne had been a sickly, asthmatic child, stuck indoors, too fragile at times to play with the others, pale and thin and wistful. But she flourished in adolescence, becoming a darkly pretty woman who hid the insecurities of her sheltered, wallflower youth behind a brassy, bold exterior and a truck driver's mouth inherited from her father, which made even her plain-talking mother blush at times. In high school, she became a cheerleader. She was an avid dancer, she entered beauty contests, she would talk to anyone. As an adult, Anne didn't just walk into a room, she made an entrance. "It's me, it's me—Anne Marie," she'd always proclaim as she passed through the door, halting whatever conversations or activities might be in progress without her.

Barely out of her teens, she had married a Los Angeles policeman and had two children. But her husband's chronic drinking problem eventually destroyed both his career and their marriage. After their divorce, Anne fell in love with a young nightclub singer, but before their relationship progressed far, her ex-husband was injured and nearly blinded on the job. He begged her for help, and Anne went back to him, remarrying him, trying to reunite their family of four while nursing him back to health. The singer was brokenhearted. So was Anne, but she said it was something she had to do.

When Anne and her husband parted company again for good a year or so later, the singer had embarked on a new relationship. He said he couldn't forgive Anne and would not leave his new fiancée for her. Crestfallen, Anne found herself alone and beset by financial problems—a repossessed car and an ex-husband who could pay no child support. All she had was a job setting hair at her mother's beauty salon, bolstered by the meager earnings of part-time cocktail waitressing. She had a fourteen-year-old daughter and an eight-year-old son, and their demands for clothes and cassettes and movies and fast food were spiraling quickly beyond her means. And then along came Art—substantial, solid, dull, punctual, meticulous Art Smith.

"But I don't love you," she told him when he proposed after six months of dating.

"You'll learn to love me," Art replied.[4]

Maybe, maybe not, Anne would later tell her friends. But it was worth the gamble, she figured. Anne needed the security, the buffer against loneliness, the help with her son and daughter. She said yes, Art, I suppose I will fall in love with you. They married on March 3, 1974.

The tyrant emerged—at least according to Anne's admittedly partisan friends and family—soon after.

It wasn't that Art denied Anne anything material. He bought her anything she wanted, and more—and he had the money to do it. He was a successful independent insurance adjustor, appraising accident damages and repairs for major insurers—a busy, lucrative industry in auto-obsessed Southern California. The L.A. freeways become gridlocked bumper-car rides during daylong rush hours, generating scores of car crashes every day, a literal insurance-claims machine. Not to mention the fact that Los Angeles is the car break-in capital of the world. Art had more offers for work than he could accept, leaving him plenty of money for vacations, clothes, investment properties, a boat.

Art was always buying and selling cars (a Cadillac and a Mercedes to the Leasures, for instance), homes, or real estate, and he kept anywhere from forty thousand to ninety thousand dollars in cash in his safe at work at all times. You never know when the opportunity for the right deal or purchase might materialize, he told his friend Bill Leasure. He bought a thirty-acre island for thirty thousand dollars off the coast of Belize in Central America, which he planned to develop into a resort with Bill Leasure's help. He owned another lake resort property in Minnesota, already in business.

He was always free with his money with Anne and the kids. At his own suggestion, he paid for Anne's breast enlargement while they were still dating. After the operation, she took her blouse off for some girlfriends and said, "Can you believe these things?" She was really proud of the change in her figure. So was Art. He commissioned an expensive nude oil painting of her, which hung boldly in their master bedroom. When her son Scott turned twelve, he started charging neighborhood kids quarters to sneak in and leer at it. Anne went through the roof when she came home one day to find four pubescent boys discussing her nipples. But Art refused to take it down.

Generous as he was with his money, Art Smith made innumerable demands in return. As Anne's friends, mother, and brother saw it, Art insisted on an unrelentingly disciplined life-style, which his wife and stepchildren chafed against and resented. He ran their ranch-style home in the upscale suburb of South Pasadena as if he was a drill sergeant and Anne and her children were raw Marine recruits. He would wake up the children if they left chores undone, screaming at them that they had let him down and insisting they drag themselves from bed to clean the dishes or vacuum the rug they had forgotten. He would run his finger on the top edge of doors, and if any dust grayed his fingertip, he would throw a tantrum. An elbow on the dinner table could provoke a shouting match. He once nearly drowned the family poodle for soiling the lawn. He beat his stepson black and blue for stealing some Christmas presents from under a neighbor's tree.[5]

At first, Anne was Art's apologist. "He's not so bad," she'd say. "He's a good provider." But after the first year or two of marriage, he and Anne began having outright wrestling matches, arguing over everything. Their sex life became an early casualty—Anne soon lost interest in Art's nightly bedtime advances, a disinterest that caused Art to pursue her ever more avidly. She complained to her friend Donna Bennett that he would never leave her alone, that she couldn't even sit in bed to do her nails without him flopping on top of her, his drawers around his ankles. "He wants sex every night," she said, bitter and repulsed. "Well, I like steak, too, but I don't want it every night." Then the weak joke turned into a simple statement of fact. "At least, not with him."

Anne never did learn to love Art. In time, she came to hate him. But when friends asked, why don't you leave, Anne would remember the days of repossessed cars and hamburger six nights a week, and say, "I have to think of the kids."

Art responded to his marital difficulties by ignoring the problem at first, then by attempting to bribe Anne with even more money and gifts. When she continued to turn her back on him in bed, he followed the example of his good friend Bill Leasure: He found a girlfriend.

Art met Bill Leasure in 1974, the same year he married Anne. His insurance business had taken off, and he found himself working with city attorneys and policemen regularly, particularly traffic officers. That year, Leasure had left patrol work for his brief tenure in bunco-forgery at LAPD's auto detail. In mid-1974, he handled a case in which a car owner discovered a repair shop had charged him for expensive new parts in his wrecked Toyota, even though they had merely put all the old, barely functional parts back in. When the car broke down a few weeks later, the motorist went to the police, and Leasure pursued fraud charges against the repair-shop owner. Betsy Mogul, whom Leasure was beginning to date at that time, prosecuted the case. Smith, the insurance adjustor for the company who had paid off the motorist's claim, was called to testify about the repair-shop owner's scam.

Leasure came by Art's Highland Park office several times to gather information on the case. Art was impressed by Leasure's dedication. "I love this work," Bill told him. "I've never been happier at LAPD." The two became close friends in short order. The friendship continued even after Leasure was sent back to patrol because superiors decided a detective was needed for the bunco job, even though Leasure's job performance evaluation had never been (and would never again be) as glowing. Leasure's friends figured he would be crushed at the demotion—giving sleazy repair shops their comeuppance appealed to him like no other brand of police work. Yet, as usual, he never protested. Nor did he try to earn the necessary promotion to get his coveted job back. He always said he wasn't interested in becoming a detective. It was one more submission to authority for Leasure, and another deep resentment against LAPD and a world that failed to appreciate him.

Impressed with the successful, monied Smith, Leasure became a regular visitor at the office, taking off time from his patrol duties to chat with Art, or to diagram accidents for him for insurance claims, or to discuss going into business together. He became a fixture at the office. Art liked Leasure's meticulous, draftsmanlike sketches of accident sequences (Leasure's LAPD supervisors repeatedly commended him for the same thing). Art Smith also liked having a policeman for a friend, and he often boasted of the "connections" he had at LAPD. Art would loan Bill a few hundred dollars now and then, sometimes a few thousand, and he provided the phone credit card for the calls Betsy wasn't supposed to know about. Bill would pay him back with the accident diagrams, or twenty or thirty dollars now and then.

Leasure, meanwhile, began to speak reverentially of Art to his other friends. "He's a self-made man," Leasure would say. "A man after my own heart." The man who had grown up in a family that lived paycheck to paycheck was always worshipful of others' wealth: He took Art's pronouncements on investments, money management, and insurance as gospel. While others found Smith boastful, self-centered, and cold, Bill remained untroubled by these traits, if he even noticed them. So what if Art monopolized conversations, listening to others only long enough to change the subject to himself? Leasure felt comfortable and at ease with Art's ramblings. He told his friends that hanging around with Art Smith was an education.

Though he was polite and cordial to Anne's face, he was less than flattering in her absence, Leasure's friends recall. As much as he idolized Art, he seemed to dislike his younger wife, and was especially critical of her "free-spending ways," a cardinal sin from frugal Bill Leasure's point of view.

"I don't care for Art's wife at all," he told his friend Flo Ong. "All she ever wants is more money from Art. I don't know why he puts up with it. I just really don't like her."[6]

Leasure, of course, was widely known as a penny-pincher. Irene Wong complained to him often because he never brought her flowers or gifts or took her to a decent restaurant. Both Leasure and Betsy Mogul would dissect restaurant tabs when they went out with other couples, pulling out a calculator to make sure they didn't pay an extra penny—no simple, even splits of the check would do for the Leasure family. When Art would complain about Anne's spending, he struck a deep nerve in Leasure.

Smith and Leasure often spoke quietly to one another at Art's office. Usually they would retire behind the closed door of Art's private inner office, out of earshot of the other insurance adjustors. Sometimes Leasure came by with his partner at the time, Big John. If someone walked in on them, a secretary with papers or an associate with questions, the conversation as often as not would stop. There was a certain tension about some, though certainly not all, of these little talks. And as Art's marital problems increased, the huddled meetings with Bill seemed to grow more frequent.[7] Some in the office thought all this suspicious. Others, though, did not, and grew tired of the gossip. "What are they supposed to do, stand in the middle of the room and talk?" one of the secretaries asked. "Of course they go into Art's office."

A few years into their relationship, Art and Bill began taking trips abroad together, including one to the Cayman Islands and two to Belize, where Leasure became entranced with Art's island and resort plans. A beautiful tropical jewel surrounded by blue-green Caribbean waters and coral reefs rife with world-class diving and swimming, Art's private paradise offered unending pleasure for someone raised near the cold and crusty shores of Lake Erie. Wild animals roamed a fairy-tale landscape of deep, vivid greens, rain forest marching to the edge of white-sand beaches, so different from the crowded, litter-strewn brown sands of Southern California. Centuries-old shipwrecks lay submerged offshore, giving up tiny bits of their treasures one by one to the tides. Beachcombing every morning, Leasure would find old clay pipes washed up by the tides from some long-lost hulk, and he'd fantasize about hunting for lost ships and riches.

Upon his return from Belize, Leasure began showing Flo Ong and other friends a photo album of the beautiful island and a neighboring piece of land he was considering buying. Little-known Belize, he said, would be the next world-class resort destination, and he intended to get in on the ground floor. "Art and I are developing it into a resort," he confided. "We have a caretaker working there and everything."

Leasure told Flo he was Art's partner in the island, and that they would make a fortune drawing tourists to a pristine idyll just waiting to be discovered. "This is my retirement plan," he boasted.[8] The plans never seemed to materialize, though—and they were actively threatened by the Smith divorce as Anne tried to claim a share of everything Art owned, the island included.

On one of their trips abroad, he and Art were joined by Leasure's young girlfriend, Irene Wong, on her first journey out of the country. Art knew all about Leasure's marital infidelities, notwithstanding his close relationship with Betsy Mogul. Art allowed Bill to use a house trailer in back of the house in South Pasadena for his afternoon liaisons with Irene and his other girlfriends—a bank officer in Pasadena and a waitress at a famous old-time Hollywood hangout Bill frequented for a time. Art had originally bought the trailer as lodging for an attractive young woman he had imported as a live-in maid, the daughter of friends in Belize. The woman had left under a cloud a year later, after Anne accused Art of carrying on with the maid in her absence. Leasure was supposed to buy the trailer and cart it away, but he ended up just letting it sit in South Pasadena, so convenient for the occasional rendezvous.

Anne, who never much cared for Leasure anyway, liked him even less when she saw him coming and going at the trailer with other women.[9] She didn't hesitate to tell Art exactly how she felt. Anne knew Leasure was married to Betsy—the four of them had dined together several times—yet Leasure baldly philandered in front of Anne, giving her a wave and a smile whenever she spotted him at the trailer with what she called "one of his Twinkies." He just assumed she would keep her mouth shut—which she did, though she resented the involuntary complicity. Leasure was just the type to make such assumptions, she griped. She suspected Art of carousing with him on extramarital double dates—and on their trips to the Caribbean.

One day in the summer of 1979, after the Smith marriage had deteriorated to the point of separate vacations and constant brawls, Anne quietly followed Art. He was supposed to be going to the island for a few days, but Anne believed he had other plans. She didn't care so much about his adultery—to tell the truth, she told Donna Bennett, it was a relief—but of late she had come to suspect something more was going on. Instinct for self-preservation overtook her guilt at spying on Art, and she decided to tail him in her prized jet-black 1970 Cougar convertible. She maintained a discreet distance and a slow burn when she realized he was heading away from, not toward, the airport. After a short drive to the neighboring small city of Alhambra, she watched him pull up in front of a condominium, where a woman was waiting for him in a parked car. Art had the key to the place, and he walked in with the woman and an armload of groceries. Anne had never heard of the condo before; when a quick call to the county tax office told her Art was the recent buyer of the property, she was furious. She had been right about more going on than simple adultery. Not only was Art maintaining a love nest for himself, but he was paying for it with money that was half hers.

In a fit of vindictiveness, she decided to burglarize the condo. "I'm not going to put up with this shit," Anne told the Smiths' young friend and tennis partner, Richard McDonough. He had known both the Smiths for years—he gave both Anne and her daughter Chris lessons and played often with Art. Now Anne recruited him to help with the break-in, and McDonough agreed.

His relationship with the Smith family was a strange one. Art had been confiding in Rich about the condo, his girlfriends, and various financial plans he was concealing from Anne in case of a divorce. He had even confessed how he asked his accountant to salt away thirty thousand dollars under another name so Anne wouldn't know his true worth when he dumped her. But Rich, in turn, was telling Anne everything behind Art's back. He liked her better than the boastful Art, but more important, he was worried about her safety. Earlier in 1979, McDonough had told her of a particularly disturbing conversation he had with Art. Although he had ultimately dismissed it as a joke, the conversation continued to trouble him enough to tell Anne.

"I know two cops who will kill anybody you want for fifty thousand dollars," Art had told McDonough. "I'm going to have them kidnap Anne and make it look like a sex fiend killing. They're going to take her, rape her, kill her, and dump the body in MacArthur Park."[10]

McDonough had looked at Art's round, serious, wrinkled face and then burst out laughing. "You're joking, right?" he asked. Of all places, MacArthur Park was known for its crack dealers and gang shootings, a place even Los Angeles policemen avoided whenever possible. Crossing its brown grass, stinking of urine and littered with debris, could be as dangerous as walking blindfolded onto the San Diego Freeway at rush hour. McDonough said, "You'd never do anything like that, Art."

"Rich, I'm tired of her," Art replied.

A few weeks later, McDonough stopped by Art's office and saw two plainclothes policemen leaving. He didn't see their faces, but he knew they were cops when he noticed the glint of a badge on one of their belts, and the butt of a gun protruding from the other's sport coat. When he greeted Art, the insurance adjustor cocked his head at the men walking out the door and said, "Those are the two I told you about." McDonough was too afraid to look at them again, but later, he dismissed it as another weird practical joke. Art was playing with his mind, he decided, trying to get an edge on the tennis court when next they played. Art hated to lose.[11]

When McDonough relayed the conversation to Anne, he assured her that Art, in his anger, didn't really mean any of it. Still, he felt she should know anyway—just in case. Anne said she wasn't so sure Art might not be deadly serious, and she made certain several of her friends knew about it as an insurance measure.[12] "Art's put a contract out on me," she told Donna Bennett. "If I get killed, tell the police."

After following Art to the condo, she bided her time for a few weeks, waiting until she could be certain he really had left town on legitimate business. Then she and McDonough donned dark wigs borrowed from the Dee Ann House of Beauty, just in case neighbors saw them and described them to Art. Then they trashed the condo, rifling through the place and taking a microwave oven, a television, a camera, and several other of Art's possessions. He was a gadget freak, and Anne knew just what to take to upset him the most. Anne didn't really want any of the stuff, so she gave it all to McDonough to keep, just to spite Art. Afterward, she knew it must have driven her husband crazy, and that he probably suspected her. But because the condo was supposed to be his little secret, he could never say a word to her.

Months later, during a temporary reconciliation, Anne finally confessed to the burglary, confirming suspicions Art had harbored all along. He said he forgave her and swore that the condo was not a "love nest," but a gift for his adult daughter from his previous marriage. He said he wanted her to have a home of her own near him, and he produced a quitclaim deed passing on title to prove it. But if Art said all was forgiven with Anne, he remained furious at Richard McDonough and refused to associate with him any longer.

Leasure had a curious response when Art told him about his tennis partner's betrayal. "Do you want him taken care of?" Leasure asked. "He could have his legs broken, or his arms, you know. Whatever you want."

Smith laughed, he would later recall, and said, "Rich is a pretty good tennis player. I wouldn't want to see that happen to him. I'd just rather forget the whole thing." He and Leasure laughed, and that was the end of it. Just a joke between two good friends, Smith would later claim. You never knew with Leasure, Art figured. That was one of the reasons he liked the guy. He was quiet, but he'd come out with the wildest things.[13]

A few months later, McDonough came to the Smith house for the wedding of Anne's daughter, Christine. Anne pulled him aside and hissed that his life was in danger, that he should get out and steer clear of Art. A few minutes later, Art spotted him and had him thrown out. Two men who said they were with LAPD kicked him out of the house. A few days later, McDonough received an anonymous threat to stay away from Anne or he'd get his legs broken. He was so scared that he moved twice, leaving no forwarding address either time.[14]

After the condo incident, Art would complain from time to time to a sympathetic Leasure about how sour his marriage had turned. He and Anne just couldn't agree on anything, he'd say. "Everything's turning to shit, Bill. And I don't know what it is." It got to the point where he dreaded going home, he'd say. As he described his home life, it was all Anne's fault. He was simply at a loss, he said—he didn't know what he had done wrong or what he could do to fix things. Yet a divorce might hurt him financially. Anne wanted too much. He already had spent a fortune on her chin job, her nose job, her eye job, and her boob job, he said. Anne was deathly afraid of growing old, and Art had paid handsomely to stave off the years. Now that he had preserved, stretched, and augmented every part of Anne's body he could, he was afraid she wanted out of the marriage. At forty-eight, he was too old to start over, he complained. "Why should I have to?" he asked.

Bill said he understood, that he knew what it was like to suffer unfairly when you had done no wrong. Then he offered to follow Anne around, see what she was up to. In the wake of the condo burglary, who knew? If she was planning anything, Art could be forewarned, Bill suggested.[15]

Smith accepted the offer, and Leasure began to tail Anne, riding behind her in shades and his silver Corvette. He watched her drive to Long Beach to meet her friend Donna one day. Another time, she drove to a mall, where she met a man for coffee. The next trip, she traveled to a narrow, crowded stretch of sand on Anaheim Bay in Long Beach, where she met someone Leasure determined to be a Los Angeles Rams football player.

The beach Anne had driven to lies along a narrow inlet and is known as "Horny Corners," where bronze weightlifters in Speedos and flat-stomached women in thong bikinis and opaque sunglasses come to sweat and sizzle in a daily cocoa-buttered display of aerobicized flesh. Horny Corners isn't a particularly pleasant beach—the water is murky from a nearby marina and the sand is a dirty brown—but the narrow stretch of ocean front there is packed daily in summer, even on weekdays, as if sunbathing was a profession. Traffic is so intense along the street opposite the beach that the police set up roadblocks in summer—the only way neighborhood residents can get their cars in and out of their garages.

With Bill parked at the end of the block, Anne stretched out on this exhaust-choked spit of sand and cooked with the rest of the sun worshipers for hours. Then she returned to South Pasadena, Leasure on her tail. There wasn't anything suspicious about it—she hadn't embraced any strange men, as Art had come to expect—but Bill reported all her movements anyway. Smith was hungry for every detail.[16]

When Leasure wasn't following Anne Smith, the welder Dennis France was. At Leasure's direction, he tailed Anne between the house in South Pasadena and an Orange County medical building, where she and her son went for family counseling. Once again, reports filtered back to Smith. Leasure told his operative France that Smith was outraged at the psychiatric bills Anne was running up.[17]

Not long after agreeing to have Leasure tail his wife, Art began accusing Anne of cheating on him. She would laugh at this, then tell him to go to hell. She began staying away from home more often, sleeping over at her mother's house next to the beauty shop or in Long Beach at Donna Bennett's beachfront house, infuriating Art further.

In February 1980, Art took another trip to Belize to check on his island. Upon his return, he found someone had broken into the office over the weekend and photocopied his ledger books and other confidential records—he knew what had happened, because he found a few crumpled discard copies in the wastebin. Art flew into a rage—those records were confidential; they should never be copied for any reason.

He was sure it had to be Anne, probably with the help of McDonough. She had recently been accusing him of keeping two sets of books, one for her and the IRS, and the real books for his own use, concealing his true wealth. It would be just the kind of ammunition she would attempt to uncover in an effort to destroy him.

But then again, he reasoned, the break-in could also have been by a former employee with a key, intent on stealing his clients. Art methodically changed his locks every month just to avoid such a break-in, but a determined disgruntled former employee—or even a current one, planning for the future—could get around that roadblock. He couldn't be sure who was at fault, and the intense interrogation of his staff that he launched that day failed to provide any answers.

"Who do you suspect?" Leasure asked the next day when Art called him up for advice.

"I don't know. I suspect everyone," Art replied. "Probably Anne. Whoever it was, if I catch the bastard, I'll kill 'em."[18]

By March 3, Art had calmed sufficiently to take his wife to dinner for their anniversary. He thought perhaps they still could patch things up. But then she asked for the divorce and the new shoes instead. Anne knew Art had taken her request too well at first, and that the peace couldn't last. She was right: The brawl over her necklace and credit cards erupted less than three weeks later, on March 23.

The divorce papers were served a few weeks after that. Art refused to accept them, so the process server just hurled the bundled complaint and subpoena onto the porch. Art let them lie where they fell all day, but finally picked them up the next morning. After reading them and conferring with a lawyer, it became clear to him Anne had been the one who broke into his office. She was using his own records against him. He had been right—she and McDonough had broken in and copied his ledgers.[19]

Art worked himself into a rage again over the break-in. His employees couldn't help but notice. They tried to steer clear of their boss, but finally, one of his part-time secretaries, Dovie Gordon, had to get his signature on a report. When she walked into his office, he made her sit down and listen as he launched into an angry, odd monologue on Anne's supposed treachery.

"I'll have her killed before she gets anything of mine," he concluded. "She wants the house, but she'll never get it. I'll see her dead first. She'll get nothing from me."

Dovie was aghast. "Art, you're angry. Surely you can't mean what you're saying?"

He looked at her, calm and cold. "You wait and see."[20]

At around the same time as that conversation, Art and John Doney had an equally disturbing talk over breakfast. Doney was one of Art's claims adjustors. Five years before, when Art had worked as a manager for a major insurance company, he had supervised Doney. When he formed the Art Smith Company and ventured out on his own, he had taken Doney with him, one of his first employees. They had become good friends, breakfasting together at a diner near the office almost every weekday before work, and socializing off the job as well. Doney, tall, quiet, and deferential, made a good audience for Art.

For the past several months, Smith had been confiding in Doney about his faltering marriage and how he wished he could work things out. But of late he seemed to have a change of heart—to cease mulling over how he could reconcile with Anne, and to start considering the best way to be rid of her. One day, Doney could see, Art seemed particularly angry at his wife. He was agitated, muttering that she wanted too much. She wanted to ruin him.

"I'm planning to have her killed, John," Art abruptly announced, leaning over their dirty breakfast dishes. "Bill Leasure and another cop will go to the house and have Anne come with them on some pretense. They'll tell her I'm sick or something. And then she'll just disappear."

Doney spilled some coffee on himself, barely noticing in his shock. "What?" he asked.

Art ignored the question. He knew Doney had heard him correctly. "It'll only cost me fifteen thousand dollars. It's worth it. I've had enough."

"You'd never do that," Doney said, laughing nervously, trying to see a joke behind Art's serious, grim expression. Then again, Doney had never really known Art to joke about much of anything—he was pretty much a humorless drill sergeant. "Come on, Art, what are you saying?"

Art just stared at his coffee cup, lost in thought.

Doney knew Leasure casually from his frequent visits to the office. He couldn't see the quiet traffic cop as a hired killer. The guy couldn't hurt a fly, Doney suggested.

"Hah," Smith said, roused from his reverie. "Bill does this kind of thing all the time. He and his partner are in Utah right now on a job. Watch the news. There's going to be a double murder there. Believe it."[21]

Now Doney was getting unnerved. "Why are you telling me this, Art?" he asked quietly.

Art seemed startled at the question. For the first time, he seemed to realize the impact he was having on Doney. He shook his head and told Doney to forget it. "It was just something Leasure offered to do. I'm too religious to go through with it. I could never live with myself. It's just talk. Don't give it another thought."[22]

Doney nodded, relieved. He liked Anne. And he liked his job. And, after all, neither his boss nor some wimpy LAPD traffic cop could possibly be a killer. For a long time, he never mentioned the incident to anyone. Why should he? It was ridiculous.

• • •

I never followed Anne Smith for any reason. That's wrong. Now, I don't think John Doney is a liar—he seems like he's trying to tell the truth. Maybe he just doesn't remember the conversation right. He didn't come forward back then. He's gotten other things wrong.

Or maybe Art was really angry that day and made something up about hiring me to kill Anne. Who knows? It just doesn't make any sense, though. They tried like crazy to find a double murder in Utah to match what Doney said. There wasn't any. So that part was made up. If Art was going to have his wife killed, why would he tell everyone in advance? He wouldn't, naturally. If he ever said anything like that, obviously it was just talk. I never heard him say anything like that. Never.

Art really loved Anne. I don't think he could ever have done anything like that. He's innocent. Just like me.

• • •

A pivotal divorce hearing in the Smith case was held on May 28, 1980. Anne had asked for a "kick-out order"—a ruling from the judge forcing Art to move out of the house in South Pasadena. She had tired of living with her mother and brother. She wanted the house. Art was just as insistent. So she had moved back in, with Art still there. The result was a constant war of slamming doors and blaring televisions, as each spouse grappled for supremacy, provoking Anne's request to have Art evicted.

Art wouldn't leave her alone, Anne testified at the hearing. She said his latest tactic was to hound her throughout the house with a tape recorder in one hand and a Bible in the other, spouting verses and curses whenever she tried to use the bathroom or pour a cup of coffee or get some sleep. Art countered by claiming Anne was abusing his beloved pet parrot, withholding the rotten bananas it preferred to eat in lieu of birdseed. He accused Anne of concocting her story about his hidden assets and double ledger books, saying the true purpose of her break-in at the insurance office was not to prove his financial deceptions, but to steal records that could prove his honesty.

The judge wasn't buying either of their stories that day. The case was too new—everything had to be sorted out in later hearings and at trial. He denied Anne's request for exorbitant spousal support and attorney's fees. But living arrangements had to be straightened out right away, and in that limited area, the judge sided, at least in part, with Anne. He wouldn't boot Art out of the house, as Anne had requested, but the judge ordered him to stay out of the master bedroom and to install a second phone there for Anne, so she could have some measure of privacy. He admonished Art to keep his tape recorder and his Bible verses to himself.

The judge in the case, to everyone's discomfort, saw himself as something of a comic—he had a tendency to crack painfully un-funny jokes during hearings and testimony. Art's complaints about parrot abuse had particularly tickled him, so when the tense and angry hearing came to a close, he concluded with an inevitable pun: "This case is for the birds." The lawyers dutifully laughed. Art Smith glared and left the courtroom, then hissed his only direct words to Anne that day: "This isn't over."[23]

"You'd better come over here tonight," Anne's sister-in-law Nicki Pontrelli suggested later that evening after Anne had called in tears. "You can't stay there. You'll never feel safe, especially if Art's been threatening you. Please, come over."

Nicki was worried. Anne had been coming to the Pontrellis' house almost weekly, hiding in the garage when Art came looking. One night a few months earlier she had appeared at the house more distraught than usual, popping Valiums like candy. Her brother Vito said she should stay the night. "You're paranoid," he said, but Anne just said, "I'm scared." Later, after 11:00, with everyone in bed, someone outside began shining a brilliant quartz spotlight into the garage and other windows in the house, terrifying Anne. Vito ran outside in his pajamas, but by the time he threw open the front door, the light had snicked off and no one was in sight. The next day he found one of Art's business cards stuck in the screen door, a note scribbled on the back: "Thanks for taking care of my wife."

"Art's put a contract out on me," Anne had whispered when she saw the note, and she explained what Richard McDonough had told her.

With that as prologue, when Anne called on the night of May 28, Nicki's natural reaction was: Get over here. Quick.

But Anne had a stubborn streak—and a temper of her own. It's my house, too, she said. I have the court order. I'll lock the bedroom door, take some sleeping pills, get some rest, then deal with Art in the morning. She said she knew what to do. Nicki wasn't so sure, but there was no changing Anne's mind once she had chosen a course.

And she did have a plan. The next day, May 29, 1980, shortly before 9:00 A.M., Anne Smith left her home and drove to the South Pasadena Police Department. She asked to see a friend of the family who worked there, Detective Budd Swapp. Later, Swapp would speculate that Anne had wanted to tell him about Art, about what she took to be his threats on her life, and to ask for his help and protection. He would have gladly intervened for her—but he wasn't in the office that morning. Anne had missed him by fifteen minutes. So many things would have turned out differently if she had just been a little earlier, or he had lingered for one more cup of coffee. Instead, she just left a message and told the desk sergeant she would talk to Detective Swapp later—he could reach her at work, she suggested. And he did call back within the hour, reaching Delores at the beauty salon. But by then it was too late.

Anne left the small police department and drove to nearby Highland Park and Dee Ann's House of Beauty. She had worked there with her mother at least three days a week, cutting and styling hair, for the past twenty years. The regulars had watched her grow up behind those sturdy blue vinyl chairs and roaring nose-cone hair dryers.

Anne arrived at about 9:15. Her mother, already at work setting an elderly customer's hair, watched Anne walk into the salon and suffered a pang of worry. Her daughter seemed to look thinner and more weary every time Delores saw her. Despite her plastic surgery, which Delores had argued against—"What's wrong with a couple laugh lines?" she had asked—her daughter's face now showed every one of her forty-one years, and more. Once again, Dee cursed herself for introducing Art and Anne. Since their marriage, her daughter's once happy, exuberant manner had been replaced by a constant stream of minor ailments and anxieties. Please let their divorce be over, Dee thought to herself. Let her have a fresh start.

Anne greeted her first customer of the day, seventy-one-year-old Eleanor Trethaway, an old family friend. Then she burst into tears when the unsuspecting woman asked Anne how she was. As Eleanor hugged her hairdresser and clucked in sympathy, Anne recounted her latest courtroom battle with Art, and how she was heartbroken that her own daughter would testify against her. After a few more minutes of tears, there-theres, and motherly pats, Anne calmed down, then set to work washing and setting Eleanor's hair.

Five to ten minutes later, a short, pale, rumpled man in an untucked denim shirt strode in through the front door. He had a cap pulled down to his eyebrows, and he hunched his shoulders, keeping his head down and face averted. Walking past the cash register without a glance and ignoring the other women in the shop, he had stepped up behind Anne and grabbed her before Delores even noticed him.

"This is a holdup. Give me your money," the man said, speaking to Anne only, as if no one else were in the room. He pulled something wrapped in an athletic sock from his belt and shoved it against Anne's back, making her gasp. The two salon patrons froze, but Delores, in her fear, absurdly continued to wind rollers into her customer's hair.

Anne reached into her purse and handed the man the few dollars she had with her. "Is that all?" the robber asked as he grabbed the money. Anne said it was. Then the man walked her to the back of the salon, to a storage area in the rear. Once there, he stopped, seemingly confused, and told Anne, "Oh, there's a cash register." Delores later remembered him also saying, "I'm nervous. I'm very nervous."

He walked Anne back to the front of the store, where he had her open the cash register and give him the seven dollars from the nearly empty till. Still jabbing that sock-wrapped object into her back, the robber walked Anne to the storage area again, warning the other women not to stare at him and not to move for at least ten minutes. He did not reach for the three other purses in the room, nor was he interested in the diamond ring glittering on Delores's finger.

Anne and the robber vanished from sight in the back. Delores thought he took Anne into the bathroom for a while, then brought her out again. To Delores, it seemed as if they were back there an eternity—later, she would guess it was five to ten minutes, though the police would call this perception a vast overestimate, a common dilation of time brought on by danger and stress. However long it was, Delores kept telling herself, surely he'd leave with the money and do nothing else. Anne hadn't struggled. There was no reason to hurt her.

Then Delores heard a single loud bang, and suddenly she was no longer frozen in place—she was running to the back room, Eleanor on her heels. Anne lay on the floor, crumpled and silent, blood spreading in a dark stain on her white-and-black-striped velour blouse. The rear door leading to the parking lot was open, with no one else in sight.

Delores kicked off her shoes and ran across North Figueroa Street to the fire station, but the paramedics who raced to Dee Ann's House of Beauty moments later could do nothing. The gunman had put his .45-caliber automatic against Anne's back and sent the heavy bullet crashing through her heart and lungs. She never had a chance.[24]

LAPD Detectives Neil Westbrook and Nelson Crowe, assigned to the case within the hour, didn't take long to settle on Anne's insurance adjustor husband as their prime suspect. They didn't buy the shooting as a robbery—not even the most stupid holdup man in town would hit a beauty shop early in the morning, before any cash was taken in, then pass on jewelry and purses in plain view.

Even more telling, the killer had deliberately targeted Anne, although she was the farthest person from the door he had entered. It could easily have been a professional hit, the detectives figured, and Art Smith seemed to have plenty of motive. Art feared Anne was trying to bleed him dry in the divorce, Delores told them. In interviews with the detectives later that day and throughout the week, Delores, Nicki Pontrelli, and other relatives said they were certain Art was behind it. Their hatred for the cold and domineering ex-Marine was undisguised, but their account of Anne's fear of Art in her final days seemed telling to the detectives, family bias notwithstanding.

Suspicions were stoked further when Art refused to speak with the police. Instead, the grieving husband exercised his constitutional rights and hired a lawyer to fend off questioning—a move that, to cops, is roughly akin to strapping on a sandwich board reading, "I did it." The final straw came on the night after Anne's murder, when the two detectives appeared at Christine's home for the usual round of routine questions. Expecting a grief-stricken daughter, the detectives instead were surprised by her odd first words: "Are you here to arrest me?"[25]

But their case against Art quickly stalled, all suspicion and no evidence. Plenty of people had heard Anne speak about Art's threats, but that was useless hearsay, inadmissible in court. To solve the case, they needed to find a missing link: the shooter.

Problem was, the three surviving women in the beauty shop, two of them frail and elderly, could barely describe the gunman. Even under hypnosis, details eluded Eleanor, and the other customer said she saw and remembered nothing. Delores's recollection was so vague she couldn't even produce a composite with the police sketch artist. There was one good lead, though: A Toyota mechanic at a dealership next door had seen two suspicious men parked behind the beauty shop in a distinctive green Chevy Nova just before the shooting. The car, a late sixties or early seventies model, had white racing stripes and the word "Rally" stenciled on its side.

The mechanic came up with pretty good descriptions of the men, too, from which composite drawings were created and distributed throughout the neighborhood and in local newspapers. But his description of a thin-faced man in a baseball cap who cut through the dealership on his way to the beauty shop, believed to be the killer, was somewhat different from the man Delores and Eleanor vaguely remembered. The case seemed headed for the unsolved files.

Delores and the rest of Anne's family had no doubts, though. They were sure Art was behind the killing, and they didn't hesitate to say so—to friends, neighbors, the police. Word got back to Art, and he began threatening them with legal action. "I can sue you for slander if you don't stop it," Vito and Nicki Pontrelli recall him saying. An anonymous woman caller to the beauty shop provided a much more direct threat to a shaking, shocked Delores: "Stop talking about Art, or you'll end up just like Anne." Click. Police said the call proved nothing, but they put recorders on the family phones anyway to see if the caller tried again. She didn't.

Then the investigation took an unexpected turn. Another anonymous woman caller phoned the police department with a new story: She claimed a drug-addicted petty criminal by the name of Charles Persico had killed Anne Smith in a botched junkie robbery. It had nothing to do with Art Smith.

Westbrook and Crowe tracked down Persico's estranged heroin-addicted wife, Elvia, whose hatred for her husband was obvious. According to Detective Crowe's report on their meeting, Elvia admitted making the anonymous call—something she would later deny. The detective also reported that Elvia said Persico looked just like one of the composite drawings in the newspaper, and that he had admitted to her one day that he was being sought for killing a lady in a beauty shop.

It was a breakthrough. After that day, the detectives seized on Persico as their target, dropping their investigation of Art, once they had made certain there was no connection between the two men. In retrospect, they reluctantly decided, Anne must have been killed in a genuine robbery after all, gunned down by a panicked junkie looking to score a heroin fix and worried about being identified. They felt the strange behavior of the robber could be explained by narcotic intoxication.

There were a few problems to be dealt with in that scenario, but no real stoppers: Persico didn't own a green Chevy Nova, for one thing. But, again, Elvia seemingly provided an answer. She said Persico's friend Arthur "Tutti" Gomez Garcia, another drug user with a long record, could have been the driver in the robbery. Did Tutti own a green Chevy Nova with stripes? Elvia said, why yes, he did. Motor vehicle records showed no such car in Gomez's name, but it was enough for the detectives.

Partly because of an apparent lack of thoroughness, partly because a key witness held back, few contradictions to their new junkie-robbery theory surfaced. Westbrook and Crowe never sought out the tennis player Richard McDonough or Art's secretary, Dovie Gordon, though they had been suggested as potential witnesses by Anne's family. And their brief interview with the adjustor John Doney did not delve into his strange breakfast conversation with Art Smith. Doney was still Art's friend and employee, and he decided not to tell the detectives about the ominous talk of contract murder. To him, the robbery-shooting at Dee Ann's House of Beauty sounded nothing like the plan Art had described to him months before. And so the detectives never heard about the threats on Anne's life or Art's hotheaded talk of hiring a policeman named Bill Leasure to kill his wife. Instead, they pursued Charles Persico and, months later, charged him with the murder.

• • •

Charles Persico killed Anne Smith. I have no doubt about that. The evidence is all there. . . .

I was nowhere near that beauty shop when Anne was killed. I know exactly what I was doing. I've always known what I was doing when Anne Smith was murdered. It was like you know what you were doing when you found out JFK was assassinated. It was such a traumatic thing. Art called me up. He was sad. If it was an act, it was a good one. When he didn't talk to the police, it was what his lawyer told him to do at the time. Art was real emotional, and it wasn't a good time to talk to the police. Nothing suspicious about that.

Anyway, the phone rang. I was outside working on the garage. I had called in sick, but I had stayed home to work on the garage. And Art told me Anne had been killed. It really affected me. I had never had someone close to me die before. And you remember things like that. I'll never forget it. . . .

Thank God Betsy keeps such good records. We have records that show what I was doing that day. And I have witnesses to prove it, too. Once people see all the evidence, I don't see how they can have any doubt.

• • •

Art Smith buried his wife in a quiet ceremony. He was the executor of her small estate and collected on her modest insurance policy. Art took Delores to court to get Anne's jewelry from her. He also took Anne's prized Cougar convertible from her mother's beauty parlor parking lot and, after Anne's family had searched it thoroughly for evidence of foul play, finding none, Art claimed he discovered a cache of pills and cocaine under the floor mat. "I flushed them down the toilet," Art told Anne's brother Vito. "I don't want to soil Anne's memory." Vito called Art a liar. "If there was anything there," he said, "we'd have found it. There was nothing." But Vito eventually swallowed his anger. Art might be an ass, he told Nicki, but he had been cleared of murder. Best to forget.

Art bought a tombstone with Anne's picture on it, a once-popular extravagance, now rare. Bill Leasure accompanied him to the funeral—as a bodyguard. This was before Persico's name surfaced, while Smith remained the prime suspect, and he said he feared Anne's family might do something rash.

As for Leasure, LAPD records would show he called in sick on the day of Anne's murder. His chronically bad stomach was acting up again, he told a supervisor, and he would need a day at home to recover before he was up to working traffic patrol again. "I have a severe case of diarrhea and will be unable to work today," his sick report read, dictated over the telephone to the desk sergeant at Central Traffic Division. The time of the report was noted as 8:50 A.M.—about half an hour before a bullet pierced Anne Smith's heart.

A few days later, Leasure's welder friend, Dennis France, decided to get his 1972 Chevy Nova painted at Earl Scheib's. Seventy bucks and change turned the old bomb into a bright orange-red showpiece—so much better than that metallic green, with those loud white stripes and the word "Rally" on the side.[26]

THE BATTERED SLICE OF south Los Angeles County that gave birth to Dennis Edward France is as insular as any rural crossroads, skirted by the rest of L.A.'s residents and invisible to the remainder of the world. It is a place you pass through—or to be more precise, a place you pass over—on a series of elevated freeways that carve through the neighborhoods like concrete cataracts, carrying a constant heavy flow of traffic between downtown and the city of Long Beach on L.A.'s southern fringe. For the vast majority of travelers on those automotive rivers, there is no reason to enter the gritty little procession of puzzle-piece towns below, except perhaps to remedy the occasional empty gas tank or flattened tire. Knowing this, those cities' planners have made certain every intersection near a freeway exit is bleakly stubbled with the marquees of fast-food restaurants and self-serve gasoline. The predominant art form is the billboard; the favored cuisine, drive-up.

This colorless, seasonless landscape of France's turf is a handful of miles from the icons of Los Angeles, yet the postcard images remained foreign to him. He knew nothing of the mansions and *haute couture* of Beverly Hills, or the gleaming, smog-shrouded skyscrapers of downtown, or the sleazy tourist traps of Hollywood—they were unreal to him, scenes not from his backyard but from the television set in his living room. Even the iron-blue waters and cooling breezes of the Pacific beaches a scant twenty miles distant seemed, to him, to be part of some other world, a place of tanned, well-muscled, department-store-catalogue bodies in which he held no place or claim. Dennis France was as Southern California as a square dance.

His home in the small city of Paramount lay inside one of four cramped apartments in a two-story brown concrete box whose cast-iron barred windows overlooked busy Orange Avenue. Sixty years before, acre upon acre of orange orchards had spread out across what had been a dry but fertile plain. Now the growers were long gone and only the street name remained, its surface soft and tarry in the ablative heat of summer. Outside the boxy apartment house, no yard or lawn covered the front, just a concrete parking pad well coated with crankcase drippings, separated from the sidewalk by a thin, weedy stretch of glass-speckled dirt and a line of stunted, faded palms.

Work at the machine shop provided little escape from this grim environment. France spent his days hunched over the brilliant blue flame of an acetylene torch, sweating behind the iron mask with its glass portal, inhaling the sulfuric odors of molten metal and burning gases. Financially, he barely scraped by, trying to support a wife and three children, one of them with a spinal defect and a clubfoot. France complained constantly of his poor medical insurance and his inability to pay for the corrective surgeries his son so desperately needed, a source of constant guilt and anguish in the France household.

For France, the California dream lay not in Los Angeles, but in escaping it. He loved nothing more than disappearing into the emptiness of the mountains and deserts to the east, to hunt deer or fish in cool fresh waters or to mindlessly plink bullets at tin cans amid the cactus and mesquite. Once a year, maybe, he could muster enough cash to take the kids to Disneyland. He imagined no other way of life.

Then Bill Leasure came along. A world populated by hundred-thousand-dollar yachts, private planes, and marina condos opened up before him. Suddenly France had access to the thrill and power of police work and policemen, something he had dreamed of but never dared think possible. He learned to speak cop talk, he rode with Leasure during patrols, spending entire shifts with his officer friend, who was only too happy to bend the rules. "Only for you, Dennis," Leasure would say, conveniently forgetting the regular squad car rides he gave to his girlfriend Irene Wong, shuttling her to college or on various errands when he should have been on patrol.[1] No matter—France wouldn't have minded sharing the experience even if he had known. The crackling urgency of police communications was better than music to him. Listening as the dramas of crime and pursuit unfolded in the cockpit environment of the squad car was like being a part of it. He came to know what a Code 7 was—officer taking a lunch break—and a 211—the California Penal Code section that defines the crime of robbery. He also learned about another penal code section—187. Murder.

Dennis France, in short, was dazzled by Leasure. He couldn't believe such a man would be his friend, would share his secrets. It made Dennis proud. It made Dennis feel important. And there came a time when he quite literally would do anything for Bill Leasure.

"I considered him my best friend," France would later say, glum but heartfelt. "Bill was the smartest man I ever knew. . . . We had some good times. I just want to make sure people realize that."

One year Leasure's senior, France met Leasure in 1976 or so, introduced by Dennis Dean Winebaugh, then France's landlord. France was thirty-five years old at the time, and he would see Leasure, sometimes in uniform, visiting with Forty-four at the apartment building. From the outset, he was jealous of Winebaugh's friendship with the traffic officer. When he was told Leasure had given Winebaugh an official LAPD portable radio, commonly called a Rover, France was envious, and continually begged to be allowed to listen to the police frequencies on it. Whenever Leasure showed up at Winebaugh's apartment, France would generally find an excuse to come over uninvited to hang around. He wanted so much to be a part that Forty-four and Leasure seldom had the heart to tell him to leave. "He's okay," Winebaugh told Leasure. "I trust him."

France's own relationship with the policeman began in earnest when Leasure bought a vintage Jeep station wagon with a modified 327 Chevy engine—much more power than the vehicle's chassis and power train were designed to carry. Leasure fashioned new, stronger motor mounts for the car, but he needed an expert welder to affix them. Winebaugh, his usual choice—not only because he was good, but because he would do the work for free—said he'd like to, but he was busy.

"Why don't you use my neighbor, Dennis France? You've met him before. He's good."

"Yeah, but do you think he'll do it?" Leasure asked, his mind on the bottom line. "I mean, for nothing?"

Winebaugh laughed, and explained France's fascination with

the Rover and how enamored he was of policemen. "I think he'll do anything you want."[2]

Forty-four had already prepped France by telling him what a "crooked police officer" Bill was. "I do all kinds of things for him," Winebaugh had boasted. "I broke a guy's legs for Bill for two hundred fifty dollars. I did such a good job, Bill gave me a two hundred dollar bonus."[3]

Later, France greeted Leasure eagerly when he came to the apartment to meet France and his family and to discuss the welding job. He happily agreed to come to Leasure's home in Northridge to weld the Jeep motor mounts, strictly as a favor, no charge.

France was a fine welder—the work was flawless. Soon Leasure entrusted him with all his Corvettes and other cars. The welding, France's fawning fascination with police work—Leasure called him a police groupie—and their mutual interest in guns formed a solid basis for a friendship.

The relationship was almost cut short soon after it began, however. In July 1977, Dennis Winebaugh abruptly packed up for a new home in Midwest City, Oklahoma. Heat from the Gilberto Cervantes killing, and some subsequent double-dealings with Tony and Paulette, had Winebaugh jittery. In the months after Cervantes's murder, Winebaugh had accepted five thousand dollars from Tony Reyes to kill his ex-wife Paulette. But instead of fulfilling the contract, Winebaugh secretly taped Tony making incriminating statements, then turned the tapes over to Paulette—leverage for her to use while she battled for alimony and child custody. When Tony failed to cave in, Paulette took the tapes to LAPD, which opened a murder conspiracy case against Tony. Then Paulette abruptly dropped the charges when she realized she was being investigated along with Tony. Ironically, all their divorce proceedings had finished by then, and Tony and Paulette were legally free of one another. So they promptly moved back in with one another.

The double-cross backfired on Forty-four, however. Tony sent the police an anonymous letter implicating Winebaugh in the Cervantes murder. The San Gabriel Police had been looking for him ever since. So far they hadn't located him. And Winebaugh intended to keep it that way.

Before leaving, he pulled France aside and said, "You oughta come, too, Birdshot." Birdshot was the mildly derisive CB handle Forty-four had bestowed upon France, ostensibly based on his preferred type of shotgun ammo—Number Four birdshot—but also a jibe at his diminutive stature. France didn't like the nickname, but he wasn't up to challenging Winebaugh.

Unsure of what he had to fear by remaining in Paramount, France said he'd think about heading to Oklahoma. He had helped Forty-four with Cervantes, sure, but Winebaugh had told him they didn't have to worry about the cops—the contract supposedly had been on behalf of Bill Leasure. Of course, France hadn't actually heard that from Bill himself. Winebaugh could have been blowing smoke, although he surmised Forty-four was telling the truth when he saw Leasure pass Winebaugh an envelope full of money after the killing. He also believed Paulette to be involved as well. And since he had driven his friend to Paulette's house time and again, France knew she and Winebaugh had been sleeping together for a time, and he guessed she was the ultimate source of the money in the envelope. Still, it was all so confusing to France. But, finally, one thing eventually seemed clear to him: If Forty-four was scared enough to flee, there must be a good reason. Less than one month later, France packed up his family and followed Winebaugh east.

Simple money problems ended the sojourn to Oklahoma. Within a few months of the move, France brought his family back to Los Angeles, unable to make a living as a welder on the nonunion wages he had found awaiting him in Forty-four's home state. France had learned there were no arrest warrants outstanding for him or Winebaugh—Leasure had checked police computer files for them, finding nothing.[4] There apparently was nothing to fear after all. He resettled in Downey, one stop down the freeway from his old stomping grounds in Paramount, got his union card with the Boilermakers' Local Number Ninety-two, and picked up where he had left off. As both he and Leasure tell it—with entirely different meanings—France simply took Dennis Winebaugh's place.

• • •

Sure I was friends with Dennis France. We went to the gun shows together. I introduced him to other police officers. I gave him some composites. That's how he knows about Anne Smith—I told him. I took him on some ride-alongs. He was a pest. He used to call me up and beg, please, please, please, until I finally said okay. So when I was working solo, I did take him, reluctantly. So probably, now that I think about it, I did take him along and I probably showed him where my friend got killed. He loved to hear that kind of stuff. He was a cop groupie. He loved to be around cops. And so I gave him everything he needed to frame me.

He was not a close friend. They want to say we were best friends, that we hung around all that time. But that is just not true. He was a casual acquaintance, really. I felt sorry for him. He has a handicapped son. He's a borderline idiot. . . . People always say I've got a fault: I always tend to see the good in people, and overlook the bad. I just didn't see what he was.

•   •   •

Early in their relationship, Leasure had thought France was mentally deficient. He told friends he felt sorry for him. But after spending time with him, Leasure eventually realized France was merely uneducated—that he was street-smart and far more capable than he'd been given credit for. He considered France sleazy, an undesirable character, yet he chose him as a regular companion and introduced him to several other police officers as well, conferring respectability on him the same way he had done with Winebaugh.

In time, Leasure introduced him to two LAPD officers who taught tear-gas classes, which France joined, so he could obtain a license to legally purchase and use Mace. Prior to the class, Leasure would buy the Mace for him. France said he needed it for self-defense, though he never made clear what he felt he was defending himself against. He just wanted it.

When France expressed admiration for the Rover radio Winebaugh used to have on loan from the Central Traffic kit room, Leasure presented one to France to keep, along with several rechargeable batteries. The little welder would spend hours listening to police frequencies, learning the codes. Leasure would bring him freshly charged batteries periodically.

Leasure and France also traded guns and sold them to one another—shotguns, automatic pistols, rifles. They reloaded ammunition together, as Winebaugh had taught them, and went target shooting, indoors and out. France bragged to friends that Leasure was holding an illegal silencer for him. And they began to frequent gun shows together as well. At the Pomona Gun Show, Leasure introduced France to Jimmy Trahin.

Trahin had been a rookie assigned to Central Traffic Division in 1971, where he had partnered at times with Leasure. Later, Trahin transferred to LAPD's Scientific Investigations Division, where he eventually became the department's premier ballistics expert, nationally renowned for his ability to match expended bullets with the guns that fired them, a principal means of linking suspected murderers to murder weapons. After hours, Trahin kept a table at the gun show and sold weapons out of his home, mostly to policemen.

France became a regular customer and gun buddy—a relationship that would become nearly as disastrous for Trahin as France's friendship proved to be for Leasure. Trahin and France even went hunting together. Like Leasure, Trahin saw France as an undesirable type, but he chose to associate with him anyway.

France, in turn, sold both Leasure and Trahin televisions and videotape recorders that his ripoff-artist brother, Jerry France, had obtained with bad checks and false I.D.[5] He always made sure his friends on the force got good deals on the electronics, still new in the box but priced as if they were used.

A sallow, bandy stub of a man, Dennis France was nervous with policemen, but always eager to please Leasure and other officers he met. He spoke ungrammatically—sentences peppered with *ain't* and *you wasn't* and other unwieldy constructions—yet the voice that uttered them was a rich, melodic tenor, a storyteller's voice, full of homey charm that didn't quite seem to fit the man. Nor did it fit his words, which so often were bellicose and violent.

Anxious to prove himself fearless around policemen, he always liked to say he was willing to bust a head when the situation demanded—his notion of how a good policeman should operate. Mostly it made people nervous. Leasure found France's behavior amusing.

When cruising on patrol—or, more often, when they parked the police car to talk and eat sandwiches or pizza in the car— Leasure would discuss his cases and other investigations underway at LAPD. He would pass on bulletins and composite pictures of suspects to France, who began his own small crime collection at home. The composites from the Anne Smith murder were the first Leasure ever gave him.

France's greatest contact with police work came with his unauthorized ride-alongs with Bill as they prowled the streets of Central Traffic Division together, an unlikely pair in a black and white cruiser. At times, France would spend whole shifts with Leasure in his one-man patrol car, fantasizing that he, too, was a cop. Often, France would berate Leasure for not being harder on traffic offenders.

"I would have written that guy up, Bill," an outraged France said after Leasure stopped a speeder, then let him go with only a warning.

"Nah, it's okay. He was polite."

"Shit, you're too damn soft." France was grumpy the rest of

the shift. It was a typical reaction. The billy clubs, the guns, the power of authority were heady stuff to France. He couldn't see holding back, couldn't see that not using the power could increase, rather than decrease, the authority. Bill tried to explain, but it was useless. "You got the badge," Birdshot would reply, "whyn't you use it?"

Leasure made no secret of his friendship with France. He met with him at Denny's Restaurant with his police partners along. Big John knew France, as did Officer Jon Herrington, one of Leasure's later partners and a co-owner of an airplane with Leasure. So did Officer Ralph Gerard, who had bought a share of the yacht *Thunderbolt* with Leasure. But the visibility of the relationship didn't make it any less perplexing. Most of Bill's friends considered France a creep. They didn't see just how comfortable Leasure was with his welder friend—and how much the misfit from Wayne had in common with him.

"Why do you hang around with him?" Bill's motherly friend, Flo Ong, asked after lunching with them at a Denny's restaurant, Leasure's and France's perennial meeting place. France had remained silent, head down, the entire meal. "Friends like that are going to be the end of you some day. You really ought to be picking your friends more carefully than you do. He's icky."

Leasure just shrugged and said, "He's okay, Mom. I feel sorry for him."

Later, France would boast to others that Leasure had wanted him to kill an elderly woman he had met at Denny's for lunch. "She's your next job," he recalled Leasure telling him after the woman had left. "I'm in her will and I'll get her house once she's dead." France said he turned down the job because he wasn't interested in blowing away little old ladies from Pasadena.[6] Like his other boasts, it was dismissed out of hand by most people who knew him: Who, after all, would hire a guy like Dennis France to be a hit man?

Well known for threatening violence as a means of impressing others, France was also famous for bragging about his past acts of aggression, real and imagined. In addition to boasting to his neighbor Bill Jennings about hitting an old Mexican, he also spoke to Jennings of people he and Forty-four had worked over. He told friends how he had "cut up a doctor real bad" for treating his son incompetently. He often claimed, falsely, to have served time as a juvenile for murder, part of a general pattern of claiming responsibility for killings he never committed. The only judicial record that mentions his name is a 1963 arrest for burglary, in which he was first considered a suspect, then became a witness, apparently through "cooperation"—that is, by informing on his accomplices. This was a part of France's personal history he wisely kept to himself. Friends like Dennis Winebaugh, for one, would have revised their opinions of France's trustworthiness had they known he had informed on others in the past.

Over the years, France attempted to impress Bob Kuns, among others, by claiming, "I killed a woman in a beauty shop." He also spoke of killing "a man for a woman." When he really wanted to puff up, France would say he had committed these two murders for Bill Leasure, claiming the traffic officer had paid him several thousand dollars apiece, though France couldn't say how much money, if any, Leasure had made personally on the contracts. He only knew that Bill had to pay for the man's killing out of his own pocket, because the woman who hired them hadn't paid up, France said. He also bragged that he had killed the woman for stiffing him, but he begged Kuns never to repeat this to Leasure. "He'll be mad at me," France said fearfully. Kuns later learned the woman was named Paulette, and that she was alive and well. And so he never knew just how much of France's jabbering he could believe.

There was more wild talk. For three thousand dollars plus expenses, France had offered to kill the stepfather of Kuns's daughter, whom the Skipper suspected of molestation. When Kuns expressed concern at the cost, France blandly suggested, "Don't worry about the three thousand. Just pay me a couple hundred bucks, take care of my expenses, and I'll go ahead and do it. You can pay me when you can." Kuns thought about it, but eventually let the proposal die by never bringing the subject up again. Leasure was not present for the discussion, and neither man ever mentioned it to him.[7]

Like Winebaugh before him, Dennis France would occasionally brag to others about his dirty cop friends and all the things they did together—without mentioning specifics. Anxious to show his competence and foresight, he often said that whenever he used a gun in some kind of crime, he would either dump the weapon in the Los Angeles Harbor afterward, or use his skills as a welder to melt the gun down.

"I always took Dennis with a grain of salt," Kuns recalls. "He liked to say he'd do anything, and not care about it. And as far as doing dirty work, he was tenacious, a little bulldog. He'd be hard to stop once he got started. But Dennis follows a leader. Someone else makes the decisions for Dennis."[8]

In contrast to his bragging of brutality, France seemed utterly devoted to his family. He doted on his children and agonized over his son's medical difficulties. He would fly into rages at any unkind remarks or taunts other children made about the boy.

Yet there also were flashes of a short-fused temper and something more—a bully's bravado and fear. One day in 1977, he came home to his Paramount apartment building's parking lot and found a child's tricycle in his customary parking spot. He had complained previously to Bill Jennings, whose son owned the tiny trike. This time, France simply ran it over with his pickup truck, snapping the handlebars and bending the wheels.

Jennings, well over six feet and 280 pounds, towered above the five-foot-seven-inch France. When he came outside bellowing at France, the welder ran into his apartment and emerged brandishing a handgun, then taunted Jennings. "What're ya gonna do about it now?" The normally mellow Jennings, becoming as irrational in his anger as France, ran into his own apartment and came out with an even bigger gun. "C'mon," he yelled. "If you're gonna do it, let's do it!" The ludicrous showdown abruptly ground to a halt when France whirled around, dashed into his apartment, and slammed and locked the door. An hour later, he called Jennings on the telephone, apologized profusely for losing his temper, and promised to buy a new tricycle for his son, which mollified Jennings, even though France never came through.[9]

Tammy Winebaugh had a similar experience with her son, Denny, who had playfully pointed his finger at the France family dog, then yelled pow-pow, as if shooting the animal. The little Brittany Spaniel reacted by barking angrily, exactly the reaction the child desired. When he kept teasing the dog, France came outside with a real pistol, pointed it at the terrified ten-year-old, and said, "Now, how do you like it? And if you ever act like you're going to shoot my dog again, I'll blow your head off."[10] The ugly scene created a lengthy, though impermanent, rift between France and Winebaugh.

If France was insecure about his size, compensating with outrageous bragging and a personal arsenal holding upward of thirty guns, his functional illiteracy was a source of far greater uncertainty and shame. It was the one thing no amount of boasting or firepower could counter.

As a grade-school student in the fifties, France had been labeled retarded and put into remedial classes. "Dummy classes," the other kids called them. The decision was both ignorant and cruelly incorrect, though not uncommon for that era. True, he did poorly on IQ tests, but the clinical scores masked an intellectual capacity that was average, perhaps better. Rather, as his special education teacher, Dale Lloyd Boyce, eventually concluded, France's scholastic problems were due to emotional and learning disabilities, in part stemming from his large and troubled family and the early death of his father, and in part from the perceptual impairment known as dyslexia, which caused France to see letters and words backward or scrambled. Well into adulthood, simple writing remained as incomprehensible as Egyptian hieroglyphics to him.

Boyce, who treated France with patience and kindness when the children around him tormented him, became a lifelong friend. He had been France's best man at his wedding. France was never a braggart around Boyce; he often called him "Dad." If Leasure was France's idol, Boyce was his confidant. And in a moment of crisis, France confided in Boyce about something terrible: murder. Not as a boast. Not as a defense. And not as a means of impressing similarly minded associates. This time, it was a plea for help.

Dennis France used to come over every weekend to play cards with Dale Boyce. One day in late 1977, shortly after his return from Oklahoma, the teacher could see his former student was troubled—nervous, toying constantly with his watchband, unable to concentrate on the card game. Boyce waited for France to speak up, then finally prodded him by asking what was the matter.

"I'm in trouble, and I can't go to the cops, Dad," France murmured. "I don't know what to do. I'm involved in a hit ring."

Boyce didn't register what France was saying at first. "A what?"

"A hit ring. A murder-for-hire ring. Killing people."

This stunned the older man. Boyce had always thought of France as a basically good person, a rough-and-ready type of guy who liked to talk about how good he was at fighting, but never vicious, never cold-blooded. In the schoolyard, France had fought the bigger boys by swinging his belt like a sling, the big brass buckle he always favored flashing at the end like a bludgeon. Later in life, Boyce noticed his friend always carried a revolver in his glove compartment, the adult version of that big old belt buckle. "It's nothing. A little fella like that tends to be that way," Boyce would tell his wife, explaining away the swaggering talk. "It's a protection they use."

But these words at the card table were something different. France obviously was terrified.

"You've got to get out of it, Dennis," Boyce finally said, slowly, commandingly—a tone he knew France was susceptible to.

Just as Leasure and Kuns had seen, Boyce considered France a born follower, and he wanted desperately to out-command whoever was telling Dennis to commit crimes. "You've got to go to the police."

"I can't go to the police. The police are part of it," France replied. "There's a LAPD cop named Bill. He's part of the ring. He tells me what to do."[11]

Boyce held the opinion that France, despite his bluster, would never lie to him about something important. He saw no reason to doubt him now. His main concern was helping his younger friend. "Look, Denny," he finally said, "I have a nephew. His name is Alan, he's an investigator for the District Attorney's office downtown. Used to be a cop in Glendale. He's got nothing to do with LAPD. You could go to him."

"I dunno . . . I don't want to go to jail. I'm afraid."

"He can help you."

"I need help," France agreed. "I'll think about it."

He said little more at the time. He gave Boyce no details about the "hits," only a litany of his fears. He was afraid of going to jail, afraid of being killed for snitching, afraid of who else might be involved at the police department, and afraid of keeping silent, because it meant doing more hits. He finally called Boyce back a few months later and said yes, he wanted to talk to the nephew. Boyce quickly set up a meeting at Little Joe's, an Italian restaurant in Chinatown, just north of downtown L.A.

When D.A. Investigator Alan Tomich took the call from Boyce, his uncle told him only that he had a friend who was reluctant to go to the police, but who "had some information on a murder." Tomich, who had been in the D.A.'s office four years, worked in the welfare fraud division—investigating murders was not his responsibility or forte at that time. But he agreed to the meeting anyway, just as a favor to his uncle. He decided to do it on his own time, though, and he brought his brother-in-law, a Glendale policeman, along for the ride. The four men met in Boyce's car in Little Joe's parking lot that same night.

Once the introductions were out of the way, France's first words shocked the two policemen: "I was hired by a L.A. police officer to murder a man, an old Mexican."

Tomich and his brother-in-law exchanged a look inside the dark, crowded car. They had expected an informant, not an admitted killer. Tomich pulled out a notebook, then asked three questions. "Where? When did it happen? Who did you kill?"

Hesitantly, France began to describe the murder of Gilberto

Cervantes—but with crucial details altered or omitted. Though less than a year had elapsed since the crime, most of his responses were oddly vague, or dead wrong. He never really had been sure in what city Cervantes lived—in the L.A. Basin, one small city runs into the next, often without clear delineation. But he named one for Tomich anyway, guessing incorrectly: El Monte, a handful of miles distant from the actual scene of the crime, San Gabriel. Then France made matters worse by providing only a general time frame in 1977 for the crime, instead of the more precise date needed for a successful records search in a vicinity with so many murders. Worse still, he could not—or would not—give the victim's name.

When it came time to describe the murder itself, there was no mention of Forty-four or any other accomplice. France told Tomich he had committed the murder alone, waiting for the old man outside his house, then shooting him once with a .357 Magnum revolver, which he subsequently melted down. A policeman had contracted for the murder, France said, but he did the killing himself. He left Winebaugh totally out of the equation.[12] France volunteered a partial name of the policeman who hired him, and said the officer could further be identified by the fact that his wife worked for the District Attorney's office as a prosecutor.[13] He said the crime had never been solved.

When France finished, Tomich had another question. "If you got away with it, why are you telling me this now?"

"Because," France said after a long pause, "I don't think it's right for a policeman to hire me to do something like this."

Tomich was less than enthusiastic about Dennis France, and asked few other questions. The story—and the man—seemed fishy to him. Worth checking out, but probably a load of bull. Crazies confessed to phantom crimes all the time, and his uncle, a heavy drinker, was not the most reliable judge of character. Tomich did not inquire about other accomplices, nor did he ask how much the policeman supposedly had paid France for his murderous services. And when France offered to compensate for the vagueness of his story by driving Tomich to the murder scene, so he could use the exact location to better track down records on the case, the investigator refused. "I'll get back to you when I know more," he told France and Boyce, ending the meeting after a mere half hour of conversation. "Then we'll see."[14]

Tomich and his brother-in-law went to the Glendale Police Department office and called the city France had named. Naturally, they found no such murder as he had described. Then they called the county coroner's office, with predictably poor results.

Harried workers at one of the largest medical examiner's offices in the country, where thousands of homicides are processed every year, needed more information than Tomich could provide. Without a name or a date, no effective search of the coroner's records was possible. The office simply responded that they could find no match for the unsolved murder of an elderly Mexican male shot in 1977 in El Monte, as described by Tomich.

When Tomich called Boyce back and said the information France had provided him could not be verified—in other words, saying it appeared to be untrue—Boyce told his nephew he would check with France, then get back to him.

France confessed that he had held back when Boyce confronted him that afternoon. "I couldn't go through with it," he explained. "If I told everything, I'd be killed. I had to lie about some things."[15]

When Tomich heard that explanation, he told Boyce he would go no further with France. He did not ask which elements of the story had been true and which had been lies. He wanted nothing more to do with France. "Tell him to go to Internal Affairs at LAPD. Or the FBI." Tomich threw away his notes from his meeting at Little Joe's and dismissed the entire strange interlude from his thoughts.

"What're you going to do?" Boyce asked afterward.

France shrugged, fearful but also relieved. "I don't know."

After that odd and ineffective meeting in a restaurant parking lot, France continued his relationship with William Leasure. Indeed, still casual friends in 1978, they grew much closer in the months and years that followed France's attempt at confession—a seeming contradiction of the fears he had expressed to his surrogate father, Dale Boyce. Bill never knew about the meeting in Chinatown; France told no one except his wife.

Within the next year or so, Leasure introduced France to his girlfriend Irene Wong—widening the circle of trusted associates who knew of his extramarital affairs, even while he was bringing Dennis home to Northridge to meet Betsy.

Irene despised France from the outset. She didn't like his unkempt hair, wrinkled T-shirt, and dirty blue jeans, and her contempt only increased when a grinning Leasure asked her if she had any Chinese friends for Dennis. "Dennis says he's never had a Chinese girl before," Leasure explained. Irene was furious and said no, but the message was clear: Bill Leasure discussed his most intimate secrets with Dennis France, even his sex life.

There were other signs of Leasure's and France's closeness, Irene saw, particularly the home-style bank account Leasure maintained for France. The welder, whenever he came into some money, would give it to Leasure to hold, Bill explained to Irene. Otherwise, France would fritter the money away. Leasure would keep a running total in his notebook of the money he owed France. He would usually give the cash to Irene and have her put it in her bank account, where Leasure stashed his other secret savings and payments as well. The whole thing left a bad taste in Irene's mouth.

"Why do you have him for a friend?" Irene asked once, her voice thick with distaste.

"He'd do anything for me," Leasure replied simply.

If the confession in Chinatown was France's attempt to shun the business of murder for hire and the influence of William Leasure—as he would later claim—it accomplished neither goal. If it served a darker purpose—to lay the groundwork for a shifting of responsibility for his crimes to Leasure—it succeeded, although that would not become apparent for many years to come. In any case, despite his meeting with Tomich and the fears he expressed to Boyce, France kept on riding in the patrol car with Bill, he continued welding Leasure's vehicles, and he was still there to help with Leasure's special problems and wayward friends. There was talk of France breaking the arms and legs of Irene's mother—a plan eventually dropped. There was the hiring of France's brother to perjure himself on behalf of Big John and another man who had been implicated in a beating death of a transient. That plan succeeded. In 1980, two years after the Chinatown meeting, there was the business with Art Smith and his wife.

And after that, there were Tony and Paulette de los Reyes. A new will had been penned. And Tony's time finally had come.

CHAPTER 9

ON THE AFTERNOON OF SEP-
tember 1, 1981, for what seemed like the hundredth time, Tony
Reyes evicted his on-again, off-again wife Paulette. When the
blowup came, they weren't even sure of what had precipitated it—
only that, after nine months of divorced cohabitation, they were
through with one another once again.

It would be their final breakup, their last fight.

They had been living in the old San Gabriel house at the time,
inherited by Tony after his mother, Natalia Cervantes, followed
Gilberto to the grave in 1979. The Munster house in Boyle Heights
had burned down mysteriously three months earlier, forcing them
to move into the overgrown ghost house on South Palm Drive.
They drifted amidst the Cervanteses' clutter of boxes and worn furniture, feeling Gilberto's crotchety presence amid the piles of junk,
still smelling hints of the cloying sickroom odor that had permeated
the house in Natalia's last bedridden days.

Within a day of telling Paulette to leave, Tony was back
together full-time with Sandra Zysman, a young woman he had lived
with off and on for the past two years—pretty much whenever he
and Paulette were on the outs. Ten years Paulette's junior, Zysman
was her opposite in every way—self-effacing, supportive, and plain,
nothing like the flamboyant, demanding, me-first Paulette. Tony was
a different man around Zysman, witty and relaxed. They had known
each other five years, since the de los Reyeses' divorce was filed in
Superior Court. Sandra knew nothing of Dennis Winebaugh or
taped talk of murder or Gilberto Cervantes's death. To Sandra
Zysman, Tony was nothing short of wonderful, and his continued

attachment to Paulette was a bafflement. But Sandra forgave Tony any transgression, and, consequently, he committed few she knew about, except for his inevitable womanizing, which she tolerated cheerfully. "How can I hold that against him?" Sandra would say to friends. "He's the most vivacious, alive man I've ever known. If he has to be nine years old to play with Aaron, he's nine. If he has to be twenty-one with me, he's twenty-one. If he has to be sixty, he can do that, too. Of course he's a womanizer. So what?"

Not surprisingly, and in spite of this open attitude, there was one woman in Tony's life Sandra could not abide: Paulette de los Reyes. The feeling was mutual, and their encounters invariably turned ugly. During periods when Tony and Paulette lived apart and Sandra had moved in, the two rivals would run into each other whenever Paulette brought Aaron to his father's house for court-ordered visits. Sometimes the four of them would endure achingly tense dinners together, with Paulette, the consummate homemaker, eyeing each dish Sandra had prepared like a dissatisfied czarina.

Shortly before the latest Paulette-Tony breakup, Zysman had come to the San Gabriel house only to stumble into a typical de los Reyes family argument. Turning her anger toward the younger woman, Paulette had greeted Sandra by calling her "Slut," then threw a glass of wine in her face. Sandra, bigger, younger, and stronger, reacted by delivering a roundhouse punch to Paulette's chin, sending her crashing into the refrigerator, then to the floor. At first relishing the shocked look on Paulette's face, Sandra became mortified when she saw little Aaron, standing behind her in the kitchen, eyes wide. Sandra had always doted on Aaron and they had enjoyed an easy friendship, but now the twelve-year-old leapt to his shrieking mother's defense and refused to look at the stricken younger woman. Tony spent the next week on the phone trying to calm Paulette, who promptly began threatening lawsuits and assault charges. Everything would be fine, Tony told her. He'd always take care of Aaron. He'd always take care of her. Yes, Paulette said. You will.[1]

Eight days after the breakup, on Wednesday evening, September 9, 1981, Tony de los Reyes drove his white Thunderbird to the Chez Nora Bar, Sandra beside him. The little nightclub in the Sherman Oaks section of Los Angeles, north of Hollywood, was a pleasant, cozy place, a dark and quiet fixture for old-time jazz, with a family of regular customers. Chez Nora was the kind of place where the owner, Nora Marcom, used to emerge from behind the bar and sing with the band at times. Tony was booked there with a trio Marcom had put together, playing his bass from 9:00 at night until 1:30 in the morning, four times a week. Then he would go home and sleep through the day. Now that the tortilla business was gone, killed by divorce and his war with Paulette, he didn't have to worry about business concerns any longer. He had plenty of money from his stepfather's estate, more than enough to live comfortably the rest of his life. He could pursue the music just for fun now, indulging his passion.

After arriving at Chez Nora that night and unloading his bass, Tony told Sandra to brace herself—Paulette was supposed to stop by the club to pick up child support money for Aaron. "Try not to kill one another," he said. Sandra promised to be civil. She had seen Paulette in the bar twice in the past week already, and there had been no fireworks yet.

Then the music began, and Tony was lost in his playing, Sandra, in her listening. She still remembers exchanging smiles with him from time to time as he stood on the stage, and their easy conversation between sets, his hard, dry hand in hers. He was finally free of Paulette, he promised. He and Sandra could settle down. They could get married. Sandra was jubilant.

By the time Tony finished his last set at 1:30, Paulette had still not come, which was fine with Sandra. Tony, though, seemed surprised. If the subject was money—especially money owed her—Paulette would never miss a date, he said. But he shrugged it off, and they packed up. After Tony had a last Scotch and water, he and Sandra walked out to the large deserted parking lot in back of Chez Nora.

The day had been oppressively hot and smoggy—air quality "unhealthful," the newspapers had said—and the Thunderbird's air conditioner had strained to make the drive to Chez Nora bearable earlier that night. But now the cool of an approaching morning greeted them as they left the stuffy bar, air lightened by a sixty-degree freshness that only the peculiar mixture of ocean and Southern California desert can create, and which not even nine million people and an army of developers' bulldozers can conspire to destroy. Once outside, Sandra and Tony stopped to chat with one of the cocktail waitresses and a singer friend of Tony's who had come to hear the trio play. After a few minutes of idle talk, the singer said good night and walked the waitress to her car, parked at the opposite end of the lot from Tony's T-Bird.

Sandra felt a vague anxiety as they approached their car. She hated that Thunderbird, uneasy about it ever since she had almost been killed sitting in its front seat a few months earlier. She and Tony had been parked outside Sandra's apartment building, talking, when someone drove by and shotgunned the driver's-side rear window. All Sandra heard was the explosion of glass, then the sound of tires screeching in the night. Tony had chased the reddish-orange car a few blocks, but gave up after Sandra pleaded with him to stop. She had been leaning forward to reach for the cigarette lighter at the moment the shot was fired, and the deadly cluster of shotgun pellets had nicked her headrest, then shattered the window beside her. "If I'd been sitting up, I would have been killed," she had whispered, brushing broken glass from her lap.

Tony told her it had been just a prank, kids blowing out the window, nothing more. Happens all the time in L.A., he said. "They probably didn't even see us in here." Sandra thought it was strange, but accepted his explanation, and even acquiesced when he told her they needn't call the polite. What could the police do? Tony just put the car in the shop the next day and had the windows fixed, and never mentioned the drive-by shooting again. Sandra dismissed it from her mind, but she never felt comfortable in that car again.[2]

Now Sandra and Tony were left alone as they walked to the big white car in the far corner of the Chez Nora lot. She had the keys and was going to drive. Tony, as usual, had downed quite a few cocktails over the course of the evening. Then, as she unlocked the Thunderbird, she realized they were not alone in the dark parking lot after all.

A man muttered something to her as Sandra opened the driver's door. She looked up and saw a shadowy figure in the corner of the lot, standing behind a waist-high wall at the lot's perimeter. She ignored him—just a street crazy, she figured. But then the man spoke louder, more clearly, and the words froze her: "Your money or your life."

• • •

There's not a shred of evidence that shows I had anything to do with Tony's murder—no motive, no witnesses—except the word of Dennis France. Nobody else says I was there, or that I was driving the car. Sandra Zysman didn't see him talk to anyone or look at anyone, the way he says he talked to me. Because I wasn't there. It's just Dennis France, involving me to save himself.

On the night Tony was killed, I have records, I had done something with two people. One person was staying at my house for about two weeks at that time. I have phone bills, toll calls, my pilot's flight log—we went flying together while he was here. . . . This is a friend of mine in San Diego. A kid I grew up with. We can prove he was at the house for two weeks, including the night Tony was murdered. He would have known if I went out late one night while he was staying there. I didn't. He'll say I didn't go out.

I can tell you exactly where I was on the night Tony was killed. I was in bed, sleeping. I guarantee it.

• • •

Long before this deadly encounter outside Chez Nora, a fearful Tony de los Reyes had taken steps which, he believed, would safeguard his life.

His fears had been prompted by Dennis Winebaugh's treachery. A few months after Gilberto's death, Tony had hired Winebaugh to kill Paulette. It had been a grave error: Paulette had been sleeping with Winebaugh, and he took five thousand dollars from Tony for the hit, then skipped town. On his way out, though, he made tape recordings of Tony contracting for the murder and passed them on to Paulette, who then tried to extort money and divorce concessions from Tony. Once Tony knew Paulette and Forty-four were in league with one another, he decided they might be plotting his death next. To fend that off, Tony had written a "dead man's letter"—a kind of insurance policy, entrusted to a trusted ally. If he should die violently, the letter would be forwarded to the authorities. It was dated July 7, 1977—right after Paulette threatened to have him arrested based on the Winebaugh tapes.

Crudely penned in Tony's hand on ruled yellow paper, it accused Paulette and Winebaugh in the death of Gilberto Cervantes, going far beyond the anonymous letter he had mailed earlier to the San Gabriel Police. Without providing a name, Tony wrote that Paulette also had hired "someone else" to kill him, and that he feared "the police might not properly investigate" if he turned to LAPD for help. He did not, however, directly say this fear arose because a policeman was involved in the plot, nor did he name Bill Leasure in the letter. But Tony clearly felt that this "insurance" offered him more protection than going to the police. If he went down, Tony told Paulette, so would she.

Later, the letter began to seem like an unnecessary precaution. Tony and Paulette had continued their peculiar relationship after Gilbert Cervantes's death. Their divorce had been final five days after the murder, and Paulette had married Big John five days after that, supposedly a union of convenience designed to circumvent the department's investigation of Tony's complaints against Big John.[3] Yet, a year later, in April 1978, with yet another murder plot and treachery behind them, Paulette and Tony walked out of the courthouse following a bitter child custody hearing, arm in arm, a couple again. They moved back in together, and all was well. For a time.

Paulette still saw Bill Leasure often, still joked now and then about killing Tony, still complained bitterly about his supposedly terrible treatment of her. Nothing had really changed. They were divorced yet living together, still warring and forgiving in cycles. She and Big John had separated a few months after marrying, and divorced soon after. Tony was waiting. "You're crazy for going back to him," Bill said. "He doesn't deserve you. It'll never last."

"You're probably right," she admitted in one conversation shortly after the de los Reyeses' reconciliation. "But I have to do this—if not for myself, then for my son. I have to make sure Tony does right by Aaron."

Paulette expressed concerns about the future—specifically, her and her son's financial future—regularly over the course of the next twelve months with Tony. When Natalia died in 1979 and Tony inherited everything, her fears accelerated. Paulette asked him to rewrite his will—leaving more (if not all) of the Cervantes inheritance to Aaron, and less to Tony Junior. At the time, Tony had a will that excluded Aaron completely, and he was not sure he wanted to change it. He liked to hold it over his ex-wife's head, an inducement to better behavior.

Later, he attempted to mollify Paulette instead of threatening her. First, he offered a truce, letting her move back in with him in January 1981 after yet another separation. Then he agreed to finance a plan of hers to open a Louisiana-style fish company. One of a string of money-making schemes she had concocted since the tortilla factory folded the year before, the fish business—like so many of her other plans—never got off the ground. To secure a fishing boat for Paulette, Tony was supposed to put up as collateral one of the commercial buildings he had inherited from his mother and stepfather. Sandra Zysman, however, sensing a potential plot by Paulette to part Tony from his real estate holdings, cautioned him to demand proof that there really was a boat to be financed. When he asked, Paulette could not provide any proof at all, not even a Polaroid snapshot of the boat, much less title and registration. Tony quickly backed out of the deal.[4]

Still, he was quick to reassure his ex-wife, promising to take care of her financially even if he had rejected the fish proposal. The Winebaugh murder-extortion business was four years in the past by then, and Tony apparently thought he could work things out on a more civilized basis. It was then, in a final effort to appease

Paulette by securing the financial future of their son, Aaron, that Tony made his mistake. He let it be known that he might be worth more dead than alive.

In April 1981, after four consecutive peaceful months of living with Paulette in Boyle Heights, Tony came home with a surprise: He said his lawyer had drawn up a new will. Instead of Tony Junior getting everything, young Aaron would be heir to the Cervantes fortune after Tony died. All but the San Gabriel house would go to him, safeguarded through a trust fund to be administered by Paulette. (The former Cervantes home was to go to a cousin of Tony's, in gratitude for her helping to care for Natalia over the years.)[5] Tony had been holding out the promise of a new will to Paulette for years; now he had an unsigned proposed draft of the new will in hand, waving it in front of his ex-wife like a flag of truce.

Paulette, who had been in the kitchen cooking for a dinner party that night, was overjoyed. The first person she told was Bill Leasure.

"Tony's finally done right by Aaron," she told Bill over the telephone. "He's finally made out a new will."

Leasure had called that evening to see how she was doing—Paulette had been complaining again to him about Tony's "horrible" treatment of her—but now she said everything seemed great. Aaron was in line for three quarters of a million to a million dollars, she said. The future was bright. Things were so cordial that Tony even suggested Paulette invite Bill to the party. Leasure politely declined.[6]

But the old pattern of the de los Reyes marriage was not so easily broken: The happy atmosphere faded quickly as distrust and violence marred the peace. Exactly who did what and when remains unclear; however, whatever the catalyst, Tony's relationship with Paulette deteriorated quickly in the spring of 1981. As she had in years past, Paulette began once again to complain to Leasure about Tony. He was beating her, and trying to get her to prostitute herself and to accompany him to gay bathhouses, she said. And when she refused, she said, he would rape her in drunken frenzies. They were living together then, but as roommates, not as man and wife—Tony was even seeing Sandra at the same time. Yet, Paulette wept when Leasure came to see her, "He still attacks me sexually all the time, like an animal." She told Leasure he began, once again, to stand over her as she slept, as he had when they were married years before, until she finally opened her eyes and saw him, red eyes glazed, hands like claws, frozen in a posture of attack.

"I wish he was dead," Paulette said, her old refrain.[7]

Paulette would later recall that Leasure seemed genuinely upset at her predicament, and that he called Tony an asshole, strong words for the ministerial Mild Bill. He even told Dennis France, during a ride in his patrol car, that Paulette's husband was beating her badly and, worse still, threatening to go to the police, to get them all in trouble. Something had to be done, Leasure said. And soon.[8]

Not long after, Dennis France's reddish-orange Chevy Nova fell in behind the white Thunderbird as Tony and Sandra Zysman drove home from a nightclub date. The Nova stayed a few cars back, blending into the light but always present freeway traffic, even at 2:00 in the morning. Tony and Sandra parked outside her apartment building in L.A.'s Fairfax District, a few blocks from the crowded stalls of the Farmer's Market and the boxy sprawl of Television City, bustling during the day, but quiet and empty at this hour. As they sat in the car, talking and smoking, the Nova approached unnoticed from behind, then pulled alongside, its passenger side no farther than a foot from the T-Bird's driver's side. The shotgun barrel emerged from the passenger's side and sent its deadly load of birdshot exploding into the other car.

Although he had downplayed the significance of the drive-by shooting to Sandra, the nearly fatal incident in the Thunderbird, so close in time to his decision to alter his will, apparently rocked Tony—and renewed his suspicions about his ex-wife. He accused Paulette of being behind the shooting, telling his old friend Addie Gomez that Paulette was trying to have him killed so that the Cervantes inheritance would filter down to Aaron. "Then she'll have control," he said. "I know what she's planning."

Just as Paulette told her best friend Bill about Tony's supposedly bizarre and abusive behavior, Tony claimed to Addie Gomez that Paulette was a murderess without conscience. "She's into black magic," Tony muttered. "She's a devil worshiper."[9] Paulette denied all knowledge and responsibility for the shooting, answering his accusations by proclaiming that there was no end to the number of jealous husbands and shady characters who might want to see Tony killed.

Not long after the drive-by shooting, another, different sort of disaster struck. The Munster house in Boyle Heights, along with two other adjacent houses Tony had inherited from Gilberto and Natalia, burned to the ground in a mysterious fire on June 17, 1981. Arson investigators were never able to determine a cause. Yet Tony seemed certain Paulette was behind it, although he could not articulate a reasonable motive for her burning down her own house.[10] Forced out of their home, Tony moved to San Gabriel. Despite his suspicions, he reluctantly brought Paulette and Aaron in tow—Paulette made it clear that if Tony wanted Aaron, he would have to take the whole package.

Two uneasy months later, Paulette and Tony had their final falling out. He evicted her from the San Gabriel house on September 1, this time, he vowed, for good. And nine days later, in the early morning darkness of the parking lot outside the Chez Nora Bar, Tony de los Reyes's life caught up with him.

"Your money or your life."

Sandra started and looked to the left at the man in the shadows. She still wasn't sure she had heard right. The words were menacing, but the man was not—he hadn't moved, hadn't done anything to back up his threat, hadn't displayed a gun or a knife. A muttering man, standing behind that waist-high wall at the Chez Nora parking lot's weedy edge—that was all Sandra saw.

She glanced at Tony. He had his hand on the passenger-door handle, waiting for her to unlock the car, saying nothing, seemingly ignoring the man. Tony always liked to carry cash—there was the little bank bag of quarters he kept, which he used to call women on nightclub pay phones during breaks between sets. And he always had a roll of several hundred dollars in his pocket, with even more cash stashed under the T-Bird's floor mat—fifteen hundred dollars total, not to mention the gold medallion, worth more than a thousand dollars, swinging from Tony's neck. He was an excellent target for a robbery.

Sandra followed Tony's cue and ignored the man. Climbing into the car, she jammed the key into the ignition, started the engine, then hit the headlight button. When she looked up again at the man, he was squinting back at her, bathed in the white glare from the T-Bird's lights. In the harsh illumination, Sandra saw a thirtyish white man with dark hair and a bushy mustache, big boned, wearing a white shirt with blue, widely spaced stripes. He seemed tall to her, anywhere from five foot ten to six foot three, but it was hard to tell with that wall blocking him off from the waist down.

As she reached over to pop the lock and let Tony into the car, Sandra heard a tremendous explosion. Looking up in panic, she saw the man at the wall was no longer in sight. Neither was Tony.

Sandra leapt from the car and ran to the passenger side of the T-Bird. Tony was lying on the ground, his body twisted unnaturally, a halo of blood forming about his head. His pink shirt, white pants, and white shoes were spattered with droplets of the dark liquid. His shattered glasses had skittered under the car. Inside the spreading circle of blood pooling on the oily asphalt, two of Tony's trademark quarters had rolled to a stop, flashes of silver in the sickly yellow illumination from the parking lot lightposts.

As Sandra stood staring and stunned, the singer they had been talking with moments before ran from across the lot to Tony's side, saw the massive wound in his head and the blood and hair plastered to the side of the car, and realized there was no hope for the little bass player's survival. Tony lay there moaning incoherently, unresponsive to Sandra's frantic question, repeated over and over: "Tony, can you hear me?" The singer loped after the waitress, who, hearing the gunshot and seeing Tony crumple to the ground, had run to the bar to phone the police. The time, recorded by the emergency 911 dispatcher, was 1:50 A.M., September 10, 1981.

Against all odds, Tony clung to life during the race to the nearest hospital. His skull was shaved clean and he was rushed into emergency surgery. But he had been struck in the head and face with the blast of a shotgun, at close range, thirty feet or less. One of his eyes had been obliterated, and he had suffered massive and irreparable brain damage. Seven hours later, he was pronounced dead, a foregone conclusion, despite his heart's refusal to stop pumping blood long after Tony Reyes was gone.

When detectives came to question the shocked and tired musicians, bartenders, and waitresses at Chez Nora, they learned no one but Sandra Zysman had seen the gunman, and that had been nothing more than a fleeting glimpse of a man frozen in the headlights of Tony's Thunderbird. Still, a composite sketch she and a police artist later constructed would be identified by the bartender as a man who had come to Chez Nora twice before the killings—the night Tony was killed and on an earlier night, September 6, which also just happened to be the last night Paulette de los Reyes had visited Chez Nora. Each time, the man who looked like the composite drawing had come in alone, ordered a single drink, spoke to no one, then left. Though no getaway car or accomplice had been seen, investigators concluded from the quick disappearance of the shooter that there must have been both.[11]

Tony's aunt, who had been baby-sitting Aaron, came with the boy to the hospital. Sandra lacked the heart to tell Aaron that his father had been shot to death. Nor would she mention her burgeoning suspicions that, somehow, Paulette was behind it. Instead, she brought Aaron to her Fairfax District apartment and explained that Tony had died of heart failure. Under the circumstances, a lie seemed the kindest way out.

After bringing his tears under control, Aaron asked to call his mother to break the news. She was staying with a friend. He made the call, then, after a few moments, he handed the phone to Sandra.

"Tony had a heart attack, Paulette," Sandra said, wondering how she would react to the lie. "He died in my arms."

Paulette reacted by laughing. She knows the truth, Sandra thought. She knows he was shot, not killed by a heart attack, because she was in on it. Finally, Paulette spoke. "I'll be by to pick up Aaron later," she said. Then she hung up.[12]

The next day, Paulette recruited Bill Leasure to help her gain entry to the house in San Gabriel, where she and Aaron once again took up residence, Tony's eviction earlier that month notwithstanding. She expected that Aaron would inherit the house once the estate was settled, along with everything else of Tony's. Bill helped her move in, comforting her and advising her on how to deal with the detectives who, he said, would inevitably be around to question her. Paulette told him over and over how sweet he was for taking care of her.

"Well, I may need a favor from you someday, Paulette," Bill replied simply.[13]

The funeral was held a few days later. Tony's family snubbed Paulette, which, unfortunately, meant Aaron was left out, too. She had to call the coroner's office to get the name of the funeral home, where the director suggested it would be best if she didn't come to the ceremonies. Paulette flew into a rage. "We'll be there," she proclaimed.

The Catholic services and burial were at the San Gabriel Mission. Tony's family and friends, including Sandra Zysman, sat in the front pews on the right side of the church. Paulette, wearing a large wide-brimmed hat and dark glasses, swept dramatically into the church and pointedly sat with Aaron on the left side. Later, there was no room made for them in the limousines that brought the family to the gravesite; she and Aaron had to bum a ride from a friend from the tortilla business who had come to pay his respects.

At the grave, Paulette stood tearfully in front of the coffin. Then, noticing Sandra weeping, Paulette turned to Aaron and said, loudly and clearly for the entire hushed assemblage to hear, "Look at the spectacle your father's whore is making of herself."[14]

Through it all, two LAPD Hollywood Division detectives stood by and watched. Funerals are a favorite observation point for homicide detectives who like to gauge their suspects' reactions under stress. Later, one of the detectives pulled Sandra Zysman aside and said, "Sandra, I promise, one day you and I will be eating popcorn at Paulette's execution."

The detective had been particularly sympathetic to Sandra, and had answered all her questions in the trying days since Tony's death. Now she looked at him and couldn't help but smile a little. "I'll even cook it," she said, "if they let me pull the switch."[15]

• • •

It's so ridiculous. They can't prove I was paid anything for these murders—because I wasn't. They can't prove it because it isn't true. They have no motive whatsoever.

So they have to make something up. That I'm some kind of thrill killer. I did all this for kicks, I got bored writing traffic tickets and decided to start killing people. I'm a big thrill-seeker. Come on! It's so ridiculous it isn't funny.

• • •

Looking at the evidence and listening to Sandra Zysman's account of the shooting, Detectives Philip Sartuche and William Williams dismissed robbery as a genuine reason for the killing—echoing, without knowing it, the previous police responses to the Smith and Cervantes murders. Though money had been demanded, there had been no actual attempt to rob Tony or Sandra before the gunman opened fire—Tony's wallet was untouched, as were the gold chain and medallion around his neck, and the money in the car.

Instead, the detectives focused on Paulette as a potential suspect in what looked to them like a professional hit.[16] They were suspicious of her failure to come to Chez Nora as promised that night, and though the police verified her alibi—she spent the night with a girlfriend named Sylvia—Williams and Sartuche decided that she must have hired a contract killer.

They soon learned of the unsolved murder of Gilberto Cervantes, and began sharing information with detectives in San Gabriel, who had also suspected Paulette four years earlier. They were sure the two crimes were linked, and they believed an LAPD officer was somehow involved—Big John, they guessed. But none of it fit together. Tony's dead man's letter, naming Dennis Winebaugh and Paulette as the Cervantes killers, ended up on the investigators' desk a few months later, just as Tony had planned. But though it confirmed their suspicions, it offered no usable proof against anyone. The case went nowhere.[17]

In fact, as far as the investigation of Paulette de los Reyes was concerned, it went backwards. Even Paulette's supposed motive for

Tony's murder seemed to evaporate. The last will and testament Tony had asked his lawyer to prepare the preceding April would, indeed, have given nearly everything to Aaron—three quarters of a million dollars in cash and real estate in the form of a trust fund, with Paulette controlling the purse strings. But there was one problem: Tony, a notorious procrastinator when it came to dealing with paperwork, had neglected to return to his lawyer's office to sign the will. After putting it off several times, Tony had finally made an appointment with his attorney to sign the will in front of witnesses, making it official. The appointment was for September 11, 1981, one day after Tony died.

The money and property Paulette had been counting on, even the house in San Gabriel in which she had been living, did not belong to her or her son, and never would. Tony's death brought her nothing; even his fifteen-thousand-dollar life insurance policy was in arrears, and netted Paulette only five hundred dollars, scarcely motive for murder. If she had contracted for Tony's death, she had jumped the gun. As it was, she was able to tell the police, Bill Leasure, and anyone else who asked, "I got nothing from Tony's death. Nothing!"

At the same time she was denying to police that she had any reason to see Tony dead, Paulette claimed in probate court, where wills are adjudicated, that papers destroyed in the Boyle Heights house fire would have proved Tony intended for her and Aaron to receive an inheritance. Whatever the merits of that claim, only a signed, intact copy of Tony's will could be accepted in court. And the only signed will known to be in existence was produced by Tony's elder son, Antonio de los Reyes, Jr. This 1977 handwritten version gave Tony Jr. everything, and Aaron next to nothing.

Outraged, Paulette sued the estate, complaining that she and her son were due a share, and claiming that, at the least, she was owed four years of unpaid child support and unpaid alimony that had been ordered in her divorce with Tony. When Tony Jr. tried to get her out of the San Gabriel house, which was slated for demolition in favor of a condominium complex, she refused to move and sought numerous court injunctions, attempting to stave off the eviction. She claimed in court that Aaron should receive the house through his "homestead" rights. Aaron eventually received a seventy-thousand-dollar settlement.

In the meantime, Ron Schines, a man Paulette had met in a Pasadena bar in the summer of 1981, a few months before Tony died, moved into the San Gabriel house with Paulette and Aaron, and began a series of failed business ventures with the widow. While living there, he saw Bill Leasure come by a number of times to see Paulette. They would speak in hushed tones, usually standing outside the house and out of earshot if Schines was around. Other times, Leasure left several urgent messages on the answering machine when Paulette was not home, saying he needed to reach her as soon as possible. He had little to say to Schines other than hello, good-bye, and excuse us, please, we have to talk.

Finally, Schines asked what all the secrecy was about. Paulette said it was nothing, but then made an odd remark: "Bill was a go-between for me and the man who killed Tony. He's just protecting me."

Schines, who considered Paulette "a schemer, very devious and believable . . . very good at lying," discounted what she had told him. There were plenty of reasons she might lie to him, he figured. He just didn't believe she could have anything to do with her ex-husband's killer—and certainly not in partnership with a Los Angeles police officer. That would be crazy.[18]

Across town some months later, Skipper Robert Kuns watched his friend Bill work on one of the Corvettes in the yard of the Leasures' Northridge home. Bill was wrestling with something under the sleek sports car's hood as he talked, trying to persuade Kuns to hire Dennis France as a yacht crewman. Kuns and Leasure were in the boat business together by then, a form of risk-taking far more lucrative than other, more shadowy pursuits Leasure had hinted at to the Skipper. Now Leasure wanted his trusted gofer France in on the action.

"Why should I hire Dennis?" Kuns asked. "I don't even know him. You can't trust someone you don't know."

"Well, I trust him," Bill said. "He's done some things for me. Heavy things. He's reliable. He'll do almost anything you want."

Kuns nodded. In his mind, something "heavy" meant breaking somebody up, or perhaps committing a major robbery. He wouldn't ask for details—that wouldn't be right, it would violate the etiquette of their relationship. And anyway, the explanation as offered was sufficient for Kuns. It was "business." And a fellow businessman—a successful one, at least—could always be trusted. With Kuns, such a story was the best way of vouching for a person. There could not be a better reference.

"Okay," Kuns said, as Leasure deftly turned his wrench. "He's hired."[19]

CHAPTER 10

BILL LEASURE AND BOB KUNS had known each other nearly four years before either of them broached subjects criminal. Instead, their conversation had always drifted easily among scuba diving, pleasure boating, and the latest Corvette Bill was working on—never a hint that either one of them might be willing to step over the line.

Leasure would occasionally speak to the Skipper about his work as a traffic officer, seemingly relishing what sounded like rather dull work to Kuns. Once Leasure proudly showed off an intersection with stop signs at each corner. "I got those signs put up," he said with the satisfaction of a climber who had scaled Everest. "There were lots of accidents here before." Kuns politely congratulated him, but silently wondered how a man could be satisfied by such mundane accomplishments without some other outside diversion. He wondered if there might be more going on behind Leasure's bland expression—he had seen glints of something else, he thought, something at odds with the starched blue uniform of LAPD—but he was not the type to ask. In Kuns's world view, you just didn't pose such questions.

And so they had remained casual friends for years, brought together in 1978 because Kuns's younger sister, Betsy Mogul's fellow assistant city attorney, decided Officer Leasure might exert a beneficial influence on the morally unanchored Skipper. No one expected the influence might end up running in the other direction.

In the summer of 1982, Kuns returned to his home in California from an extended stay in British Columbia, Canada. He had been living aboard his new sailboat berthed there, a two-hundred-thousand-dollar ketch-rigged clipper he dubbed *Poor Little Urchin*, after his personal fondness for cutoff shorts and broken-down flip-flops as dockside attire. Upon his return, Kuns came to Northridge to visit his old friend Leasure.

When he described his new boat, Leasure became intensely curious about the fifty-one-foot Morgan—a sleek fiberglass-and-teak rich man's toy that should have been far beyond Kuns's means. Leasure knew the Skipper had been making only a modest living in the yacht maintenance business before leaving for Canada and, of late, had been doing very little work at all.

"Where do you get the money to buy something like that boat, Rob?" Leasure asked when Kuns came over to Northridge for a visit. The pointed question made it clear that the money-conscious Leasure was both envious and suspicious—enough so to make him pry, which was something neither man did often. For one of the few times in their relationship, Kuns felt he was in the presence of a police officer, a potential adversary.

Alarmed, Kuns shrugged and uttered some platitude about scrimping and saving to buy the boat—which was ridiculous, since Leasure knew Kuns well enough to be sure that the Skipper could never have saved enough money to buy a toy boat, much less his two-hundred-thousand-dollar dream yacht. For as long as Leasure had known him, Kuns either had a ten-thousand-dollar roll tucked into the pocket of his chino pants, or he was trying to bum a ten-spot off of Bill to get him through the week. There was no in between, and, both men knew, no way Kuns legitimately could have bought such an expensive yacht. He was incapable of saving.

Still, Kuns couldn't just tell Bill the truth about *Poor Little Urchin*'s origins, at least not without feeling him out first, testing whether his loyalties to a friend, or to LAPD, would be the stronger. A paroled bank robber with thirty-five months of federal time under his belt, Kuns was practically twitching at Leasure's question.

But Leasure sensed Kuns's unease immediately. He knew the only way to get the Skipper to open up about the Morgan would be to reveal some secret about himself—or, at least, make it seem that way. So Leasure told Kuns a story supposedly from his past, designed to prove to Kuns that their moral compasses were in tune with one another's.

"I've done a few things here and there in my day, too," Bill began—and Kuns's suspicions about Leasure's other side suddenly seemed confirmed. "I would understand if you had done something to get that boat."

As Kuns recalls it, Leasure told him he had burglarized documents from a law office for a woman he knew in Michigan, in order to extricate her from some legal problems related to her sale of some movie rights. Then, Leasure said, there was Dennis France and his "heavy" work. By Kuns's lights, these seemed very impressive credentials indeed.

"So now you tell me something, Rob," Leasure concluded. "How did you get enough money to buy that sailboat?"

Kuns considered the possibility that Leasure was making up a tale of burglary and intrigue just to entrap and arrest him. But somehow he didn't think so. He had seen a kindred spirit in Leasure's eyes. And he also knew Leasure's tightness with a dollar. That gleam in Bill's eye wasn't suspicion, it was avarice, Kuns decided. The guy didn't want to miss out on a good business opportunity.

"I'll just throw caution to the wind and tell you, Bill," Kuns finally said, then drew a deep breath. "I didn't get the money to buy that boat. I just took it."

Leasure barely reacted, just nodded, then asked how Kuns had managed this feat, his voice carefully neutral. The Skipper proudly explained the system he had developed for exploiting a loophole in the government's method of recording boat ownership, allowing him to exchange phony bills of sale for genuine registration cards. Other people laundered money; he had figured out how to launder boats. He had done it twice so far—once with his first boat, the *Shori Ryu,* and more recently with the Morgan. Perfect crimes, he said.

When Kuns finished outlining "the business," Leasure nodded and smiled and, as Kuns would later testify, said exactly what the Skipper had hoped to hear:

"If you're going to do something like that again, Rob, I'd like to come along."[1]

By the time Leasure met him, Kuns possessed the aspect of a man who had spent his entire life on or near the sea, from his Captain Ahab beard and Mr. Clean scalp to the capable economy of motion with which he knotted a line and raised a sail. But, in truth, Kuns had taken on the mariner's persona late in life.

Born in Bristol, Pennsylvania in 1945, he had spent his youth landlocked in Arizona and Colorado, where his father ran a dude ranch. He finally ended up at New Mexico State University, where he spent two years majoring in food science before dropping out. It was during a two-year stint in the Navy aboard an aircraft carrier homeported in San Diego that he finally developed his tastes for the ocean and Southern California. When college and a first marriage failed to work out, he left New Mexico in 1970 and took a job in San Diego at a health spa. When a second marriage crumbled, a third grew shaky, and the spa went belly-up, putting him out of work, Kuns decided to go for some fast money. Ever since he was a child, he had been fascinated with the idea of committing the perfect crime. Now was the time to try one, he decided.

The bank branch he patronized in La Jolla, north of San Diego, seemed ideal. Convenient to major highways in four directions, it received a major delivery of currency once a week, always at the same hour, so customers could cash their paychecks. The bank took minimal security precautions. It was really amazing how carelessly large sums of money are handled, Kuns marveled. He rented a nondescript yellow Ford Pinto for a getaway car, substituted makeshift cardboard license plates he had copied from another yellow Pinto he had seen on the freeway, then headed to the bank.

Wearing a ski mask, a Marine Corps fatigue jacket, jump boots, and an ammo belt picked up at a Navy surplus store, Kuns marched into the bank with an AR-15 automatic rifle and cleaned the place out just after the armored car dropped off its load of cash. He left with $52,648. Terrified bank employees later described the robber as a muscular, five-foot-nine, 180-pound wild man wielding a shotgun. Two inches shorter and forty pounds lighter, the wiry Kuns walked into the bank the next day in his usual beach bum garb, made a deposit with some of the bank's own money, exchanged smiles with one of the same tellers he had robbed the day before, then left, completely unrecognized, the adrenaline rush of it all making the blood pound in his temples.

The hapless motorist whose license plates he had copied did not fare so well: a Vietnam vet who owned a yellow Pinto, a Marine fatigue jacket, and a physique that exactly matched the bank tellers' erroneous description, he was arrested and nearly charged with the robbery before the FBI finally accepted his alibi. Nothing motivates a cop more than being made to look foolish: FBI agents painstakingly tracked down every other person who drove a yellow Pinto south of Los Angeles at the time of the robbery, until they happened upon a laid-off health spa worker who had just bought a new Pantera sports car for himself, a Lotus Europa for his wife, and had rented a four-bedroom house on the beach—all without any legitimate source of income. "God, I was stupid," Kuns recalled later. "I must have wanted to get caught."

The police staked him out, then busted him while he was on his way to rob an armored car, a sawed-off shotgun, a .357 Magnum revolver, and a hundred rounds of hollow-point bullets in his trunk. In August 1973, three glorious months after the bank job, Kuns was arrested and eventually pleaded guilty to bank larceny. He drew a ten-year federal sentence, but as part of his plea bargain and because of his otherwise spotless record, he became eligible for parole the day he walked through the prison gates. He was out in just under three years.

After a year tending bar in one of Los Angeles's high-end yacht harbors, Marina del Rey, Kuns decided working with boats was what he wanted to do with his life. He started hiring on as a menial at boat yards, then learned to scuba dive and taught himself how to perform underwater repairs and maintenance on pleasure vessels. He moved south to Newport Beach in Orange County, California's monied Republican enclave, where he became one of the best-known working divers in town. Kuns specialized in servicing the expensive, seldom-used yachts of the developers, real estate magnates, and other assorted tycoons who docked their boats in Newport Beach, lined up hull to hull like trophies in a case.

In May 1978, he had been successful enough to start his own custom-yacht maintenance business. Three months later, he bought his first boat. He christened the thirty-seven-foot trawler the *Shori Ryu*—Japanese for "Victorious Dragon."

That fall, his sister Kay mentioned to her friend and supervisor at the City Attorney's Office, Betsy Mogul, that her brother had bought a new boat and was planning a dive trip that weekend to Catalina Island, just off the Southern California coast. Kay asked, "Why don't you and Bill come along?" Betsy agreed, and that weekend, she, Leasure, Kay, two other city attorney employees, and the newly divorced Skipper and his girlfriend piled onto the *Shori Ryu* and spent a pleasant, if uneventful, weekend at Catalina. Despite LAPD policies against officers socializing with known felons, neither Betsy nor Bill seemed to think hanging out with the Skipper would pose any ethical dilemmas.

Kuns and Leasure sized each other up quickly and apparently liked what they saw. They both loved Corvettes and diving, and they were both fairly quiet, although compared to Leasure, Kuns was positively garrulous. When they returned to Newport Harbor Sunday afternoon and the group piled off the boat, Betsy pulled Kuns aside and said, "I'm so glad you and Bill got along so well."

"Really?" Kuns replied. "We couldn't have said more than twenty words to each other the whole trip."

Betsy smiled. "Believe me, he likes you. He wouldn't have talked to you at all if he didn't. He'll go to a party and not say a word to anybody."[2]

In the months that followed, Kuns joined Leasure and Betsy on a dive trip to Cozumel, Mexico, organized by a group of LAPD officers. They embarked a few days after Kuns married for the fourth time—the trip was the new couple's honeymoon, a wedding gift from his sister, with Bill and Betsy in tow. Leasure even went to Kuns's parole officer to vouch for Kuns's safe return from abroad. The following year, in spring 1981, a similar trip brought Kuns and Leasure to the Cayman Islands in the British West Indies, one of several trips the two men would make to the island dependency, known as a tax haven for investors—and, because of its strict banking secrecy laws, for money launderers.[3] Kuns fell in love with the Cayman Islands on that trip and began talking of settling there someday.

By then, Kuns had been out of prison and living straight for five years. But he was beginning to chafe at existing solely to service the rich. At the end of each day, he would emerge from the water and pull the brine shrimp from his bushy reddish beard, having spent long hours scraping barnacles or straightening propeller shafts. He'd put in twelve hours a day, six days a week, then watch the huge yachts he could never afford glide by, captained by men in blue blazers and white pants, sipping wine with women twenty years their junior—the sort of life he had envisioned for himself driving that new Pantera so many years before.

So in the spring of 1981, he took his boat up to Santa Barbara, a two-hour drive north of Los Angeles. There he changed the name of the *Shori Ryu*, altered the serial number engraved on its hull, and left it in a rented boat slip. A short time later, he had a friend drop him in the water between the mainland and Catalina Island, where he bobbed in an inflatable raft for hours. Finally, a group of weekend sailors on a charter fishing cruise spotted him. "My boat sunk," he told them as they pulled him on board, wet and shivering. "Thank God you spotted me."

The insurance adjustor who took his claim did not try to hide his doubts about Kuns's story. He knew something was wrong. But he had no evidence to dispute Kuns's tale of shipwreck and watery ordeal. Whatever investigation the insurance company conducted, if any, it failed to ascertain that Kuns, rather foolishly, had been seen by dozens of people painting away in Santa Barbara on a boat remarkably similar to the *Shori Ryu* a few weeks after the "sinking." Eventually the insurance company cut him a sixty-thousand-dollar check. Not long afterward, he reregistered the altered *Shori Ryu* under its new name, then sold it for thirty-five thousand dollars up in San Francisco. Despite his mistakes, his scheme had worked.

He had planned to use the proceeds of this fraud to buy the sailboat his latest wife said she wanted. She told him not to bother, she was leaving him anyway. By then, Kuns realized he didn't care. He had become fascinated with the possibilities his scam with the *Shori Ryu* had raised. Why buy a sailboat? Why not just take one? And on June 13, 1982, he did just that. The fifty-one-foot Morgan sailboat *Juliana*, the prize possession of a prominent Los Angeles developer, disappeared from its slip in Marina del Rey, resurfacing in Sidney, British Columbia, a few weeks later as *Poor Little Urchin*.

Kuns felt no guilt at the theft—he figured the owner of the *Juliana* would be compensated handsomely for his loss from insurance coverage. And if he did feel a pang, it was quickly soothed by the pleasure of his new acquisition. He had the boat of his dreams—along with a new business. Bob Kuns Custom Yacht Maintenance was history. From then on, Kuns would take what he wanted, from the very people he had slaved for over the years.

Not long afterwards, he went to visit Bill Leasure in his cluttered home in Northridge. He left with a new partner.

• • •

My theory, as far as modifying the boats, changing ID and all, he had a crew to do that before I ever saw the boats. He'd steal them, change them, then get me to crew for him. He claims that we did those changes on the boats while we were at sea. It's ridiculous. Anyone who tells you they can make those changes while underway is a liar. There's no way . . .

He used me, really. I did do some DMV [Department of Motor Vehicles] stuff for Kuns. He'd ask me to run a boat on the computer and I'd do it. He'd say it was to check the title on a boat he wanted to buy, to make sure it was clean. Actually, he probably was checking to see if the owner lived near the boat, or on the boat, so he could steal it. But I didn't know. I've never stolen a boat in my life.

Dennis France and I used to call Kuns "Dummy" all the time. Not to his face, no. Just when he wasn't around. It wasn't to be mean, though I guess it kind of sounds that way. It was just that Kuns spent his money like water. If he had a girl, and he had two hundred fifty dollars, and that was all he had in the world, he'd figure it was fifty dollars for dinner for the two of them, then he would spend the other two hundred to send her a flower arrangement. Then the next day, he'd be flat broke and borrowing money from everyone. Now you tell me. Isn't that a dummy? He was really a weird individual.

• • •

The first boat deal after *Poor Little Urchin* involved a trip to Colombia. The customer was an old friend of the Kuns family who operated a casino there. The customer wanted a pleasure boat for hauling his high rollers out to sport-fish in the warm South American waters between bouts at the gaming tables. He advanced Kuns twenty-six thousand dollars to bring him one, with a similar balance due on delivery. The buyer assumed Kuns was going to make a legitimate boat purchase for him.

Kuns had other plans. Months before, he had set up a dummy corporation in the Cayman Islands called Custom Sail Dive Charters, for which he claimed to be an employee. His cover story was a stroke of genius: Custom Sail, he would tell people, had its own boats, operating primarily off the coast of Mexico and in the Caribbean. After years of charter trips, these boats would approach the end of their useful service lives and would have to be sold—at a discount price, of course, Kuns would say. With a single stroke, he had created a plausible reason why he would have lots of boats to sell, as well as explaining why he could always offer them cheap enough to assure quick sales. Neither the casino operator nor any of his other customers would ever have reason to suspect Kuns was a thief unless he told them so.

Kuns, Leasure, and a friend of the Skipper's known only as "John from Boston"[4] sat down and planned the deal. Kuns had selected a forty-two-footer docked in Newport Harbor for the Colombia customer. It matched the buyer's specifications exactly, and a few weeks' surveillance of the boat had established that the owner seldom visited the yacht, making it ripe for the taking with a minimum of risk.

Because Leasure had never done anything like this before, Kuns decided Bill should wait on the dock, keeping watch for nosy neighbors and the Harbor Patrol, while he and John broke in and boarded the yacht. That way, at least Bill could get away if there was trouble, Kuns suggested. But, by Kuns's account, an insistent Leasure objected.

"Let *him* wait on the dock," Leasure is supposed to have said, nodding at John. "I want to go in."

"But why, Bill?" Kuns asked, surprised. "That's the most dangerous part."

And that's when Leasure quashed any lingering doubt Kuns might have harbored about his policeman friend's loyalties, the Skipper would later say.

"No, Rob," he recalls Leasure replying. "That's the *fun* part."[5]

Toward the end of 1982, Leasure took some vacation time from LAPD and told his wife Betsy—and his girl friend Irene—that he was embarking on a sailing trip to San Andrés, Colombia, with Kuns. Leasure was to be a crew member, a chance for him to gain some hands-on experience at sea, he said—something he had never done before. Best of all, he said, it would be a financially painless vacation: Kuns was covering his expenses and paying him two thousand dollars.

The owner of the targeted yacht had a habit of leaving a sliding window cracked open on board, something Kuns had taken careful note of, just as he had charted movements and deliveries at his bank nine years before. Around 11:00 on the evening of departure, by Kuns's account, he and Leasure slithered through the window. Once aboard, they turned on the lights, unlocked the doors and windows, and generally assumed the appearance of boat owners performing some late-night repairs—people who had nothing to hide and belonged on the vessel, should anyone be watching. Let's be bold about it, Leasure suggested, and Kuns agreed.

Kuns unzipped a duffel bag and pulled out some tools and a spare ignition switch and key. He and Leasure quickly pulled out the yacht's existing ignition switch, replaced it, and started up the engines. John hopped on board, and they were off.

On the way south to San Diego, according to Kuns's subsequent testimony, he and Leasure stood on the swim step at the stern of the boat and went to work on the name painted on the transom. As the yacht chugged southward, they used paint stripper and sandpaper to remove the old name, then covered the abraded area with teak plaques Kuns had prepared in advance, emblazoned with the ship's new name—*Jimmy K*—in gold-leaf lettering. The next day, they rented a slip in San Diego, where they finished Kuns's patented transformation—a new color for the sheer strip along the top of the hull and, affixed to the railing, a stainless-steel plate engraved with new serial numbers, for which Kuns had already obtained registration in the Cayman Islands. Finished with the modifications, they departed, hitting international waters before anyone even noticed the boat was missing.

Both Leasure and the Skipper would later recall the trip as

their most enjoyable voyage ever, notwithstanding the bad weather and near disasters that plagued the entire trip. No other foray into "the business" would be as much fun—from the heart-pounding rush of the flawless break-in and getaway to the lush ports of call along Mexico's Pacific coast as they made their way south. The highlight came in Cabo San Lucas, on the rocky fingertip of the Baja Peninsula, where Kuns had the pleasure of seeing—for the first and only time—Bill Leasure get drunk. A day on the beach wolfing down tacos and drinking deceptively potent piña coladas had tee-totaler Bill laughing convulsively as he tried, unsuccessfully, to pilot a dinghy out to the *Jimmy K*. He ended up traveling in circles, unable to straighten out the rudder, nearly falling into the ocean several times before Kuns finally pulled him on board.

A few days later, while en route southward again, Leasure's chronic seasickness—there was never a trip when Bill didn't become violently ill—turned into something more serious. He was feverish and hardly able to move. Kuns put in at Acapulco, where a Mexican doctor diagnosed Leasure's problem as "liver amoebas" and prescribed a drug that seemed to help. Back in the States, his doctor would later say there was no such thing as liver amoebas, but, in any case, Leasure was useless for the rest of the voyage. Kuns dropped him at the Acapulco airport and sent him home, continuing the voyage without Bill's help.

Before leaving, though, Leasure told him what their next job should be. "I know a guy who wants a boat," he said. "A friend of mine, Art Smith."[6]

The Smith deal was a more complex one than the Colombia trip. In April 1983, before even acquiring a boat, Kuns, Leasure, and Smith flew to the Cayman Islands to create a dummy corporation called ASCO (short for Art Smith Company). Then, in ASCO's name, they registered a fifty-two-foot sailboat, the *Santine*, presenting phony bills of sale and a phony builder's certificate of completion for a yacht that did not as yet exist. Among other benefits, Cayman registry meant no property or sales taxes would have to be paid on the "purchase" of the boat, which was being "bought" by ASCO from Kuns's Custom Sail Dive Charters.

The four-day trip was not all business: Bill brought Irene Wong with him, and Kuns brought his girlfriend, Kathy. Leasure had a broken leg at the time, which gave him time off from work, but didn't stop him from motorcycling all over the main island of Grand Cayman, with Irene on the seat behind him. It was her first trip abroad and she was thrilled to be visiting such an exotic island. Bill obviously had been there before—he proudly showed her all the sights. As far as Irene knew, the trip was all pleasure. She knew nothing of the yacht-related machinations.

Afterward, back in the States, Kuns, Leasure, and Smith strode through Marina del Rey on a "shopping" trip. Art had seen actor Sylvester Stallone's boat once, and announced that he wanted a yacht just like the star of the Rocky movies. Like a salesman displaying his wares, Kuns showed Smith a series of different sailboats—other people's sailboats—until Smith decided on a fifty-one-foot twin-masted yacht called *Lucky Star*. Smith would later admit embarking on this shopping expedition, but would tell police he thought Kuns was showing him boats that were legitimately up for sale. Kuns, however, would describe in detail how he pulled out a bolt cutter, sliced the *Lucky Star*'s cabin lock off its hasp, and brought Smith and Leasure on board for a tour. "I want this boat," Smith said when they were through.

Later, Leasure handled the financial negotiations alone with Kuns. "He's a friend of mine, Rob. What will you do it for?"

"Fifty thousand. It's worth three times that. More."

"Come on," Leasure wheedled. "You can do it cheaper than that. I'll go along and I won't charge you. So will Art. So you won't have any crew expenses." Leasure's fee for crewing to Colombia had been two thousand dollars, but now that he was experienced, Kuns was prepared to go as high as ten thousand a trip.[7]

Kuns mulled it over, then finally said, "Okay, I'll do it for thirty thousand."

Leasure seemed surprised that his friend had come down so far so easily. Then a sly expression stole over his face. "Really?" Kuns recalls Leasure saying. "Well, how about I tell Art forty thousand, and keep the extra ten for myself?"

Kuns was caught. He had already agreed to a lower price. What could he say but "Okay"? It would not be the last time Kuns felt Leasure had taken advantage of him financially.[8]

Nor, as it turned out, was it the first. As far as Kuns knew, the boat was to be solely Art Smith's. But the ASCO corporate papers Leasure filed for Smith in Grand Cayman list Leasure as a co-owner, and later, when papers were filed in Oregon to give the *Santine* U.S. registry, Leasure filled them out, listed himself as co-owner, and put down his own address under Smith's name. A month after the Caymans trip, once Art, Bill, and the Skipper had stolen the *Lucky Star* and transformed it into the *Santine*, Leasure brought Irene to see it. "This is my new boat. I own it with Art," he told her. "But don't tell Rob. As far as he knows, it's just Art's. He'd get really mad if he knew. He would have charged us more."[9]

The yacht, moored in San Pedro, just north of Long Beach, became a regular rendezvous point for Irene and Leasure. A typical dinner date would end with them rolling around together in the large main stateroom—a far more luxurious setting than the trailer in back of Smith's house. Irene never saw Smith on board the *Santine* during these visits. Part of the reason she put up with Leasure's cheapness and tendency to make their dates into perfunctory preludes to sex was his apparent wealth, she would later admit. Leasure represented security to her, if not love. She would see this fantastic yacht, or his high-performance plane, or all those cars, and say to herself, someday this will be mine, too. And she would make excuses for Leasure's conduct.

Irene was not the only person who believed the *Santine* belonged to Leasure, at least in part. Several of Leasure's fellow police officers, as well as Betsy Mogul's city attorney colleagues, would later recall that both the Leasures referred to the *Santine* as "our boat." This point—and Leasure's subsequent insistence that he had no financial stake in the yacht—would eventually take on profound significance, for it showed a financial connection with Art Smith that Leasure was anxious to deny.

After the *Santine* deal, Leasure finally persuaded Kuns to hire Dennis France for future boat trips. At first Kuns disliked France's bluster and violent talk, but in time he learned to accept it, once he saw that France really was dependable and willing to follow orders. If anything bothered him, it was Bill's odd attitude about France, a combination of protectiveness and threat.

"Remember," Leasure told him more than once, "Dennis is my friend first. He lets me know everything that goes on."[10]

The first job that included France as crewman took place early in October 1983 in Sidney, British Columbia, Canada, where the trio flew in order to pick up a $160,000 motor yacht called the *Peggy Rose II*. While casing the job, Kuns and France stayed aboard the Morgan. Leasure found a girlfriend in nearby Tacoma, Washington, and stayed with her. Kuns, like many other friends of Leasure's, marveled at his success with women. "Whatever it takes, he has it," Kuns remarked to France.

The owners of the *Peggy Rose II* did not notice it was missing for weeks. Leasure, Kuns, and France were long gone by then. En route to Southern California, the name of the forty-foot yacht was changed to *Tortuga*. The hull identification number was removed and replaced. The new number matched a fictitious thirty-seven-foot trawler Kuns had preregistered with the California Department of Motor Vehicles, claiming it had been built in 1981 by a nonexistent Tacoma, Washington boat builder, Hewitt Marine, Inc.

There are thousands of boat builders worldwide, small and large, with dozens going in and out of business every year, and no comprehensive central directory listing them. Kuns knew the state bureaucracy would never try to verify whether a Hewitt Marine had ever existed or not. In fact, Hewitt Marine was simply a post office box Kuns had rented and a pile of blank forms he used for creating phony builder's certificates. The government's review of these records was so slipshod that Kuns was able to file one boat builder's certificate that was signed and dated 1981—even though a line at the top of the page plainly showed the fill-in-the-blanks form had been printed in May 1982. The form was an obvious and sloppy forgery, yet no one noticed.[11]

While Kuns steered the *Tortuga* southward, France and Leasure packed all the personal possessions on board—magazines, fishing tackle, scuba gear, cooking utensils, recipe books, small appliances, plates and cups—into large plastic trash bags. They stopped in Long Beach and unloaded the bags into Bill's pickup truck, which had been left at his marina condo. Leasure promised to dispose of the property later.

Next, they brought the yacht into Newport Beach and listed it for sale through a local yacht broker. Kuns sold it to the owners of a cable television firm two weeks later for seventy thousand dollars. Leasure was strictly an employee, not a partner, on this trip: He was paid four thousand dollars plus expenses.[12] France was paid fifteen hundred.

While Kuns busied himself with the sale of the boat, Leasure took care of the booty in his pickup truck. But instead of hurling it into the marina Dumpster, as he had promised Kuns he would do, Leasure cruised over to Irene Wong's house and told her to pick whatever she wanted from the truck—one of his few gifts to her, ever. When she hesitated, he began packing her a box full of goodies—cookbooks, a toaster, plates, Corningware, and a pressure cooker. Now that Leasure had gotten her an apartment in Glendale, just a short drive from his home, she needed to stock up, he told her. When Irene asked where all the things had come from, Leasure said it was just stuff off of one of Rob's boats, things the new owner wouldn't need. Irene was glad to have it, although she thought the cookbooks, half in French, half in English, seemed odd. She put them on a shelf and forgot them—for the time being. The innocuous gift would come back to haunt Leasure much later.

The next boat deal came two months later, an insurance scam, similar to Kuns's first foray into the illegal boat trade with the *Shori Ryu*. Instead of stealing a boat, Kuns rented a trawler from a friend of his in Newport Beach. He and Leasure made a conversion of the boat's number and name, then "sold" this boat, now dubbed *Sunshine*, to France. The sale was just on paper—no money actually changed hands.[13]

The boat stayed parked in Long Beach for the next two months, insured for fifty thousand dollars. Then Kuns picked it up, repainted it back to its original condition, replaced its old hull number, and returned it to the owner. A week later, France went to the marina, stood in front of his empty slip, and screamed, "My boat is gone!" He reported the boat stolen and, eventually, was paid a forty-nine-thousand-dollar insurance settlement by an insurance claims adjustor who was certain France was a crook, but who had no proof. Bill and Dennis each received ten thousand dollars; Kuns kept the rest.[14]

After that, the thefts and scams became increasingly regular and routine, as Kuns recalls it, as the threesome perfected their technique and rampaged throughout the monied marinas of Southern California, taking what they wanted, picking and choosing as if prowling through a vast marine smorgasbord. Police and insurance companies gradually noted a boat crime wave was underway, yet nothing could be done. The thieves were careful in choosing boats that were of common design and, because the owners lived far from their vessels, would not be missed for a week or more. The time lag between theft and discovery rendered impractical the sort of air and sea searches insurance companies are willing to launch when thefts are discovered immediately. There would be too much area to search to be practical.

Officer Leasure became an important asset to the operation at this point. Kuns would select a boat he liked, then, when Leasure went to work at Central Traffic Division, he would use LAPD computers to access motor vehicle registration files and track down the owners of the yacht Kuns had his eye on. For a policeman with a reputation for doing little work and disappearing on his shift, finding time for a little unauthorized play on the computer was no trouble. If the would-be theft victim lived aboard the boat or had a home nearby, Kuns would cross that yacht off the hit list. If the owner lived far from the marina, the "team," as Kuns called the three of them, could be assured that the owner was a weekend boater, leaving the door open for a weeknight theft.[15]

Shortly after the Caymans trip, Irene began noticing that Bill would disappear for several days every month or two. He would tell her he was "bringing another boat down" from Northern California, then she wouldn't see him for the next week. He told a similar story to his friend Flo Ong, saying he was keeping busy bringing boats to Southern California for friends. Flo thought it strange that Leasure was able to get so much time off, but then he had always seemed like the type to avoid work whenever possible.

"You're not exactly my idea of an ideal policeman," she chided him just before he left on one of these trips.

Leasure looked hurt. "I'm a good cop," he said—a refrain he often repeated to Flo whenever she questioned his dedication to LAPD. "I'm really a good cop." And he would explain, as he had many times before, how he preferred not to write tickets but to give warnings, and how his sergeants always accused him of dodging work because he preferred to treat civilians nicely. Flo would nod and say uh-huh, but she knew better. Barbara Sanchez, who worked with Flo at a Los Angeles beverage plant, had already told her how Bill would spend hours chatting about boats and guns and offering her yacht rides when he was supposed to be out on patrol.

Beginning in 1984, and continuing for the next three years, Leasure took sick leave, vacation time, and other days off at an increasing rate, juggling his schedule at Central Traffic in order to make boat trips with Bob Kuns. He didn't hide this from his colleagues; indeed, he boasted about his new marine activities. However, he always claimed to be ferrying boats south from Northern California, which was generally the exact opposite of the route he and Kuns took. In any case, his performance on the job, even-keeled if unspectacular for most of his tenure at LAPD, began to sag. He was given poor ratings five times for failing to take his firearms qualifications test on schedule. But his sergeants had come to expect less than exemplary performance from Officer Leasure, and little came of it. They were used to him calling in sick, complaining of nausea or other debilitating stomach problems, and no one really questioned him about his time off. Nor did anyone notice the missing Rover portable police radios and battery chargers that vanished from Central Traffic Division, and which, Kuns says, Smith and Leasure used to keep watch during the *Santine* theft.

Pumped up with adrenaline, the thieves would march boldly onto another person's boat as if they owned the entire marina. Other times, they would wear dark clothes and watch caps, and smear their faces with greasepaint, like commandos on a raid. Bolt-cutters would slice through locks like butter; wrenches would loosen the ignition switches. At Kuns's insistence, they got the operation down to under ten minutes, from boarding to start-up to departure.

During one theft in Long Beach, Kuns later recalled, he and Leasure decided to take their time before departing, pausing to throw the owner's blankets and china and other personal property into a trash bin in the marina parking lot. It was after midnight, and three local police squad cars had congregated in the lot. The officers sat, drank coffee, and watched Kuns and Leasure finish disposing of evidence. Bill and the Skipper waved pleasantly to the cops. The cops waved back. Look like you belong, Leasure advised, and no one will ever question you—sage advice from a man who had spent his entire existence blending in.

When the boat pulled out of the marina, its engines thrumming loudly in the quiet, darkened harbor, Kuns recalls himself and Leasure giving each other a high five, then laughing aloud. Nothing could stop them, it seemed.

Next, Kuns announced, they would find a new boat for Leasure.[16]

CHAPTER 11

By all accounts except his own, Bill Leasure's extracurricular activities assumed a feverish pace as the holiday season approached in 1984. His friends and LAPD co-workers marveled at his frequent vacations and sick leaves—and his increasingly out-of-character boasts of yachting exploits and investment coups. It was as if Mild Bill was trying to compensate for a lifetime of blandness with a flurry of wild excess.

As the months passed, he seemed to be juggling more and more balls. There was the increasingly time-consuming boat business with Kuns. In addition to his hobby of collecting Corvettes, he began his own similar car "business," inspired by his success with the yachts. He had his private planes, and a vintage military Sabre jet on order. Juggling girlfriends and wife took the organizational skill of an air traffic controller. He spoke often of building the island resort in Belize with Art Smith. He acquired an interest in a second yacht. And then there was the separate set of scams he began working with his sometime police partner, Officer Ralph Gerard.

It got so that the outside business endeavors began to spill over into his workday at LAPD, leaving less and less time for police work. He would cruise to Denny's in his patrol car, ask his partner to wait a minute, then discuss a new job with Dennis France, or pay him for the last one.[1] Or he would show up at Flo Ong's workplace, in uniform, to claim a parcel he had had delivered to her under an ironically chosen false name—"Bob Law." When Bill unwrapped the package, his expression was like a little boy's, she thought, as if he was thinking, "Oooh, here's my new toy." On one occasion Flo was horrified to see a gun and what she took to be a silencer kit. Bill eagerly began assembling it right there in front of her. Another time, it was a driver's license for Irene Wong—under a false name—delivered to Ong's house.[2]

Also at this time, as the yacht business became a near-monthly endeavor, Leasure began showing up regularly at the bank where Irene Wong worked as a teller. He would arrive in uniform, march to Irene's window, then have her deposit his money in her personal account. Most of the initial deposits were checks from Kuns, drawn on his Cayman Islands bank account. When Irene asked why he didn't use his own bank account, Leasure said, "Well, this is more convenient. And it gives me an excuse to come see you during the day."[3]

Leasure's explanation to Kuns was far different: "I have to have my play money. Betsy watches my paychecks like a hawk." The other obvious bonus, unspoken but perfectly clear to both men, was that potentially incriminating transactions between the two of them went to an unsuspecting Irene Wong, leaving no trace under Leasure's name. If investigators ever suspected Leasure, there would be no paper trail linking him to Kuns, and vice versa.

Kuns had observed Irene on the trip to the Caymans. She was quiet, shy and sweet, he thought, and she clearly worshiped Leasure. Kuns liked her. He also couldn't think of a better person for Leasure to use. She would believe anything he told her. She was perfect.

It bothered Kuns, though, when Leasure would talk, rather crassly, he thought, about what a "good lay" Irene was. The long sea cruises would pierce Bill's silence—he would open up, and the strangest things would come out, words drifting through the darkness and the slosh of the waves. The girl he was dating at a popular Los Angeles restaurant was gorgeous, "but a cold fish in bed." Irene, however, was hot—she'd do anything he wanted, Leasure said.

The Skipper winced at such talk. His criminal background and tolerance for business-related mayhem aside, Kuns fancied himself a gentleman bandit. He professed to hold Old World mores and a traditional notion of behavior, as if he modeled himself on the pulp novels he consumed about well-mannered assassins and international superspies. He didn't think it was right to speak poorly about someone you supposedly cared about. Lying to and using them was fine, for he had done the same with his own loved ones ("I couldn't very well tell my mother I was stealing boats, could I?"), but the way Leasure talked about Irene, and others close to him, violated Kuns's personal mercenary's code.

Leasure had no such code, as Kuns saw it, no moral anchors

at all. He was a nice man, gentle and kind—never violent, never physical. Yet, as Kuns became closer to Leasure, he came to the conclusion that Leasure had killed in the past—or, rather, engineered killings—without compunction or guilt. The only reason he had stopped was because stealing boats was easier, safer, and more profitable, the Skipper deduced. In truth, none of this bothered Kuns much. Business was business. What bothered him more was the way Leasure would talk about France when the welder wasn't around: Quiet, kindly Leasure called his good friend Dennis "the idiot." At other times, he derided as sex objects all the women in his life, except Betsy, whom he cheated on and lied to, though he spoke of her reverentially. Kuns didn't know it, but when France and Leasure were alone, Bill referred to the Skipper as "Dummy," because of Kuns's capricious way with money—and for letting Leasure cheat him so easily, so trustingly, on their boat deals. The nice-guy image sagged at such times.

Kuns considered Leasure his best friend, but when he heard such talk, a small voice in the back of Kuns's head kept asking if trusting in Mild Bill was really such a good idea.

• • •

I helped him five times crewing on boats. But I didn't know the boats were stolen. The stuff in my garage was just junk: knickknacks, pans, that sort of thing. Nothing of value. Nothing worth stealing. He was getting rid of it. So I hauled it home for garage sales. It wasn't that much stuff, not the thousands of items the police claim. And it doesn't mean I stole the boats.

Rob was not my best friend. Not at all. We were really just casual acquaintances. I was much closer to his sister. I used to go see his father all the time. The vacations to Cozumel and the Caymans were with his sister. He just came along.

You know, Kuns might think we were best friends. From his point of view, he might have considered me his best friend. I think that's pathetic, really, that he had so few other friends that he would think that. But it really wasn't that way.

• • •

In October 1984, another yacht was pirated from Newport Beach, this time a white and blue cruiser called the *Tribunal*. The eighty-five-thousand-dollar vessel had been bought just a few months before by a young couple, Dan and Sharon Dupuis. It had previously belonged to a Los Angeles Superior Court judge who had contracted cancer and could no longer use the boat. In years past, Kuns had worked for the judge, maintaining and servicing the yacht. He targeted it for theft, thinking it still belonged to the ailing jurist. Knowing the layout of the boat in advance gave him an even greater edge when it came time to steal her.

Leasure and Kuns sailed the yacht to Richmond, California, in the Bay Area, where the Skipper already had rented a slip, and where, a year and a half later, the two of them would meet their downfall. At the time, though, the half-empty Marina Bay Yacht Harbor seemed a perfect spot for a hot boat stolen from Southern California to cool off before they attempted a sale. Transforming it en route into the *Deliverance*, supposedly built by the mythical Hewitt Marine Inc., Bill and Rob waited a few months, then returned the vessel to Long Beach, parking it a scant twenty miles from the scene of its theft. They used Leasure's own condominium slip to house it. Once again, the bags of personal property—easily identifiable if the original owners ever saw it—were loaded into Bill's pickup truck for disposal. And once again, instead of throwing it all away, and without telling Kuns, Leasure carted the treasures and bric-a-brac that had belonged to the Dupuis family to his eight-car garage and stacked the stuff in a corner. None of it was terribly valuable—a buck knife, two big red pipe wrenches, a barbecue, a barometer, a box of sheets and pillowcases—yet Leasure couldn't resist keeping it.

Bolder still, instead of immediately parting with the boat, Leasure and Kuns decided to run another insurance scam first, certain they could not possibly be caught. Rather than risk their own jobs and liberty, though, they sought a third partner in the fraud. France had done it once already, so he was out, and Smith already had a boat. Leasure said he couldn't do it, Kuns would later recall, because he'd never be able to explain his ownership of an expensive yacht to Betsy. So he suggested his LAPD partner, Officer Gerard, might be a good choice as the "owner" of the yacht. Gerard, another veteran traffic officer who, like Leasure, showed little ambition, already had a troubled history at LAPD, with several brutality claims against him. His career was going nowhere, and he had been envious of Leasure's rich man's life-style. He jumped at the offer.

Gerard knew nothing about boats, but he trusted Leasure implicitly. One month after the *Tribunal* was stolen and became the *Deliverance*, Gerard went to his bank and requested an eighty-thousand-dollar loan. When the bank turned him down, he called back a few days later and said he could get the yacht cheaper after all—for thirty-two thousand dollars. Although Kuns expected the bank to ask questions about the sudden shift in price, his worries were unwarranted: The bank approved an eighty percent loan—twenty-five thousand dollars, no questions asked. Once again, Leasure and Kuns marveled at the capricious manner in which large sums of money seemed to be handled.

Although Gerard told the loan officer he was going to make up the rest of the purchase price with a cash down payment, no other money ever changed hands. Gerard simply handed the loan check over to Leasure, who then split it with Kuns.[4] The Skipper, in turn, gave Bill a receipt saying he had sold the boat for thirty-two thousand dollars to Gerard. Then, as in the *Sunshine* deal with France months before, arrangements were made to have the *Deliverance* insured. As a matter of routine, the insurance company required a survey of the vessel—a marine equivalent of a real estate appraisal—before issuing the policy. Sure enough, the boat was valued at eighty thousand dollars, the amount Gerard originally sought to borrow. Once again, a glaring contradiction failed to sound an alarm: The insurance company issued a policy for the full amount, never questioning the huge disparity between the supposed purchase price and the actual value of the boat.

Once it was insured, the boat just sat for a while. A theft too soon after the sale would have raised undue suspicions, even if the victim was a Los Angeles policeman.

In the meantime, a vintage 1927 Studebaker roadster appeared in the Leasure garage, surrounded by boxes of boat property, car parts, and airplane equipment. Leasure told a friend he had bought the sleek white Art Deco car at an auto show and auction in Reno.[5] But its true owner, Mickey Blowitz, had reported the car stolen from a Northridge swap meet parking lot a scant mile or two from Leasure's house. Blowitz cashed in a twenty-thousand-dollar insurance policy on the car even as it sat in Leasure's garage.

Leasure sold cars as well as obtained them. Kuns bought a pair of Corvettes from him—one for the Skipper's own use, and one for his girlfriend, Kathy. At least one of the Corvettes was a stolen car, police would later discover. Inspired by Kuns's method of altering boats, Leasure switched the serial number on a stolen Corvette with the number of a wreck he had picked up for a few hundred bucks years before. With the numbers switched, he was able to claim the mint-condition 1975 Corvette Stingray was a restoration job—the wreck supposedly returned to life. When Kuns registered the car with the state, he had to provide a sworn verification form from an official who had examined the car and determined that its serial number was proper and properly attached—in other words, that the car was legitimate. The official who signed the form for Kuns was one Officer William Leasure, LAPD Serial No. 14996.[6]

At about the same time, Leasure picked up a 1963 split-roof silver Corvette, beautifully restored and in perfect condition, except for its expired plates. He approached his friend Flo Ong and asked if he could store it in her garage. "Mine's full, Mom," he said, and Flo told her "second son" fine, it's yours, anytime, and gave him a key.

When he repeatedly cautioned Ong not to open the garage door or let anyone near the car, she thought it odd, but again said okay. She knew he was a fanatic about his cars and that he was afraid to drive his most prized ones for fear they would get nicked or scratched. This one, he had proudly announced, had seventeen coats of lacquer on it—a four-thousand-dollar paint job, he claimed. "Whatever you want, Bill," Flo said.

Leasure checked on the car now and then, turning over the engine and polishing its waxy sheen, sometimes just standing and admiring it—but as far as Flo knew, he never moved the thing from her garage, except to occasionally top off the gas tank at the nearest station.

Later, when Flo told her about Bill's request, her co-worker at Arrowhead Water, Barbara Sanchez, asked, "Don't you think that's a little suspicious?" Flo shrugged it off, saying, "You know Bill." But still, she wondered. Ultimately, her decision to give Leasure a key to her house would destroy their friendship.

Flo Ong had always been willing to give Bill the benefit of the doubt—maybe because of the way he had treated her daughter after the accident, maybe (before she learned he was married) because she thought he was potential son-in-law material, maybe simply because he listened to an older woman's troubles and seemed sympathetic. When Bill moonlighted with Big John years earlier as a security guard at the Pioneer Market near Dodger Stadium, she had brought him huge meals to get them through the night. Once someone crashed into her car in the market parking lot while she was visiting him, then tried to flee—but Bill chased the hit-and-run driver down and forced him to make good on the damages. She couldn't get over it. Flo had never seen Bill move fast for anything, but, suddenly, he had been transformed into a serious, authoritative policeman. Maybe he was a good cop after all, just like he always insisted.

And she did feel sorry for him. Not only because of the shabby way he claimed Betsy treated him, but because he seemed so often to Flo to be a wounded puppy. He always had some get-rich-quick scheme that never panned out, Flo recalled. There was the island he was always talking about developing with Art, and the gold mine he and Big John were hunting for but never found, and the plan to buy and restore a fleet of old planes. Leasure's notebook was full of calculations for that one.

Even small things seemed to elude Bill, Flo thought. He had asked her to throw a birthday party for him once, complaining that Betsy never acknowledged his birthday. Leasure had given her a list of people to invite—policemen, his flying friends, Art Smith—at least ten men and women he wanted to be there. Flo cooked a huge prime rib dinner for them. Only Big John showed up. Bill was stricken, but they tried to make the best of it. John ate so much, he had to stretch out on the floor like a beached whale, waiting for the food to digest. Flo gave Bill a present of a tiger's-eye ring. Leasure spent most of the evening in silence, and Flo felt awful for him.

But, little by little, her indulgent attitude toward Bill Leasure changed. Maybe, she began to suspect, he wasn't the "poor boy" she had thought.

The first hint came during a visit to Safari Land, a little thing, really, but it stuck in her mind. Leasure, Flo, and Leasure's young daughter from his first marriage had gone to a wild-animal park south of Los Angeles for the day so the girl could take a pony ride. While waiting in line, Leasure spotted a dollar bill lying on the ground near the woman selling tickets for the ride. Instead of picking up the money and giving it to the woman, who had obviously dropped it, Leasure told his daughter to go stand on the dollar bill until no one was looking. "Then put it in your pocket," he said.

"Bill!" Flo whispered when the girl had left to follow his instructions. "What kind of example is that?"

Leasure looked at her blankly. "What do you mean?" he asked. She told him to never mind. He hadn't a clue about why it bothered her. After that, she would later say, "My guard went up."[7]

In 1984, when Flo's daughter was badly in debt and looking for her mother to bail her out one more time, Flo wanted to help, but didn't want to seem like an endless source of blank checks to her free-spending daughter. So she gave Leasure three thousand dollars, then asked him to pretend he was loaning his own money to Cheryl as a temporary bailout. That way, she would be sure to pay it back, instead of stiffing her mother, as she had in the past. Leasure leapt at the chance to appear to be the rescuer—for free, no less—and Cheryl gladly accepted the money, though she continued to treat Leasure terribly despite his apparent generosity.

Perhaps that was why he decided to further ingratiate himself by telling Cheryl not to worry about paying back the debt—without ever asking Flo, much less repaying her himself. Flo was outraged, but Bill never offered to reimburse his surrogate mother, and Flo was out the money. "And the thing was, Cheryl still couldn't stand him," she recalls.

Then there was that odd drive to Big Bear in the San Bernardino Mountains, where Flo kept a cabin three hours' drive from L.A. Bill had agreed to drive out with her one day in the early 80s for one of her periodic checks on the place. On the way back, Flo had thanked him for coming with her, and told him what a nice person she thought he was for doing it. After they had been driving down the mountain in silence for a while, Bill replied to her compliment with a remark so strange, it would stick in her mind for years, though she would attach no real significance to it until much later.

"What would you say if I told you I killed someone?" Flo Ong recalls Bill asking in his quiet way.

For a moment, Flo took her eyes off the winding road she was negotiating so she could look at him. She wasn't sure she had heard him right, and had to think about what he had said for a second before the words registered. Then, as Ong tells it, she answered, "Well, Bill, if it was something to do with the war in Vietnam or in the line of duty, that's something I could understand. But if it was anything else . . ."

Bill just nodded and dropped the subject. Flo assumed he had been talking about something from the war. Neither of them ever brought it up after that. But, again, it left her wondering whether she really knew Bill Leasure as well as she thought she did.[8]

The final blow to their relationship came in the first half of 1985, when Flo came home from work to find Leasure, uninvited, in her living room, hurriedly tucking in his shirt, while Irene Wong, blushing furiously, stood next to him trying to straighten her disheveled hair. Obviously, Flo concluded, Bill had used his key to the garage to get in the house for an extramarital liaison with Irene, whom Flo had never met before. Flo was furious at the invasion.

"I didn't go for that sort of thing with my kids, and I don't like it now," she fumed. "If you consider yourself my son, you'll take her out of here and go."

Bill mumbled apologies and turned to go. Flo asked for her keys back, and told Leasure to take his Corvette away. She said she could no longer trust him. It was the last time she would see Leasure, except, a year later, when he appeared on her television during the 11:00 newscast.

A few days after her falling out with Bill, Flo was going over her phone bill. She saw someone had made a number of toll calls over a period of several weeks—apparently Bill had been using her house and her telephone without telling her for some time.

"He's just not the person I thought he was," Flo later told her daughter. "Bill used me."⁹

Irene Wong was just as surprised. Leasure had told her he had rented out the house in Northridge—he claimed the Ong house was *his* home. He had a key, he acted as if he had free run of the place—he brought Irene there all the time on "dates." The one thing she had never understood was why he always insisted they enter the house through the garage. . . .

* * *

Flo Ong was a real good friend. She used to bring me lunch, a car full of food. It was really something. She always hoped I'd marry her daughter someday. Now she says, Oh, I didn't really know Bill. That's what all my friends say. It's because the police go to them, and tell them that they didn't know the real Bill Leasure, that I've done all these bad things, so they'll turn against me. It really hurts me.

We did take a trip to Big Bear. We were coming down the hill, and Flo was saying what a great guy I am. "Well, Flo," I said, "I'm a policeman. Sometimes I may have to hurt someone. Sometimes I might be called on to shoot someone. What if I was in Vietnam and I had to kill someone? What would you think of me then?" That was it. Totally innocent.

But now she talks to the police and it's all changed around. . . . It really, really hurt me.

* * *

It was a busy time for Leasure. When he wasn't dealing with yachts and cars, he was acquiring firearms—some legal, some otherwise. He continued to frequent gun shows. He bought a whole series of commemorative LAPD weapons, issued by the department on special occasions. He bought and traded several .45 automatics from Dennis France, a risky proposition, given France's predilection for boasting about violent acts. Several other firearms turned up in his gun room—a shotgun and a revolver—that had been taken from stolen yachts. Then there were the guns Kuns had lost up north.

At the Skipper's request, Leasure contacted the Canadian Mounties in order to retrieve a pair of weapons that had been aboard the *Poor Little Urchin*. During a routine inspection of the sailboat, the Mounties had found an AR-15 automatic rifle and a .45-caliber Detonics automatic handgun—both of which were registered to Leasure, who had bought them for Kuns. A matching .45 with a consecutive serial number—the one that would be seized later aboard the *La Vita*—was hidden on board apart from the other weapons, and the Mounties missed it, just as they failed to notice they were poking around a stolen vessel. All they did was seize the guns they had found, then let Kuns go. Kuns gave Leasure enough money to pay off the resulting fines so he could retrieve the weapons, illegal in Canada. Leasure wrote the authorities asking for his guns back, but later told Kuns that the Mounties failed to return the firearms, despite his payment of the fines. The weapons were worth more than two thousand dollars, but Kuns wrote them off as a loss and moved his precious sailboat to Brookings, Oregon, away from the now-suspicious Mounties. Only much later would he learn that Leasure had gotten the guns back after all, and was keeping them for himself in his gun room at home, hidden with his silencers. Dummy had been ripped off again.

One gun Leasure did get rid of in early 1985 was a revolver he gave to Irene Wong. "You need to be able to defend yourself," he told her, then showed her how to load and shoot it. Irene never felt comfortable holding it, much less firing it. She put it in a drawer and left it there. The gun, police would later determine, had been stolen at least once and had been used in robberies in Los Angeles and New York. They never figured out how it came into Bill Leasure's possession.

•   •   •

I didn't do the boats. I didn't do the murders. Silencers, I did. They found them in my house. I can't very well deny having them. I had them, and it was wrong. But I could name twelve policemen with a lot worse things—like live hand grenades, mortars, fifty-millimeter Brownings. They're toys. I justify it like a lot of other cops. I'm a good guy. I'd never do anything wrong with them. They're just really neat toys. They're fun to own, and fun to sell.

I'm a collector, not a shooter. My guns are not touched by human fingers. I put them in a closet and I sell them after two years. I've done some bad things—I had those silencers, and the AR-15s. But I certainly didn't do anything with them.

•   •   •

The yacht business continued steadily. In April 1985, Kuns sold a stolen yacht named *Sans Souci* in Richmond, where the Skipper made his first sale to Mervin and Gloria Gray, the yacht brokers who would later set a trap for the gang with the Oakland Police. Leasure did not participate in the *Sans Souci* trip.

A month later, Kuns, Leasure, and France traveled to Sidney, British Columbia, where Kuns had his eye on an expensive sport fisher. As the Skipper tells it, they planned the job like kids playing Army, sneaking into the well-lit and guarded marina with an inflatable raft paddled softly under the piers. Their commando-style entry in black clothes and blackened faces was a success, but they were stopped in their tracks by the most prosaic of problems—they couldn't get the boat started. As Kuns would later recall, they worked on it for hours, then had to abandon the effort when the tide withdrew too far for the big yacht to safely exit the marina. They came back the next night, but found that the owners had been on board and had discovered their tampering. Suspecting a trap, the thieves fled.[10]

Upon their return, Kuns spotted a twin-engine trawler named the *Billy G,* berthed in Dana Point south of Newport Beach. "That one would be perfect for you," he told Bill. "I'll take you to see it."

"That's okay," Bill replied. "I don't need to see it. Whatever boat you think is best will be fine."

As Kuns would later testify, Leasure said he was not really interested in keeping the boat. Its most important characteristic would be its value as an investment. Six months to a year later, they would rip it off from themselves, collect on the insurance, sell it up north, and then Bill could go after a really nice boat. "This is just a temporary," Kuns recalls him saying. The Skipper shrugged and agreed.

The *Billy G* was stolen just after the 1985 Memorial Day weekend. Leasure and Kuns sailed it up to Richmond—after dropping off the hefty bags of fishing gear, clothes, pots and pans, televisions, even Christmas decorations, all of it destined for Leasure's garage. The *Billy G*'s owner, William Lofthouse, noticed its absence a week later and fruitlessly combed local marinas, taking a week off from work, hoping to find the thieves and the *Billy G,* but coming home empty-handed. Leasure and Kuns had changed its appearance radically. Canvas and paint were replaced in new colors, and the prominent blue dome of the Raytheon radar system above the cabin had been exchanged for an entirely different, red Furuno model, taken from the *Deliverance,* which was by then ready to be stolen anew. Kuns had prepared papers and new name boards to convert the *Billy G* to the *Tiara,* but, in his only expression of opinion about his new boat, Leasure rejected Kuns's feminine name choice in favor of something more macho.

"I'm calling my boat *Thunderbolt,*" he proclaimed. "What do you think?"

Kuns had to laugh at his friend's incongruous choice. "It's you," he said.

After a month out of circulation in Richmond, Leasure decided it was time to bring the new boat down to his slip in Long Beach. He flew up north with his friend Gerard, and they crewed the boat south together. At the same time, Kuns and Dennis France removed the *Deliverance* from Leasure's slip and headed north, installing the *Tiara* name boards Bill had rejected earlier onto Gerard's now twice-stolen boat. In Morro Bay, midway between Los Angeles and San Francisco, the two boats crossed paths. France forgot they were supposed to ignore one another and yelled and waved, until Kuns silenced him with an exasperated hiss.[11]

While Kuns sold Mervin Gray the *Tiara* in Richmond, Leasure and Gerard berthed the *Thunderbolt* in Long Beach, then Gerard called the police to report his yacht stolen. He waited five more days before calling his insurance company on July 16, 1985. Due to the delay, the company decided against launching a search for the missing boat, and eventually paid off the eighty-thousand-dollar policy to Gerard, after deducting twenty-five thousand for his bank loan.

Of the remaining fifty-five thousand dollars, Gerard secretly funneled almost all of it to Leasure and Kuns, through Irene Wong's account, Kuns would later testify. Leasure then gave Gerard a half share of the *Thunderbolt.*

Between July 1985 and March 1986, four more yachts mysteriously disappeared from the Los Angeles area—pirated, Kuns later testified, by the team of Leasure, Kuns, and France. All were sold in the San Francisco Bay Area.

During the same period, on August 1, 1985, a nearly new Corvette Stingray vanished from its parking spot on a Los Angeles street and ended up in back of Leasure's house. There was no more room in his garage, so jammed was it with the booty from stolen yachts. Even Kuns had finally relented on his seldom-enforced policy of disposing of all evidence from the yachts. He kept a gaudy floral-print couch taken from the yacht of an Orange County dentist and installed it in his Newport Beach apartment.

Boats were stolen in October, December, and January. In February 1986, Kuns and Leasure traveled to Oregon to register the *Thunderbolt*. Phony builder's certificates were filed in the process. Leasure also filed the document indicating he was co-owner, with Art Smith, of the *Santine* on that trip.

That same month, Gerard's fourteen-thousand-dollar leased Ford Thunderbird ended up in his partner Leasure's garage, key in the ignition. Gerard's wife later reported it stolen, and Gerard filed an insurance claim. The only attempt to disguise this apparently bold scam was to remove the license plates from the car. There might have been plans to alter it further, but time ran out for Bill Leasure soon after, and the car just sat, collecting dust, awaiting the police.

After one more yacht theft and sale in Richmond in March 1986, Kuns remembers telling Leasure he was quitting the business. "You take over. I'll live in the Caymans and be your consultant. But for me, it's time to get out."

As Kuns would later recall, Leasure grew alarmed at the Skipper's desire to retire. "Don't quit now," Kuns remembers Bill saying. "We're just getting our system down. We can make so much more money. How can you quit now?"

Kuns had given no hint in the past of wanting to leave the yacht business. But he was getting more and more worried. The odds that they'd be caught climbed with every job, he figured. "I just think it's time to get out, Bill."

"Come on, one more year," Leasure responded. "Let's really go at it one more year, and retire millionaires. Just like you wanted. What do you say?"

Leasure knew just how to push the Skipper's buttons. Kuns's fantasy of late had been to score big, then retire to the private island he, Leasure, and Smith had spoken of so often, off the coast of Belize. With enough money, they could even become a sovereign island nation unto themselves, detached from the mainland government, independent, Kuns theorized in his spare time.

Then Leasure, France, and Kuns could form what the Skipper called "The Victorious Dragon Society," a private little three-man Mafia that would commit crimes worldwide, just once every year or two, scoring big each time. Kuns had even sketched a design for gold dragon medallions for the three of them to wear, icons for their secret society. In between jobs, Kuns would write a novel based on their exploits. He would call it *Fun and Games*.

Leasure never bought into this fantasy, other than wanting to invest in an island paradise. Beyond that, it was Kuns's private little dream, not his. But he knew Kuns was a hopeless romantic. It didn't take much pleading to persuade him that twelve more months of the yacht business would be a good idea, a way of realizing his dreams.

"All right, Bill," Kuns recalls telling Leasure. "One more year."[12]

They sat down in Leasure's den in Northridge and planned out more than a million dollars' worth of jobs in the next few months, Kuns would later recall. There were to be insurance frauds with the *Thunderbolt* and the *Santine*, a four-hundred-thousand dollar combination yacht theft and insurance scam in Kuns's name, and assorted other straight pirate jobs and resales. Another LAPD officer wanted a trawler like the *Thunderbolt*, while yet another officer wanted Kuns to look into acquiring, cut-rate, a million-dollar commercial shrimping vessel. Leasure was going to buy a vintage military surplus Sabre jet and get certified to fly it; then they were going to begin stealing corporate jets and vintage restored airplanes, worth hundreds of thousands of dollars apiece, according to Kuns. Using the same technique he pioneered with the serial numbers from wrecked Corvettes, Bill was going to buy old aircraft hulks; then they would steal mint-condition airplanes of the same type, later claiming to have restored the wrecks. Then they could cash in on the resales. Leasure was talking about getting hangar space in the Mojave Desert north of Los Angeles, near the barren moonscape of Edwards Air Force Base, home to the primordial dried lake beds used for Space Shuttle landings. And Kuns already had a customer lined up for a Learjet—the casino owner in Colombia who had bought the *Jimmy K* years before would take delivery of the plane as soon as they could get one.[13]

"We're going to have it made, Rob," Kuns recalls Leasure saying when the planning session had concluded. "Then we can both retire."[14]

A few weeks later, as Kuns tells it, they began their big year by slicing through the locks of a sleek blue and white yacht in San Diego called the *Holiday*, then headed north through the darkness. When they arrived a few days later in Richmond on May 29, 1986, on a yacht they had rechristened *La Vita*, The Life, the police were waiting for them, and the plans were spoiled. There would be no Victorious Dragon Society, no island paradise, no millions made through cleverness and nerve. There would be only loss and scandal, disappointment and betrayal. And there would be a roomful of officers in LAPD's Central Traffic Division saying, no, not Bill. Not Mild Bill.

• • •

I could have used better judgment in choosing my friends. But you know, I introduced Kuns and France to other cops, I brought them to gun shows. I wasn't hiding anything.

Some people asked, why would you ever want to hang out with scumbags like them? Most policemen tend to be real conservative. But, you know, I've said this before: I tend to see the good in people. Most cops see only the bad. I'm a nice guy. I'm not the sort of cop who beats up people. I think I'm probably the exception of L.A. police officers. I'm so gentle. I'm so mild. I don't shoot people. . . . And now I'm going to suffer because of it.

PART III
1986-1987

WEIGHT
OF THE
EVIDENCE

Depend upon it, there is nothing so
unnatural as the commonplace.
        —SIR ARTHUR CONAN DOYLE,
            "A Case of Identity"

CHAPTER 12

CROWDED AND MUSTY, ITS sole wall decor a balding wild boar's head, the homicide squad room at the Los Angeles Police Department's downtown headquarters possesses all the charm of a vigorously chewed pencil. There is no Hollywood glitz, no gleaming high technology, just men in wide ties and shoulder holsters huddled over telephones and stale coffee. Business is brisk, and the detectives sit crowded two by two into cramped desks that look less like the workplaces of LAPD's elite, and more like discards from some poorly endowed junior high school library.

The homicide squad room's size and configuration were frozen sometime during the 50s, when the murder rate was one tenth its current tempo and street gangs settled their differences by rumbling instead of spraying one another with Uzis and AK-47s. Today the room bursts with the men, women, and paperwork necessary to chart the unrivaled carnage of America's second-largest city.

Most of the floor space is taken up by four long rows of a dozen gray, battered desks, laid out in a rough horseshoe shape, their scarred tops mostly invisible beneath leaning piles of files. The stacks of files never leave the desk tops because there are fifty to a hundred new pending cases under investigation at any one time, but filing cabinet space sufficient to hold approximately seven of them. Each detective has to himself precisely one desk drawer the size and shape of a modest woman's jewelry box, useful for holding virtually nothing related to police work. One of the greatest battles detectives would wage in building a case against Officer William E.

Leasure would be their largely fruitless quest for a filing cabinet or two.

Shelves and cabinets lining the squad room's walls already overflowed with blue three-ring binders known as "Murder Books"—each of them a complete history of a homicide investigation, from the initial desperate phone call to 911 onward. In LAPD's labyrinthine Parker Center headquarters, the homicide detectives can always be picked out from the other suits on the creaking elevators—they're the only ones who carry those sky blue schoolboy notebooks. When a case is solved, a "case cleared" report is placed in the binder and the Murder Book is shipped to a warehouse. Open Murder Books stay in the squad room forever. There are hundreds of Murder Books accumulated there, some dating back to the 40s, all of them officially open and unsolved, providing a strange history of the City of Angels told through its most violently dead. The infamous Black Dahlia case is there, unsolved for four decades, along with the mystery of Julie Cross, a Secret Service agent slain in an ambush by an unseen attacker in 1980. There are hundreds of others, both famous and anonymous, posthumously equal in the obscure immortality of LAPD's files, a final resting place for the likes of, among others, Tony Reyes, Anne Smith, and Gilberto Cervantes.

It was to this jumbled haven that Detectives Addison "Bud" Arce and Henry Petroski were summoned by telephone at 5:00 p.m. on Friday, August 8, 1986. They had already gone home for the weekend—the workday officially ends at 3:30 at Robbery-Homicide Division—and they were busy pounding nails into a new garage roof at Petroski's house when the phone call came. They were not informed what was up. The detective on the other end of the line simply told them to get their asses back into work, as soon as possible.

They pulled their ties and suits back on, stopped for their traditional pick-me-up—some plastic tubs of bitter black coffee and a bag of huge, sugary apple fritters from Winchell's Donuts—then began the twenty-mile drive in from Petroski's home in the San Fernando Valley to downtown Los Angeles. Arce (pronounced like the letters R-C, accent on the R) and Petroski had been partners for seven years by then, and they had accumulated the shared intuitions and mutual habits of a middle-aged married couple. During the drive to Parker Center, they played their "what-if" game.

"Okay, what if the daughter of the president of some airline's been kidnapped?" Arce started.

"Yeah, yeah," Petroski said, building on the fantasy. "And we solve the case, and this guy, he's the president of TWA—"

"No, United," Arce said.

"Yeah, United. He's so grateful to get his daughter back, he says, these guys are really terrific guys."

"And he says, boys, you can fly wherever you want, whenever you want. Here's your passes."

They laughed and washed down their fritters with coffee. It was sophomoric and they knew it, but when you're called at 5:00 on a Friday and they won't tell you what's happening over the phone, you know it's bad. Homicide investigators tend to spend all too much time staring down at the torn and battered husks of bodies that have been shot, clubbed, stabbed, burned, or killed in countless other ways—they knew firsthand that the imagination of destruction never ceases in its inventiveness. They had seen children beaten to death because they cried in the night, and whole families wiped out with shotgun blasts just because someone wanted to take their money or their TV set. Best to find a reason to laugh now, while they could. Who knew what was waiting for them at the other end of their drive?

They walked into the empty squad room only to learn they were wanted up on the Sixth Floor—the level where the chief and the rest of LAPD brass reside. A conference room had been set aside, and a group of administrators—captains, lieutenants, and the deputy chief who oversaw all of LAPD's detective squads—was waiting for them. A bad sign.

Once seated, Arce and Petroski were told they would be in charge of investigating an LAPD traffic officer suspected of engineering three murders for hire. An informant had just come forward to Internal Affairs investigators. They had spent all day interrogating the man. Then it had been decided that experienced homicide detectives ought to handle the case. Arce and Petroski had been at the top of the on-call list, so they were to be the lucky ones. Needless to say—the unusual assemblage of brass in the room spoke for itself—the chief would be taking an "active interest" in this one, the detectives were told.

"Who's the officer?" Petroski asked.

"William Leasure, out of Central Traffic. Right now, he's up in Martinez on a boat-theft charge. The informant's terrified Leasure will have him killed. Says that's why he decided to come forward."

The detectives were only vaguely familiar with the Leasure boat-theft case. Leasure's arrest had made headlines two months earlier, a major scandal at LAPD. A spate of news stories had followed, suggesting other policemen had been implicated and were under investigation as well. But the initial buzz about the laid-back traffic officer with a taste for Corvettes and oceangoing yachts had died down after two weeks, replaced by more pressing news. Arce and Petroski had soon forgotten about it, like the rest of the city. There had been the briefest suspicion of violence and murder when Jerry France sold his bill of goods about bodies dumped at sea, but that had been dismissed within a day or two, and the case had been left to the Internal Affairs Division.

Now that had changed. The brass gave the two detectives a brief overview of the homicide case to date. At the time, the "case" consisted of a rambling, sometimes contradictory tale of murder, conspiracy, and extortion spun by an unlikely hit man by the name of Dennis France. The only other thing LAPD officials knew then was a growing sense of dread that the department, which prided itself on a corruption-free reputation, was going to receive an enormous black eye when this latest development hit the news.

"This case is to be top secret," the deputy chief told the detectives. Internal Affairs feared other officers were involved with Leasure. The informant had said he and Leasure had friends on the ballistics unit and the bomb squad, who may have helped them conceal their crimes by tampering with evidence, Arce and Petroski were told. So any weapons testing on the case had to be farmed out to other police agencies. And because no one knew who else might be involved, they were not to discuss the case with anyone in the chain of command except Deputy Chief Barry Wade, who then oversaw the Internal Affairs Division. They were to report directly to him.[1]

Then the detectives were told to head down to the fifth floor—Internal Affairs—for further briefing and to meet the informant. That was it. To be instructed not to report to your lieutenant, captain, and commander—all of whom lay in the normally inviolate LAPD bureaucratic chain between detectives and deputy chief—was extraordinary, and troubling. Arce and Petroski filed out of the room wondering what they had gotten into. Their what-if game had suggested some wild possibilities in the past. But they wouldn't have guessed they'd be investigating one of their fellow officers—for murder, no less, and in secret, with others in the department under suspicion as well.

As they discussed the briefing in the elevator, they realized the greatest mystery confronting them would not be the usual murder-scene puzzle of whodunnit. The bodies were too cold, the cases too old for that. No, this would be a "whydunnit"—why would an LAPD officer like Bill Leasure turn to crime? What in his background or his makeup had eluded detection by the thousands of officers around him, even while he committed murder? Assuming, of course, this Dennis France could be believed.

"I feel a long night coming on," Arce muttered to his partner.

• • •

From the first day Dennis France came forward, they based their case on whatever he told them. Everything flowed from the assumption that what he said was true. Everything they could find that would support what he said, they used. Anything that would prove he was a liar, the police ignored.

Well, Dennis France is a big liar. He made up a lot of bad things about me to get himself out of trouble. It's so obvious. Why were they so eager to believe him? . . .

You know, it's like the detective up in Oakland told Kuns. We accidentally got a tape disclosed from [Oakland Detective Arthur] Roth, mixed up with the other stuff we were supposed to get from discovery. They claim there is no such taped interview with Kuns. But we have it. So they lied. They still claim it doesn't exist. The tape is intermittent, there's stuff missing, but at one point, Roth says, "We want Leasure, not you. He's the cop. It's the code. We've got to fuck him in the ass." . . .

That's what happened. They wanted to get the "dirty cop." They're not interested in finding the truth. They just wanted to make their case.

• • •

Forty-two, husky and dark, Arce had perfect black hair and well-tailored suits whose fashionable lines were marred only by the Barreta nine-millimeter automatic he wore in a hip holster. Arce had been born in Norwich, England, during the last year of World War II, to a Scottish-born mother and a father in the U.S. Army Air Corps. His nickname of Bud originated with his mother's family, who, before the Arces left for Los Angeles in 1949, habitually referred to him as "our little Buddy from America." Genial to all, even suspects, Bud Arce's trademark at LAPD was his unrelenting politeness, counterbalanced by a toothpick planted firmly in the corner of his mouth, its tip barely visible but always present, giving him a disconcerting tendency to speak out of one side of his lips.

Three years his senior, Hank Petroski was the classic rumpled detective—the perfect foil for the dapper Arce, never appearing quite comfortable in a suit and tie, the circular bulge of a tin of

Skoal always pushed into a back pocket. He had come up through
the detective ranks, settling into homicide to finish out his twenty-
five-year career at LAPD. His round face had grown lined on the
job, and his brown hair was graying. Known for wisecracks—
intentional and otherwise—his "Petroski-isms" were legendary in
the squad room. "Who's in charge?" some VIP touring the department once asked Petroski as he sat in Robbery-Homicide. "I am,"
the detective replied. "Can't you see I'm doing the crossword puzzle?"

At the time, Arce and Petroski were one of the most respected
detective teams at LAPD's Robbery-Homicide Division. They were
pulled off an investigation of threatening letters sent to another police officer—in itself a high priority—in order to take over the
Leasure homicide case.

When they arrived at the fifth-floor Board of Rights hearing
room—a small auditorium where in-house police misconduct trials
are held—eight people were already at the table discussing the case.
Deputy Chief Wade, whose command included supervision of Internal Affairs, and several other high-echelon supervisors were
there, along with three other homicide detectives, listening to the
men from I.A. talk. Detective Tom King, who had met with
Dennis France that morning at Denny's restaurant, and his supervisor, Sergeant David Wiltrout, were briefing the group on the
highlights of their lengthy interrogation of the newfound informant.

Arce and Petroski were struck—and alarmed—by three things
as they listened to the briefing. First, as Wiltrout and King described the informant's statements, France's story sounded much
too vague on key details, considering the fact that he was describing some of the most traumatic events in his life. His story of three
contract murders sounded remarkable, but it had yet to be verified
in any meaningful way—the victims had not been identified, since
France said he could not remember their names. Considerable digging would be necessary to locate police files that corresponded to
the killings he had described, if any existed, and France's vagueness
was a serious—and curious—handicap. In the detectives' experience, such events were generally seared into the memories of the
people who lived through them.

Second, as Sergeant Wiltrout spoke, it seemed clear to the detectives that he resented the arrival of the newcomers from homicide. Internal Affairs had wanted to run with the case on its own.
But Wiltrout had been overridden in favor of the homicide squad
by supervisors already concerned over serious flaws in Internal Affairs' two-month-old investigation of Leasure's yachts and cars—

including a botched search warrant that threatened to render key evidence in the case useless. Listening to Wiltrout, Arce and Petroski began to foresee problems when it came time to share detailed information with Internal Affairs, which, because of its in-house policing mission, already tended to be insular and secretive in its dealings.

Finally, the deal France had struck—total immunity for three murders—disgusted them. "We were shocked," Arce would later say. "There's no way he should have gotten immunity."

In Arce and Petroski's opinion, the "sweetheart deal" France got was an example of why the administrative types at Internal Affairs, trained to perform personnel investigations rather than to deal with serious crimes, should never be allowed to call the shots on criminal investigations. If homicide had been called in immediately after France started talking about hypothetical murders—as standing LAPD policy required—the detectives would have negotiated with France, attempting to get him to cop to a lesser charge in exchange for his testimony. Indeed, King, an experienced detective on loan to Internal Affairs, had wanted to make just such an attempt, only to be overridden by Sergeant Wiltrout.[2]

Instead, alone, untrained, illiterate, and fearful, Dennis France had negotiated for himself a deal that would become the envy of every high-powered defense attorney in town. He had admitted to three cold-blooded professional murders, yet he would not serve a day in jail. Furthermore, the police had agreed to help pay his rent and moving expenses—he said he was afraid Leasure would have him killed if he and his family stayed in one place too long. He could buy new guns and—his most ardent condition for cooperation—he could keep his hunting license. Such sweeping immunity for a killer was unprecedented. Yet he had received it in a matter of minutes.

"I asked Dennis later if he would have agreed to some sort of plea bargain to a lesser charge and a lower prison sentence than murder," Petroski would later say. "He said, 'Sure I would have. But no one ever asked me.' That floored us. They never even asked him."[3]

Eight hours before Arce and Petroski were called in on the case, the legally immunized Dennis France began telling his story to police at 10:47 that morning, in a dingy cubby hole at the District Attorney's Office on the seventeenth floor of the County Criminal Courts Building in downtown Los Angeles. He spoke into a tape recorder for hours, haltingly and with frequent breaks, as Deputy District Attorney Robert Jorgensen, Detective Tom King, Detective Gilbert Hetrick, and Sergeant Dave Wiltrout listened and asked occasional questions.

France's story stunned his interrogators, and later, after much of it proved verifiable, it would become the cornerstone of the case of *People* v. *Leasure*. But there were also serious problems with his story, and part of the fault lay with the flawed manner in which his first interrogation was conducted.

In any criminal investigation, this first on-the-record encounter would be the most crucial stage—the initial interrogation of a key witness. Although its primary goal was to get information about Bill Leasure's alleged crimes, the statement would serve another purpose: It would become the benchmark against which all of France's future statements and testimony would be measured and compared. It was important, then, to get as full and as detailed a rendition as possible, with any inconsistencies cleared up as they occurred.

A simple principle of criminal investigation lay at the root of this: If the story changes, defense lawyers would argue, then France is lying. Even witnesses who are being truthful will have inconsistencies in their accounts and can be made to look like liars in court. Furthermore, if a witness provides new information at a second, more detailed interrogation, defense lawyers can argue that the witness was "fed" information between sessions. Experienced detectives know the secondary purpose of any interrogation is to seal off avenues attorneys like to exploit.

But this did not happen during France's initial interrogation. The meandering interview was rife with unnoticed contradictions and vague claims. More than once in the coming months, Arce and Petroski would wish they had been present for that first round of questions and answers. They felt they could have addressed some of the inconsistencies and omissions then and there, and posed some of the questions left unasked. As it happened, they could only listen to the long hours of tape made by Dennis France before they were called and shake their heads, knowing it could come back to haunt them.

Nervous and in need of frequent assurances that he wouldn't be prosecuted, France had started that first interview by describing his introduction to Leasure in 1974 or 1975. His neighbor, Dennis Winebaugh, "told me he knew a crooked police officer" who paid him "to do things."

"I thought it was a lie. But that's how I met Officer Leasure."[4]

He then described driving Dennis Winebaugh to the city of El Monte, where, he said, Winebaugh used a .357 Magnum to kill a man who owned a tortilla factory. Bill had set up Winebaugh with a woman named Paulette and her ex-husband, who wanted the tortilla maker killed so they would inherit his factory and money, France said.

France could offer no other names, no address, and no date, other than saying it was about seven years ago. (It was actually nine, and, as would later be revealed, the city was not El Monte.) He didn't know the name of the victim and said he had not been paid to act as the getaway driver—he didn't even know Winebaugh was going to kill anyone until after it happened, France swore.

He said Winebaugh was paid three thousand dollars, a thousand of it by Paulette, another portion by Leasure, and still another part of the money by Big John, whom he described as a policeman friend of Leasure's who had married Paulette. Big John had to pay because Paulette had shorted Winebaugh, France said. "He had to get that money or Dennis was going to do her in."

But in later discussions, France would say Leasure paid Winebaugh five thousand dollars for the job by leaving an envelope of money at his Paramount apartment building. And he said Winebaugh then passed on to him two thousand for driving the car, a serious contradiction.[5]

After the killing, France said, he grew frightened about being involved and talked to a D.A. investigator—which Arce and Petroski would later confirm as the unproductive meeting in Chinatown with Dale Boyce's nephew, Alan Tomich. "I wanted help," France said. "I was scared. . . . He didn't believe me. He said, 'Adios,' so I adiosed."

Then the interrogators asked France to describe "the next unusual thing" he did with Leasure.

"Bill had come to me and told me Paulette's ex-husband wants her killed," France said. "And that Paulette's ex-husband is going to tell we had killed his father. And so Paulette was willing to pay fifty-five hundred dollars to have him killed."

France said he told Bill that he didn't want to do it, but Leasure insisted. Leasure drove France's car to a bar in West L.A. one night, France recalled, where he shotgunned the man.

The Internal Affairs investigators didn't catch it at the time, but France had just made the first of many serious factual errors in his recitation of the murders. He described the murder of Tony Reyes as the first time he pulled the trigger for Bill—"the next unusual thing" after Winebaugh shot Gilberto Cervantes. When

France claimed, a few minutes later, to have killed a woman in a beauty shop at Bill's behest, the interrogators did not notice he had just contradicted himself.

Without names or crime reports, they had no way of knowing that the beauty shop shooting—the murder of Anne Smith—had occurred over a year before Tony Reyes died. France tried later in the taped interview to correct himself, but his account remained so muddled that when it came time to brief Arce and Petroski, the I.A. investigators still described the beauty shop murder as the third and final killing France performed for Leasure.[6]

France repeated and compounded his mistake later in the tape when, describing his feelings about being asked to kill Tony, he said, "I was scared. . . . At that time, the only thing I had done was drove a car for Bill—I mean, for Forty-four. But, like Bill told me, 'Hey, you're just as involved—they're gonna hang you just the same [whether you drove the car or pulled the trigger].' And I don't know what the law is on that. I'm not a lawyer, so I believed him." Once again, France was saying there had been no killing between the Cervantes shooting and Reyes's murder: Before Tony, all he had done was drive a car.

Arce and Petroski eventually would dismiss France's slips as simple memory lapses. "Dennis gets confused," Arce would say— many times—over the next five years. But others would interpret it as a key miscue in a web of lies. Either way, a fundamental element of Bill Leasure's legal defense had just taken root. And the more France spoke, the more it would grow. His account of being paid for the murders constantly changed: One moment, he said Leasure paid him three thousand five hundred dollars after the beauty shop killing; at another point, he said he received twelve hundred dollars up front, and a similar amount a few days after "the job." There were inexplicable variations in his account of killing Paulette's husband, too: At times he recalled being paid in full, but he also claimed, "Bill still owes me fourteen hundred on it."

If such inconsistencies gave the first set of interrogators pause about trusting France and basing a case against Leasure on his account, they didn't show it. What struck them instead was the small price Leasure placed on human life, assuming France was telling the truth: three lives snuffed for something on the order of twelve thousand dollars. This, too, would prove to be a crucial point in Leasure's defense. Dennis France might be expected to kill for a paltry few thousand dollars, but why would a man like Bill Leasure risk so much for so little? It made no sense, nor could France help on this point. He said he knew nothing of what Leasure might have earned as the alleged engineer of professional killings. He thought a big inheritance or insurance policy might have been at stake, but he didn't know if Leasure ever collected a share. And while he spoke at length about why various people might have wanted to hire Leasure to commit murder, he offered no clue as to why Leasure would agree to do it.

He only knew his own motives with any certainty. He said he had been too afraid ever to disobey Leasure. Leasure made clear that the price of refusal would be arrest—or death, he said. Every time he resisted Leasure's commands, France said, the veiled threats began. You'll end up in jail, Dennis. You already accepted the money, Dennis. You've got to do it. We had a deal.

Although he seemed clear on Paulette's motive—inheritance— France seemed confused about who hired Leasure to have the woman in the beauty shop murdered and why. "Bill told me it was the husband. Or the boyfriend. Her boyfriend. . . . He said she had been cheating on the guy and running up a lot of psychiatric bills." In subsequent tellings, France would mention the divorce. But not in his first statements—allowing defense lawyers to raise the specter of a witness being fed information.

France also told police that a ballistics expert at LAPD, Jimmy Trahin, had supplied information to his friend Leasure about evidence in the beauty shop killing. Leasure had called Trahin to ask if a casing found at the scene could be analyzed and linked to a murder weapon. Trahin, according to France, said, "Yeah, I can make the gun." It was this statement—combined with the involvement of Leasure's partner, Officer Ralph Gerard, in the stolen yachts—that created a panic among LAPD higher-ups, and led to their insistence on maintaining secrecy in the case. Trahin, as an internationally reputed firearms expert, was entrusted with sensitive cases at the department and used as an expert witness across the country. If he was involved, the logic went, there was no telling how far the tentacles reached.[7]

After consulting with Trahin, France said, Leasure took the .45-caliber automatic used to kill Anne Smith. "He was going to destroy the whole gun," France recalled. He added that Trahin was not an accomplice—he merely had been chatting about the case with his friend Bill. "Jimmy Trahin didn't know anything," France said. The ballistics expert remained adamant when investigators later questioned him about France's story: Trahin said he never discussed the case with Leasure. (It would take months before the department accepted that assertion. Trahin's previously exceptional career would be seriously damaged in the process.)

There was one point France made over and over for his interrogators. Each time he had participated in a murder, he claimed, he did so reluctantly, and only because Leasure forced him into it with threats of exposure or violence. Each time, France claimed, he put off following through for weeks at a time, making continual excuses for not killing—until Leasure actually got behind the wheel, drove him to the scene, and said, "You've got to do it. Now." Thus the man who once openly boasted to Robert Kuns about murders was now minimizing his own responsibility, making Leasure the sole active force behind each of the killings—the master pulling the puppet's strings.

After describing the three murders, France went on to tell King, Wiltrout, Hetrick, and Jorgensen about other crimes he claimed he discussed with Leasure. Through these shocking, if vague, claims, the investigators began to form their theory that Leasure's Mild Bill persona at LAPD was a mask, hiding a callous, calculating criminal willing to risk everything for a profit.

First, France said, there was a plan for Bill to blow up the tortilla factory so they could collect on the insurance. But that fell through.

"Then I was asked by Bill to beat up his girlfriend's mother. He told me he would give me five hundred dollars if I'd break her leg or her arm. She was an elderly woman, Oriental, and I said no. I couldn't do it. . . . He told me his girlfriend's mother was a real bitch, and she was talking against him."

France said that the girlfriend, whose first name he remembered as Irene,[8] was not involved in any crimes. Then he added the interesting detail that Irene had cashed checks for Leasure, putting them in her account instead of his. The Internal Affairs investigators already knew this from questioning Irene Wong in their investigation of stolen yachts. The fact that France knew it too suggested he was on very intimate terms with Leasure. It made him seem all the more credible.

Another time, France recalled, Leasure had described a man who wore an expensive gold chain and pendant. Leasure wanted the piece of heavy gold jewelry, and instructed France to rob the man outside a bar near Los Angeles's Farmer's Market. He wanted France to hit the man, knock him down, and make off with the jewelry while Leasure waited nearby in his patrol car, ready to drive France to safety. France said he refused.

Yet another time, France said, Leasure wanted him to team up with Winebaugh to kill a young woman who had married a wealthy "old coot with one foot in the grave." The man's family wanted her killed before he died and she inherited all the money. But Winebaugh and France had moved to Oklahoma at that time, France said, and by the time Leasure found them, the old man had died of natural causes, foiling the plot.

"Bill told me, 'I could have got you twenty thousand dollars.' "

He said Winebaugh had bragged about beating and killing other people for Leasure before France joined the team. Even more ominously, France said, Leasure "wanted me to do something for a police officer." This unnamed policeman wanted his wife and daughter killed, France said. "She was divorcing the guy and I guess she was going to take him to the cleaners. . . . I told him no. Get someone else." France didn't know if Bill fulfilled the contract himself or not.

At the time, no one thought of asking why France, who was supposedly too afraid of Leasure to spurn any request, was able to blithely refuse these murderous assignments.

The one other incident he described in detail, at least in terms of names and places, involved Bill's friend and former LAPD partner Big John, who by then had left the force. A few years back, John had moonlighted as a security guard at a market, France said. One night, John and another guard beat up some wino and the man died. Leasure wanted France to testify that Big John was innocent, France said. Instead, France volunteered the services of one of his brothers, Terry (not to be confused with Jerry), who agreed to do it for five hundred dollars. Bill supplied a magazine article on how to beat a lie detector test, which Terry subsequently passed, France said. Big John was eventually exonerated and, though he had been fired earlier, his status was changed to stress retirement and he regained his pension, even though "they beat that guy to death," France said. (A subsequent review of LAPD files by the Internal Affairs team showed France's account to be essentially correct. Evidence suggested that Big John watched while the other security guard, Louis Lee Sandidge, fatally clubbed the man with his baton. On the strength of Terry France's testimony, the D.A. reversed an initial decision to prosecute and declined to file charges against Big John, while Sandidge received a plea bargain that netted him thirty days in jail and three years probation for involuntary manslaughter for the August 6, 1981, beating death of Roberto Chavez.[9])

The interrogators were horrified by this litany once France was finally through. It was worse than anything they had imagined when the little welder first came forward, worse even than the tale they had rejected from his brother Jerry. France had portrayed Bill Leasure as a virtual Murder Incorporated, and LAPD as riddled with crooks and conspirators.

"I can imagine the pressure you've been under, just knowing all this," one of the interrogators said.

"You couldn't believe it," France sighed. "I really want to sit here and cry. I'm just holding it back."

"Do whatever you want to do," a detective said.

"I'm so happy now," France said then, not a trace of irony in his voice. "I really am."

But France also showed that he had not forgotten the bottom line, the real reason he was there. "Can Bill testify against me now?" he had asked moments before.

"No," came one of the interrogators' telling reply. "It's who raised their hands first."

Was that what it really came down to? Had Dennis France come forward simply to beat Leasure to the punch, fearing that, if he waited—if he didn't raise his hand first—Bill might try to parlay similar information about France to get himself out of jail up north on the yacht case? When Arce and Petroski had been briefed on the results of that first interrogation and went off to talk to France on their own, this was among the questions nagging at them. Could France be coloring his story to deemphasize his own culpability while overstating Leasure's—a common tactic employed by informants?

Arce and Petroski saw disturbing signs that this might be the case—France's claim that he had tried to go to the police and they said adios, for one. That seemed patently unbelievable, as did his claims that he didn't really want to kill anyone. The discredited I-was-only-following-orders defense just didn't wash with the detectives. The man was a gun nut—he owned a small arsenal and would sit for hours patiently reloading bullets to save a few bucks. He had lived with his murderous role in silence for a decade, only coming forward when his friends were behind bars, his house had been searched by police, and his weapons had been seized. Until then, he had stayed friends with Leasure for years, stealing boats with him, socializing with him, trading guns with him. And despite his nervousness during the interrogation, his accounts of the killings were related with a certain callousness, as if he was discussing the plot of a movie he had seen too many times. He was fearful, yes—of being punished. But Arce and Petroski thought he showed little sign of conscience—again, hardly the type to hesitate to kill for profit. His story, at least on that point, did not ring true.

It worried them. Just what had LAPD bargained for when they traded Dennis France immunity?

When their turn with him came, they brought him into the homicide squad room. France took in the baleful glare of the boar's head amid the musty silence of the room, but said nothing. They escorted him into one of the two interrogation rooms near the entrance to the squad room—a barren, windowless, bathroom-sized box with gray walls covered in discolored and chipped acoustic tile, a lumpy table at its center, a buzzing fluorescent light overhead. Its sole features were the door, which locked from the outside, and a ludicrously prominent thermostat mounted on one wall, which just about every interrogation subject over the age of seven correctly deduced to be a hidden microphone.

"All right. Let's start from the beginning," Petroski said. "We want to go through everything you told the others."

Once they heard France's story for themselves, they could see if the department had files on the murders, presumably unsolved, that France described. If such files existed, then they would know, first of all, that France had not fabricated the incidents. And with the files in hand, they could test France's version of events against evidence and witness statements gathered at the murder scenes years earlier.

"What happens then?" France asked.

"What happens then," Arce bluntly told France, "is we decide if we believe you."

Once again, France walked through the crimes for the detectives, remembering—and altering—the story in ways that would later prove important.

He described the Cervantes killing first. Recalling a previously forgotten detail, he mentioned that an old woman walking a dog had seen him and Winebaugh as they sat in France's pickup truck awaiting the victim's return from church. This was the sort of detail—if it checked out—that France could know only if he had been present at the murder, the detectives decided.

But when they moved on to the next murder, once again the order of events became confused. Petroski asked, "Now, the second case is in reference to the son being murdered. Right? The daughter-in-law killed her husband?"

"Right," France replied without hesitation, again suggesting that the first murder he committed after Cervantes was the killing of Gilberto's stepson, Tony Reyes. He corrected himself later.[10]

In describing the killing at the beauty shop, France said he had walked in the front door while Leasure waited in a back alley in the green Nova, parked next to a Dumpster. France said he walked directly up to the intended victim—Bill, he said, had shown him a picture of the dark-haired woman he was supposed to kill—then took her at gunpoint to the back of the shop. At Leasure's command, he said, he had stuffed his Smith and Wesson .45-caliber Featherlight into a white athletic sock in order to catch the shell as it was ejected. He said he at first forgot that Leasure wanted the hit to look like a robbery, so he had to walk the victim back to the front of the store to get to the register, then return with her to the back of the shop, France recalled.

He said he then shot the woman in the back, putting his gun right up against a bra strap. He ran out the door as she crumpled to the floor. Then he offered another detail that detectives would later interpret as crucial:

"Bill told me if she was wearin' a, a necklace, to take that from her because he wanted it," France told Arce and Petroski. "But she didn't have it on, I don't think, because I don't remember . . . I don't remember seein' it." When they drove off after the killing, France said, Leasure yelled at him for not bringing him the diamond pendant.

Despite the precaution of placing the pistol in a sock, the bullet casing fell out of the fresh bullet hole as France got into his Chevy Nova, he said. He wasn't sure where the casing rolled. That story would change later too, to France's detriment. This was the casing about which Leasure supposedly called their friend in LAPD's ballistics lab, Jimmy Trahin. Because the casing could be matched to the murder weapon, Leasure took the gun away and melted it down, France said. When they learned France's car had been spotted and described, he said, Bill paid him to have the green Nova painted red.

Next, when he described killing Paulette's ex-husband, whose name he suddenly remembered as "Tony," France recounted going to a bar late one night, with Leasure driving the now-red Nova. Again pretending to be a robber at Leasure's instructions, he said he asked for Tony's money as he came out of the bar with a girlfriend, then shotgunned him. Accurate to that point, France again tried to minimize his guilt by claiming he deliberately tried to miss the victim. He said Bill told him later that a single pellet pierced Tony's eye, and that Tony died of a heart attack on the operating table. This, the detectives would soon learn, was utterly false. (And yet, as they would later learn, it matched the lie that Sandra Zysman had told Paulette: He died in my arms of a heart attack. Arce and Petroski wondered, had Paulette passed on the lie to Leasure? Who passed it on to France?)

At other times in this second interrogation, France provided details that initially sounded incredible, causing the detectives to doubt him. Later, they would find out these details actually bolstered his credibility. Chief among these was his account of an earlier failed attempt to kill Tony. Bill had made up some boards with nails driven into them, which they had placed under Tony's Ford, France said. When the car's tires went flat, they were going to blast Tony as he got out to check the flats. But the tires did not go flat—France couldn't say why—and they had been forced to follow Tony until he parked with his girlfriend near the Farmer's Market. Leasure prepared to pull up next to Tony's Thunderbird, and, according to France, said, "When I stop, cap him."

"But I'm gonna hit the woman, too," France recalled saying. "So what? Do it!"

France then fired his shotgun into the car, blowing out a rear window, missing Tony on purpose, he told the detectives. He had hoped the resulting furor would put a halt to the murder attempts, France recalled. But he later learned from an amused Leasure that "this dummy didn't call the police." So they went on to make the successful hit on Tony Reyes, France said.

Arce and Petroski found this account difficult to accept. Once again, France had portrayed Leasure as a cold-blooded killer, with himself as the reluctant puppet. Yet, their doubts notwithstanding, the detectives found they were beginning to look at Leasure in the same way. Even if France was shading his story to his own benefit, he obviously was easily manipulated. And as the welder described riding with Bill in the police car, speaking gleefully of being allowed to push the siren button now and then, it became clear he had idolized Leasure, that their activities together had an air of adolescent prank to them. And, bottom line, the detectives just didn't think France was sophisticated enough to make all this up.

Throughout his recitation, France had provided no last names. There was a reason for that, he said, in addition to the fact that Leasure never shared that information with him. He said he was unable to read, and was just beginning to go to school to become literate.

For that reason, he told the detectives, he hadn't read the victims' names in the newspaper after the murders. When Bill gave him a composite drawing of the killer and driver in the beauty shop case, he had been unable to read the information written under the pictures. He claimed he hadn't even known Bill's last name for years, because he didn't know how to read his LAPD name tag.

At 10:00 that evening, Detectives Arce and Petroski finally finished taking France's second taped statement. He had been interrogated by then for over twelve hours. Arce and Petroski had what they felt were detailed descriptions of the crimes, but, still without names, places, or dates, they had no real way to check out France's story. They decided to go see the actual crime scenes. Then they would know where to find the bodies—at least on paper.

"Can you show us where these murders happened?" Arce asked, setting aside his fifth or sixth cup of coffee and stifling a yawn.

"You bet," France said. "I'll do anything, as long as you don't leave me alone here."

The three of them rode down to LAPD's basement garage and climbed into an unmarked car. Then Dennis France directed the detectives out onto L.A.'s night-dark streets, to give them a road map for murder.

Two and a half hours later, Bud Arce and Hank Petroski had driven with France from the quiet residential streets of the Valley to the raucous strip of bars west of Hollywood, crisscrossing the heart of Los Angeles in search of France's violent past. Then they brought their exhausted informant to his home, then in the pleasant suburb of Downey south of L.A., a vast improvement over the shoddy apartment in Paramount. At 1:00 in the morning, the two detectives returned wearily to the empty glare of the homicide squad room, where they began a bleary-eyed review of LAPD murder logs from 1977 to 1982 to check France's story.

The case did not look promising to them at this point, and France's performance in the car had been less than stellar.

First, France had taken them to the address where he claimed to have driven Winebaugh to shoot Paulette's father-in-law ten years earlier. It had not been in the city of El Monte, as France said, but in San Gabriel. The scene of the murder was supposed to have been an old house with an unkempt lawn. But there was no house standing where France had brought them, only a condominium complex.

"I swear it was here," France mumbled. "We parked right here."

The detectives said nothing. They circled the surrounding blocks, supposing France could have been off in his directions and that the house was nearby, but they found nothing.

Then they went on to the next stop on Dennis France's hit parade, as they came to jokingly refer to that night's drive—a bar in the Hollywood area called Pat's. France said the bar where Tony had been killed looked like this Pat's, but that he wasn't sure it was the right place. There were so many bars along this strip of Ventura Boulevard and adjacent streets in this northwestern corner of L.A. They drove on through the area, but there was no other place nearby that resembled the nightclub France remembered. "I know it's around here somewhere," France insisted, but to the detectives, he again sounded disturbingly vague.

When they finally gave up looking for bars, the three of them were too tired to seek out the beauty shop. They decided to skip it. That was the one location France had described in fair detail—in Highland Park, on Figueroa at Avenue Sixty, near a fire station. The detectives were confident they could find that on their own by checking LAPD sources.

They found it all right, as soon as LAPD's Northeast Division opened for business that morning. "You guys work a murder of a woman in a beauty shop about four, five years ago?" Hank Petroski asked one of the Northeast detectives over the telephone.

The detective didn't hesitate. "Sure, Anne Smith. She was killed during a robbery over in Highland Park. She used to be married to a detective out here. All the guys knew her."

"You're shittin' me," Petroski said. "A cop's wife?"

"Not when she got killed. They'd been divorced for years. She was married to some insurance guy when she died. Why do you want to know?"

"Well," Petroski said, "we might have a lead on the case."

"A lead?" the perplexed Northeast detective exclaimed. "Shit, Hank, some hype pleaded guilty to that three years ago. That case is solved."[11]

CHAPTER 13

Bud Arce saw the look on his partner's face as he hung up the phone. "Trouble?"

Petroski nodded and told him what he had learned about the Anne Smith murder. True, Dennis France had told them he believed someone else had confessed to the murders. Leasure had even boasted of arranging this phony admission. Bill had laughed about it, France said.

But, like so many other things he had told them, France had been vague on this point, and Arce and Petroski had tended to dismiss it. If there had been such a confession, it undoubtedly would have been disregarded at the time as unreliable, they assumed.

Police departments receive ersatz confessions regularly from people who feel compelled to admit to others' wrongdoing. In years past, this has led to horrendous miscarriages of justice. For this reason, a fundamental principle of American law forbids criminal convictions on the basis of confessions alone. There must be independent evidence to support the admissions, to weed out the false confessions, and to make sure the truly guilty party has come forward.

With this in mind, neither detective had expected to hear that the beauty shop case had been cleared by arrest and conviction. Such a resolution meant there had to be substantial, independent evidence that someone other than France had killed Anne Smith.

It meant Dennis France, quite probably, had lied to them. And that their case was headed for the toilet before it had even started.

"All we can do is pull the file, and find out what's what,"

Petroski sighed. The long night was rapidly becoming a long day as they sat alone in the squad room, desolate on a Saturday morning, unoccupied desks piled high with the unending flow of paper that murder creates. "We just might be screwed."

As a solved case, all the files on the Anne Smith murder had been shipped to the LAPD warehouse. During business hours, they could be obtained through a phone call. But on Saturday, Petroski had to go over himself and fetch the beaten manila envelopes crammed with paper, photographs, cassette tapes, and lineup cards.

They spent the next few hours sifting through the voluminous file—with remarkable results.

On March 3, 1981, just over nine months after Anne Smith was shot to death, LAPD Northeast Division Detectives Nelson Crowe and Neil Westbrook had arrested a heroin addict named Charles Fred Persico. The Anne Smith Murder Book, retrieved from the warehouse five years later by Arce and Petroski, showed that Arthur Gayle Smith had been the prime suspect in the first days after the killing. But then an anonymous caller who had seen a composite drawing of the killer in the newspaper put the detectives onto Persico and his estranged wife Elvia. The original investigating detectives, particularly Crowe, had then seized on the longtime addict, well known in their precinct, as the likely killer. For them, Art Smith had ceased to exist.

Crowe had talked to Elvia within a few weeks of Anne's death. The police reports Crowe wrote after that meeting stated that Elvia believed her husband looked like the composite drawing of the murderer, that he had admitted to her to being wanted for a murder and robbery in a beauty shop, and that he had a friend, Tutti Gomez, who drove a green Chevy Nova with stripes, just like the getaway car described in news accounts of the crime. It was on the basis of these reported comments of Elvia's that questioning was cut short of witnesses who knew of Art and Anne Smith's messy divorce and ugly threats.

Yet nine months passed without the detectives taking any other action, although Persico had been in and out of jail several times on heroin charges during that period—and was presumably an easy target for arrest. Why, Arce and Petroski asked themselves as they read the old file, didn't the other detectives arrest Persico right away? It made no sense—unless something was wrong with their case.

At his trial, Persico's lawyer suggested the original detectives hesitated because a case was being manufactured during those nine months. The detectives could have showed a photo lineup of Persico to the two women right away, rather than wait for him to be arrested. But they did not. This, Arce and Petroski recognized, was a departure from normal police procedure and, again, seemed to cloud the case against Persico.[1]

Still, Persico's fate had seemed sealed after he was placed in a physical lineup at Parker Center. When Delores Garofola, Anne Smith's mother, and Eleanor Trethaway, Anne's customer on the day she died, stood in a darkened room behind one-way glass and stared at six sullen men on a stage, both of them said Persico looked like the killer. Delores was so sure Persico was the man, she fainted in the parking lot after picking him out of the lineup.

He was three or four inches taller and darker than the five-foot-seven-inch man they had initially described nine months earlier, but nevertheless, they said, he's the one. Even though, on the day of the murder, their initial recollection of the gunman's looks was too vague to produce a composite—Eleanor had been too scared to look up and had only seen his reflection in a mirror—they said they could identify Persico as the killer, no doubts at all.

There were composite drawings and more exact descriptions, however, based on the recollections of a Toyota mechanic working next door to the beauty shop, who saw two men in a green Chevy Nova. Persico did indeed seem to resemble one of the men the mechanic had described.

Persico's conviction, however, was far from assured. He had a possible alibi, if a shaky one, for the time of the murder—he claimed to be at a methadone clinic with his girlfriend that day. And his wife, Elvia, a heroin addict like her husband, eventually said Detective Crowe lied in his report and coerced her with drugs and violence into falsely accusing her husband. She claimed she never said the things Crowe had attributed to her.

The prosecution's case was weakened further when the mechanic, a conscientious young man named Thomas Rumbaugh, said Persico definitely was not one of the men he had seen in the Chevy Nova. Although he had tentatively identified a photo of Persico as the passenger in the green Nova, once he saw the man in person—both at the lineup and in court—Rumbaugh said Persico definitely was not the culprit. And Tutti Gomez wasn't the driver, either, the mechanic said. (In any case, car registration records showed Gomez had never owned a Chevy Nova.)

Rumbaugh's description and resulting composite drawings were what led to the breakthrough in the case in the first place—the anonymous caller, after all, whether it was Elvia or someone else, had said she was responding to the composite in the newspaper. If Rumbaugh said Persico was the wrong man, the whole case was called into question, regardless of what Anne Smith's mother and customer said.

In an eleventh-hour plea bargain just before the jury began its deliberations, the prosecutor offered to plead the charges down from first-degree murder to manslaughter. If Persico agreed, he could be out of prison in three years with credit for time served and other built-in sentence reductions, rather than risk life in prison without the possibility of parole. Persico, who had already spent half his life staring through bars (for a multitude of drug offenses, but never for a violent crime), knew a good deal when he saw one. He took the offer. In effect, just as France had told Arce and Petroski years later, he had been persuaded to "confess." It was not Leasure's persuasion, though, as France had thought, but the normal courtroom bartering that lubricates a creaking justice system.

Years later, the file spread out on their desk, Arce and Petroski decided the odds were good that the jury, had it been given a chance to reach a verdict, would have acquitted Persico. As far as they could see, he had been charged solely on the basis of the most questionable type of evidence there is: eyewitness identification. Long experience questioning multiple witnesses to crimes had taught them that, for every witness, there would be a different— sometimes radically different—account of events. It was a simple rule of human perception. People see what they expect, and remember what they wish. The Persico witnesses' testimony was all the weaker because of the inexplicably long passage of time between the crime and the lineup. If eyewitnesses are notoriously unreliable within a few hours of a crime, then waiting nine months made their testimony practically worthless as far as Arce and Petroski were concerned.

Apart from those eyewitnesses, there was no physical evidence, no murder weapon, no fingerprints, no getaway car— nothing else to link Persico to the crime. And the most reliable of the three eyewitnesses, the one with the best description of the gunman and the least emotional involvement in the case—the mechanic—had said Persico was innocent.

On the other hand, France had described the getaway car perfectly, right down to its stripes, exactly as Thomas Rumbaugh had described it six years earlier. France even produced an old color snapshot of the car, long since sold, with his family posed in front of it, but its green paint, stripes, and the word "Rally" on its side clearly visible. Any possibility that France was fabricating his involvement in the Smith murder evaporated in the minds of the detectives once they saw that photo. You can't lie a six-year-old picture into existence.

Furthermore, France, not Persico, was the height Delores Garofola had initially given police in her description of the murderer—five feet seven to five feet eight inches tall. France had described wearing light blue clothing and a baseball-style welder's cap—very similar to what the witnesses in the beauty shop had recalled after the crime. And, just as he described taking Anne Smith to the back of the shop, then up front to the register, then to the back again, so had Delores described the same odd pattern—so unreasonable for an addict intent on committing robbery, but quite understandable for a nervous killer who briefly forgot he was supposed to pose as a robber.

From Arce and Petroski's point of view, every important element of the crime France had described seemed to match events described in the old Murder Book—right down to the Speer brand bullet casing found in the parking lot and the diamond pendant Anne Smith usually wore, but left with her mother that day. Any inconsistencies in France's story paled in comparison, the detectives decided.

How could Dennis France have known all this, the detectives asked one another, unless he had been there? And since France said he and Art Smith hadn't known each other, there had to be some other link between the killer and the man who wanted them killed. Who else could it be, they asked one another, but Officer William Leasure?[2]

"It's got to be mistaken identity," Petroski told his partner. "There's no way Persico should have been convicted."

"There's no way he should even have been *charged*," Arce replied.

They had found not just a killer, but an innocent man wrongly convicted of murder.

Their elation at having found France's story largely accurate when compared to the facts of Anne Smith's murder soon faded, however, when they realized its true implication. They were not trying to convict Dennis France. They were pursuing Bill Leasure. So what if they now could prove France, not Persico, had killed Anne Smith? Maybe an innocent man might get out of jail because of their efforts, but it did little else. If the case against Persico had been weak, the evidence against Leasure was far scantier. Not a shred of physical evidence linked Leasure to that murder. No witness was going to identify him. The balding, pale Leasure looked nothing like the Hispanic driver with a full head of hair described by the mechanic. Nor could any bullet be matched to any of Leasure's many guns, seized and catalogued in an LAPD warehouse months before. Once Persico was convicted and his appeals had been exhausted, all physical evidence in the case, including the spent casing found at the beauty shop, was destroyed. And besides, France had said the murder weapon had been melted down by Leasure, leaving nothing to test even if the casing had still existed. Just for the sake of thoroughness, the detectives eventually shipped all of Leasure's weapons off to the FBI in Washington for test firings—the LAPD lab couldn't be trusted because of the allegations against firearms expert Jimmy Trahin. The tests, as expected, yielded nothing useful. The guns were clean.

So all they had was Dennis France's word that Bill Leasure was pulling the strings. And, once again, they had to ask themselves just what the uncorroborated word of an admitted murderer would be worth once they got to court—*if* they got to court. The answer was clear. It would be worth nothing.

A similar pattern played out with the other two murders, as Arce and Petroski pieced together France's information and found unsolved murder files at the San Gabriel Police Department and in LAPD's own Hollywood Division. France had been right about the location of Gilberto Cervantes's demise, after all—the San Gabriel investigators confirmed that the old, unkempt house had been torn down in favor of condos. Likewise, the Chez Nora Bar had been torn down and was to become the site of a bank branch. Pat's Bar, where France had brought them, was about two miles away from the empty lot that had been Tony Reyes's last gig.

As in the Anne Smith murder, France had been stunningly accurate about many details of the killings, with a few inconsistencies that did not, at the time, seem important to the detectives.

The Cervantes file was a wealth of information. The original investigators of the March 1977 murder had found that, just as France said, the only witness was an elderly woman walking her dog, who had seen two men sitting in a light blue pickup truck with a camper shell—again, just as France had said. The San Gabriel investigators had considered Tony and Paulette de los Reyes prime suspects because of the inheritance at stake once the ailing Natalia joined her husband in death—again, matching France's account.

Both Tony and Paulette had been evasive and uncooperative when questioned, though each provided an alibi that checked out.

The file at the small San Gabriel police station also included the anonymous letter that accused Dennis Winebaugh of killing Gilberto, and named the trucker Bill Jennings as someone who knew Winebaugh—again, exactly as France had told Arce and Petroski. The posthumous letter from Tony, accusing both Winebaugh and Paulette of the murder, was attached to the file, too, apparently provided by Tony's eldest son after the bass player's murder.

The detectives were disappointed at finding nothing pointing directly to Leasure—they thought, at the least, that Tony's letter should have mentioned him. According to France, Tony Reyes had known Leasure might be trying to kill him. The two of them had talked on the phone, France said, and Leasure had pretended he was willing to kill Paulette if Tony would outbid her. To Leasure, it had all been a delightful game of seeing which of the de los Reyeses would pay the most to murder the other, France told his interrogators.

The game ended, France said, when Tony threatened to go to the police. "If Tony talks, we're gone," France recalled Leasure warning. "We're goin' to jail. We've got to do it. I've promised her [Paulette] I'll do it tomorrow." If true, though, Arce and Petroski wondered, why didn't Tony's dead man's letter mention Leasure?

But though the Cervantes file failed to provide any direct evidence against Leasure, the homicide detectives were surprised to find a nine-by-twelve glossy of another LAPD officer, Big John, who had been a suspect in Gilberto's death from day one, thanks to the name "John" found scrawled in pencil on Gilberto's truck at the murder scene. Several witnesses had told the San Gabriel investigators about arguments between Paulette, Big John, and Gilberto over control of the tortilla factory, but no real evidence against him was ever found, either.

Still, the presence of a photo of Leasure's good friend and LAPD partner in the file showed just how close the undermanned suburban police department had come to breaking the case open.

"They knew an LAPD cop was involved," Petroski would later say. "They just had the wrong one. It made us feel we really were on the right track."

Arce and Petroski were puzzled, however, at finding little in the file in the way of documented efforts to find either Winebaugh or Bill Jennings, other than going to the Paramount apartment where the two men had lived with France and coming up empty-handed. Nine years later, the two homicide detectives were able to return to their squad room and locate both Jennings and Winebaugh after a few hours of phone calls.

The detectives also tracked down an old LAPD file on the October 1976 Hollywood bombing of Tony's car. Big John had been a suspect in that crime, too, although again investigators never made a case against him or anyone else. France had described the bombing, saying Leasure had claimed he and Big John did it to scare Tony during Paulette's divorce.

The LAPD detectives investigating the September 1981 murder of Tony Reyes had joined forces with the San Gabriel police, focusing on Paulette and Dennis Winebaugh as potential suspects, Arce and Petroski found once they had unearthed those old files at Parker Center. They tracked down the only eyewitness in the case, Sandra Zysman, Tony's old girlfriend. She was living in a dirt-floor cabin in an isolated pocket of gold rush country outside Sacramento called Pioneer, near the rolling hills surrounding Lake Amador. Five years after the killing, she was still mourning Tony's death. Although her description of the murder was essentially the same as France's, it differed in one key respect: As far as she could tell, the gunman was alone. She never got a good look at his face in the dark parking lot, so she couldn't identify—or rule out—France. But she was adamant about the fact that he did not talk over his shoulder to an accomplice, something France had insisted he did as he sought instructions from Leasure before reluctantly shooting Tony.

Worse still, from the detectives' perspective, Zysman had never heard of Bill Leasure. Tony Reyes had never mentioned him.

But the seesaw of doubt and belief in Dennis France's story tipped in favor of credibility with Zysman's recollection of the drive-by shooting France had described earlier. Sandra had nearly forgotten about it because Tony had been so blasé about the incident. Just a prank, he had said. But once the detectives jogged her memory, she said, yes, someone had driven by the car and fired a shotgun inside, missing but terrifying her. They had never reported it to the police, and when Tony was killed, she hadn't even thought to mention it. She couldn't even remember when it happened— anywhere from two years to a few months before Tony's death, she has estimated at various times.[3]

It was enough for Arce and Petroski. France demonstrated knowledge of a key detail no one else could know. It wasn't even in the police files. No living person knew about it other than Zysman, France, and, presumably, Leasure. France had to have been there.

On that same trip to the Sacramento area, the detectives tracked down France's old friend and schoolteacher, Dale Lloyd Boyce, who was then serving a state prison sentence for child molestation in Jamestown, California. France had told the detectives that Boyce could verify much of his story. And, sure enough, Boyce confirmed that France had fearfully confided in him about being involved in a murder ring nearly ten years earlier. Boyce recalled France showing him two thousand dollars paid to him by "Bill," an LAPD officer, and that France had told him about several murders.[4] Boyce led the detectives to his nephew, D.A. investigator Alan Tomich, who confirmed France's unlikely story about trying to go to the police after the Cervantes killing, only to be told, "Adios" (figuratively, not literally). Tomich said he had met with France to talk about the murder of an old Mexican and the involvement of an LAPD officer, but that the story had not checked out. He had, in essence, told France to get lost, Tomich recalled.

But the tug of war between France's credibility and doubt about his veracity continued for Arce and Petroski when the D.A. investigator's recollections did not match France's on some key points—like the name of the policeman involved in the murder.

"If he gave us a name [of the policeman], it was a common one, like Jones," Tomich told Arce and Petroski—a troubling detail. Obviously, "Leasure" was not a common name. (Then again, Dennis France claimed that, because of his illiteracy, he only knew Leasure as "Bill" at that time.)

Tomich recalled that France had claimed sole credit for physically gunning down the old man, and that "he was the only one involved in the actual shooting."[5] Once confronted with this inconsistency, France recalled that he had lied during the Chinatown meeting with Tomich, omitting Winebaugh's role in the Cervantes killing. He said he had wanted to avoid implicating Forty-four until he was sure Tomich would protect him from retaliation. Arce and Petroski found this explanation reasonable, though it would prove to be yet another contradiction with which defense attorneys would hammer away at his story.

Even with Zysman, Boyce, and Tomich providing partial corroboration of France's account of the Cervantes and Reyes murders, Detectives Arce and Petroski still had the same problem as with their probe of the Anne Smith killing. They had convincing proof that Dennis France was involved, but nothing to put Leasure at the murder scenes—or even behind the scenes—except for France's word.

And the detectives knew this failing went beyond mere questions of credibility, or whether a jury would believe France's story. A fundamental legal hurdle stood in the detectives' path. In a kind of corollary to the rule that requires confessions to be supported by independent evidence, Dennis France's story also required independent corroboration before his accusations against Leasure would hold up in court.

In legal terms, the police believed France and Leasure were co-conspirators—that is, they planned murders together. The law requires that the testimony of one conspirator against another must be corroborated by physical evidence or through the testimony of someone outside the conspiracy. The reason for this is simple: If, for example, France killed Tony Reyes on his own, he could fabricate a story about a conspiracy, then point the finger at some innocent person in exchange for immunity. In theory, requiring independent proof weeded out such false accusations.

And so, as much as Arce and Petroski came to believe France had told them the truth on most significant points, they knew the law required them to find some independent evidence to support his claims. They had to find some way to prove Bill Leasure was involved in three old murders, cold evidence, destroyed casings, dead-end leads, faded memories, and the conviction of Charles Persico notwithstanding.

Otherwise, they wouldn't have to worry about whether jurors would believe Dennis France's story, because a jury would never hear it. Without more hard evidence, Detectives Arce and Petroski couldn't write Bill Leasure a ticket, much less charge him with murder.

The question was, where would they go from here?

• • •

You know what gets me? They never even tried to talk to me. No one from LAPD ever came up and asked me a question, not about the boats, and not about the murders. Not to this day. Why didn't they try to talk to me? I might have told them something. What did they have to lose?

But they weren't interested in what I had to say. They still aren't.

■ CHAPTER 14

AFTER BILL LEASURE'S AR-
rest aboard a stolen yacht—but before Dennis France came forward with his tale of contract murder—LAPD had tried to build a
portrait of Leasure as a mediocre cop turned master thief and
fraud. The department had showed unbridled enthusiasm for ripping into—and ripping apart—the lives of Leasure and everyone
around him.

Although it had a long and well-documented history of wink-
ing at brutality, racism, and sexism within its ranks, LAPD was
equally well known for rabidly pursuing the slightest hint of police
thievery or corruption. Chief Daryl Gates had made it clear he
wanted to set an example in the yacht case. And so an internal investigation of unprecedented magnitude had focused microscopic
attention on the professional and private lives of William Leasure.
His friends, his fellow officers, and, in particular, his wife were all
considered fair game. The simple taint of knowing Leasure, of
showing up in his personal phone book or having traded guns with
the man, threatened whole careers. A total of twenty-five search
warrants had been issued in the case, and teams of Internal Affairs
investigators had rifled through Leasure's home three times, his
LAPD locker, his phone records and bank records, as well as the
homes and possessions of Kuns, France, and several of his fellow
officers. It had been the repeated searches and questioning about
stolen yachts that helped push Dennis France into coming forward.

Two months later, in their quest to corroborate France's story,
Bud Arce and Hank Petroski turned for answers to the efforts of
this investigative task force, which had accumulated a mountain of

paper in its special "Leasure Room" down the hall from the chief's office. After several days' delay and an angry exchange with Petroski over who outranked whom, Internal Affairs Sergeant David Wiltrout finally provided the homicide detectives with copies of its reports and witness interviews.

The portrait of Leasure that emerged from those voluminous documents was as interesting for what it lacked as for what it contained.

On the one hand, there seemed to be little doubt that Leasure was, in Petroski's bottom-line terminology, "a crook." Internal Affairs investigators reported finding his home, garage, and boat crammed with stolen property. He possessed stolen cars, a stolen yacht, stolen guns, stolen clothes, stolen furniture. A search of the home of his friend Rob Kuns similarly revealed the Skipper to be a crook. His friends Dennis France and Dennis Winebaugh were crooks. His partner on the force, Officer Ralph Gerard, was co-owner of Leasure's stolen yacht *Thunderbolt,* so he, too, was labeled a crook. The notion that Leasure might have acquired the yachts and other possessions without knowing they were stolen never received serious consideration. To Internal Affairs, such a proposition seemed ludicrous. He was a cop, they said. He had to know.

On the other hand, in seventeen years on the job, Leasure had shown no hint of being a corrupt cop. That, too, seemed inconceivable. His Marine Corps record was equally unblemished. His childhood history, at least as far as it was known, was bland. His psychological testing at the police academy had been unremarkable. Other than an occasional comment about poor work habits, no one on the force, or among the citizenry he dealt with, seemed to have a bad word to say about him. Quite the opposite: He had done his job, kept his head down, stayed out of trouble.

Outside the workplace, he had an apparently loving wife with a sterling reputation as a government prosecutor—she had even run for the office of City Attorney the year before Leasure was arrested. (Typically, Leasure managed to find time during his workday to deliver legal papers related to her campaign.) Yes, he might have seemed dull and mediocre to his colleagues, but that didn't make him any different from several thousand other invisible men wearing uniforms at LAPD. But it did make him a most unlikely suspect.

In two months of investigation, Internal Affairs had made little headway in reconciling this duality. If anything, the stark contradiction between the allegations against Leasure and the rest of his life had only grown stronger as the investigation progressed, and all the more so once Dennis France came forward. Leasure would later say the police should have deduced from this that they had the wrong man, that he was being framed. Instead, the notion that Leasure led a psychopath's double life would be advanced by Internal Affairs investigators. At home, there was Mild Bill with his pet bunny, his lawn-munching pygmy goat, his endless tinkering in the garage. Then on the streets with his cutthroat friends, Leasure's mask came off, leaving him free to steal, bomb, and kill with conscienceless glee. This theory seemed an uneasy fit at best, an oversimplification of a complex man. But at that point in the case, nothing better came along.

As far as the thefts went, evidence of Leasure's guilt seemed compelling. Evidence to *explain* his guilt, however, seemed nonexistent. No gambling debts, no drug or alcohol abuse (he abstained from both), no childhood abuses or disasters pocked his past— nothing. Legally, the police are not required to prove motive in order to convict a person of criminal acts. But they always look for it just the same, and failure to find it troubles investigators.

And there was another point in this disparate picture of Leasure that troubled the homicide investigators as they looked for clues to their suspect's motives and personality: The order of events was all wrong. The murders occurred *before* the yacht and car thefts. There had been no gradual descent from less serious property crimes to graver acts of violence. If that had been the case, then at least a logical progression would have emerged, the sort of pattern that appeals to commonsense notions of the evolution of criminality. If a cop goes bad, popular wisdom held, he or she would undoubtedly begin small, then work up to major crimes later. A mortal sinner is not born overnight, the argument went.

But no such pattern applied in the Leasure case. The first stolen boat was in 1982, the last murder in 1981. If Dennis France was to be believed, Leasure had started with the most serious crime of all, then switched from professional hits to theft on the high seas.

"That part didn't make sense," Detective Tom King, one of the original Leasure task force members, would later concede. "You just don't wake up one day and decide to start killing people. There's got to be more to it than that. Something had to have come before."

But what? Arce and Petroski searched the voluminous Internal Affairs files, looking for that elusive key.

Dennis France had given his own startling portrait, to start with. The inoffensive Officer Leasure, according to France, transformed himself into a callous and bold criminal who took an almost childlike delight in his exploits.

"He told me that him and Big John had gone over and blew up Tony's car," France would later testify.[1] "And how 'neat' it was for him to sit in the car and count off the seconds.

". . . And he was telling me he likes going in [to work at Central Traffic Division] after doing something like that, when they have their police meetings. And they say how big of a genius he is for blowing up these devices. And he likes hearing that. They don't know it's him doing it. And he gets a big kick out of it."[2]

Apparently there had been other bombings, though France could offer no specifics.

France also told Arce and Petroski, "Bill would pick me up all the time, and we'd ride around in the patrol car all the time." On one such ride, France said Leasure stopped his patrol car at a construction site. Looking through the chain-link fence, he saw a temporary utility pole with some industrial plugs hanging from it—a special type of curved, two-foot-long plug that allows workers to tap directly into main power lines. The plugs cost all of thirty or forty dollars apiece.

"Bill said he wanted one," France said. "So he stopped and said, 'Dennis, jump over that fence and take it.' I said, are you crazy? What if someone calls the cops?

"And he said, 'Don't worry, I'll just buy the call.' "

To "buy a call," in cop parlance, is to tell the police dispatcher that you'll handle a crime report that comes over the police radio. So, with Leasure's assurance that he'd keep him out of trouble, France jumped over the fence, got the plug, and returned to the patrol car, booty in hand. A smiling Leasure threw the plug into the trunk.

"It was just one of those things," France said. "That's what Bill wanted, that's what you got."[3]

Another time, France said, he was the one who wanted to steal something while they were cruising around in Bill's patrol car. They were on a lonely stretch of highway, and France saw some kind of warning sign that he wanted. He didn't have any real use for it, he just wanted it. So Leasure pulled his police car over and, according to France, the little welder clambered onto the hood of the cruiser, stood on his toes, and yanked the sign from its post. He threw it in the backseat, and they left—a silly, outrageous theft, in broad daylight, in full view on a public highway.[4]

The detectives listened to these stories and couldn't help but think, not of serious criminals, but of adolescent boys playing pranks, showing off, committing mischief simply because they knew they could get away with it. The way they would whoop it up and high-five one another after a successful yacht theft possessed the same flavor. It was all so frighteningly childish, as was the notion of Leasure committing crimes, then showing up at roll call to hear his handiwork discussed, smirking to himself at his ingeniousness and the fact that only he knew the culprit's secret identity. Was this same immature and secretive joy also at work in the murders? Was that the underlying motive—adolescent thrills, boys with guns?

It fit, the detectives thought, but only when they viewed events through the filter of Dennis France's claims. The problem was, there was a mound of evidence that painted just the opposite picture of Bill Leasure. The cops who worked with him every day saw no sign that he was a criminal, felt no suspicions even as he amassed cars, yachts, and planes, called him the exact opposite of a thrill-seeker. He was dull. He was quiet. They felt Bill Leasure would do no wrong. Their assessment would be powerful testimony if Leasure ever mounted a good-character defense—a division full of hardened cops saying, no way.

Perhaps closer to Leasure than anyone at LAPD at the time, Officer Jon Herrington had worked with Leasure, socialized with him, rented an aircraft hangar with him at a small airport. He had gone to dinner with Bill just a few days before the fateful yacht trip to the Bay Area in May 1986, and had planned to crew for him aboard other yachts (though scheduling conflicts always seemed to get in the way). He borrowed money from Leasure, and had owed him twenty-two hundred dollars at the time of the arrest. Because of this closeness, Internal Affairs investigators were so convinced Herrington must be involved with Leasure's alleged crimes somehow that they read him his Miranda rights against self-incrimination before questioning him. They later conceded he was innocent of any wrongdoing. His only sin, in their eyes, was liking Bill Leasure.

They had worked together as traffic officers since 1982. Like the other officers at Central Traffic, Herrington had nothing bad to say about Leasure. He, too, saw nothing suspicious in his boating activities or his Corvettes. Most of the cars were junkers, Herrington said. The bank account in Grand Cayman was just "for tax purposes," not for any criminal endeavors. As far as Herrington was concerned, Bill and Betsy were living well within their means. Leasure was just a guy with a bad stomach and a hernia who called in sick now and then because he got nauseous, and a few more times so he could take boat trips. That didn't make him a criminal, Herrington said.

"We all believed that once a guy is arrested, that he is ninety-nine point nine-nine percent guilty, that's true," Herrington told Internal Affairs after Leasure's arrest. "He's been a good friend of mine. Some of these allegations are just incredible for me to believe. Everybody says he's hung, he's out to dry, he's going to jail for twenty-five thousand years. . . .

"But maybe it's all lies . . . all made up. I've heard stories."

Herrington was younger and less experienced than Leasure, and the older cop felt he was a role model for him. They had grown very close. Herrington had met Art Smith, France, and Robert Kuns, and never heard any talk of stealing or killing, just Kuns bragging about fast cars and fast motorcycles. The bottom line, Herrington said, was that the Bill Leasure he knew was not the same fellow Dennis France had described.[5]

But, like so many other people who spoke out on behalf of Bill Leasure, there were a few points that raised questions in the minds of the investigators. Some of them were minor—like Leasure lying to Herrington about Kuns's bank robbery conviction and prison term. Leasure had told Herrington the Skipper was the victim of a misunderstanding, and had served only pretrial jail time before being exonerated—a clear fabrication. And Herrington admitted being aware that Leasure habitually lied and cheated on Betsy Mogul. Sergeant Jim Berg recalled Leasure bragging that his yacht, the *Thunderbolt,* was worth a quarter million dollars—twice its real value. And another Central Traffic officer told Internal Affairs that Leasure once asked him to authenticate the serial number on a Corvette he said he had restored. It turned out the vehicle was stolen and its number had been altered—Leasure had made his fellow officer an unwitting party to theft and fraud. "He was a user," Detective Tom King would later observe. "He used people shamelessly."

Then there was the business with Leasure's police locker, which left even a stalwart supporter like Jon Herrington wondering. Reluctantly, he described the incident for Internal Affairs investigators when they questioned him for the second time a month after Leasure's arrest.

Leasure had called Herrington three times, collect, from the Contra Costa County Jail shortly after his arrest. Open up my locker at Central Traffic, Jon, Herrington recalled Leasure asking. Take out my personal things. I'm worried my wife Betsy might find out there's a picture of Irene Wong in there. You've got to help me.

Herrington told investigators he had hesitated, his worry that honoring such a request would get him in trouble conflicting with his desire to help a friend. He knew Bill had girlfriends—at

Leasure's suggestion, Irene had become Herrington's roommate a few months earlier. So it didn't surprise Herrington to hear Leasure had some photos or personal phone numbers he didn't want anyone else to get hold of. Nobody wants their lives turned into an open book, he reasoned. At the time, he decided, there was nothing suspicious about the request, and Herrington didn't think to inform his superiors about it. Yet, for some reason, he couldn't bring himself to go to the locker.

A few days later, a man telephoned Herrington, identifying himself only as "Andrew," an inmate jailed with Leasure who said he had agreed to make calls for him. Andrew said Leasure wanted Herrington to "tell everyone at work that he was not guilty of stealing any of those boats." Then he gave Herrington the combination to Leasure's LAPD locker and asked him to remove some specific items: Leasure's field officer's notebook, a small pad that every cop at LAPD is issued; any photographs; and anything in the pockets of Leasure's LAPD uniform shirt hanging in the locker. Then Andrew added that Leasure wanted any items removed that might implicate him in crimes—and that was when Herrington got scared. Something was wrong, he knew. But still, he thought, it might only be that Leasure was worried that the contents of his locker would be misconstrued, or, worse, would make Betsy Mogul divorce him.

In mid-June, Herrington screwed up his courage, waited until the locker room was empty, and opened Leasure's locker—only to find Internal Affairs had beaten him to it. A search warrant and property receipt sat inside, left behind by investigators who had searched and emptied the metal locker. Herrington shut the door without touching anything. When Leasure called back the following week, Herrington told him what he had found. Leasure still wanted him to go back and get his "personal stuff"—shirts, pants, boots— that the investigators had left behind. But Herrington refused, and, after a few more tries, Leasure dropped the subject. "That was it," Herrington said.[6]

To Herrington and Leasure's other friends, the request to clean out his locker seemed reasonable. Bill didn't want his wife to find out about his girlfriend, didn't want his private phone directory scrutinized, didn't want his personal things thrown away or lost. What was wrong with that?

Plenty, according to Internal Affairs. The search of Leasure's locker had turned up evidence not only of Leasure's infidelities, but of his involvement in yacht theft. Inside the pocket of his uniform shirt were printouts of boat registrations, taken from an LAPD police computer. One of the printouts, made in December 1983, concerned a stolen fifty-one-foot sailing yacht—the *Lucky Star*, which had become Art Smith's *Santine*. This was one of the registration checks Leasure eventually admitted performing for Kuns, and, at the very least, it suggested that Leasure knew for years that his friend's boat was stolen.

In the same pocket was a flyer distributed by the owner of another stolen vessel, the *Billy G*—a boat that had been transformed into Leasure's yacht, the *Thunderbolt*.

The documents suggested to the investigators that Leasure had gathered information to assist in stealing yachts and covering his tracks. Yet the question remained: Why would he keep such documents once he had used the information they contained? They served no useful purpose, other than to incriminate him should they ever be found.

Unless, investigators theorized, they were souvenirs. Trophies of his conquests.

Search warrants served at Leasure's house in Northridge turned up similarly perplexing finds. There were three separate searches in the ten days following Leasure's arrest in Oakland—it took that many before LAPD figured out exactly what they were looking for.

The first time, going on the error-riddled story of Dennis France's brother Jerry, they were looking for evidence of boat thefts and related homicides, under the mistaken belief that yachtsmen had been murdered and their bodies dumped at sea. Police seized only a few guns at that time—ones Leasure had bought from Dennis France, plus his three illegal silencers and an AR-15 assault rifle converted into an illegal bullet-spewing machine gun. Later, they returned to seize forty more weapons—shotguns, pistols, rifles, plus boxes of ammunition, bayonets, and knives. Then they came back a third time, having been thoroughly briefed by the Oakland Police on the huge scope of the yacht thefts. They seized more than one hundred items apparently taken from stolen boats.

The dozen investigators who descended on Leasure's home to conduct those searches were frankly mystified by Leasure's house. They found the bewildering hodgepodge of plane parts, dismantled cars, and other assorted junk in the large, weedy backyard—a look that suggested less a master criminal and more "Sanford and Son." But the big discovery lay in the eight-car garage/workshop Leasure had built in his backyard. The searchers found piles of tools, fishing gear, artwork, furniture, cooking utensils, and other items, all taken from the string of stolen yachts. Even William Lofthouse's box of Christmas decorations, last seen aboard his beloved *Billy G*, docked in Dana Point south of Los Angeles, was found stored in Leasure's garage. Lofthouse's treasured Chinese paintings were hanging in Betsy's home office, there was a stolen fifteen-thousand-dollar Chinese vase in the house, and the revolver Lofthouse had kept aboard his yacht was found in Leasure's gun room. There was even a name board from the transom of one of the other stolen yachts, and a fishing reel with a yacht owner's name and driver's license number inscribed inside. The owners of the stolen yachts had been brought to LAPD's Parker Center headquarters to walk through the truckload of possessions seized from Leasure's home, garage, and boat, identifying their clothes, guns, blankets, and cooking utensils in what the police call a "property show-up." All these stolen possessions, Internal Affairs deduced, provided hard evidence of Leasure's involvement in the boat thefts.[7]

Very little of it was of any monetary value, strangely enough—it seemed more like the stuff people spread out on blankets at swap meets, which is exactly what Leasure would later say he and his wife planned to do. Kuns had just given him discards from boats about to be sold, Leasure would say. "I had no idea any of it was stolen. That should be obvious. If I had known, I never would have kept that junk." (Kuns, however, would say later that Leasure was supposed to have disposed of the things, but secretly hoarded them instead. "He's a pack rat. When they brought all that stuff in court, I couldn't believe it.") Once again, the police had to ask themselves: Why would the guy save the stuff? It made no sense.

They also found two allegedly stolen cars, including the Ford Thunderbird, keys in the ignition, previously reported stolen by the wife of Leasure's partner at LAPD, Officer Ralph Gerard. Gerard already was under investigation as the co-owner of the *Thunderbolt*. The other car was a stolen Studebaker, a vintage 1927 model, which had disappeared from the California State University's Northridge campus during a weekend swap meet on its grounds a year earlier. The owner cashed in a twenty-thousand-dollar insurance policy he had purchased for the Studebaker, although the car was worth, at most, six thousand dollars. More strange dealings, but, in any case, LAPD had some more felony counts to file.

Evidence at the house led them to a third car—a 1984 Corvette with a modified serial number—that had been stolen the previous summer. It was found later abandoned in Tijuana, just across the California-Mexico border. Normally, cars are stolen and vanish at the border with regularity, but the abandoned Corvette was so suspicious that any would-be thieves must have figured it for a setup or sting, and they left it alone. Mexican police eventually recovered it and turned it over to LAPD. Leasure's old machine shop friend, John Wieland, told the police that Leasure had Corvettes hidden all over Los Angeles.

The reports on the cars and the searches of Leasure's home were of special interest to Arce and Petroski as they read through the Internal Affairs reports. Dennis France had told them that Betsy Mogul telephoned him after her husband's arrest, asking France to help her dispose of stolen cars and property. But when he arrived at the Leasure home, he found the place swarming with police. He made a U-turn and left, he told the homicide detectives. (According to Bill Leasure, Betsy Mogul denies ever asking France to come over or to dispose of any property.)[8]

Working with the Oakland Police, LAPD had identified a total of ten stolen yachts linked to Leasure and Kuns. The pattern of stealing from Southern California, then altering the yachts and selling them up north, was well established early in the investigation. LAPD investigators were able to trace several of the trips up the coast, finding slip rental receipts signed by Kuns or a witness who remembered chatting with Leasure. The paper trail of phony registrations, much of it sloppy, seemed ridiculously easy to spot once investigators knew what to look for. And even more telling than the property taken from the stolen yachts and stashed in Leasure's garage was Leasure's personal notebook, which helped document the thefts in revealing detail.

One particularly significant page, in the minds of investigators, read as follows:

PROFITS	
Columbia	2,000
Art & Me	10,000
Canada	4,000
Dennis	10,000
Ralph (Deliverance)	237
	250
	1,500
(Sell Deliverance)	9,430
Thunderbolt:	
(Profit on Exp)	1,259.63
(Profit on Loss of Deliv	
Less Cost of Thunderbolt)	12,000.00
Total	50,676.63
+(4,000 Total)(Mikes Boat)	1,000
+Ocean Spirit	10,000
Total	$61,676.63

The I.A. investigators and the Oakland Police had no trouble deciphering these entries: "Columbia" was the first boat trip Leasure took with Kuns aboard the *Jimmy K* for a two-thousand-dollar fee. "Art & Me" was the sailboat *Santine* and the extra ten thousand dollars Leasure tacked onto the purchase price, preying on both Smith and Kuns. "Canada" was the trip to the Vancouver area and the theft of the *Peggy Rose II*, transformed into the *Tortuga* and sold in Newport Beach. "Dennis" represented the ten thousand dollars Leasure earned from an insurance fraud with Kuns and France with the phony yacht *Sunshine*. The next few entries pertained to profits Leasure earned from the stolen yachts *Deliverance* and *Thunderbolt*, co-owned with "Ralph" Gerard. There was no way for Leasure to have made a "profit on loss" on the *Deliverance* unless there was a fraud behind it.

"Mikes Boat" was an apparent reference to a stolen yacht sold to a San Diego resident named Mike Maseline, and the *Ocean Spirit* was a stolen yacht taken from Southern California and sold in the Bay Area.

Investigators were especially amused by the line labeled "Profit on Exp," which was interpreted as Leasure's account of how he cheated his friend Gerard by inflating his expenses for stealing and altering the *Thunderbolt*. A separate page showed he was charging Gerard about twenty-eight hundred dollars in expenses, while, in a separate entry, he showed a "true" expense total of approximately fifteen hundred dollars. Right down to sandwiches and cans of Coke, he charged—and overcharged—his partners in crime every penny he could.

Another damning notebook page was labeled "Withdrawles" (sic), which listed a series of seven checks and cash payments from Ralph Gerard to Leasure. The payments appeared to concern the *Deliverance* and *Thunderbolt*, totaling just under fifty thousand dollars.

The investigators probing the boat thefts soon realized that the amounts and dates listed on this notebook page exactly matched deposits Leasure had made to Irene Wong's bank account. They knew this because the FBI, followed by LAPD, had found Leasure's young, now outraged Asian-American lover shortly after his arrest in May 1986. She had not obeyed Leasure's telephoned request to destroy bank records and letters involving him. Instead, they became damning evidence against Bill Leasure. And beyond producing hard evidence of his and Kuns's boat theft profits, Irene Wong, in Arce and Petroski's opinion, more than anyone else would lend credibility to Dennis France's contention that Bill Leasure had led a double life.

In a way, Irene Wong's ignorance of whole areas of William Leasure's life was as telling as the narrow spectrum about which she had complete and demonstrable knowledge. The same young woman who had become pregnant with his child, who dated him for six and a half years, who knew his closest friends—including Dennis France and Robert Kuns—and who was engaged to him for at least half that period, had no idea he had been married three years before they ever met. She firmly believed his home in Northridge was rented to others, and she thought he lived in a home that actually belonged to his friend Flo Ong.

In a series of six interviews with the FBI and LAPD in June and July 1986, Irene, initially hesitant, would let out a few more details in every session with the investigators probing the boat thefts. Slim, slight, and fearful, Irene said she had wanted to come forward right away, but hadn't because Leasure's friend Officer Jon Herrington had warned her to wait for police to come to her. Otherwise, he said she should "keep her damn mouth shut," she told investigators.

Throughout, Irene sounded confused and worried about her future. All her hopes of a family and a stable life with Bill had been shattered, as had her image of the "moral" man she had always believed him to be. As late as Thursday, May 29, 1986—the very day Leasure was arrested—Irene was waiting for him to return to L.A., where they had made plans to go to the hospital together to determine the extent of her latest pregnancy. But he failed to show up. She heard the following day of his arrest, and then, one day later, learned of Leasure's long-standing marriage to Betsy Mogul, the woman he had sworn was just an evil ex-girlfriend. Two days later, an FBI agent was sitting in her living room, tipped by a friend of hers and Leasure's.[9]

The FBI became involved because of the suspicion—later dismissed as unfounded—that Leasure and Kuns were drug or arms smugglers, and the initial belief that their yacht thefts involved interstate crimes. Kuns's personal yacht, dry-docked in Oregon, had secret compartments—the hallmark of smugglers—and police searching Leasure's home had found several LAPD "Narcoban" kits for the testing of cocaine and marijuana. There was no legitimate reason for a traffic officer to possess the kits, inflaming suspicions. Later, I.A. investigators reluctantly dismissed their presence

as part of Leasure's overpowering instinct to hoard things both valuable and useless. Finally, when it became clear the thefts, frauds,
and resales of yachts were confined almost exclusively to California,
the FBI backed out of the case, leaving it to local and state authorities.

But their initial interviews with Irene established her long-
standing affair with Leasure, and she became a font of information
on his habits, his vacations abroad, and his use of official time and
equipment for personal profit. He was always driving her around
town in his police car—an echo of France's story—or visiting her,
in uniform, at the bank where she worked as a teller. In hindsight,
Irene told investigators, she supposed Leasure was able to keep her
in the dark about his marriage by spending part of the night with
her, then leaving, presumably returning home to his wife—a juggling act for which investigators expressed a grudging admiration.
"I was just his good-time bimbo," she would later say, still bitter
years after they had parted. "It was the most humiliating experience
of my life."

Detectives Arce and Petroski could see she had never felt comfortable questioning Bill. He was older, an authority figure, a savior
to her in so many ways. And, also, Leasure had that way of quietly
listening and asking questions that encouraged openness in others
while at the same time discouraging any probing of his thoughts
and feelings. Only in the month or so before Leasure's arrest had
she finally begun to doubt his intentions. And even then, she had
accepted his vow that she was the only woman in his life.

Every time she had tried to challenge him on his distant ways
and reluctance to show any firm commitment to her, he would
break down and cry, begging her not to pressure him. When she
asked why he would disappear for weeks, then show up unannounced for sex, Leasure would exclaim that he faced death in the
streets daily. He had a crazy ex-girlfriend plaguing him, threatening
to ruin him. "And now you're starting, too," he would complain,
his eyes wet. "I can't take the pressure." Irene would end up begging him for forgiveness, not realizing until later that Leasure had
turned the tables on her, turning the true victim of their relationship into the heavy.[10]

The police didn't need Irene to tell them of her close relationship with Leasure. The contents of his locker had told them that
much. In his personal phone book, Irene's phone number and address were listed under a disguised name, so that no one else could
recognize it as a woman. (Paulette de los Reyes was listed in a similar manner—as "Paul.") And police had, indeed, discovered pho-

tos of Irene Wong in Leasure's locker, just as he had worriedly suggested might happen to Jon Herrington. There was one color snapshot of Bill in his deep blue LAPD uniform, hugging a slim and attractive Irene as they stood before a police squad car. The second picture showed Irene vigorously polishing Leasure's souped-up World War II training plane in its hangar at Whiteman Airport north of L.A. And picture number three was the one Leasure undoubtedly had feared most that his wife might see: Irene Wong, naked and brown from the sun, languidly stretched out for Bill's camera on a double bed in a richly appointed ship's cabin— "his" *Santine*. Leasure had kept the photos in a place where he could look at them or show them off whenever he wished, while remaining safe from discovery by his wife.

Yet throughout their six years together, Irene told the FBI and LAPD, she found nothing surprising about Leasure's ability to buy boats, planes, and Corvettes, to take her to the Cayman Islands, or to consider buying beachfront property in Belize. "He was frugal with his money and could have saved large amounts of his salary," she told police.[11]

If this partial testimonial disappointed investigators, they were pleased when Irene produced the canceled checks and other bank records showing how transactions apparently related to boat thefts were filtered through her account, always in amounts under ten thousand dollars. Cash transactions over ten thousand trigger reports to the Internal Revenue Service—by splitting a fifty-thousand-dollar transfer between Ralph Gerard and Bill Leasure into seven separate transactions, these telltale reports were avoided.

Irene also turned over to LAPD Internal Affairs investigators the French-English Canadian cookbooks, toaster, pressure cooker, and other household items Bill had given her years before. They soon were identified as property last seen aboard the stolen Canadian yacht *Peggy Rose II*.

When the investigators asked her if she could testify against Bill, Irene said she'd rather not. "But he used me. He lied to me. I'll do whatever I have to do."

Two months later, when Arce and Petroski saw Irene Wong's statements, they realized she probably had no knowledge of the murders—she didn't even know the yachts were stolen, when, from their point of view, only the most naive of people would have failed to suspect Leasure of questionable financial dealings. Still, they were struck by a few key details Irene had mentioned that corroborated Dennis France's tale of crimes with Leasure.

For one, Irene recited the tale of Big John and his security guard friend, Louis Sandidge, beating a wino to death at the Pioneer Market. She said Leasure had spoken of hiring someone to falsely testify on Big John and Louis's behalf. Her story exactly matched France's—and LAPD records on the case.

She also told of Bill introducing her to a slovenly welder named Dennis. She didn't know his last name, but there was no question it was France. Leasure told her that Dennis's son had a clubfoot, and that Dennis "took a knife to his doctor" for mistreating the son. Other witnesses would relate the same, apparently apocryphal, story about France.

Later, Irene mentioned to Arce and Petroski that Leasure drove her in his police car to Art Smith's house several times. She hadn't known Art's wife had been murdered, but she did remember hearing him complain about his wife and the divorce they were going through—which, he said, was costing him "a bundle." The homicide detectives thought that point helped corroborate France's statements about Art's motive for murder, however slightly.

Even more interesting to Arce and Petroski were the phone calls Leasure had made to Irene. Bill had called her from jail and begged her to dispose of any records of his use of her bank account. Cut them up and flush them, she recalled Leasure telling her. To the suspicious minds of detectives, these requests could only be made by a guilty man.

Yet, more important to Leasure—and, perhaps, what hurt Irene the most—was his plea that she tell no one about their relationship or her pregnancy. No one must know, he told her—ignorant of the fact that she had already been visited by the FBI. Above all else, she recalled Bill pleading, don't reveal our relationship to Betsy.

Assistant City Attorney Betsy Mogul was the final piece of the puzzle confronting the homicide detectives when they examined the inconsistencies of Leasure's life and personality assembled by Internal Affairs. A successful and powerful senior prosecutor for the city, known for her tough stance on crime, she even had lectured LAPD officers on correct legal procedures. Mogul was an unlikely conspirator. Then again, as Chief Daryl Gates would later put it, she had shared a life and a home with Leasure, and she was neither blind nor stupid. "You have a lot of miscellaneous stuff lying around, you've got to ask for an explanation," the LAPD chief remarked in one press account. "My wife would."[12]

Some of the property from aboard the stolen yachts was found in what the police decided was Betsy's home office, in their living room, and in other common space shared by Leasure and Mogul—it was not just confined to Leasure's workshop and garage, where Betsy seldom, if ever, ventured. Some of the stolen property was found piled in boxes stenciled "Special Operations Unit," the division of the City Attorney's Office in which Mogul worked. Two of the policemen who searched the Leasure house had written afterwards, "The amount and location of the property involved dictated that Betsy Leasure [Mogul] knew of its presence. William Leasure was found to have kept financial records regarding the vessels and autos. One such document was found to have 'Betsy owes me' written across the top."

But Betsy, in conversations with her boss, City Attorney James Hahn, convinced him she was innocent. To Hahn, she seemed surprised and crushed by the allegations against her husband—not to mention the revelations about her "Billy's" girlfriend. Later, she would become her husband's champion, insisting not only on her own innocence, but on his. At the time, though, it appeared that the two might be on the verge of splitting up.[13]

Betsy Mogul, not surprisingly, was devastated and confused by her husband's arrest. In three successive searches, openly hostile teams of policemen had arrived at her home and, from her point of view, ransacked her privacy and her possessions. Detectives began showing up at her workplace, questioning friends and fellow workers about her character. The police department she had worked with day in and day out as a prosecutor for years now seemed bent on her destruction. Acquaintances, friends, and relatives throughout California were called and questioned about her life-style and activities. She eventually took the public stance that Leasure was being framed. Although a marital separation agreement was drawn up within months of Leasure's arrest and the revelation of his affairs, no divorce papers were filed. Instead, Mogul stayed with the marriage, and became a harsh critic of the LAPD's and the District Attorney's tactics.

"They formed an entire Betsy Mogul task force," she would later say. "They wanted to find something on me, desperately. But they couldn't."

Investigators at LAPD didn't buy any of her protests of innocence. Early in the case—even before Dennis France came along—Deputy Chief Barry Wade had warned Betsy's boss about her possible involvement in Leasure's crimes. He made it clear the department wanted Mogul barred from handling criminal cases—a move City Attorney Hahn initially refused to take because of his belief in Betsy's innocence.

In fact, there was no hard evidence linking Betsy to any criminal acts. The page from Leasure's notebook that mentioned Betsy was strange, perhaps suspicious, but not in itself incriminating. It read:

BETSY OWES ME

DMV Reg.	2 84 Vettes	$565.
El Toro Glass	" "	$350.
2—84 Vettes		$10,000
2 Batteries M.B.Z & Vette		$84.
VCR (s)		$250.
"T" Bird—Dennis		$500.
84 Vette—Dennis		$500.

To Detective Tom King, the page clearly demonstrated Betsy's involvement in Leasure's stolen cars, VCRs, and other chicanery. But others, including a prosecutor assigned to the case, would eventually interpret the notebook entry as a possible reference to old Corvettes Leasure had refurbished on Betsy's behalf. Everyone knew she watched his spending like a hawk, and that he often would have to come to her, hat in hand, for a loan to buy car equipment. Perhaps he had let her invest in some of the Corvettes. In that context, the "Betsy Owes Me" entry would be completely innocent.

At the time of its discovery, however, the police thought otherwise. The two detectives assigned to investigate Mogul, Sergeant Larry Hinrichs and Detective Al Brethour, did little to conceal their belief in her guilt as they questioned her friends and co-workers. "How could Betsy not have known? What's going on here?" they began virtually all of their interviews, as they flashed evidence photos of stolen property taken from the Leasure home. And yet, even with that suggestive investigative technique, the vast majority of people LAPD investigators questioned about Betsy still argued in favor of her innocence. If Bill Leasure was a crook, they said, Betsy Mogul probably didn't know about it, no matter how bad things looked.

"I think these two people had totally separate existences to a great extent," former Assistant City Attorney Kay Kuns, the Skipper's sister, told the detectives. Kuns said Mogul frequently complained of Leasure's secretive ways. "She said, 'I'm so damned mad at Bill, because he won't bring home his work schedule . . . I don't know if he's off a day until he's off that day.'

"It's not real conducive to sharing a lot of time with your husband, particularly when you don't share it anyway because of his job. . . . There were weekends when Bill was supposedly working, in hindsight, he probably was with his mistress."

Catherine Vale, at one time Betsy's supervisor at the City Attorney's Office, told the investigators she was confident Mogul had no idea what her husband was up to. Devastated and in tears, Mogul—whom Vale described as "one of the toughest birds in the office"—had said, "It can't be so. It can't be so. This can't be happening."

"It shocked the hell out of me to even think that quiet little Bill Leasure could be involved in these things," Vale said. "I will stake my life on the proposition, as crazy as it is, that she didn't know anything about it."

Like Kay Kuns, Vale saw Betsy and Bill as leading separate lives. "I don't think Betsy knew anything about anything her husband might have been doing," Vale told Hinrichs and Brethour. ". . . He would be gone for long periods of time. So far as Betsy was concerned, he had an absolute right to be away, she never got on his case about that. . . . She's deeply in love with her husband. She absolutely adores him. She views many of his little escapades . . . with the kind of indulgent affection that you would see in a mother speaking about her teenage kid."

But Vale's husband, Bob, who was a friend of Leasure's, had a slightly different view—it was not so much Betsy overlooking things as being deceived outright by her unassuming husband. He recalled Leasure saying, "Betsy doesn't know half the things I do. . . . If Betsy ever knew I had a couple thousand dollars extra, she'd want to put it into some sort of savings account or securities."

"In a courtroom," Bob Vale said, "it's pretty hard to fool Betsy on anything. . . . But she believed in Bill."

Friend after friend expressed similar opinions to Hinrichs and Brethour. They didn't really think Leasure was guilty, but if he was, they were even more sure Mogul was either deceived, or blinded, by her husband's easy way of explaining things and deflecting questions.

One assistant city attorney and casual friend of Betsy's, Christine Patterson, was less charitable. Mogul was known for her moralistic approach to the law and her intolerance of any rule breaking, Patterson said, yet Mogul nevertheless had used her prosecutor's credentials to sneak into the jail to see Leasure. Patterson said Mogul should be fired for that breach of ethics.

"I can't make up my own mind whether or not she has suffered the world's greatest injustice from a spouse," Patterson said, "or whether she's leading some double life, that they'll make TV movies about. I don't know."[14]

Then there was Dennis France's story about a meeting he claimed to have had at Denny's restaurant with Betsy shortly after Leasure's arrest. He said she questioned him about guns and other crimes—writing out notes rather than speaking aloud, then burning the notes in an ashtray. One note asked, *Do you know about the cars?* Another: *Do you know about the boats?* All of this, of course, was based on France's word, which was always open to question. To the homicide detectives, it suggested guilt on Betsy's part, but who knew? It didn't fit the picture of Betsy Mogul everyone else painted, but then again, neither did a murderous Bill Leasure fit his image at LAPD. Leasure and Mogul would later brand France's story a lie. But even if you believed France, what he described did not constitute a crime, the detectives knew.

There was only one certainty about Betsy Mogul, Detectives Arce and Petroski decided: They could expect no help from her. Whether that made her an accomplice, or a loyal wife, they were not prepared to say.

• • •

Betsy stood by me so far. If she stuck by me through this, she'll stick by me through anything. Which makes me feel even worse about [Irene Wong]. I'd never do anything like that again.

I feel guilty over the harm that's been caused to Betsy's career. I wish I could undo that. They've pursued her and said terrible things about her, and none of it's true. She's never, ever done anything wrong. . . . Really, I was more concerned about her than I ever was about my murder charge.

• • •

As they finished reviewing the Internal Affairs investigation reports, Detectives Arce and Petroski came to feel certain that Leasure had been involved in yacht thefts and other property crimes. No other explanation fit the evidence as far as they could see. Obviously, he was not who he seemed to be at LAPD or anywhere else—not with his wife, his girlfriend, his buddies. Was it then such a leap, they asked themselves, to think Mild Bill might be capable of worse crimes than theft? Of murder, perhaps?

So they settled on a portrait of Leasure as a man who led a bizarre double life, a man whose two halves were completely opposed to one another, and whose driving motivations were making money, deceiving people, and accumulating power over others. His treatment of Irene Wong, the finances he kept secret from his wife, his request to Jon Herrington to clean out his locker, and abundant other instances of his manipulative skills seemed to show that he was willing to use people without remorse, concealing his actions with a mask of mildness and good cheer.

But in all that, Detectives Arce and Petroski found nothing to support the charges of murder. In all the mountain of papers in the Leasure Room, they had found little to disprove Dennis France's story—but even less to corroborate him. They were faced with the same problem as before: How would they prove the words of an admitted murderer?

Finally, after consulting with the D.A. assigned to the case, they decided on a risky strategy, one that would put their star witness under even greater pressure and scrutiny. Nervous, uneducated, semiliterate Dennis France was going to become their undercover agent. Wearing body wires and hidden microphones, France would try to get Leasure and the other conspirators to convict themselves.

CHAPTER 15

To the homicide detectives' surprise, Dennis France immersed himself in his role of undercover agent with unexpected aplomb. The same police groupie glee he had demonstrated while riding in Leasure's patrol car or listening to crime dispatches over his bootleg LAPD Rover radio made him a willing sidekick and pupil for Detectives Arce and Petroski.

France's eagerness to betray his old friends Bill, Forty-four, and the others, along with his startlingly effective performance as an undercover operative, was invaluable to the detectives. But it also left them feeling slightly queasy about their star witness.

If Bill Leasure had led a double life, Dennis France proved himself no slacker in that area, either. Right before the detectives' eyes, he became a chameleon.

Deputy District Attorney James E. Koller, however, freshly assigned to the case and eager for new breaks, considered France's acting talents an unequivocal godsend. Anything less, and the Leasure case—the case of a career—would have stalled. And so it fell to Koller to "script" France's performances after he was enlisted to work undercover.

Three days after Dennis France came to the police with a halting story of murder and a plea for immunity, the deputy D.A. had returned from a brief vacation in the mountains with his wife and children, then assumed primary responsibility for the newly expanded Leasure case. He initially found it an exhilarating process. "I'm having the time of my life," he would come home and tell his wife day after long day of trying to "think like Bill Leasure."

Bill Leasure, in his LAPD blues. He was known to visit his hit-man friends Dennis France and Dennis Winebaugh, in uniform and with his black-and-white police cruiser, while on duty.

Top: Leasure's garage, piled high with property taken from stolen yachts. Paintings, fishing gear, kitchen utensils, clothing, weapons —anything imaginable, both valuable and worthless—were found salted away here when officers from Leasure's own department arrived with a search warrant. *Middle:* Another view of the Leasure eight-car garage. The white, vintage Studebaker had been reported stolen by its true owner. Leasure claimed he bought it legitimately, but police computer printouts he had sneaked out of LAPD showed he knew the car was stolen. *Bottom:* The Leasure house in the Northridge section of Los Angeles. Its innocuous exterior belied the stolen property and other evidence of crimes found inside.

Left: The yacht **Billy G,** before it was stolen by Leasure and Kuns and transformed into **Thunderbolt.** *Right:* The stolen yacht **Billy G** was altered and transformed into the **Thunderbolt,** which Leasure claimed to own with another police officer at LAPD. Both men were charged with stealing the boat and committing insurance fraud.

The owner of the yacht **Billy G** passed out these flyers in an attempt to recover his stolen boat. A copy was found in Leasure's police locker.

Left: Anne Smith and her husband, Arthur Gayle Smith, who would be charged with hiring Bill Leasure to kill his wife. *Right:* Anne Marie Smith, opening a birthday present a few years before her murder.

Anne and Art Smith, and Anne's two children from her first marriage.

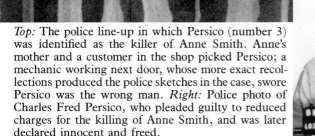

Top: The police line-up in which Persico (number 3) was identified as the killer of Anne Smith. Anne's mother and a customer in the shop picked Persico; a mechanic working next door, whose more exact recollections produced the police sketches in the case, swore Persico was the wrong man. *Right:* Police photo of Charles Fred Persico, who pleaded guilty to reduced charges for the killing of Anne Smith, and was later declared innocent and freed.

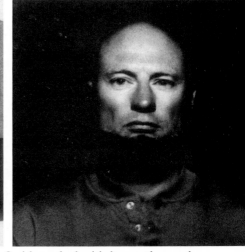

Left: Dee Ann's House of Beauty, where Anne Smith worked with her mother, and the scene of her murder. *Right:* Robert Denzil Kuns, "The Skipper," a paroled bank robber befriended by Leasure, who perfected a nearly foolproof method of stealing millions of dollars worth of yachts.

Tony Reyes, who once played with the big bands, was shotgunned to death on September 10, 1981, after concluding a late-night set at the Chez Nora Bar in the Sherman Oaks section of Los Angeles.

The hit man Dennis France's Chevy Nova, parked beneath a sequoia tree bridge in Northern California. The Nova was green with stripes until it was used as a getaway car in the killing of Anne Smith. It was painted reddish orange and used in the Tony Reyes killing.

Paulette de los Reyes was arrested in May 1987 for hiring Bill Leasure to kill her ex-husband, jazz musician Tony Reyes, six years earlier. Through a plea bargain and agreement to testify for the prosecution, her charges eventually were reduced to solicitation to commit murder.

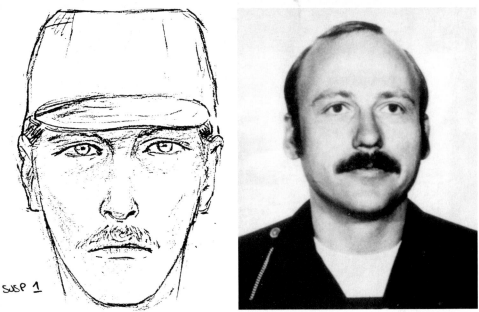

Left: Police sketch of one of the two men seen outside Dee Ann's House of Beauty at the time of the Anne Smith murder. The witness said the thin-faced man with the cap was the shooter. The drawing resembles Leasure, who was alleged to have driven the getaway car, rather than firing the fatal shot. Dennis France, the gunman in the Smith killing, who was a protected witness and could not be photographed, more closely resembled the witness's sketch of the driver. The prosecutor in the case suggested the witness simply confused the positions of the two men. *Right:* William Ernest Leasure, in his official LAPD identification photo.

The gold badge of a veteran Los Angeles Department officer. Leasure's badge number was 3047.

Betsy Mogul, a city prosecutor and Bill Leasure's wife, was arrested for perjury in February 1987. She was accused of filing a false document with the state in order to avoid taxes on a used Mercedes, which she had purchased from murder and yacht theft suspect Arthur Smith. Mogul was fired by the Los Angeles City Attorney, but she was acquitted of perjury after Leasure swore he had falsified the tax document alone.

Detectives Addison "Bud" Arce and Henry "Hank" Petroski of the Los Angeles Police Department Robbery-Homicide Division spent nearly two years investigating Bill Leasure.

Deputy District Attorney James Koller, the prosecutor assigned to the Leasure case.

Orchestrating a probe of unsolved murders, pushing police investigation and surveillance techniques to the edge of legality, and flirting with coercion and entrapment without stepping over the line seemed like the most exciting prospect imaginable for the then thirty-five-year-old prosecutor. Koller already occupied a high-profile position in the District Attorney's Special Investigations Division, which specialized in prosecuting government corruption and police misconduct. The Leasure investigation, a case drawing considerable press attention as potentially the worst example of corruption in modern LAPD history, presented a once-in-a-lifetime opportunity, as Koller saw it.

He huddled with Detectives Arce and Petroski in his seventeenth-floor office at the county Criminal Courts Building. With the three of them hatching and discarding ideas in hours-long sessions, Koller began scribbling out a file full of scripts for Dennis France to use for cover stories as he tried to trick Leasure and the others into incriminating themselves. With the right script and a convincing performance, they decided, France could crack the case open.

Taking such an active role in an investigation, as Koller did from the outset, is unusual for a prosecutor. In most cases, a district attorney is handed a completed investigation by a police agency, then uses the resulting witnesses and evidence in court—a separation of process so complete that it sometimes makes for misunderstandings and frosty relationships between the District Attorney's office and LAPD.

Koller, however, took more of a hands-on approach to his cases, not because he was a frustrated cop at heart, but because he felt it was his duty to become involved. Although much of his work at the D.A.'s Special Investigations Division involved prosecuting dirty cops—a surefire method of engendering ill will among policemen—he still was able to maintain good working rapport with LAPD detectives through his willingness to get his hands dirty. He would share their long, boring hours of surveillance and stakeout, then retire with them to the "Code 7," the seedy tavern near Parker Center favored by policemen, to continue hashing out the case over beers or whiskey.

Koller had been supervising the stolen boat and car cases against Leasure almost from their inception. Back when Internal Affairs investigators found a truckload of stolen property at the Leasure home, they realized the legal expertise of a prosecutor would be essential to avoid mistakes, and Koller had drawn the assignment. Indeed, he had to work hard to extricate LAPD from an embarrassing legal screw-up almost from the start: With every top official at LAPD looking over I.A.D.'s collective shoulder, the officers who wrote the first search warrant for Leasure's house had failed to list his garage as a place they wanted to search. As a result of this carelessness, all of the stolen property found there could have been thrown out of court. The yacht case would have been decimated.

Koller, however, persuaded a judge to rule that the search of the garage was valid, relying on the newly adopted "good-faith exception" that permits police errors so long as they are inadvertent. "That search was disastrous," Koller would later say. "It almost destroyed our case. We're still using it as an example in training courses to show how *not* to prepare a search warrant."

Koller rode herd on the Leasure investigation after that, and by the time Dennis France came along, he was immersed in the life of Bill Leasure. Had he not been on vacation, the task of dealing with France's request for immunity would have fallen to him, rather than to colleague Robert Jorgenson. As it was, he was happy to have been absolved of responsibility for that unpopular call. Once the murder case opened, he became even more involved in the day-to-day investigation, becoming, in effect, a third detective, joining forces with Arce and Petroski to choreograph the intricate legal ballet France was about to perform.

The targets were easy enough to choose: Art Smith, Paulette de los Reyes, Dennis Winebaugh, Betsy Mogul, and, of course, Bill Leasure. If France was telling the truth about their involvement, Koller had to assume they would be nervous over Leasure's arrest up north, and that they would be suspicious if Dennis France suddenly just popped by for a heart-to-heart. He decided France should telephone each of the targets, one by one. Each would be led to believe they were the only one France was calling. And the script Koller crafted for his "friendly," the term police prefer to the more pejorative "snitch," was designed to allay suspicions while simultaneously prodding incriminating statements. "Tell them you're scared because some homicide detectives came around to question you," Koller instructed. "Tell them you're worried Leasure might rat on the rest of you. Then ask to meet, so you can get your stories straight."

Throughout the telephone conversations, a tape recorder would capture every word. If any of the targets agreed to meet him, France would don a body wire, and a special van with remote recording equipment, parked nearby, would pick up the conversations. If it worked, France's story would be corroborated in the best way possible—through the words of the very people he had accused of participating in theft and murder. What could be more damning?

Dennis France nodded and smiled when the plan was explained to him, not bothered a bit at the prospect of lying to and betraying his friends and benefactors. "Just tell me what to say," he said. "And let's get goin'."[1]

Arthur Gayle Smith was targeted first. There was no particular strategy at work in singling him out, other than the general consensus that, of all the players in the case, Smith could be most likely to spill his guts and sell Leasure out if the police could uncover enough evidence against him.

Certainly he had the most to lose. While Paulette de los Reyes had gone broke after Tony Reyes's death, with a lost home and a string of failed business ventures behind her, Art Smith had prospered since his wife was murdered six years earlier. He had continued to operate his profitable insurance business for years. He had sold the house in South Pasadena he had fought so hard to keep from Anne and moved to the neighboring town of Alhambra. He had remarried shortly after Anne's death, then divorced, then married his fourth wife, the twin sister of a childhood sweetheart. Though he was not on friendly terms with Anne's family, he had stayed close to her daughter, Christine, who lived with her husband next door to Art in a house he rented to them. The investigators considered him ripe for a setup.

At 10:00 in the morning on August 27, 1986, nineteen days into the murder case, Koller, Arce, and Petroski arrived at France's most recent abode, a small frame house on a tidy suburban street in Downey. They briefed him on Koller's favored script: France was to call Smith at home, tell him a homicide detective had left a message asking to talk to him, and say he was afraid. Maybe Bill was talking, France was supposed to suggest. To add to the verisimilitude, they decided to walk France to a street-corner phone booth near the house, with plenty of traffic noise in the background, so France could tell Art he was afraid his home phone was tapped and that he was reluctant to speak freely for fear of being recorded. Koller told him he should not immediately blurt out details of the murder, but that he should back into the subject slowly. Art Smith already had his guard up. Detective Tom King and other LAPD investigators had repeatedly questioned him about yachts after Leasure's arrest, and the *Santine* had been impounded. He knew he was under scrutiny, and would no doubt be highly suspicious of France. Just hint at the murder, Koller instructed. If France was telling the truth, a hint would be all they needed. Smith would provide the rest.

The phone rang thirteen times at Art Smith's house before someone picked up and brought Art. France impatiently counted off the electronic bleats for his audience. Passersby stared at the strange assemblage—three men in suits towering over a short, stout, T-shirt-clad man at a pay phone.

"Hello, Art?" France said in his oddly rich voice, speaking naturally and with warmth, as if addressing an old friend. "This is Dennis. I don't know if you remember me or not. With, ah, Bill?"

Smith mulled it over a moment, repeating France's last words. "With Bill."

"Yeah." France looked at his three law enforcement companions, who were listening to the conversation through the speaker on their recording device.

"Which Bill?" Art asked.

"Leasure."

"Oh, I know. Yeah."

One issue had just been resolved. Contrary to future assertions by Smith, he did know Dennis France, at least in passing.

"Okay, you know Bill's in jail?"

"Yeah."

"Okay, ah," France hesitated, exchanging a look with his coaches, then pushing on, once again as natural and believable in his lies as an accomplished actor or con man. "I had some people come out to my house and they left a business card, for some, ah, robbery-homicide thing. . . . And I don't know what they wanna talk to me about. But I'm scared, and I don't have anybody I can go to, you know? And I don't know if Bill's talking or not."

Art's voice revealed no surprise at France's words. He said, "I have not talked to Bill. And, all I know, you know, is his wife called me and said that he was in jail. . . . And they were down to my boat, and my boat has been confiscated."

Yes, France said, but the policeman seeking him out now wasn't interested in boats. "This is about somethin' else," he hinted. " 'Cause this is robbery homicide. . . . And I'm, I'm in a phone both, because I'm afraid to talk on my phone."

"Yeah. Yeah, well, it's not good to talk on mine, either," Smith agreed, leaving an opening for France to suggest they meet in person to discuss matters. Smith agreed—later in the evening, about 8:00, they would rendezvous, he suggested.

Still circling around his subject, France repeatedly stressed the fact that the police detective wanted to talk to him about a murder, not about boats. He pretended not to be able to pronounce Petroski's name—instead, he painstakingly spelled it out from the business card he claimed he found on his door, and then described a note on its back as saying the detective wanted to see him at 9:00 the next morning. France complained that he was afraid to go to the meeting alone, but that he couldn't afford an attorney, "like I told Betsy." Mostly, though, he was just plain frightened, he told Smith. "I'm not goin' to lie to you," he said with an earnest tremor in his voice. "I'm scared."

None of this was scripted—it was France ad-libbing, and doing a job so convincing that Koller, Arce, and Petroski found themselves exchanging expressions of wonderment. The bit about spelling out Petroski's name was a beautiful touch. France's reading ability, apparently, had come a long way.

Then France let loose a little bit. "I would just like to find out who knows what, and what is going on, you know? And, I don't know what Bill has said about the beauty shop, or anything, you know? I really don't."

Art Smith, the man whose wife had been gunned down in a beauty parlor six years before, did not gasp, did not ask France what he was talking about, did not express bewilderment of any kind at the mention of Bill talking about "the beauty shop"—as an innocent man might be expected to do. Instead, he told France, most emphatically, "Don't say any more."[2]

In Koller's mind, that remark nearly nailed shut the case against Smith. Who but a man with something to hide would say that? A little more, Koller figured, and he'd have what prosecutors like to call a "slam dunk"—a case so firm that there was no way to miss scoring a conviction.

France and Smith closed their conversation by agreeing to meet that night outside an International House of Pancakes restaurant in Pasadena, near Smith's house. Smith was calm and unconcerned throughout the conversation—closing the phone call with a casual, "Talk to you later." With luck, the detectives would capture on their tape recorder a more direct admission by Smith at the pancake place, something that would cinch the case and clearly corroborate France's story.

But it was not to be. France sat outside the coffee shop for hours that night, the detectives nearby, cramped and cranky in a van, sipping cold coffee and grumbling. Smith never showed. His new wife answered the phone when France finally called back. She said Art had gone out with his daughter that night. In the days that followed, Smith never returned France's increasingly desperate messages.

Still, the tape already in hand would be quite damaging if it were played before a jury. They pronounced their first "phone stiff" in the case a success. That's what France had just performed, a phone stiff. The expression dated back decades at LAPD, where the technique was originally likened to "stiffing" someone for a bill in a restaurant. In this case, the stakes were infinitely higher: One conspirator was "stiffing" another into accepting responsibility for murder. The bill could run as high as the gas chamber.

That same day, France tried to stiff his old buddy Dennis Winebaugh, too. The detectives joked that he was going for a "two-fer."

His orders were to get Winebaugh to admit killing the tortilla magnate Gilberto Cervantes, and to say the contract was made at the behest of Bill Leasure and Paulette de los Reyes. France pronounced himself ready, and they tried to reach Winebaugh that same afternoon while they waited for the night's appointment at IHOP.

There was a problem, though—Forty-four Magnum no longer had a telephone. When France dialed, he could only reach the phone company's mechanical woman's voice, droning endlessly that the number was out of service. Winebaugh had ripped the phone out of the wall in a fit of anger, he would later say.

Undeterred, France and his law enforcement escorts drove to a Western Union office and had a Mailgram dispatched to Winebaugh's home in Del City, Oklahoma, just outside Oklahoma City. "You must call me," the message said—composed by Koller, but signed by France. "It's an emergency." Winebaugh did eventually call back, and after much telephone tag and several missed messages, France got Winebaugh's phone number at work—a car dealership in Oklahoma, where Forty-four worked as a night security guard.

On the evening of September 10, 1986, the fifth anniversary of Tony Reyes's death, the Winebaugh phone stiff began. France placed the call from Arce and Petroski's desk in the homicide squad room, the two detectives and Jim Koller at his side. France was supposed to say he was calling from a pay phone.

"Remember," Arce told France as the informant dialed. "Don't talk to us once it starts. You talk."

"Right, I won't," France assured them.

The conversation with Winebaugh started then, with Winebaugh answering, "Officer Dennis" in that unmistakable midwestern country-boy drawl, and France joking that the greeting scared him for a minute. They both laughed. Their words were jovial, warm, just two old friends jawing about old times, hunting, guns, their jobs, their families. Winebaugh wanted to know how France's ailing son was doing. Scoliosis, France said. Had to get two steel bars surgically attached on either side of his spine. It was a bravura performance. If anything, France was more assured and convincing than he had been with Art Smith two weeks earlier.

With the pleasantries out of the way, France gradually turned the conversation toward murder, ensnaring his friend in a web of admissions. First France expressed concern about Winebaugh's ex-wife, Tammy. Would she talk? Did she know anything?

"Yeah, she knows I did a hit," Winebaugh said, the sort of frank admission that prosecutors kill for. "She doesn't know when or anything else."

"She doesn't know it was Gilbert?" France asked.

"Don't say no names," Winebaugh urged—an echo of Art Smith's warning, and one that had Koller grinning.

"Huh?"

"Don't say any names!" Winebaugh repeated.

Then France began his tale of woe. The police had come out to his house, he said. They wanted his fingerprints, his guns, pictures of him from ten years ago. "They asked me if I, I knew you, they asked if I knew, uh, Bill Leasure, they asked me if I knew Paulette."

Winebaugh told him not to worry. No one could identify them, no gun could be traced, no witnesses could be produced. Neither of them could have left any fingerprints, he said. The only place he had ever left fingerprints was at the house of a woman named Paula (his name for Paulette de los Reyes), with whom, he said, he had an affair. Bill Leasure had introduced them, Winebaugh recalled. "He set me up with her, he told me she was a good piece of ass," Winebaugh said.

Throughout this attempt to ease France's professed worries, Winebaugh did not come out and describe the murder explicitly. But his next words would leave no doubt as to what he was talking about.

"There could be absolutely no prints of any kind . . . and if you remember right, I had gloves on."

"That's right, you did, didn't you?" France said. "I forgot all about you wearing gloves. That day was so screwed up for me."

"Yeah," Winebaugh agreed, "it was your first one." And they both chuckled.

This statement was especially telling to the detectives and Koller—it seemed to be a direct admission by Winebaugh of his role in the "first" murder, Gilberto Cervantes. It would fall to others to point out that it also suggested France had lied about a key element of his story—he had claimed in his interrogations that he had no idea Winebaugh was going to kill Cervantes when they drove to San Gabriel. He had said he thought Forty-four was just going to beat someone up. Now Winebaugh seemed to be saying France knew all along, and had been nervous at the prospect. France added to that impression by saying:

"Yeah, yeah, I was so damn scared." But then he drew Winebaugh further along in his admissions. "Let me ask you something else, too. Do you remember when we were sitting on the corner?"

"Yeah?"

"Okay."

"The woman and the dog?" Winebaugh asked, without further prompting, recalling the old woman described earlier by France—and by the old San Gabriel police reports.

"Right."

"There's absolutely no way she can ID," Winebaugh said. ". . . Nope, no goddamn way. Do you realize how many years that's been, Dennis? That old woman's got to be eighty years old, seventy years old now. She's senile."

This small detail held immense importance for Arce, Petroski, and Koller. There was no way Winebaugh could have known about that woman unless he had been there. And he had not been prompted by France. Rather, it had come out naturally, in the way two old friends might reminisce about an old shared adventure, one they had retold so many times that very little needed to be said. With that, Koller felt he had enough to convict Winebaugh then and there. And France's credibility had soared.

But then some ambiguities crept into the conversation. They had Winebaugh nailed, but what about their primary target? Where was the evidence against Leasure? Just because France was telling the truth about Winebaugh didn't mean he was telling the truth about the traffic officer's involvement. And when France zeroed in on that all-important area, the results were, once again, less than convincing.

"The only other thing I worry about," France said, "is what, what . . . Bill Leasure and what Paulette says if they, you know . . ."

"Bill does know—" Winebaugh began to say, then was interrupted by France.

"Me and you have to get our story straight for ourselves," France said.

"Bill knows nothing for certain," Winebaugh said, seemingly contradicting what he had started to say a moment earlier. Koller and the detectives listened more closely. This was not what they had expected to hear.

"Yeah? Didn't he pay you something?"

"He turned me on to her," Winebaugh said, an apparent reference to Leasure introducing him to Paulette. ". . . For a piece of ass and that's all. The rest of it is hearsay. . . . He don't know for sure. He was told, but I didn't tell him. . . . She did. She made up the story and told him."

France hammered at the point. He had already told the detectives that he saw Leasure give Winebaugh an envelope of money after the Cervantes slaying. He repeated that for Winebaugh.

"No, he didn't give me anything," Winebaugh insisted. Was this proof that France had lied? Or was it, Arce, Petroski, and Koller wondered, merely Winebaugh's unwillingness to make any more explicit admissions over the phone? Eventually they decided to believe the latter.

France then described—in roundabout terms—the hit on Tony Reyes, comparing it to the Cervantes killing. "The second one, you know, Bill Leasure was with me. . . . He had my job and I had your job. He drove for me. And I stepped out." Meaning Leasure waited in the car as France shot Tony, just as France had waited in the car while Winebaugh took care of Gilberto.

Winebaugh hastily cut him off. "Yeah, okay, that's enough."

The point, France said, was that he was worried Leasure might now try to inform on them in both murders in order to extricate himself from jail.

"He didn't have nothing to do with it," Winebaugh explained of the Cervantes killing, "other than introducing me to her. . . . The first time, he's got nothing . . . 'cause he wasn't there. The second time he was there and he may make a deal. It's very, very unlikely, but even if he does, he's still got nothing. I mean, it's his word against yours. You were somewhere else."

This statement by Winebaugh was more to the detectives' liking. Only later would they notice that, once again, the killing of Tony was referred to as the "second one"—omitting Anne Smith, and, once again, raising doubt about portions of Dennis France's account of Leasure's crimes.

Then Winebaugh suggested a story line for France, to explain why Leasure might lie about him being involved in murder: "He's mad at you for screwing around with this woman of his. That's all you know."

". . . Was she a good piece of ass?" France asked.

"Real good," Winebaugh assured him.

"Heh, heh, heh. Okay, so I can tell them that truthfully, then, she was a good piece of ass."

Then they began talking about guns and hunting and family again, and how Winebaugh really wanted France to visit him in Oklahoma, with France agreeing heartily. Suddenly a beeping sound halted their conversation. As Arce, Petroski, and Koller froze, horrified, the prosecutor's pocket pager went off, signaling a phone message. Koller fumbled frantically to silence the unmistakable beeping sound, and did, after just one beep. But the damage had been done.

"Uh, I hope that wasn't a tape recorder that just whistled," Winebaugh said, sounding shaken.

France didn't miss a beat, thinking faster than the three professionals at his side, who stood by dumbstruck. "No, it wasn't a tape recorder that just whistled because there's nobody." He looked around the homicide squad room, then shut his eyes. "Tell you where I'm at. I'm in a mall and I'm in a phone at a mall and there's no one else around but people working inside the mall."

And that was it. Winebaugh bought it. Someone had just walked by with a beeper or something. And they went on talking, natural and at ease, with Winebaugh bragging about his personal arsenal, asking about France's guns, and even joking about a particularly powerful rifle France owned.

"It's to shoot can," Winebaugh drawled. "Mexi-can, Afri-can." And both of them laughed at the abysmal racist joke.

Slowly, France steered the conversation back to Cervantes and Leasure, but, again, with mixed results.

"I don't know what Bill knew," France said.

"He knows all," Winebaugh pronounced. "But he can prove nothing. . . . It's just hearsay. It's what he thinks. All we have to do is say . . . it's not true. It's our word against his."

The same was true for Paulette, Winebaugh suggested. "She don't know for sure. She didn't see us do it. . . . It's her word against ours. Fuck, I don't know what you're talking about, you're talking about somebody else, it ain't me."

"Yeah," France said earnestly. "Because then that just boils down to me and you, guy, and we're going to watch each other's back."

"You bet," Winebaugh said. "No matter what they say, you don't know what the fuck they're talking about."

Then he urged France to come see him soon. His heart was bad—he had had coronary bypass surgery the year before—and he didn't have long to live, he told his friend. Better make it soon. France heartily promised to come out, knowing, of course, that it would be policemen, not he, who soon would be banging on his friend's front door.

Winebaugh closed the conversation with a pep talk: "It's doubt and fear that nails you. . . . There's only two people that really know what happened, and that's me and you. And that's the only two people in the world."

"I ain't talkin'," France piped in.

"Me neither."

"I, I can't afford to," France added.

"No," Winebaugh agreed, unaware that he had just finished talking himself into a murder charge. "I can't either."[3]

When they hung up—the two killers saying "bye-bye" to one another—Arce, Petroski, and Koller were upbeat. They felt they had Winebaugh, open and shut. He had admitted his role in the Cervantes killing. And he had named Leasure as his connection to Paulette and, by extension, to the plan to hit Cervantes. In the rush of the moment, Winebaugh's denial of receiving payment from Bill, and his curious contention that Bill knew about the murder but could prove nothing, did not seem very significant. They had accumulated more pieces of the puzzle and, once others had been added to the picture, these minor discrepancies wouldn't matter, they figured.

At the same time they were setting up Winebaugh and Smith, the detectives also kept pursuing Paulette de los Reyes. But France's scripted attempts to make contact with her proved fruitless. Message after message produced no response. She had no regular address or phone number, and she moved often, depending upon the favors of men she met in bars to provide housing for her and her son, Aaron, who by then was in high school. A stakeout team had been trying to track down the two of them for weeks, so far unsuccessfully. Paulette had apparently pilfered or squandered her son's seventy-thousand-dollar inheritance settlement from his half-brother, Tony Jr., and she had no clear means of support, so far as the detectives could determine.

An attempt to stiff Betsy Mogul also failed. After repeated calls, France persuaded her to meet him outside the Los Angeles City Hall East Annex, where she worked. France was wired with a microphone, and an LAPD van equipped with video surveillance gear was trained on the building alcove where they met. But Betsy, jumpy and suspicious, had little to say to France, and left after only a few minutes. Certainly nothing she said was incriminating—not at all like the note-burning meeting France had claimed took place.

In truth, the Betsy Mogul task force had come up dry, all suspicion and no evidence. The worst thing Detective Tom King and Internal Affairs could find was a false declaration on a Department of Motor Vehicles form she had signed, which said Betsy Mogul had obtained her aging Mercedes from her father, exempting her from sales tax. The "father" was listed as Arthur Gayle Smith.

Koller put the information aside. Although no one had ever been prosecuted for such a minor offense—the amount in question was, at most, five or six hundred dollars in unpaid taxes—filing such a false document was, technically, perjury. If that was all they could find against Betsy Mogul, they would use it.

In the meantime, the investigative team decided to leave behind, for the moment, the supporting cast of characters, and to turn their efforts toward their prime target: Bill Leasure himself. It was time for a trip up north, to the cool green hills, pastures, vineyards, and small towns that surround the concrete box of the Contra Costa County Jail, Bill Leasure's home since Memorial Day weekend.

It was time for Leasure's good friend Dennis France to pay him a visit.

•   •   •

Art Smith had nothing to do with anything. He would never do anything like this. He's just a really, really nice guy, who's been framed by Dennis France. That conversation with Dennis France that's supposed to be so incriminating doesn't prove a thing. Art Smith was so guilty, he brought his son-in-law along to the meeting that night—and his son-in-law was an Alhambra police officer. Is that what you do if you're guilty of murder? They spotted the LAPD stakeout, realized something was wrong, and left. It's impossible for Art Smith to have been involved in killing Anne.

. . . Dennis Winebaugh has said he's innocent in the Cervantes

case. And Dennis France told the D.A. investigator right after the killing that he shot Gilberto Cervantes, by himself. Now, the tape with Winebaugh sounds pretty bad, but it's possible France did the shooting and Winebaugh drove. Who knows? I think Winebaugh was involved, but all I know is that Winebaugh says he talked to Dennis France another time, and that France said he shot Tony all by himself. Winebaugh says, "Bill's innocent, and I'm not gonna say he's not."

Now if anyone could cut a deal to get off, it would have been Winebaugh. They wanted him to testify against me. But he wouldn't. He's facing life in prison, but he decided to tell the truth, instead. As far as I'm concerned, he's the only one in this case with any principles.

CHAPTER 16

SHORTLY AFTER DENNIS France started working for the police, Bill Leasure had telephoned him from jail. They hadn't spoken in months—not since a week or so before Leasure's arrest—but both men tried to project warmth and reassurance, picking up where they had left off, conversing about wives, jobs, and family. All the while, an LAPD tape recorder spun silently, connected to France's phone.

Leasure apologized for waiting so long to call. He had been reluctant to phone any of his friends after being arrested, he told France, because he was afraid the police would accuse him of rounding up people and concocting a defense. So he had waited sixty days, then called a few close friends like Dennis, confident that enough time had passed to avert any suggestion that he was trying to influence potential witnesses. France said he understood.

When Detectives Arce and Petroski listened to the tape of this conversation, they recognized this claim as a blatant, if casual, lie. This was Leasure's way of making sure his friend didn't feel slighted: I wasn't avoiding you, he was telling Dennis, I didn't call anyone. But the truth was, the detectives knew, Leasure had called Irene Wong shortly after his arrest, and Officer Jon Herrington a few days later, with his request to empty out his locker. Numerous other friends had been called as well, LAPD employees among them. Leasure simply hadn't found it necessary—or wise—to call Dennis France at that time. He only phoned the welder after France, mimicking panic, begged Betsy Mogul to have her husband call as soon as possible.

The story about waiting sixty days might have been a simple

white lie, but it was uttered with conviction and sincerity, and the detectives thought a glimmer of Leasure's supposed hidden personality, the "master manipulator," was peeking through on that tape.

By the time a jailhouse visit was engineered between France and Leasure, the two men had talked on the phone twice. However, France turned on the tape recorder LAPD had installed on his phone for only one of those conversations, he would later claim. "I forgot," he told Arce and Petroski.

In any case, the one telephone conversation he did record sounded innocuous enough. Leasure knew jail phones were often monitored, and he suggested France's phone might be tapped, too. Throughout the conversation, after his apology and explanation for not calling, Leasure repeatedly stressed his innocence and accused the police of persecuting him and all his friends. At times it seemed as if Leasure was delivering a testimonial for himself. Clearly, he assumed others were listening in.

"They think I'm a bad guy, probably," Leasure said at one point. "And they're going to go through everything they can to try to prove it. And you know what, in the end, they're gonna prove I'm a pretty good guy."

"Yeah, yeah," France said, a pillar of support. "Probably will."

"You know, I've been seventeen years and never had a complaint, other than six personnel complaints against me, and they're not, you know, neglect of duty. One of those was because when I broke my glasses and I couldn't go to work, they said I failed to properly notify them. Big deal, you know? . . . And four of those is because I neglected to go down for my monthly shooting. . . . But you know what, I'm one of fifty police officers ever in LAPD, since the day it began, and right now they've got like seventy-five hundred people . . . that can shoot perfect scores."

France dutifully marveled at this feat. Petroski told Arce it made him want to throw up. It was a spiel Leasure would apparently commit to memory and repeat, time and again, almost verbatim: They'll look and look, and in the end, they'll realize what a great guy I am.

Although his standing instruction was to get Leasure to speak about the murders, France seemed oddly reluctant to bring the subject up, and did not even come close to broaching it in over a half hour of conversation. The nearest he came was mentioning two of his old guns that had been seized from Leasure's house. At least with Smith and Winebaugh, he had eventually come around to the subject of murder, after a fashion. But this time, with Leasure, the two friends spoke mostly about France's brother Jerry, with Leasure complaining bitterly about how he had lied about them, falsely linking them to wild and provably false allegations. France even assured Leasure he'd wring Jerry's neck if he could ever find him, giving Leasure an opportunity to demonstrate his peaceful nature.

"You don't want to do anything like that," he chided France. "It'll blow over." Arce and Petroski winced when they heard this— Leasure was sounding like a saint.

Most of the rest of the conversation focused on the stolen yachts. Leasure professed to be a victim in the case, jailed by mistake. "It's all Rob," he said, referring to the man he was arrested with, the Skipper, Robert Kuns. Leasure said he was certain to get off, however, because Kuns promised "he's gonna take the fall for everything."

"He's over there crying his eyes out because he got me in trouble," Leasure said. "He never wanted to get me in trouble. . . . And I'm cryin' my eyes out because he got me in trouble. I'm gonna punch him out, you know." Then Leasure and France chuckled at the prospect.

A short time later, Leasure made an observation that would come back to haunt him at his trial, when he would try to cast Skipper Kuns in the role of rogue and liar. This day, though, he spoke far more admiringly of Kuns, portraying him as the honorable thief stoically protecting his friends: "Rob is going to tell the truth," Leasure said with certainty. "Rob is not one to . . . lie on somebody to get a deal for himself."

"I still want to be friends after it's all over," France said a short time later.

"Well, I don't want to be friends with Rob anymore," Leasure said. "But I'm going to be nice to him until it's over."

France would later explain his failure to mention the murders by saying he had been alone at home when the call came. Without his coaches and scripts, he was unsure what to say. "I was too nervous," he told Arce and Petroski when they had listened to the tape and pronounced it useless. "I'll do better next time."[1]

Next time, the investigators decided, should be in person. Leasure would speak more freely that way, they reasoned.

On September 18, 1986, just over a week after his successful talk with Dennis Winebaugh, France boarded a ninety-minute flight to the Bay Area. He was accompanied by Bud Arce and another LAPD homicide detective. Hank Petroski and Jim Koller remained in Los Angeles, working other leads and witnesses.

France's cover story this time had him visiting his sister in Sacramento, then making the two-hour drive into Martinez to see how Leasure was doing. Leasure had no reason to doubt France—the welder had told him he had twelve brothers and sisters, and the notion of one living in Sacramento was not at all suspicious.

Once again, Arce instructed France to steer the conversation around to the murders. A tape recorder was secreted under France's chair on his side of the jail visiting area, and a second mircrophone was placed on Leasure's side of the booth, to ensure that both ends of the conversation would be recorded.

When Leasure was escorted into the visiting room that morning, he was genuinely glad to see France waiting there for him, a broad smile on his thin face. Other than his lawyer, no visitors had come to see Leasure since his arrest in May. He had only spoken long distance with his wife, and those conversations had not always been happy ones, he said.

"So what's up, you been working?" a clearly delighted Leasure asked.

"No, I'm up here visiting my sister right now. And I wanted to get away from the house," France said. Then he told Leasure the police had been to his home. "They found, uh, composites at my house."

"So?" Leasure replied. "No big thing."

"It isn't?" France asked. He hadn't mentioned Anne Smith by name, but this was, the police assumed, a reference to the composite drawings Leasure had given him years before, depicting the two men seen outside the beauty shop before and after Anne Smith's murder.

"Why should it be?" Leasure asked lightly. France laughed uneasily.

Then Leasure abruptly turned the tables on the police. He had walked in with a piece of lined yellow paper and a pencil, and at this point in the conversation he began to write notes to France.

The sound of his pencil can be heard clearly on the tape, but the contents of the notes are known only to France and Leasure. Obviously, Leasure wasn't talking, and France was unable to recall the notes' contents very well once the visit ended and Arce tried to debrief him. Suspecting that the room was bugged, Leasure resorted to notes throughout the visit whenever France tried to steer the conversation toward something incriminating. After each note was shown to France, Leasure would erase it, then write over the same spot with his next note. In that way, if the police had seized the paper, they would have found it impossible to tell what had been written. At several points in the conversation, France could be heard asking Leasure what he was looking for, then suggesting that it would be illegal for the police to bug the visiting room. "You never know," Leasure said at one point, then later, after craning his neck around again, said, "I'm just checking."

As he wrote, Leasure continued a spoken patter of innocuous comments, protesting his innocence and the police department's attempts to smear him and all his friends, so that the tape, once again, was more testimonial to his good character than admission of crimes.

"They're just harassing all my friends, and you're just one of my friends that they're harassing, that's all. Don't worry about it."

This time, though, France drew nominally closer to the subject of murders—though he was still far from explicit. Leasure kept shushing him every time he started to say something directly, France later reported to his LAPD keepers.

At one point, though, he told Leasure that the police had questioned him recently, and that they had mentioned having a witness from Avenue Sixty—the location of the beauty shop in which Anne Smith was murdered. This line of questioning had scared him, France whined.

"Well, see, they'll try to get anything they can," Leasure responded. "They can say anything they want to say, you know. They'll lie about anything. And they try to do that just to trip you up. . . . If they think they have something, they'll question you about it and they'll make it sound like you're guilty, because they want you to confess, that's all." Then Leasure made an odd remark, one of the few non-self-serving comments he would utter, all the more curious because of his obvious certainty that his words were being monitored. He said: "Even if you did something, I wouldn't confess to anything."

A short time later, France returned, albeit obliquely, to the subject of the Anne Smith murder. "What about the mechanic?" he asked, referring to the Toyota mechanic whose recollections spawned the composite drawings.

Leasure's answer came in the form of another note.

After a pause, France replied, "Yeah, but why are they looking at us if he confessed to it? That's what I'm wondering. Why are they, you know, if somebody confessed to it, why are they looking at us?"

"Well," Leasure said aloud, "because it's just something for them to do."

To Detective Arce, this exchange seemed to suggest Leasure had knowledge of the Anne Smith murder—and of Charles Persico's guilty plea. The note, apparently, had said someone else had admitted to the murder. But it was so oblique. Arce had been working the case for more than a month, and he was just getting a handle on all this. How could they expect a jury to even begin to understand these subtleties?

France next asked about "the forty-five casing"—an apparent reference to the expended bullet casing found near Anne Smith's body. Again, Leasure seemed to respond like an accomplice, the detectives decided. France later told them that Leasure wrote a note to the effect that, "One was left at the scene."

As the tape would later reveal, France exclaimed, "Well, I know it was left there. I'm asking if you got it? Because you said you were friends with somebody and he could get it out for you." This was a reference to ballistics expert Jimmy Trahin.

"Oh, yeah," Leasure said, then began writing another note. France would later tell the police the note read, "That gun's gone," a reference to the forty-five that, by France's account, had been melted down by Leasure, rendering the casing at the scene meaningless.

"Oh. And you did what you said you was going to do?"

"Yeah," Leasure said adamantly.

A final note was written before the end of the conversation. France told Arce later, as they drove from the jail to the airport, that the note asked him if he was trying to work a deal with authorities. "He asked me if I had copped out to the police," France recalled. During the visit, he told Leasure with complete sincerity that there was no way the police would deal with him, or vice versa.

"I was the shooter," he pointed out. "You wasn't."

Bill's reply was a hissed, "Shhh."[2]

It was the closest France came to a straightforward comment about the three murders he was supposed to be discussing with Leasure. Once again, he failed to mention directly the word murder or hit, nor did he refer to Anne Smith, Tony Reyes, or Gilberto Cervantes by name—the very subjects he had been instructed to talk about.

He had used the words "mechanic," "composite," and "the casing," but those were only indirect references, ones that seemed to pertain to the killings but which were open to any number of interpretations. Arce and Petroski, with reservations, approved of France's oblique approach—they couldn't risk spooking Leasure. But that meant the case still boiled down to France's word—only he could explain what the conversation and the notes meant. If you didn't believe Dennis France, then the tape was useless, which put the police right back where they had started. To an outsider, the meeting at the Contra Costa County lockup sounded like nothing more than two friends talking, with one of them complaining, loudly and with great feeling, that he was being framed.

"Stop by again if you have time," Leasure said as his friend departed.

• • •

If you were to go out and kill a person yourself, would you hire Dennis France? No way.

I never had any idea he was setting me up, though. I was concerned about those two forty-fives he had sold me. I was afraid Dennis had used them in something, and that I might be in trouble because of it. That's what I was talking about. That's why he could never come out and say anything about murders. He knew I wouldn't know what he was talking about.

. . . There's nothing suspicious about writing notes. My wife and I write notes to one another all the time. I write notes to my mother! I still write notes. It just means I thought somebody was listening in—and I was right. They were. And it wasn't because I had something to hide, it's because it's nobody's business what I say to my wife, or to anyone else. And because I know that something you say can be taken out of context and twisted and used against you. Which is what they're doing to me.

• • •

Leasure's note-writing gambit threw Arce and Petroski. They had placed great hopes on France's visit with Leasure, and were bitterly disappointed with the results. They glumly reported the findings to Jim Koller the next day. But sitting in the D.A.'s office, they came up with an idea that might allow them to use Leasure's cleverness against him.

They would set up another visit between Leasure and France, but this time, they would videotape the encounter and capture the notes Leasure wrote. Koller was gleeful at the prospect. Nothing mesmerizes a jury more than rolling in the big-screen TV and allowing them to see the defendant's own words and actions. "All we'll have to do is pass out the popcorn," Petroski joked. If France asked the right questions and they recorded the notes Leasure wrote in response, then there would be no doubt about Leasure's role in the murders. Or so they thought.

Out of an abundance of caution, Koller obtained a search warrant before setting up the video visit. The warrant asked a judge to allow them "to visually, photographically and audibly seize any conversation between Dennis France and William Leasure." The warrant was a safety measure, since most appellate courts have found that an inmate has no "expectation of privacy" in a jail visiting area. Police, in other words, can listen in with impunity, and without a warrant. Koller, however, wanted to make doubly certain that there was no way the videotape could be excluded from evidence. Even then, with so much more investigation to be completed, he sensed his case might boil down to whatever the camera saw when Bill Leasure and Dennis France next met.

As it happened, Leasure had been brought to Los Angeles a few days before Koller got his warrant, to be arraigned on new charges, accusing him of receiving stolen property—three cars. Koller had hastily filed the charges in L.A. after a Contra Costa County judge, supervising the stolen boat case up north, lowered Leasure's bail from one million dollars to ten thousand. Leasure quickly posted bail and would have walked out of jail had Koller not stopped him by filing the new charges. Bail in the Los Angeles case was set at half a million dollars—unusually high for such a case—because investigators from Internal Affairs filed sworn statements saying new, more serious charges would be filed, and that Leasure had planes and offshore bank accounts that made him a high risk for jumping bail.

Bringing Leasure to L.A. served a second purpose: It also allowed Arce and Petroski to set up the video camera over one of the glass-walled visiting booths at the Los Angeles County Jail, instead of flying up to the Bay Area for another visit. On October 14, 1986, with a portable home video camera positioned above the visiting booth, France and Leasure spoke again.

Once again, Leasure seemed happy to see his old friend Dennis. And once again, he used notes to communicate sensitive— and seemingly incriminating—statements.

The visiting booths at L.A. County jail separate visitors from inmates with a smeary pane of safety glass. Grimy telephone receivers anchored with steel cords have to be used for the inmate and his visitor to hear one another. The camera was installed just above the glass, on France's side, pointing directly downward at the countertop between the two men, where Leasure would write his notes.

"So how you been?" Leasure asked.

"Not too bad," France said. "How about you?"

"Oh, pretty miserable," Leasure answered as he finished his neatly penciled first message, then turned it around for France to see.

"Hold it up," France requested.

The note read: *Don't say anything.* A moment later, he wrote, *Taped.*

The innocuous verbal conversation continued as Leasure wrote another note. Aloud, he complained about the class of criminals he was incarcerated with—the Night Stalker serial murderer among them. Meanwhile, he flashed another note, which said: *Did you have any brass from that one?*

This would be interpreted by the police as a question about whether bullets and brass casings seized by the police from France's home included any that might match the "one" found at the Anne Smith murder scene.

France answered, truthfully: "Yes, I did." The police had, in fact, seized a nearly empty yellow plastic box of Speer brand bullets identical to the one that killed Anne Smith. They had also seized empty brass cartridges, previously used, which France had planned to reload.

Then the conversation shifted to bail. Leasure said, "Right now, it's five hundred thousand. You don't happen to have any extra cash, do you?" As they both laughed, Leasure showed another note: *Your phone is tapped. Mine too.* He began methodically crossing out the words with his pencil, then erased the marks one by one.

As Bill erased up to where the word "brass" had been, France stopped him and said, "That one there . . . Did, uh . . ." Then France wrote with his finger on the glass, spelling out the word G-U-N.

In reply, Leasure wrote a single word on his little piece of paper, printed neatly in capital letters: *Melted.*

The police saw this as a direct admission and confirmation of France's story two months earlier, that the murder weapon had been melted down by Leasure.

"Okay, okay, I got it," France said, nodding, but then, puzzled, he referred back to Leasure's question about the brass. "Why did you ask me about that then?"

Leasure scribbled another note in response: *They have the one.*

That would be the "one" .45-caliber brass casing found near Anne Smith's body, Koller, Arce, and Petroski would surmise.

Aloud, as he showed France the note, Leasure said, "I, you know, I'm just kinda at a loss for words right now, kinda emotional, you know?"

France, using his index finger on the glass, spelled out "Ave. 60"—the beauty shop location.

While Leasure spoke aloud of Betsy and how well she was holding up, he wrote yet another note, apparently in response to France's finger-spelling: *Did they get casings and Rover?*

"Whole box, yes you do," France said promptly.

"Shhh," Leasure responded, sounding alarmed.

Later, Leasure had to clarify what "Rover" meant when France seemed not to understand the word. Leasure wrote: *police radio.* France told him no, the police didn't get it.

There was a chilling moment on the tape after that, one that had nothing to do with France's mission, but which, in the context of their apparent discussion of murder, seemed to border on the ghoulish.

Leasure was speaking, once more, of his anger at Jerry France. "He said that you and me and Dummy stole boats, took the people on them out to sea, and killed them," Leasure said, accurately summarizing Jerry France's initial statements to the police. Then he started to laugh, and France joined him.

"I know, it's funny," Leasure sputtered, laughing so hard he could barely speak. "He's saying that me and Bob were wearing uniforms." At this point Leasure was giggling and snorting with laughter. France was cackling.

"You were what?" France asked.

"Wearing police uniforms," Leasure said, still laughing. "That's what he said. He said that, you know, we, we killed the people and sold the boats. He said that, that me and you were splitting about four million dollars."

After more guffaws, France coughed, "Hey, I want my two. You owe me."

"I wish I had it," Leasure said, and finally the gales of laughter subsided. ". . . I don't think they're believing it. Nobody could believe this. The things that he said are incredible."

The fact that Leasure spoke of these unfounded allegations by Jerry France did not in itself reflect badly on him. But Koller instantly knew, when he saw and heard the tape that night, that the way Leasure laughed, so obviously enjoying himself with France, would send a powerful message to jurors. Here was a man who laughed about murder, who was so sure he wouldn't be caught that he found Jerry's allegations—which, after all, weren't that far off the mark—amusing.

Later, Arce and Petroski had to ask who "Dummy" was. "That's what me and Bill called Rob Kuns," France said. " 'Cause he couldn't hold onto his money." Apparently Leasure was through being nice to the Skipper.

As the conversation continued, there were a couple more notes. The final one, though, just before Leasure leaned forward and spotted the lens of the camera protruding ever so slightly from its hiding place, seemed especially telling to the police. It read: *Dump everything illegal.* Very much like his parting words to Irene Wong.

When he saw the camera and listened to France say don't worry, it's a pipe, even though the "F-stop" markings on the lens were clearly visible, Leasure remained calm and mild to the last. He sat a minute or two longer, speaking in monosyllables and carefully erasing every mark from his folded square of paper. Then he picked it up as he was escorted from the visiting room. He sounded sad, not angry, when he bid Dennis France a muted good-bye.

"Just take care of yourself," Bill Leasure said. "And I'll give you a call or something."[3]

It was the last time they ever spoke.

The investigators were initially exhilarated to have the tape. But after viewing it repeatedly, they grudgingly admitted to one another that, though it was terrific stuff, it was not quite conclusive. It looked bad for Leasure, of course. He was behaving like a guilty man, writing notes, hiding things. Such an appearance in itself would be damning, they said to one another. And Leasure's penciled messages did seem to correspond to the murders—at least to the Anne Smith murder.

But the ambiguity of those notes also suggested a problem: France's failure to ask Leasure more directly about the killings. He had circled round and round, nipping the edges of the subject, but never came out and said, Do you think they'll get us on Tony? On the beauty shop? And now there could be no fourth try. Leasure had seen the camera. He had to know they were investigating the murders, and he had to know France was working with them. Their friendly's cover was blown.

Ultimately, though, they dismissed France's failure to ask

about the murders directly as unavoidable, attributed to Leasure's repeated shushing and gesturing for France to be quiet. If France had pushed it too hard, Arce told his comrades, Leasure would have clammed up much sooner. France had handled it the only sensible way, it seemed.

Perhaps—but the ambiguity of the videotape, as well as all the other recordings of Leasure, also left room for other interpretations more generous to Leasure's defense. There was no direct admission of anything criminal in those notes, just hints and inferences that might mean anything. In large part, the strength of the tape and the secretive little notes still rested on what Dennis France said they meant—which was the one great weakness with the entire case. Would it be enough to convict Leasure?

Perhaps not, Koller reluctantly decided. The case that had already consumed their lives with twelve-hour days and one-day weekends was far from over, he said. "You guys have to keep digging."

"So," Arce asked, "what's new?"

• • •

What happened was, I'm sitting there in the visiting room, and we're looking at each other through the glass . . . and his eyes just keep darting up there. So I just leaned forward and saw something. He kept saying, it's a pipe, it's a pipe, it goes all the way up to the ceiling. I said, Dennis, it's a camera. That doesn't come out on the tape, it didn't pick everything up, but I said it. . . . I was just baffled. It's a camera. Why is he saying it's a pipe? It didn't even dawn on me that he was setting me up then. What was going through my mind was that, how can I see it's a camera, and he can't see it?

If I was a bad guy, I would have probably said some things to clear me then. But I wasn't involved in homicides, so I was just baffled. It took me a while, probably a week or so, before I realized what he had been doing.

You know, he was told by Arce and Petroski and Koller to get me to talk about those two murders. That was his sole mission. And he didn't do it. He couldn't come out and say, "Bill, I'm scared, we did those two murders and now I'm scared." He couldn't say that, because I would have said, "What the hell are you talking about, Dennis?" And he knew that.

Arguably, he said some things that refer to Anne Smith. He says Avenue Sixty, hoping I'll say something incriminating, which I didn't. I didn't know what he was talking about. But there's no way he could say anything about the Tony de los Reyes murder, because I didn't know anything about it. I thought he died of a heart attack. He never mentioned anything to do with Tony. Nothing.

He testified that, "Koller told me to get him to talk about murders." Period. He didn't mention murder once. He just said, I'm scared, they took some composites. He's scared, they suspect us of something, he's scared, they're gonna run down my car. What does that tell me? If you didn't know anything about the Anne Smith murder at all, would any of that mean anything to you?

No. Of course not. And it didn't mean anything to me, either.

CHAPTER 17

EARLY IN THEIR PARTNERSHIP, Hank Petroski and Bud Arce coined a term—they called it the "Burchell Syndrome"—to describe detectives who allowed their preconceptions to influence their investigations. They believed there was an unfortunate tendency among some detectives to gather facts in order to prove their theory of a case, rather than to find out what really happened. The Burchell murder case, years before Leasure came along, allowed Arce and Petroski to discover this syndrome firsthand—by falling prey to it.

Arce, the storyteller of the pair, likes to spin the tale for neophytes over drinks. White wine for him, Scotch whiskey for Petroski, toothpick in place, and he begins. A man—Burchell—failed to show up for his job at a loan company after a long Labor Day weekend. This was back in the early 80s, in the first year or two of the detectives' partnership at Robbery-Homicide. A worried colleague drives over to the man's apartment to see if he's okay. In a panic, he calls the police: Burchell's dead, has been for days. He'd been shot.

The detectives talked to the other residents in the apartment complex. Every one of Burchell's six neighbors say they observed a stream of male visitors coming and going at the dead man's apartment at all hours, right up to the weekend he died. He's gay, they say, it's obvious. The detectives agree with that conclusion.

The six witnesses also warn the detectives not to bother talking to the apartment manager. She's nuts, they say. Liable to say anything.

But in the interest of thoroughness, they do talk to her. And, sure enough, not only is she odd both in manner and voice, but her statement diametrically opposes everyone else's in the building. "I saw a pregnant woman coming out of there," the manager says. You sure? Absolutely.

"So six people say, males in and out all the time. One crazy lady says, yeah, I saw a pregnant woman," Arce says. "Now, what do you believe?"

Arce and Petroski choose to follow the majority opinion. They assume they've got a lovers' quarrel that escalated to murder, a falling-out among homosexual men. There's no room in that scenario for pregnant women, so they dismiss the apartment manager as a flake, and continue their investigation by talking to the victim's male acquaintances, looking for someone with a grudge. They hit dead end after dead end.

Several days later, there's a break. LAPD patrol officers stumble on Burchell's car. A woman is driving it.

Arce and Petroski are called in to question her. They find out she went to the hospital and gave birth the day before. Then she cops to being in Burchell's apartment that Labor Day weekend—it turns out she was the girlfriend of a man who posed as a gay pickup, then killed and robbed the victim. They even spent the weekend in the apartment with the dead body sitting there in front of them, the woman says. It was not a homosexual killing at all. It was a robbery by a stranger, and the presence of a pregnant accomplice was not at all inconsistent. They had been looking in all the wrong places, and solved the case only through a lucky break.

"Preconceptions," Arce concludes. "We became so narrow-minded looking for guys, that we failed to see the whole picture. . . . We were adamant about not doing that with Leasure."

Arce and Petroski felt they had come into the Leasure case with eyes open. The Burchell Syndrome, in their opinion, was the reason Charles Persico had been convicted of killing Anne Smith years before. The detectives who arrested Persico had settled on him as their suspect and forgot to look for the truth. They were out to make a case against the junkie, ignoring anything that didn't fit their theory, Arce and Petroski concluded.

But they saw their efforts in the case very differently. They were not out to prove Dennis France was telling the truth, they told themselves. If anything, they had been predisposed to *disbelieve* France—not out of a wish to protect a fellow officer, but simply because France had so many "squirrely" qualities, as Petroski called them. Everything he told them was questioned and tested and subjected to verification, the detectives would later say. They bristle at any suggestion to the contrary. They didn't even like Dennis France.

Although Arce forced himself to treat France with professional solicitude throughout the investigation, Petroski barely concealed his distaste for the man. He hated being around France, hated having to work with him, even though he grudgingly accepted it as a necessary evil. "He's a moron redneck," Petroski would mutter when France wasn't present. "He wants to be friends with us. I can't even stand being around him. He's killed two people, and no remorse. It's like a game to him."

"You work with what you get, Hank," Arce reminded him. "And what we got is Dennis France."

"Yeah, but he keeps asking me why I don't like him," Petroski said in disgust.

These personal feelings notwithstanding, Leasure and his lawyers would later accuse Arce and Petroski of falling prey to the very syndrome the detectives said they were determined to avoid.

"I don't think that's true," Petroski would later muse. "We attacked France's story from every angle we could think of. Dennis France knew things about the murders he couldn't possibly have known without being there. That's what convinced us about him telling the truth. . . .

"But for a long time, we were never sure we could prove the case at all. It wasn't looking very good those first couple months. Then we got the videotape. That cinched it for us. Leasure writing stuff down for Dennis France convinced me he was guilty. That's when we said, 'Oh, yeah, proof!' "

• • •

I know if I wasn't a policeman, none of this would have happened. They had to prove LAPD could clean its own house. . . . Leasure's the cop. That's the code. We've got to fuck him in the ass. That's what they said. And that's what they did.

. . . I don't believe they just gave Dennis France immunity without knowing what he was going to say. That's their story, but I don't believe it for a minute. I think what happened is, he said, "I'll give you Bill Leasure if you give me a deal." And they said yes.

. . . Now they're lying about it. Just like they lied about taking my legal motions. They [Internal Affairs Sergeant David Wiltrout and Detective Gilbert Hetrick] *took my papers and kept them for two*

weeks before they finally gave them back. I said, "You have no right to
take my legal motions." And Hetrick said, "You have no rights."
That's the way they think. And it's not right.

• • •

The videotape may have erased any lingering doubts the detectives might have harbored about Leasure's guilt and France's
truthfulness. But that still was a long way from being able to march
into court to prove Leasure guilty beyond a reasonable doubt.

The detectives still had hopes that some candid (and taped)
conversations between France and the elusive Paulette de los Reyes
might solve their problems, but in the meantime, Jim Koller suggested they look outside the circle of conspirators. Some close
friends of Leasure's might know about the murders without having
anything to do with committing them. Such a person, if he or she
could be persuaded to testify, would be able to provide the crucial
legal corroboration, since he or she would not have taken part in
the conspiracies to commit murder. As a fellow conspirator,
France's testimony alone was insufficient to support charges against
Leasure. They needed someone else.

One man immediately came to mind. Someone who was close
to Bill Leasure, who had committed crimes with him, who was facing a heavy prison sentence, and who therefore had a lot to gain
from cooperating with the police: Robert Denzil Kuns.

Dennis France already had told the detectives that he believed
Kuns knew about the murders. The welder had recalled bragging
about his exploits a bit to the Skipper, and he said he thought
Leasure might have done the same. The detectives repeatedly asked
France if Kuns had anything to do with the homicides, because if
he did, he would be useless as a corroborative witness. Absolutely
not, France assured them. Rob was a thief, not a killer.

On October 21, 1986, one week after France and a video
camera stiffed Leasure in a Los Angeles County Jail visitors booth,
Detectives Arce and Petroski flew back to Contra Costa County to
see the Skipper. Talking to Kuns posed a calculated risk for them.
There was always the chance he would tell them to get lost, then
turn around and tip off Leasure. In the end, though, they decided
it wouldn't matter: If Leasure was as guilty as they believed, he already had been tipped off about their homicide investigation the
moment he spotted the camera. And failing to see Kuns also held
risks, too. If he had something to say, the investigators wanted to
lock him into a story right away, before Leasure had a chance to

coach him. So they decided to head up north again, this time to see what Kuns had to say.

The results were less than promising.

"We want to talk to you about Bill Leasure and homicides," Petroski said.

"I don't know anything," Kuns told the two detectives, then refused to elaborate.[1]

He had been hauled down from the inmate segregation unit at the jail—"the hole," he called it—and brought to an interview room where the two detectives waited for him. He had let his hair grow in. The gleaming, shaven scalp lay hidden now beneath a thick and wavy auburn mop, making him look younger and more pleasant, less like a pirate.

"We've got him," Petroski said, pushing on. "We just wanted to know if you knew anything that might help. If you did, the District Attorney might be willing to consider working something out."[2]

"I don't know anything about it," Kuns repeated.

"Well, if you recall anything," Petroski said, "any conversations regarding this, give us a call." And he handed Kuns a business card. Then the brief meeting ended.

"Well, that was a wasted trip," Petroski groused afterward.

"I'm not so sure of that," Arce said. "He might change his mind after the preliminary hearing."

Kuns's and Leasure's preliminary hearing on the Contra County yacht theft case had just begun. The purpose of such a hearing is to determine if sufficient evidence exists to bring a case to trial—every defendant charged in California is entitled to one. The hearing amounts to a mini-trial, and theirs was still in its early stages when the detectives came to call. At that point, Kuns still thought there was a chance his case would be dismissed—leaving him little or no incentive to talk to the detectives about anything.

But Arce and Petroski knew something Kuns didn't know: Some nasty surprises were in store for him at the preliminary hearing. Those surprises would come courtesy of Bill Leasure.

And then, Arce told his partner, we'll see who wants to talk.

The preliminary hearing for *People* v. *Kuns and Leasure* was held in Richmond, California, before the Honorable Douglas E. Swager, judge of the Contra Costa County Municipal Court. Judge Swager's wood-paneled hearing room in Richmond's low-slung, no-frills courthouse was a scant half mile from the marina in which

Leasure and Kuns had docked four and a half long months before, only to have their yachting career summarily halted by arrest. The murder investigation was still secret at that point. As far as anyone in Contra Costa County knew, boat theft was the most serious charge anyone could level against the traffic cop from L.A.

At the start of the hearing, Kuns was charged with ten counts of grand theft and receiving stolen property; Leasure was charged with a total of six felony counts. In legal terms, there really was not much difference—the potential punishment was the same for both men, a maximum prison term of about twelve years.

The first day of the hearing was October 16, 1986—two days after a stunned Bill Leasure had seen the video camera in his L.A. County Jail visiting room. He returned to Northern California in chains, forlorn and depressed, his confidence that he would elude the charges against him shaken for the first time. The preliminary hearing would, in the end, do little to cheer him.

First came the parade of a dozen victims in the case. There were the people in Southern California and Canada who lost the yachts Kuns and Leasure took to the Bay Area. They were followed to the witness stand by their counterparts in Northern California, the unfortunate buyers who unwittingly purchased the altered, stolen vessels from Kuns or his broker, and who had lost both their money and their yachts to police seizure. One married couple from Tustin, California, near Los Angeles—Marie and Gene Robinson—suffered the double indignity of having bought a stolen vessel from Kuns, only to have it pirated from them less than three years later, so Kuns and Leasure could bring it up to Northern California for another sale.

The loss of the yacht they knew as the *Tortuga*—Spanish for tortoise—had been devastating for the Robinsons. Finding out that Kuns was the culprit only added to their pain: He had been a friend for years. They had dined together; he and his girlfriend had been to the Robinsons' home. The Skipper had captained the *Tortuga* for three years in a row in the elaborate Christmas boat parade held each holiday season in Newport Beach. Nine days after celebrating that last Christmas together, the *Tortuga* was gone, and a young couple in the Bay Area had bought a yacht they thought was called *Ocean Spirit* at what seemed like a tremendous bargain, almost too good to be true. Which, of course, it was.

So the first few days of the hearing went. But this phase of the testimony, however damaging, was exclusively leveled against Robert Kuns. Bill Leasure had never taken part in any of the transactions these people described. None of the victims even knew him.

For that matter, the testimony was not conclusive against Kuns, either. It showed only that Kuns had possessed and sold yachts that were later determined to be stolen. No one actually said they had seen him steal the boats.

But then a procession of detectives from L.A. and Oakland testified next, showing just how thorough their investigation of the boat thefts had been. Crawling through bilges and cramped engine compartments, investigators had used engine serial numbers to establish the true identity of the stolen yachts, despite the altered external serial numbers. Several of the yachts' true identities were ascertained by consulting with the engine manufacturer Perkins Marine, which, ironically, was located in Leasure's hometown of Wayne, Michigan.

Worse still for Kuns, the Oakland investigators trotted document after document into court—papers Kuns had personally filed in Oregon and California in order to register these same yachts. Detectives had followed the Skipper's five-year-long hot yacht paper trail and found that the records he filed were filled with phony names, phony boat building companies, phony serial numbers, and non-existent addresses. These papers purported to document boat sales that had never really occurred. They described yachts that didn't exist at the time the papers were signed—that is, yachts that hadn't yet been stolen. Though not all the records bore Kuns's name, a fingerprint expert testified that the Skipper's prints were all over them. Clearly, Kuns had been up to no good.[3]

And yet . . . and yet, there still was no witness who actually could say, I saw Robert Kuns steal a yacht. He may have possessed stolen yachts, he may have played fast and loose with registration records. But he still had some wiggle room. And, halfway through the proceedings, Bill Leasure was hardly implicated at all. His fingerprints weren't on any of the records. He had never directly sold any of the yachts in this case. All the authorities seemed to have on him was his presence on board the last stolen yacht, the *La Vita*— still leaving open the possibility that he was merely an innocent crew member, helping out a friend in need, just as he had told the police on the night of his arrest.

"I'll be getting out soon, Rob," Leasure told Kuns at one point in their courtroom holding cell. "I'll think of you when I'm free."[4]

Leasure even scored a small victory against the LAPD officer he considered his archnemesis—Internal Affairs Sergeant David Wiltrout, who had been called to testify about the search of

Leasure's home. Leasure's lawyer got a taciturn Wiltrout to admit on the stand that he caused a search warrant—which is filed by police officers under penalty of perjury—to describe Jerry France, Dennis's hot-check writing, heroin-addicted brother, as a "confidential reliable informant."[5] Wiltrout labeled Jerry France as such even though he had no firsthand knowledge of whether or not the man had been a reliable informant in the past, and despite the fact that he had just discovered that France had lied to him about Bill Leasure's alleged crimes (not to mention Jerry's totally erroneous physical description of Leasure). In other words, the portion of the warrant that listed Jerry France as reliable—and which linked Leasure and other policemen to the sale of stolen video recorders and other crimes—was probably invalid.[6]

Emotionally, seeing Wiltrout squirm on the witness stand was satisfying for Leasure. Long before he knew Wiltrout had been pivotal in the decision to grant Dennis France sweeping legal immunity, Leasure had focused much of his hatred and anger on the tall, authoritarian I.A.D. sergeant. Leasure had accused Wiltrout of destroying evidence that might have shown his innocence—a sales receipt for one of the hot cars he was charged with possessing in L.A. (Accusations of concealing key evidence would be raised against Wiltrout by another policeman involved in a related case as well.)

But what really got to Leasure was the trip to Los Angeles, when Wiltrout shuttled Leasure to his arraignment on car theft charges and his eventual date with a video camera. At the end of the trip, Wiltrout had taken away a thick file of legal papers that Leasure obsessively carried with him everywhere. The file was Leasure's one small piece of privacy in a penal system that offers no moment, no space, and no possession you can call your own. Only legal papers are supposed to be exempt from jailers' prying. Reading and rereading that file of dog-eared motions, memoranda, and notes he had jotted down for his lawyer let him think, however briefly, that he had a measure of control over his fate, that he possessed one thing that could not be invaded by his keepers. When Wiltrout took that away from him, Leasure was livid. He felt naked. On the stand in Contra Costa County, Wiltrout admitted taking the file, but said it was standard procedure when booking suspects into the holding jail at Parker Center. He denied reading the file, saying he merely searched it for weapons, then booked it into the property locker.

As gratifying as all this was to Leasure, it had little legal effect on the case. Even if the Jerry France portion of the search warrant for Leasure's home was invalidated by Judge Swager, more than sufficient evidence remained to justify his upholding the rest of the warrant—and the crucial evidence it yielded, defense attorney William Gagen conceded.

And, just as quickly, Leasure's brief triumph was forgotten as the most damning evidence of all was presented to Judge Swager, forcing the traffic cop and the Skipper to realize for the first time just how badly off they were. The fact that this evidence existed because of Leasure's actions, not Kuns's, did not escape either man. Leasure was stunned by it. Kuns was furious.

First, there was Terry Staley, a trucker in L.A., one of Leasure's best friends. They had grown up together in Michigan. Years later, Leasure had urged Staley to move out to the West Coast and had helped pay his way to Los Angeles. Once there, Staley let Leasure use his trailer home for trysts with Irene Wong. And, finally, Leasure had recruited Staley to serve as crewman aboard two of the yachts in question—the *Tortuga* and the *Wildcat*, in January and March 1986.

The point of all this was to show that Staley had every motive to protect, not condemn, Bill Leasure. Yet his testimony was pivotal in proving the charges against his friend. Staley testified that Bill Leasure had paid him seven hundred dollars after each of the trips aboard the yachts. A reluctant witness, he nonetheless testified that Leasure had told him that he and Kuns were in the boat-ferrying business together. Assistant District Attorney Joseph Campbell then produced Leasure's checkbook, with stubs showing the two payments to Staley, one of them annotated with a yacht's false name, *Coruba*.

Staley's testimony was devastating for two reasons—it showed that Leasure was in partnership with Kuns, issuing checks to crew members, as opposed to being just an innocent fellow helping out a friend with a boat. And the dates of the trips Staley made were very close to the times of the original boat thefts, meaning there was little or no room for someone other than Kuns and Leasure to have performed the thefts.

Even worse for Leasure, Staley's testimony directly contradicted the traffic officer's initial statement to the Oakland police. At the time of his arrest, Leasure had known it would be crucial to show he had never been aboard a stolen boat in the past, so he had said, "I have never crewed for Robert before and know nothing of his dealings."[7] Staley proved that was a lie. The two times Staley had crewed, Leasure had been aboard, too. Listening to Staley, it became clear that Leasure had been aboard yachts with Kuns on more than those two occasions, as well—Staley testified that Bill had asked him to crew on other trips, but that he had turned down the offers because of other commitments.

The emotional low point for Leasure and his lawyer came with the next witness for the prosecution—Irene Wong.

"It was not anticipated. We didn't know she'd be there until she walked into the courtroom. That was really a bad moment for us," attorney Gagen would later say. "Evidence was developing constantly, even while the hearing was going on. We didn't understand it at the time, why they just hadn't closed the book on this case. Usually once charges are filed, that's it. It just wasn't that big, we thought, yet they kept digging. Now, of course, we know why."[8]

With Irene came testimony on the extensive deposits, withdrawals, and checks exchanged between Kuns, Leasure, and Ralph Gerard—all of which seemed to correspond to boat deals, and all of which used her account to disguise the transactions. She also testified that Leasure had told her as early as 1983 that he was in the boat-ferrying business with Kuns—just about the same time the thefts began. Then she brought in a box of household goods—a toaster, pressure cooker, mugs, cookbooks, and other bric-a-brac—given to her by Leasure in the autumn of 1983. The owner of the Canadian yacht *Peggy Rose II*, stolen in October 1983, identified the property as hers. Most of the items bore French-English labels, proving their Canadian origin.

But the most damaging things Irene had to say had nothing to do with the thefts, and everything to do with Leasure's character and state of mind. She described, among other things, the string of telephone calls she received from Leasure shortly after his arrest.

"I told him I was approached by the FBI and that I had talked to them and that they wanted anything I had on him. That they wanted any kind of records I had."

"And what was his response to that?" prosecutor Campbell asked.

"He told me to destroy everything. . . . Just to cut up everything and flush it away. . . . He said do not tell anybody that we are intimate. And that I do not know him."

Defense lawyer Gagen, in trying to show that Irene had a motive to lie about Leasure out of anger at him, ended up making Leasure look even worse.

"In your relationship with Mr. Leasure for the five or six years that you had a relationship, you didn't know a whole lot about what he did in his day-to-day activities, is that true?" the lawyer asked.

"No," Irene answered in a small voice, she didn't know much about his activities.

"For example," Gagen asked, "you never learned that he was married, is that correct?"

"That is correct."

". . . You were very angry with him, correct?"

"Yes," Irene said quietly, glancing at Leasure one of the few times during the hearing. "I was very hurt."[9]

Listening to her speak, Leasure looked as if he had been punched in the stomach. The slight, soft-spoken Irene, who had to be told repeatedly to speak louder in order for the court reporter to hear her, appeared near tears at times. Leasure could not look at her.

As bad as Irene Wong's testimony was, in the end, Leasure himself turned out to be the source of the most devastating evidence of all.

His notebook was brought into court. One page contained the notation "Run," next to the registration numbers of two boats: 4371HC and 7215GW. The first number belonged to the *Holiday*, stolen from the Island Harbor Marina in San Diego in mid-May 1986. This was the boat that became *La Vita*, on which Leasure and Kuns were arrested. The other number corresponded to a different boat in the same marina—suggesting that Leasure and Kuns were casing the place for more thefts.[10]

Then a computer printout of boat registration information was introduced into evidence. The paper had been one of several found in Leasure's uniform pocket in his LAPD locker. It did not correspond to the notebook entries, but concerned the yacht *Wildcat*, and had the name and address of its owner. This registration printout had been "run" on an LAPD computer on February 26, 1986, just before 11:00 P.M.—about two weeks before the twin-engine $140,000 *Wildcat* vanished from its slip in Long Beach.[11] The *Wildcat* was sold in disguised form as the *Coruba* in Northern California a week later. It had been Leasure's next-to-last yacht expedition.

And if there were any doubt about whether Leasure knew this boat and the others were stolen, his notebook erased it. Part of a page from his handwritten notes detailing money owed him by a variety of friends read:[12]

OWES ME

ROB: 11-85 Mike's Boat		$3000.00
1-86 (Terry's Exp. Ocean Spirit)		700.00
	Bal.	$3700.00
+ 3-8 (Terry's Exp. Caruba)		+700.00
		$4400.00

(+Wildcat Boat)

The entry was damning. Terry was paid his first seven hundred dollars in January (1-86) when the yacht *Tortuga,* fresh from being piloted by Kuns in a Christmas parade, was stolen and resold as the *Ocean Spirit.* The entry for "Caruba" (sic) was dated March 8—for a boat that wasn't even discovered missing by its owner until March 9. And if that wasn't enough, Leasure's notes included both the name *Wildcat*—the yacht's true name, before the theft—and *Coruba,* the name (slightly misspelled) Kuns had christened it with after the theft. There seemed to be no explanation for this notebook page other than that Bill Leasure had to have been aware of and involved in the theft of the luxury yachts.[13]

Because the page heading suggested Rob Kuns owed Leasure forty-four hundred dollars, plus an undetermined sum for the "Wildcat Boat," the notebook also directly implicated the Skipper.

Kuns would later say he had no idea Leasure had kept such detailed records of their transactions. "We were supposed to avoid leaving that kind of trail," he said.[14] It was at this point in the preliminary hearing that Kuns began a slow burn, bewilderment at this evidence gradually turning to outrage. The man he had promised to protect by confessing was turning out to be the source of their undoing—all because Leasure had felt compelled to keep meticulous records of the money owed him. They had been friends, Kuns thought to himself. They were supposed to trust one another. So why write all that down? "Did Bill think I'd gyp him?" the Skipper later speculated. "I just couldn't understand it." To Kuns, it seemed like a slap in the face, a betrayal.[15]

The crowning blow came next, through what defense attorney Gagen came to call "Bill's little treasures"—the incriminating contents of the Leasure garages.

"The boat theft operation was very shrewd, almost perfect," Gagen observed after the hearing. "Except for one thing: the way Bill elected to store his 'treasures.' It was almost laughable when they brought in that photo of that double garage, filled with everything imaginable. I told the judge I wanted to show this to my wife—she thought my garage was bad.

"The Skipper had to be upset. I can't believe any . . . accomplice would want to keep this stuff, which provided a virtual road map of the crimes."

A road map it was. Boat owner after boat owner identified cooking utensils, blankets, wet suits, patio furniture, knives, firearms, clothes, artwork, even a stuffed turtle, the mascot of the yacht *Tortuga*—all of it taken from the stolen vessels, and all of it found in one of the Leasure garages, or the Leasure house, or Leasure's yacht, the *Thunderbolt*. Police even found a plaque ripped from the hull of a stolen yacht—the nameplate that read *Wildcat*. According to prosecutor Joseph Campbell's argument, the fact that Leasure hoarded all this under lock and key showed he knew the articles were stolen and, therefore, was a participant, not a dupe, in the boat thefts. With such overwhelming circumstantial evidence, the prosecutor said, the lack of an eyewitness to the thefts didn't matter.

There was little the defense lawyers for either Kuns or Leasure could do. Judge Swager agreed with the prosecutor. The evidence, as William Gagen later conceded, was "compelling."

"There is probable cause to believe that Mr. Kuns is guilty of the offenses," Swager ruled from the bench on December 4, 1986, the final day of the preliminary hearing. "In regards to Mr. Leasure, for the purposes of this hearing, where only a strong suspicion has to be shown . . . I am going to find that there is a strong suspicion to believe that Mr. Leasure is guilty of the offenses."

Leasure and Kuns, the judge ruled, would have to stand trial for yacht theft before a jury of their peers.

"Bill is one of the most unusual defendants I've ever met," his lawyer, William Gagen, would reflect much later. "Forget the homicides, it was just inconceivable to me that he could be involved in boat thefts. It didn't fit. He was so unassuming, unimposing, softspoken, and modest. He seemed like the guy next door—not at all what you think of as the prototype of the macho L.A. police officer. Just the opposite. Butter wouldn't melt in his mouth.

"Now, I'm not saying it has melted, but by the time the evidence was in, that image had worn pretty thin."

Gagen is a bright and good-humored man, with a successful law practice in the picturesque small town of Danville, California. He has been both prosecutor and defender, and harbors no illusions about human nature. But Leasure has him stumped.

"Who is Bill Leasure?" he still wonders, years after the hearing ended. "As a defense attorney, you don't really want to know the answer to that. But you couldn't help but be fascinated by him. Any reasonable person would look at the evidence and find it conducive to guilt. Yet, it was very important to Bill that I believe him. The evidence was so compelling, we were at that stage where, okay, let's stop fencing, we've got to talk turkey. But he was adamant.

"Here was a very intelligent man, lots of interests, well read. He was a tinkerer—a Renaissance man, in his own way. But for the nature of the items in his garage, and the other evidence that linked him to the crimes, he was very, very persuasive that he was just a tinkerer. And nothing more.

"But in the end, I couldn't understand, neither could the D.A., or Mr. Kuns, or co-counsel—why did he keep that stuff? Why?"[16]

Throughout the month of November 1986, as the preliminary hearing continued in fits and starts, Kuns and Leasure had gotten occasional brief opportunities to speak privately with one another. They could not talk in the courtroom, but back in the holding cell, between court sessions and before they were hauled to their separate cell blocks back at the jail, they could sit, handcuffed and waiting on hard metal benches, and swap stories and observations on the case.

At first these little talks were cordial. Early on, while he remained unaware of the truckload of material the police had hauled out of his friend's garage, Kuns continued to assure Leasure that he planned to live up to his promise to take the rap. If the case against them was a slam dunk, he said, he would tell the police he masterminded the thefts, and that Leasure had no idea the boats were stolen. "As long as nobody just absolutely turns witness against me, and they have a solid case against me, no reason anybody else should go down," Kuns said.[17]

Later, Leasure began confiding in Kuns about his new legal troubles in L.A. Fresh from the video visit with Dennis France, Leasure told the Skipper that their mutual friend was working with the police. "There was a camera down in the visiting room in L.A. County Jail. He's trying to set me up. . . . Someone's trying to connect me with some homicides down there."[18] A few weeks later, in late November, Leasure told Kuns his lawyers said there was no doubt about it, he was under investigation for murders. Kuns could see Leasure was very upset at the news.

At one point in these hushed conversations, Leasure mentioned the name "Paulette," saying he had introduced France to her, and that the two of them might be involved somehow.[19] Kuns and Leasure discussed it for a few minutes more, then they were escorted off to their separate areas of the jail. Later, Kuns's recollection of that conversation—and, more importantly, his interpretation of it—would prove crucial to Bill Leasure's future. And his own.

As the hearing drew near an end, and it became clear that Leasure's friend, Leasure's lover, Leasure's notebook, Leasure's police locker, and, most of all, Leasure's garage comprised the most damning evidence against them, Kuns began to rethink his position on protecting Bill. As Kuns's lawyer, Terri Mockler, put it after the preliminary hearing ended, "Everybody thought in the beginning it was my guy Kuns at fault, and this poor LAPD officer who was just along for the ride. Then they had their searches, and they checked the bank accounts, and it became clear Leasure was just as deeply involved. Personally, even though Kuns said otherwise, I always felt Bill Leasure was the mastermind. Kuns had the specific skills, but, by the time they were arrested, I think it was Leasure who was calling the shots."

Kuns put it another way. When all the evidence was in, he turned to Leasure in the holding cell and said, "I oughta punch you in the nose."

His anger at Leasure was made all the worse by personal grief. His girlfriend was devastated by his arrest, and his mother had died while his preliminary hearing dragged on. Kuns's pleas for a temporary release to visit his mother in Southern California as she neared death had been rejected by the court, as was his subsequent request to attend her funeral. His bitterness over this made it all the easier to consider cutting a deal with the authorities. From the jail, he called his father first, then his girlfriend, then his sister, and asked each of them the same two questions. Would they think less of him if he turned informant? Would their relationship end? If any of them had said yes, Kuns would later say, he would have kept silent. But each of them said, do what you have to do. Just tell the truth.[20]

Two days before the preliminary hearing's final session, Kuns told his lawyer to call LAPD.[21] There were some detectives there—homicide detectives—who wanted to talk to him, he told his lawyer. And he was ready to talk back. It was time to deal, he said.

"I came to understand that Bill was going to fall . . . no matter what I said," Kuns would later testify, offering a simple explanation for his decision—self-preservation. "So I figured he's going to fall anyhow, there's no sense in my sinking also."[22]

On the last day of the preliminary hearing, after secretly having his lawyer arrange a meeting with Detectives Arce and Petroski, Kuns found himself back in the holding cell with Leasure once more. Both men were depressed at the outcome of the hearing.

"Everybody's rolling over on me," a dejected Leasure said. Kuns would later describe him as looking like "a puppy dog begging not to be kicked again." Leasure pleaded, "You wouldn't do that to me, would you, Rob?"

"No, Bill," Kuns lied. "I don't think I could."[23]

• • •

When I was brought down to Los Angeles for my arraignment, I knew what might happen to me. So when I went to court, I made sure I said, on the record, that I was aware of LAPD's and prosecutors' practice of using informants and jailhouse snitches, and so I wasn't going to talk to anyone about my case. And if anyone said I did, they're liars.

And then, right after that, I go up north for my prelim, and Kuns claims I confessed everything to him. Now does that make sense?

. . . What really happened is, back in the holding cell, I just told him, something's up. I didn't know what. I was scared. I mentioned seeing the camera to Kuns when I went back up to Contra Costa County, and not understanding what was going on. And that's when Kuns told me about Dennis France saying to him a long time ago that he killed a man for a woman—and not to tell Bill about it. Kuns told me this, I didn't tell him.

I said to him later, after I thought about it, and after I talked to my lawyers and they told me I was being investigated for homicides, that maybe it could be Paulette [whom Dennis France was referring to]. 'Cause I introduced France to Paulette. . . . And then Kuns talked to the police and twisted it all around, so he could get a deal.

• • •

On December 9, 1986, five days after the preliminary hearing ended, Robert Denzil Kuns and his lawyer sat down with Deputy District Attorney James Koller, Detectives Arce and Petroski from Los Angeles, and Deputy District Attorney Joseph Campbell from Contra Costa County.

Sitting opposite this group, Assistant Public Defender Terri Mockler, young and inexperienced at the time, felt she was in over her head. She even let Kuns talk to them for a while before she arrived. For the most part, she sat quietly and listened to Kuns negotiate his own deal, as he shouted and argued with the detectives, painfully hammering out an agreement. "It was awful," Mockler later said of the meeting. "But eventually, everyone got what they wanted."

At first, Arce and Petroski demanded that Kuns talk without getting any promises. If the information checks out, then you'll get a plea bargain, they said. Clearly, they didn't want a repeat of the Dennis France immunity fiasco.[24]

But Kuns was just as adamant. No talk until we have a deal, he shouted. Otherwise, get on the plane and go home.

After an hour of haggling, a compromise deal was finally worked out. Kuns would tell them everything he knew about Leasure and homicides. When the time came, he would testify against Leasure in any murder cases that were filed, as well as in the boat cases north and south, and any other prosecutions filed against Leasure or others connected with the case. In return, Kuns would get a plea bargain on all yacht theft charges, in Contra Costa County as well as in L.A., with a guaranteed maximum sentence of five years—which meant he would be out in a little more than two under state sentencing guidelines. Kuns also would receive immunity for any admissions he made about his crimes—but with an "anti-France provision" built in that prevented him from, literally, getting away with murder. The immunity would evaporate if any evidence surfaced that proved the Skipper had participated in crimes of violence. In that case, he would be prosecuted on all charges. "Above all else," Koller wrote in a letter formalizing his deal with Kuns, "it is intended this agreement obligate the defendant to do nothing other than reveal the truth."[25]

When Kuns began his story, he started with how he met Leasure on a boat trip in 1978, then how Leasure persuaded him to hire Dennis France in 1982. Kuns asserted, with some pride and no apparent irony, that "since all of this has started coming down, Bill believes I'm the only person he can trust. . . . Look at the number of years we've been friends, he said things to me he shouldn't have said."

With that setup out of the way, he went on to the murders. He said Leasure had spoken, in bits and pieces over a period of years, about several murders he had set up. The first killing Kuns described sounded like the hit on Tony Reyes, with some distortions.

"I don't know the time reference in here," Kuns said, "but over the next two or three years, Bill would make several references to me about a gal. . . . She had contacted Bill to have her husband executed for the insurance money. Bill contacted Dennis [France] and let him do it.

"What surprised me is that he'd say it to me, not that he had, you know, done it. Bill was a very quiet, mellow, kicked back guy. But the mercenary type."

Kuns recalled Leasure telling him that, after the murder, France became upset because he hadn't been paid all his money. Leasure ended up paying France twenty-eight hundred dollars out of his own pocket, Kuns said. The total due was supposed to be thirty-five hundred, he said. Kuns said France told him basically the same story, in bits and pieces—with the added element that he wanted to kill the woman for not paying his full fee.

Kuns said he did not know the woman's name until the last time he and Leasure were in court together. "After we went back to the holding cell, Bill went to see his attorney, who said, 'Hey, they've got somebody down in Los Angeles that's implicated you in a murder.' When he came back to the holding cell, he was really upset, and he let the name 'Paulette' slip out. I said, 'What's this Paulette?' Bill said, 'You know who it is, it's the gal Dennis was talking about.' "

Next, Kuns claimed some knowledge about the Cervantes murder, that Leasure told him there had been a hit on "this gal's father-in-law." He had little more to say on the subject, moving on instead to the murder of Art Smith's wife.

Leasure, Kuns recalled, had said, "Art's wife . . . was going to divorce him and take him to the cleaners.

"Bill . . . never came right out and said he had anything to do with Art's wife, just always gave me the impression that him and Dennis had done it. Dennis was the triggerman, and he being the driver. He did tell me that the guy that went to prison didn't do it, but he put him up to it. . . . It wasn't what it appeared to be. . . . It was a fake robbery on the beauty shop. She was shot in the process.

"One day," Kuns told the detectives, "I said, you know, I suspect you and Dennis did the job on Art's wife, and he gives this, ahhh, just with a kind of look of, 'I'm a good driver.' "[26]

These admissions consisted of "body language" and hints— not direct statements of guilt, Kuns said. Yet it was clear what Leasure had been saying with gestures and words, Kuns explained: He was saying he and France did Anne Smith. Whether it's true or not, I can't say, Kuns said. It's just what Leasure told me. As for Smith, I only know him from selling him the *Santine,* Kuns added, not from any discussions of his wife's demise. And that, Kuns said, is just about all I know about murders.

Kuns hadn't thought what he had to say amounted to all that much, but the looks on his inquisitors' faces as he finished his story told him he had hit pay dirt. For Koller, Arce, and Petroski, Kuns's statement was irreplaceable.

Whether he realized it or not, Kuns was the corroboration they so desperately needed to get their case into court. Kuns was not a conspirator in the murders—he just had knowledge. Kuns's story, plus France, completed the legal formula: His word would legally sustain the charges against Leasure. Boiled down, Koller saw, the Skipper's testimony would be shattering: Leasure told him that he had arranged the murder of Paulette de los Reyes's husband, and that he had even paid Dennis France for it with his own money. This was exactly how France remembered it (at least in one of his many versions). The corroboration on the Anne Smith killing was shakier—body language and impressions, and a claim that Charles Persico was coerced into confessing. Still, it would be enough, Koller and the detectives decided. Despite his thief's background, Kuns came across quite credibly, a far better witness than the nervous, furtive Dennis France would ever be. Kuns didn't know it, but his statement had just made a homicide prosecution of Bill Leasure possible.

Though they garnered little attention at the time from the elated detectives and prosecutor, there were three other interesting points mentioned by Kuns toward the end of his official statement on December 9, 1986. The first of these suggested that Bill Leasure was into more strange and deadly things than anyone previously had imagined—among them tank-smashing missiles and other military hardware.

"Bill once asked me if I had access to L.A.W. [Light Anti-armor Weapon] rockets, Claymore mines. I told him I did not. Bill said that would be a good business to get into." Elsewhere, Kuns had already spoken of their plans to get into the stolen jet and military plane business—an assertion corroborated by Leasure's notebook entries on the profitability of trafficking in planes, as well as Leasure's old sergeant, Jim Berg, who recalled the traffic officer speaking of a half-million-dollar scheme along similar, though legitimate, lines.

The two other closing remarks Kuns made, however, had the potential for hurting, not helping, the case against Leasure.

"Bill tried to call Paulette [from jail], but she must have changed her telephone number," Kuns said offhandedly, then added something defense attorneys would later seize upon. "This was after the newspaper article."

Kuns was apparently referring to one of two articles that appeared in Los Angeles newspapers on December 6 and 7, which detailed the murder investigation of Leasure, Winebaugh, Paulette, and Art Smith. Much of what Kuns told the police about the murders was described in those articles.

As with every other advance in the case, the deal with Robert Kuns also brought with it liabilities. The final topic Kuns broached involved Dennis France's preferred method of disposing of murder weapons. "Dennis told me he used to cut up his weapons with a torch. . . . He said the torch was the only sure way to get rid of the guns."[27]

In other words, by Kuns's account, it was not Bill Leasure who melted down guns to cover up his crimes. It was Dennis France.

CHAPTER 18

THEY FINALLY TRACKED down Paulette de los Reyes by tailing her son home from school. She had been staying with friends and moving frequently. Paulette's two latest business ventures—a garment company called French Fancies and a nonalcoholic beverage business—had failed, leaving her without home, job, or income. But if Detectives Arce and Petroski believed such misfortunes would make the long-suffering Paulette an easy mark, they were disappointed.

The detectives left telephone messages for her (invariably unanswered), dropped their LAPD "Robbery-Homicide Division" business cards in her mailbox with a notation saying they would return, and called to question her friends, knowing word would get back to her—all in an effort to rattle her into making a mistake or an admission. Each attempt failed.

At the same time, their operative, Dennis France, still pursuing his pseudopoliceman's role, also began calling Paulette, leaving urgent messages about needing to speak with her. When they finally connected, France told her he was a friend of Bill's and Forty-four's—a name she seemed to recognize. He said they needed to talk about Bill, Tony, and why the police were asking questions about murders. Paulette immediately agreed to meet him. She said she was anxious to avoid talking on the telephone, for fear hers might be bugged.[1]

The stumpy, plain-talking welder and the giddily melodramatic woman met on a chilly autumn night on a street corner in Pasadena, near an ice cream and hamburger stand. The detectives found it strange she so readily acquiesced to the meeting—France was supposed to be a stranger to her—but they eventually decided that a person guilty of murder would agree to just such a clandestine meeting.

Dennis France's script for the evening called for him to convince Paulette that someone, possibly Bill, was telling the police they were involved in the murders of Tony Reyes and Gilberto Cervantes. Under his jacket, France had a body wire taped to his chest, with a microphone and transmitter to capture anything incriminating Paulette might say. Detectives Arce and Petroski and prosecutor Koller sat hidden in an unmarked van down the street with a radio receiver and tape deck, listening to the conversation, groaning when blasts of static or traffic noise would drown out the words. One thing came through with complete clarity, however. For whatever reason, this encounter with Paulette was far different from France's previous tape-recorded sessions with Smith and Leasure. This time, France was not the least bit ambiguous.

"I had the police come over and ask about Gilbert (sic)," France began matter of factly. "I don't know if you know, but I'm the one that did Tony. I'm the one who shot him. I also drove for Dennis during Gilbert. Okay? So, the thing I need to know, is how many people know? 'Cause somebody's doin' some talkin'."

Paulette's response succinctly summed up her state of mind. She said, "Forgive me for doing this, but I don't know who you are, and I don't remember you. . . . You're talking about a lot of things that scare the life out of me." And then she reached out and rubbed the front of France's body—a pat-down. She immediately encountered something hard and square beneath his clothes: the hidden electronic eavesdropping equipment.

"No," France said quickly, alarmed, stepping away. "That's a gun. . . . I didn't pat you down, don't. I don't want to."

"I don't know that that's a gun," she said a few moments later. "It could be anything under there."

"Well," France replied lamely, "it's not a recorder, if that's what you think."

To no one's surprise in the nearby van, Paulette then told France repeatedly and adamantly that she didn't know anything about what he was talking about.

France's cover, it seemed, had been blown before he had a chance to pump her for information. Surely, the detectives and Koller whispered to one another, Paulette had to realize she was being set up after feeling that box under France's coat. Yet the strange thing was, Paulette didn't leave. She continued to talk with France for more than two hours, as cars and buses whizzed by the ice cream stand and France came tantalizingly close to prodding her into an admission.

After frisking France, Paulette said, "I'll help Bill any way I can. . . . He has been there for me." Then, in an odd digression about Leasure's personality, she said, "I think the world of Bill. Bill's the kind of man, he should have been in . . . olden times. He's almost like a pirate. An adventurer. That's what Bill is like. . . . I love that man. He's been a prince."

Even France was taken aback by this description. Bill Leasure a prince? A Bluebeard? He finally told her to stop "rattling on" and steered her back to the subject at hand—whether or not the police were on to them for killing Tony. She again denied knowing anything. She also asked if she could feel France's clothes again. He refused.

Yet she still kept talking to him, running at the mouth, really—as if she was talking to an old friend or a father confessor. She said she wanted to close the door on the past, that Tony had been "a paradox," that he "drank like a fish," that she had found him in bed with other women, that she had been terrified of him, that he had beaten her, and that there was a fine line between love and hate. And interspersed with it all, over and over, she said she didn't know anything about any murders, or anything else. And no matter who asked her, that was all she was ever going to say. "I don't know anything. Period."

Yet when France complained that the police had been by to see him twice, her response was, "If you don't know anything, don't say anything." This, *after* he had told her he was the man who killed her ex-husband.

When France mentioned how, years earlier, he had driven "Forty-four" to Paulette's house for numerous sessions of "patty-cake," Paulette, with great concern in her voice, asked, "How is he?" Not good, France answered. Dennis Winebaugh, the man who had shot her father-in-law ten years earlier, was in Oklahoma dying of heart disease—and Paulette sounded genuinely worried about him. This, too, was an interesting contradiction for the detectives. Arce and Petroski had dug up some old files at LAPD, from when Paulette reported Tony's plot to have her killed ten years before. Then she had sworn she had never met Winebaugh, except for the time he gave her the tapes of Tony hiring him for the hit. (She did, however, tell the police at the time that Winebaugh spared her because he fell in love while stalking her.) Now Paulette and Winebaugh's relationship sounded as if it must have gone a bit farther.

When they parted, Paulette told France, "Whatever you want me to do, I will do." And she offered to throw a big party once everything was over. The man who said he had killed Tony Reyes would be invited, she promised. France said he'd look forward to it.[2]

Good evidence, all in all, Jim Koller told his detectives when the tape-recorded meeting ended. It got even better later, because Paulette did not call the police after the meeting—which, arguably, would be the reaction of an innocent person who had just heard a man confess to murder. But the tape was maddening as well, because it simply was not conclusive, they decided. And though there clearly was incriminating material on the tape, the detectives and Koller missed quite a bit of it. The South Pasadena Police had approached their unmarked van and tried to arrest them for attempted burglary toward the end of the stakeout. The locals thought the three men were casing a business for a break-in. The eavesdroppers, preoccupied with explaining themselves to the suspicious patrolmen, missed the part where Paulette expressed concern for Winebaugh's health, as well as the party invitation to a confessed murderer. As a result, they ended up dismissing the tape as insignificant, never fully putting it to use in court.

Instead, what would come to be known as "the Paulette breakthrough" came as Arce and Petroski sat in the Robbery-Homicide squad room asking themselves, "Now, how do we lock Paulette in?" Arce suggested, "We have to convince her she's going down— that Bill's bringing her down." (Arce and Petroski had never met Leasure, but, in the peculiarly personal, one-way bond that develops between detectives and their suspects, they had, without really thinking about it, begun referring to him by his first name.)

After discussing some of Paulette's comments to France, an idea struck—a ploy they had never tried before, or even heard of. They could cook up a series of phony police reports to convince Paulette that the police were about to arrest her and that Bill had sold her out. The doctored reports could be leaked to Paulette. Then they could wait for the inevitable reaction.

They called Jim Koller at the D.A.'s office with their plan. He decided the ploy would be legal—if barely—and quickly approved. France had already primed Paulette for such a ploy during their meeting, when he told her the police had found Bill's diary. She had been shocked at the news, and asked France, "Why didn't he stick it somewhere away from the house, where only he could find it?"

Back at the squad room, Bud Arce painstakingly penned a

replica of Leasure's little black notebook, in which diary entries on the boat thefts, stolen cars, and other assorted reminders were kept. Most of the entries were copied verbatim from Leasure's own notes—but Arce added several fictional ones pertaining to Paulette: "Thursday: Paul wants rush on Tony." "Tuesday: Check bar for lights, entrances and exits. Run Tony's car." The entries were unmistakable references to the shooting of Tony Reyes at the Chez Nora nightclub.

Elsewhere in the book, to make it clear who "Paul" was, Arce copied a genuine entry from Leasure's phone book: Paulette's old phone number and address, under the name "Paul," recorded in this manner so Betsy wouldn't know he had a lover's number so handy.

Then Arce and Petroski typed up a phony police interview report on Leasure. It detailed a fictitious conversation between the detectives and their suspect, in which Leasure accused Paulette of paying Winebaugh to kill Gilberto Cervantes, then paying France to murder Tony. In this phony report, the detectives had Leasure claiming knowledge of the murders while denying any direct involvement. The report concluded with him eagerly offering to testify against Paulette, Art Smith, Dennis France, and Dennis Winebaugh, as long as he didn't have to go to prison. "I can't go to prison," the report quoted Leasure as saying. "Being an ex-policeman, I'd be killed myself."

When the reports were ready, Arce and Petroski stuffed photocopies into an envelope, then drove France to Paulette's latest address. He shoved the packet into the mailbox—material supposedly leaked to France from a friend at LAPD. France scribbled a note asking her to call him. Then they sat back and waited, assuming she would get back in touch.[3]

Instead, a few days later, an LAPD investigator from Detective Headquarters Division, David Scroggins, approached Arce and Petroski in the hallway near the third-floor elevators at Parker Center. Detective Scroggins, a twenty-year veteran on the force, looked uncomfortable and started to say something to the detectives, but then began to stammer in a low voice.

"What's the matter, Dave? What's goin' on?" Arce asked.

"Well, uh, I have this lady friend," Scroggins said, giving the two detectives a hard look. "And we had this talk, and she showed me this. Asked me what I could find out about them. I was amazed she could have something like this."

Then Scroggins pulled out the cover page from the phony reports delivered earlier to Paulette. He handed it to Arce.

"Jesus," Arce said.

"I didn't think it was right that she had them," Scroggins said accusingly. He had thought Arce and Petroski might be dirty, releasing secret reports for money or favors.

"Dave, you'd better come in and sit down," Arce said, directing the other detective, who knew nothing about the Leasure case other than what Paulette had told him, into the homicide squad room. And there, beneath the glazed stare of the wild boar on the wall, they filled Scroggins in. Relieved to hear that his fellow detectives were clean, he explained how he had thought Paulette was being victimized by a lying Leasure, or, worse still, by Arce and Petroski.

Scroggins explained that he had met Paulette earlier that year in a Pasadena bar, and that they had struck up a friendship. He had even helped initiate an investigation of someone who had written her a bad check a few months earlier. He told the detectives they were friends, but not romantically involved; Scroggins was a married man.

Paulette had called him the night before, saying she was in trouble and needed help. Scroggins already felt sorry for her and Aaron—they were destitute and had been reduced to living in someone's garage by then. He agreed to meet her at a restaurant, where she showed him the page from the phony reports, which she said had appeared mysteriously in her mailbox. She assured him she was innocent, and begged him to look into it. He was a policeman. Surely he could do something to protect her, he recalled Paulette saying. Scroggins had told her he would see what he could do.[4]

Paulette had only given Scroggins a single sheet from the batch of phonies—a cover-page summary of the more detailed reports that had been attached. The single page she handed over merely said Leasure was willing to give information on several unsolved murders in exchange for a deal on the stolen yacht charges. Although her name was mentioned as being "involved," the cover sheet did not detail any allegations against Paulette. She told Scroggins she was being set up, and that she had nothing to do with any murders. He had no reason to doubt her.[5]

"I thought she was a very nice person," Scroggins later said. "I was fearful for her."[6]

Once Scroggins explained his relationship with Paulette, Detectives Arce and Petroski asked if he would be willing to help them go after her. Scroggins agreed.

Now they had another undercover agent, one whose credibility as a witness seemed infinitely better than Dennis France's. This time their operative wasn't a killer. He was a cop. Arce and Petroski could barely contain their glee.

Their good mood quickly wore off, however, as they realized just how daunting a prospect they faced in getting the rambling, wordy Paulette to say something succinctly incriminating.

The Leasure case had already insinuated itself into every cranny of their lives—Arce, Petroski, and, nearly as often, Koller, were putting in twelve- and fourteen-hour days, plus another hour or two winding down over beers after work, still talking about the case. Then they would wearily drive home and crawl into bed, to dream about what made Bill Leasure tick. And now, one day after hearing from Scroggins, they found themselves back in the cold dark of the surveillance van, past 11:00 at night, listening to Scroggins and Paulette over a remote transmitter strapped to the detective's body.

Paulette met him in the parking lot of a Pasadena restaurant, inside Scroggins's car. When he told Paulette he had done some digging, she said, "Oh, God, this is getting exciting. I gotta tell you, my heart is beating a mile a minute." The odd eagerness in her voice was unmistakable. She was embarking on a new adventure.

Scroggins had a script that night, just as Dennis France had. He told Paulette that Dennis Winebaugh had been arrested in Oklahoma and brought to L.A., and that both Forty-four and Leasure were trying to get deals by snitching on her. One of them apparently had tapes of her plotting Tony's murder, Scroggins said.

"But David, I haven't done anything," Paulette protested, just as she had told France. "Why would someone be trying to make me into something when people have done things *to* me?"

But gradually, at Scroggins's insistence, Paulette's story began to change. "I know a lot of things about Bill, that Bill told me in confidence," she said. Then she admitted that Leasure had planted a bomb under Tony's car in 1976. "It was just a small little thing," she said. "Bill . . . told me, what he really needs is a scare."

Getting such nuggets during the two-and-a-half-hour conversation was a tedious chore. These valuable snippets were wrapped within long, sometimes surreal diatribes about how badly Tony had treated her, about her illnesses and misfortunes, about her son and her boyfriends. Once again, she spoke about Bill Leasure's qualities admiringly, saying she had been his confidante, marveling at how his wife must have known about all of Leasure's girlfriends yet put up with him anyway. She called the traffic officer a "very strange paradox."

"He doesn't look like he knows very much, but he's a . . . very bright man. Very well read. He's just a very quiet—I mean, I'm surprised that Bill is doing all the things he did do."

This was not the sort of material Scroggins was supposed to be getting, but the more he pressed, the more Paulette seemed to deny and digress. At one point in her ramblings, she even spoke at length about the habits of nocturnal birds, and began hooting like an owl in order to make her point. Scroggins's side of the conversation was reduced to hoarse, uncontrollable guffaws as Paulette warbled, "Hooooooo, hooooo."

Finally, though, instead of pleading with Paulette, Scroggins tried a new tactic. He said he might be able to help her by destroying the tape recordings LAPD was going to use against her. Paulette eagerly agreed to this scheme. But Scroggins set a condition: The only way he would take the enormous risk of destroying evidence on her behalf was if she would come clean to him. When Paulette still insisted she knew nothing, he began to scream at her, reducing her to sobs, a questionable police tactic at best. "You can't even entertain the thought of holding back on me," Scroggins yelled, " 'cause I gotta know how to cover our ass. You understand? Do you understand?"

She finally conceded that she may have talked about wanting Tony dead. "I might have said it even to Bill. . . . Maybe we should just wipe Tony out and get him out of my hair. . . . I may have asked, what does it cost, what does it cost to do something like that?"

". . . Did he say he'd do it?" Scroggins asked.

"No."

"You see, we can turn it all around to him," Scroggins wheedled, suggesting that she could be cutting the deal against Leasure rather than vice versa—if only she would talk. Then he asked again, "Did he say he'd do it?"

There was a long pause, the silent ticking of mental calculations. Then Paulette said, "I don't remember." And after still more prodding, she finally said, "He might have."

Then she made the most incriminating statement of the night. After insisting that this conversation about Tony's demise was two or three years before the actual murder, and therefore could not possibly be related to the hit on Tony, Paulette admitted, "I said, yes, I want him dead. Go ahead and do it. . . . He even said yes, sure, all right, no problem."

But as soon as she made this apparent admission, she backed away from it. "You know, we used to kid each other like that all the time. But it was only an outlet."

The bottom line, she insisted, was that she was an innocent woman being framed. Any talk of killing had been just that: talk.[7]

After Paulette and Scroggins bid each other good night, Arce, Petroski, and Koller huddled with their new undercover operative in the van. The past few hours had been excruciating—and mostly unproductive. They had no choice but to come back for more.

Before Scroggins was through, there would be two more taped meetings with Paulette, in restaurants and cars, over seven hours of conversation in all. At one point, Scroggins shouted obscenities at Paulette, slurring his words as if drunk, banging on the car like a madman.

Finally, in a bizarre turn, Scroggins offered to arrange for Leasure's murder so that he would be eliminated as a witness against her. But before he would do it, Scroggins said, Paulette had to assure him that Leasure was the one who had the knowledge that would convict her—in other words, she had to tell him outright that Leasure killed Tony at her behest. Otherwise, Scroggins promised Paulette, he would refuse to help her, and she could march right into the gas chamber.

"Does he need killing? Does he or doesn't he, goddammit?" Scroggins shouted.

"Yes, he does," Paulette finally agreed. "I guess he does."

Scroggins then demonstrated how he would arrange Leasure's death at the jail: He pulled a knife out of his glove compartment and briefly held it to Paulette's throat. Paulette gasped. "[They'll] shank him right in the gut at the handball court," Scroggins said. "It's over, gone, finished."

"David, that would really be the end of everything?" Paulette asked.

"They'll never get you," he promised.

Throughout this exchange, Arce and Petroski, scrunched inside their cold surveillance van, were miserable. This new murder plot was not in the script. Scroggins was winging it, and the two homicide detectives were horrified. They had sat Scroggins down after the first two taped meetings with Paulette and said he had to stop her from avoiding the question. But they had never envisioned anything like this, the screaming, the constant, manic refrain of "Tell me, goddammit, tell me," the banging on the dashboard. Arce would later say he could practically feel the shiv going into Leasure's ribs as he listened, so compelling was Scroggins's description. "Oh, God, we knew, we knew it was going to be tainted. But what could we do?" Arce recalled. Although agreeing to have someone killed is a crime, Scroggins's method of proposing it to Paulette clearly constituted illegal entrapment. And any jurors who listened to Scroggins's offer—combined with his shouting, cursing, and threats, as well as his and Paulette's alarming tendency at other times to kiss and to call one another "darling," "sweetheart," and "boobala"—would have to ask themselves, Who was worse, Paulette, or Detective Dave Scroggins? Yet Arce and Petroski were helpless to intervene. There was no way to communicate with Scroggins without blowing his cover until Paulette was gone. They could only sit and listen, surprised to find themselves wishing they were dealing with Dennis France instead of their fellow detective.

Paulette, meanwhile, began to open up a bit more—the image of Leasure dying on a handball court at the jail had accomplished that much, at least. Some admissions surfaced, sandwiched between outbursts about her willingness to kill herself, her claims that she had undergone "out-of-body experiences," her recollections of a voodoo doctor Tony had hired to bewitch her, and her desire to write a book about her experiences. Paulette recalled Leasure saying, "Sure, sure, sure, he could kill him. That was Bill, that's the way he talked. He was always very smooth, very laid-back. He said things like this all the time. . . . There was nothing he couldn't do. . . . He'd always talk about Vietnam and things he had done and people he had killed and so forth in Vietnam. And half the time it was like we were kidding and half the time it was like it was real."

But, maddeningly, each such admission was followed by a disclaimer. When Scroggins tried to pin her down by asking if she ever discussed paying him for the killing, Paulette said, "No.

"I didn't give him money, I never gave him any money," she swore—an echo of Kuns's statement that Leasure, not Paulette, had come up with the money to pay France. "We weren't even having that much of an affair, it was just a very brief . . . We were friends, our affair was very brief."

After seven hours of high-pressure tactics over three separate meetings with Scroggins, Paulette was still denying there had been a contract with Leasure to kill Tony.

Scroggins, meanwhile, sounded beside himself with frustration. Growling and increasingly slurring his words, he began to tell Paulette he would kill *her* if she held out on him. Then he said he was going to take her home and refuse to help unless she told the truth. Paulette, alarmed and crying, begged him not to abandon her, then explained that she was "afraid to trust anyone."

"Everyone I've ever told my deepest thoughts, or whatever, has always turned on me," Paulette whispered tearfully. ". . . Have you ever been so afraid in your life that you're afraid to even tell what—what you want to tell?"

Here was the moment they had been waiting for, Scroggins decided, as did Arce and Petroski on the other end of the body wire. And, finally, Scroggins found an inspiration that worked. He delivered a speech that Jim Koller would come to refer to as "the sermon on the mount," which seemed to move Paulette into an actual, unequivocal admission of wrongdoing.

"Somehow, some way, sometimes, you got to trust somebody," Scroggins said, his bluster and curses gone, replaced by a quiet, measured tone, almost a whisper, heartfelt, nearly prayerful. " 'Cause you can't make it on your own. If you feel equipped to make it, then you go ahead and do it by yourself, babe. You go ahead. 'Cause you don't need me. I'll just go on home, and I'll make it. You see, because, uh, I don't even know why in the fuck I'm helpin' you. I think because of that kid."

"Yes, I did," Paulette said suddenly, interrupting Scroggins. Her voice sounded small and meek.

"Yes you did what? . . . What'd you do, darling?"

"I asked Bill to kill Tony."

"Okay. And how did it come about?"

"I don't know any details. I don't know anything. . . . They never told me anything."

Paulette still insisted that she never paid Leasure, but she conceded there had been discussions about money. "He asked me about things, and I said yes, eventually I would get another—I'm sure there is a will." But they learned too late that Tony had never signed the will giving Aaron his money. There had been no inheritance. She had gotten nothing from Tony's death, she said. And she paid Bill nothing.

But she told Scroggins that Leasure still had asked for something. "He asked me afterward, he says, Paulette . . . I may need a favor from you some day."

"You asked him to do it and he did it," Scroggins said a few moments later. "You sure?"

"Yes."

There it is, Arce and Petroski said. Paulette had locked herself in. Shakily, but it was there, they decided. She still insisted she had nothing to do with the Gilberto Cervantes murder—she blamed that solely on Tony—but she had copped to planning her ex-husband's death with Bill Leasure, in return for inheritance money or a favor. There were problems aplenty with the tapes and Scroggins's over-the-top tactics, but it would have to be enough. Scroggins wrapped up this third and final taped meeting a few minutes later.

"If I do Leasure, is it over?" he asked.

"Yes," a sobbing Paulette said.

"He's the only one that knows?"

"The only one that knows."

As they said good-bye, Paulette thanked Scroggins and said, "I love you, David."

"I love you, too, babe. Take care. It's all gonna work out. Okay?"

"You think God'll ever forgive me?" Paulette asked. "I don't know."

". . . All will be forgiven," Scroggins promised.[8]

• • •

Paulette, I don't know what to think. Was she involved in murders? I don't know. I know this: Her Scroggins tape is not believable. She'd say anything to him, because they gave her phony reports of me confessing, implicating her. It was a setup. It's outrageous. The police can lie, cheat, set people up. They can do anything, and nobody holds them accountable. It's incredible what they did to try and get me.

Scroggins threatened her, he held a knife to her throat. Nobody could believe those tapes with him. How could they? And even with all that, Paulette kept saying I was innocent. He practically had to force her to say anything bad about me. She was scared. She goes to Scroggins for help, and he pressures her. And she still never really said, I did it. She was just throwing him a few bones, so he'd help her.

He offered to have me killed. An LAPD detective. That's his way of getting to the truth, supposedly. Can you believe that? That's the kind of evidence they want to send me to the gas chamber with.

• • •

Even with Robert Kuns on board and the questionable Paulette tapes to bolster their case, the investigators desperately wanted more. Actually, they didn't want more evidence so much as they wanted different sources for it.

They needed a different sort of witness than the Skipper or Paulette or Dennis France. They had to find at least a few normal, law-abiding people to round out the case, the sort of witnesses whose credibility could not be called into question because of their crimes, or their legal immunity, or the leniency they had earned in exchange for bringing Bill Leasure down. Lawyers call this favorable quality in witnesses "jury appeal." Convicting a policeman of murder or, for that matter, convicting a man like Art Smith, who seemed to be a pillar of the community, would be difficult at best with nothing but unappealing witnesses and some incriminating tape recordings.

Rooting through old Murder Books, trying to rekindle leads long abandoned in the disused files, Detectives Arce and Petroski methodically hunted for these witnesses, interviewing dozens of people through the fall and winter of 1986 and into the New Year. The unprecedented process of reopening and combining three old and previously unconnected murder investigations was a plodding, leaden task, with more fruitless paths than a lab rat's maze. They would pound the bricks and knock on doors, spending hours on the freeway to track down a potential witness, fast-food bags and paper cups accumulating in the back of their unmarked car. And when they finally arrived at some witness's last known address, more times than not they would be told the person had moved or died or was in prison. Other times, they would be told through a barely opened door, I don't know nothin'. Slam.

Still, the witness list slowly grew, until Arce and Petroski found some people with stories to tell who weren't admitted felons.

The breakthrough came when the detectives talked to Anne Smith's sister-in-law, Nicolette Pontrelli. She had spotted an article in the newspaper written on boat theft allegations against Art Smith and Bill Leasure—an article that also mentioned newly surfaced allegations about the Smith murder. Pontrelli put down her newspaper, all the old suspicions flooding back, and immediately called Deputy District Attorney Jim Koller, who had been quoted in the news story. At his direction, Arce and Petroski called her back, and they discovered a gold mine.

Though she would not be a witness in the case—all her information was secondhand hearsay, and therefore inadmissible in court—she turned the detectives in new directions. Blonde, compact, and energetic, she had a flawless memory, a natural storyteller's ability to describe events, and a dead certainty that the truth about Anne Smith's murder had yet to be told. She was more satisfied than stunned at the news that the supposedly solved case had been reopened.

"We knew it was a hit," she told the detectives. "We always thought Art was involved somehow. From the beginning."[9]

Nicki Pontrelli gave the detectives the names of three people who might have information about Art Smith's involvement in murder: John Doney and Dovie Gordon, who had worked for Art, and Richard McDonough, their tennis instructor and friend. Arce and Petroski realized later that all three of those names were in the old Anne Smith Murder Book, but that Westbrook and Crowe had never gotten around to interviewing two of the people. Tracked down years later, all three witnesses had a stunning story to tell, offering leads Arce and Petroski felt LAPD should have uncovered and tracked down years earlier.

The first witness they talked to in this group was John Doney, the insurance claims adjustor who had worked for Art Smith. They tracked him down at an insurance company in Anaheim, near Disneyland. Doney had been interviewed briefly years before by Westbrook and Crowe, but had offered nothing of interest then. As far as he knew at the time, Anne Smith had been killed in a robbery. He had not mentioned the bizarre breakfast conversation with Art, in which Smith spoke of having Anne killed. Besides, he was a friend and employee of Art's then. Seven years later, though, they had been through an angry parting of the ways. Smith had threatened him after Doney called him a murderer, warning his ex-employee to "keep your mouth shut." Now Doney was more than willing to tell Arce and Petroski all about it.

"He said that Bill Leasure offered to do it for fifteen thousand dollars," Doney told the detectives. "Art said that Leasure and his partner 'Big John' were going to do the murder. Leasure was going to go to Anne's house, kill her, then get rid of her body."[10]

By himself, Doney could be dismissed as a disgruntled former employee out for vengeance, the detectives knew—though his demeanor and apparent sincerity seemed to belie that. However, Richard McDonough, the Smiths' tennis partner, who had no connection to Doney, told virtually the same story.

"Art said he could get two cops that worked Northeast Station to kill anyone for fifty thousand dollars," McDonough told Detective Arce in a telephone interview two weeks after the interview with Doney. "Art said he was going to have the cops kill Anne. . . . Somehow the cops were going to arrest her, take her to a secluded place, rape and kill her. They were going to dump her in MacArthur Park. It would look like a sex fiend killed her. I didn't believe Art."[11]

Finally, the police talked to Dovie Gordon, Art Smith's former secretary. She recalled Art's bitterness over the divorce, and his statements that he would see Anne dead before she got his money. He had been hiding assets from her, she said, and keeping her in the dark about his resort development in Belize. "I know Art was serious, because when I asked him if he really meant what he said, Art said, 'You just wait and see.' "

Art and Bill Leasure used to have secretive meetings at the office, Dovie Gordon told the detectives. "Anne was afraid of Bill Leasure. . . . She believed that Bill Leasure was following her. I asked if she was sure, she said she had seen Bill following her in a car."[12]

Gordon, McDonough, and Doney all told roughly the same story. Art wanted his wife dead, and Bill Leasure was involved. Any one of them could be dismissed as a flake, a liar, or a well-intentioned citizen with a poor memory, but together their overlapping stories were impossible to explain. As far as the detectives were concerned, they provided compelling evidence of premeditated murder by Art Smith and Bill Leasure—and invaluable corroboration of Dennis France's story.

• • •

I think John Doney was trying to tell the truth. I don't think he's lying. I just think he's got things wrong. Look at how he got the message from Art Smith wrong. He probably made the same kind of mistake with the conversation he had with Art. A lot of time has passed, who knows? McDonough and Dovie Gordon—there really isn't much there. Their stories don't hold water. It's not anything like what Dennis France said. And even if Art did say anything like what they say, it was just talk. Because I know it didn't happen. . . .

• • •

After the Paulette–Scroggins saga ended, Detectives Arce and Petroski collected a few more witnesses and bits of information to help complete—or in some cases, complicate—the puzzle of Bill Leasure and the other suspects.

There was Ron Schines, a former business partner and boyfriend of Paulette's, who told the police that Paulette had spoken of Bill Leasure as the "go-between" with whoever killed Tony. Leasure was "protecting her," he said.

Then there was a curious lead on a series of old unsolved burglaries in the area where Leasure made his home. In the seventies, "Caspar the Northridge Burglar" had specialized in ripping off homes of jewels and other valuables, then vanishing into residential neighborhoods. During the Leasure investigation, a patrolman came forward and said that years before, he had stumbled on the mysterious burglar in the middle of a job, almost catching him before the elusive rip-off artist slipped away. Years later, when he read about the Leasure case in the papers, the patrolman recognized the traffic cop's house: He had lost Caspar when the burglar leaped a fence and ran into Leasure's backyard. It didn't really prove anything, and the patrolman had never gotten a good look at the suspect's face. Still, it made the detectives and the Internal Affairs investigators wonder.

They also had to wonder about some comments Bob Kuns made in a later interrogation with Internal Affairs, when he recalled discussing the "Hollywood Burglars" case with Leasure. The Hollywood Burglars were a group of LAPD cops in the 1970s who robbed stores of televisions, stereos, and other valuables while on duty, stashing the booty in their patrol cars' trunks, then pretending to investigate the break-ins. An internal investigation caught them in the act, on camera. One of the officers turned state's witness and was to testify against his former comrades, but he was killed when his car was run off the road before he could take the stand. Foul play was never proven. Kuns recalled Leasure speaking knowledgeably about the death, saying it had been no accident. Either Leasure had been involved in something, the Skipper said, or he was just puffing up, talking big. Again, this proved nothing. But it raised more disturbing questions.

The detectives also found Flo Ong, Bill Leasure's "second mother," who said she had trusted him with her life—until she found him fooling around with Irene Wong in her house and realized he was storing a stolen Corvette in her garage. Flo told the detectives about her strange conversation with Bill years before, while they were on the way home from Big Bear in the San Bernardino Mountains. "Bill said to me, 'What if I told you I murdered someone?' I told him if it was in the Marine Corps or in the line of duty it was okay. Bill dropped the subject."

And then there was the strange story of Mark Schwartz.

Schwartz had worked with Art Smith in the insurance business. He took a midlife crisis time-out, quit his button-down job, and became the caretaker on Art Smith's island off the coast of Belize, to help Smith build his resort. This was the same island paradise Leasure boasted about to some of his friends, claiming to be a partner in the project. And it was the same island Anne Smith had threatened to take in the divorce just before she was killed.

Schwartz spent a year in this tranquil oasis, then trashed the island and its buildings, stole a boat Art kept there, and abandoned his post without a word.[13] John Doney told Arce and Petroski that "Art said he wished Mark would return to the Los Angeles area so he could get even."

On July 11, 1981, Mark Schwartz, age thirty-four, tall and lean, with a shock of dark curly hair, was found in his scuba diver's neoprene wet suit, facedown in the surf at the beach at Malibu, a .45-caliber bullet lodged in his brain.

The case had been worked in 1981 by the Los Angeles County Sheriff's Department, which has jurisdiction on the pricey beachfront of Malibu. Their files showed the case as still unsolved. The sheriff's detectives had never even heard of Art Smith when Bud Arce called over to ask them about it. To Arce and Petroski, the killing sounded like a Leasure-France special, with all the hallmarks of a contract murder. But Dennis France denied being involved or knowing about the killing of Mark Schwartz, and the detectives could never find any evidence linking either Smith or Leasure to the crime. Nevertheless, suspicions about Schwartz's death fueled the general consensus at LAPD that there were other bodies out there, waiting to be found and linked to Bill Leasure and his friends.

Finally, there was William Jennings, the former neighbor of Dennis France and Dennis Winebaugh, who had worked at the tortilla factory so many years before. The detectives traced him to Panama City, in the Florida panhandle, and they flew out to interview him. He, too, was a gold mine. He said France and Winebaugh had boasted to him about killing Gilberto Cervantes, and that Paulette definitely knew Dennis Winebaugh, contrary to her claims to Scroggins and others. He also mentioned knowing Bill Leasure and recalled how France and Winebaugh had told him, "You better hope that Bill doesn't find out you know anything."[14]

Bud Arce, Hank Petroski, and Jim Koller would never be entirely satisfied with their witnesses and their tapes. They would always feel that they should have found more, that there was still something or someone out there that would cinch the case—and that would explain why a man like Bill Leasure would turn to murder. Here and there, witnesses would give some insight into his character. More often than not, he remained remote from them, incomprehensible. They were satisfied he was a murderer, but they could not really say why he had taken that path. Was it for money? Thrills? The need to promote the image of being a fixer, a man who could get anything done, a man who could claim that even theft and murder were a "piece of cake"? The detectives and prosecutor had the feeling there was more to it than that, much more—that an important key to Leasure's behavior lay out there somewhere, beyond their reach. What it was, they couldn't say. Ultimately, they knew, the facts of the case, not the motive for the crimes, had to be proven. That was all the law required, and that was all they could do. And when they had gone as far as they could toward that end, the detectives and the prosecutor uneasily, but with a measure of relief, decided there had been enough investigation. It was time to start arresting people.

It was time to walk into court, to see if they could prove their case.

• • •

It's obvious why they told Bill Jennings that I better never find out anything. Because Dennis France and Dennis Winebaugh knew I'd arrest them if I found out anything. . . .

I can't imagine ever being convicted. I really can't. I can't see how twelve people can look at this kind of evidence, at the way the police handled this case, and not realize what the truth is: that I'm innocent. I've thought that from the moment I was arrested.

PART IV
1987–1991

THE BEST
FACTS

I've never killed anyone. I'd never hurt a fly.

— William Ernest Leasure

CHAPTER 19

ON THE SECOND FLOOR OF the Los Angeles County Jail, windowless and abuzz with the white bath of fluorescent tubes, sits a special, ninety-inmate section commonly called "7,000." Also known as "High Power," this section is the jail's celebrity wing, the protective-custody unit where professional athletes, movie stars, and television actors end up when they are accused of crimes and can't make bail. Otherwise ordinary defendants in highly publicized cases are imprisoned there, too: Raymond Buckey, for one, spent five long years in 7,000 awaiting his eventual acquittal in the infamous McMartin Preschool molestation case. A more briefly tenured resident was Charles Keating, the savings-and-loan king convicted of securities fraud—and whose S&L collapse would eventually cost taxpayers two and a half billion dollars in bailout money. Such high-profile guests of the county are considered potential targets of violence from more mundane prisoners, and therefore must be kept isolated.

This odd combination of inmates is made all the more peculiar by the third class of prisoners relegated to High Power: police officers. Cops accused of crimes are housed here, too, away from the other inmates, who tend to view policemen in their midst with something less than enthusiasm.

Bill Leasure would become the elder statesman of the 7,000 block once the homicide charges were filed and he was shipped down from Northern California to face the more serious case. By the time he was brought to trial, Leasure had lived longer in High Power than any other inmate in the lockup. This was no small accomplishment in the massive L.A. County Jail, a foreboding citadel that holds more *accused* felons than most state prisons hold convicts.

In the process, Leasure saw most of the big names come and go: the Night Stalker serial killer, the "Cheers" television show co-star in for drug possession, the former regular of "Bonanza" accused of dealing coke, and a string of fellow peace officers accused of everything from drunk driving to drug dealing to rape to murder. Even a relative of Hank Petroski's coincidentally ended up housed with Leasure for a few days on a drunk-driving beef. Neither man realized the connection when they exchanged hellos in the day room. When Detective Petroski found out, he quietly asked his colleagues at the jail for a discreet move.

High Power is no country club: The special status conferred upon its inmates limits, rather than increases, privileges for them. In all the time he would be confined while awaiting trial, five long years between his arrest and his day in court, Bill Leasure would barely see the sun. There was only an occasional glimpse through the smudged windows of the jail bus during the four-block ride to the courthouse and back. For years, the brief exercise periods on the jail roof for the residents of 7,000 came only at night, three times a week, when no other inmates were around. By the time of his trial, Leasure had all the color of a mushroom.

Visits were limited for Leasure, as was medical care and access to the most basic of jail privileges—library, newspapers, telephones. Numerous court orders to the contrary, Leasure could not get the jail to bring him to a civilian dentist for root-canal work. Leasure declined the jailhouse dentist's offer to yank the offending teeth, instead opting to periodically pop and drain the abscesses in his gums with a sharpened pencil. Jail confinement, he soon learned, not only removes a person's freedom, it saps his dignity. You find yourself groveling for a cold slice of pizza from a guard's leftover take-out. Residents of 7,000 must be handcuffed whenever they are moved about the jail, supposedly for their "protection." But ordinary inmates—the ones most likely to strike out at the cuffed and defenseless High Power prisoners—are not restrained, making attacks on the High Power people that much easier. As a working cop, Leasure never gave a thought to the conditions facing the "bad guys" he arrested. In jail, any illusions he might have had about coddled criminals vanished in the miasma of body odor and cleaning fluid that filled the jail.

Gone, too, was the confident stride of an LAPD officer. As the months bled into years, Leasure came to walk and sit with a jail-house hunch, the round-shouldered slouch long-timers invariably develop. Once you've been in long enough, you rate the coveted bottom bunk in your cell—but the tradeoff is, you develop chronic poor posture to avoid banging your head against the upper berth. Leasure got it bad: He began to look shorter than his five feet ten inches, as if the weight of all that restraining concrete and steel around him was slowly compacting him. During visits, his mother repeatedly reminded her son to sit up straight on his side of the glass partition. It was embarrassing for a man a few months shy of his forty-fifth birthday, but he smiled and nodded and said, "Okay, Mom," and tried to comply. Later, alone and stretched out on his narrow bottom bunk, he would dream of eating good pizza or maybe a decent hamburger, or flying one of his airplanes or driving fast in one of his beloved Corvettes . . . or of sitting up straight, his face to the sun.

Tucked under his bunk, a hoarder to the last, Leasure had accumulated what he liked to call his "ticket to freedom": an ever-expanding row of cardboard file boxes, each one crammed with police reports, interrogation summaries, and transcripts of witness interviews and surveillance tapes. This was the "discovery" in his case—copies of the state's voluminous evidence in the *People* v. *Leasure.* By the time his trial started in 1991, he had amassed eight such boxes, each the size of a large filing cabinet drawer, representing the investigative output of Detectives Arce and Petroski on the murder case (slightly less than two boxes), with the rest coming from the massive blitz of paper, tapes, and transcripts generated by the Internal Affairs team assigned to probe every other aspect of Leasure's life and times.

When he wasn't chasing mice and bugs from nesting in his six-man cell—the rodents had a habit of depositing discarded shells from the guards' sunflower seeds in his shoes—Leasure spent his time in 7,000 block obsessively reading and rereading the discovery files. With little else to do, he continually made entries in a bulging diary he called his "theory book," scrawling notes to his court-appointed attorneys, advising them on how best to structure his defense. Periodically, he penciled long, neatly printed letters to the judge presiding over his case, accusing the District Attorney's Office of withholding key evidence and of covering up police misconduct at Internal Affairs. Throughout these diatribes, Leasure pointedly misspelled Detective Arce's name as "Arse."

When Leasure spoke with his wife, his friends, his lawyers, his private investigators, or anyone else who cared to listen, he would say the contents of his boxes did not, as LAPD claimed, prove him to be a thief and a murderer. No, he would say, he was certain he could use the state's own files to disprove the charges against him. He was being framed, Dennis France was a liar, and the many inconsistencies in the state's case proved it, Leasure said over and over. And with an air of mystery, right up until the jury in his case was seated, he promised a few surprises—evidence that would not just dismantle the case against him, but would prove his innocence outright. In his mild, insistent, reasonable way, Leasure won more than a few converts.

"It's all there. All you have to do is look at the evidence—their evidence," Leasure would say shortly before his trial began, his hazel eyes bright behind metal-rimmed glasses, his voice patient and reasoned and restrained. As always. "There's so many contradictions, so many lies. . . . If you look at everything, I don't see how any reasonable person could not see the truth.

"And the truth is, I'm innocent."[1]

Dennis Winebaugh had been the first to fall in the murder case. Detectives Arce and Petroski arrested him in November 1986, charging him with killing Gilberto Cervantes.

They had settled on Forty-four Magnum as their logical starting point. Because of his tape-recorded admission that he killed the tortilla magnate, the evidence against him was clearcut when compared to the other suspects, and, therefore, his conviction seemed the most assured. Furthermore, the detectives decided, while sufficient proof existed to go after Winebaugh on the Cervantes hit, they could not charge anyone else with hiring him for the job. There was no corroboration of France on that killing, so no charge against Leasure could be filed—as yet. But by arresting Winebaugh, they hoped to persuade him to cooperate—to testify against Leasure and Paulette de los Reyes, just as they had dealt with France and Robert Kuns before him. Then, when the time came, they could charge their rogue policeman with three murders instead of just two.

Arce and Petroski flew from L.A. to Oklahoma City to make the arrest. With them was Detective Mike Hudson of the San Gabriel Police Department, which still held jurisdiction for the Cervantes murder. Winebaugh was working at the time as a suburban car lot security guard for a company with the down-home name of "Andy's Security." A pair of Del City, Oklahoma police patrolmen knew Winebaugh from their beats—they used to stop by and share coffee with him now and then at the car lot—and they agreed to help out. They brought the California cops by

Winebaugh's house as if for a social call. Forty-four ambled out to the car happily. "Hi, I'm Dennis Winebaugh," he drawled, putting out a hand toward Hudson, who had stepped from the car to greet him.

"Hi, I'm Mike Hudson of the San Gabriel Police Department," the slight, sandy-haired detective announced. "And you're under arrest for murder." It was a classic setup, the kind cops cherish and recount over beers for years afterward. Hudson could see Winebaugh's face fall as his life lurched to a sudden and unexpected halt. He had probably been napping or watching TV, not a care in the world, a man who had gotten away with murder, Hudson thought. Now he was looking at life in prison, which was just fine as far as the cop from San Gabriel was concerned. But then, as he snapped on the handcuffs, Hudson looked up and saw Winebaugh's new wife and stepchildren staring from the doorway, uncertain and afraid, unaware of Forty-four's past. And the sweetness of solving a ten-year-old murder shriveled into something hard and cruel.[2]

A search of Winebaugh's house turned up numerous weapons and, more important, a direct link to Leasure: a note in Leasure's handwriting describing the physical appearance, car, address, and workplace of Carlos Sepulveda, the man Leasure had wanted Winebaugh to beat up for annoying Betsy Mogul so many years before. LAPD mug shots of Carlos were attached. Winebaugh didn't explain to the detectives what the paper meant, but his ex-wife, Tammy, who still lived in the Oklahoma City vicinity, did. She told them about Leasure's request that Winebaugh take care of Carlos, and she also recalled numerous secretive meetings between her exhusband and Leasure. More important, she recalled Winebaugh having an unexplained three thousand dollars shortly before they moved from L.A. to Oklahoma in 1977—which, the detectives knew, was shortly after the hit on Cervantes.[3] Dennis France had already told the detectives that Winebaugh had earned five thousand dollars for the hit and gave him two thousand of it.

But any hope that Winebaugh would become another witness against Leasure faded by the time they got him back to the local police station for questioning. Forty-four was a different breed from the other suspects in the case—not a fearful follower like France, nor a dreamer and schemer like Kuns, nor was he like Leasure, who thought he could explain his way out of anything. Forty-four didn't panic when the police showed up at his door, nor did he show any hint that he was willing to cut a deal.

Ten years after the Cervantes hit, Winebaugh looked at first blush to be nothing more than a short, ailing man with a triple bypass operation under his belt and a heart with only a few years' worth of beats left in it. There were deep dark bags under his eyes, and his hair was gray and thinning. No one would mistake him for the Hollywood image of a hit man. "But when you take a good look at him, you see his eyes are steel, cold and calculating, inside that dumpy old man's head," Detective Petroski would later recall. "I looked at him and saw a born killer. It wouldn't faze him a bit."

At first, Winebaugh said he was willing to waive his rights and make a statement to the police. He readily admitted knowing Bill Leasure, even teaching him karate. "I think Bill was involved in stealing Corvettes," he said. He also admitted knowing "Paula," saying Leasure introduced them, and that he "slept with her a couple of times." But he said he knew nothing about any murders. This was exactly the cover story he had spelled out for Dennis France during the phone stiff two months earlier. After hearing these denials from Winebaugh, Arce and Petroski pulled out a transcript of that tape-recorded conversation and showed him the parts where he described the murder of Cervantes and how Leasure knew all about it.

"I recall parts of this conversation," Winebaugh said after glumly reading it through. "You're not going to believe this, but I thought it was a joke. Paula is eccentric. That was probably a robbery we tried to do. I better not say any more."[4]

And that was it. Winebaugh was brought back to Los Angeles to face a charge under Section 187 of the California Penal Code: murder. On the plane trip, he wavered briefly, telling Detective Hudson he did have a story to tell, an incredible tale of sex and multiple murders. But once they landed, he backed off his offer to talk, clamming up for good.[5] There would be no deal with Dennis Winebaugh. If Arce and Petroski were going to get Bill Leasure, it would be without his help.

Prosecutor Koller, though not ready to go public with murder charges on the Anne Smith and Tony Reyes killings, was nevertheless eager to up the ante against Leasure and his accomplices. So three months after Winebaugh's arrest, on February 27, 1987, he filed a new series of yacht theft and insurance fraud charges in Los Angeles involving the motor yachts *Deliverance* and *Thunderbolt*, and the sailing vessel *Santine*. Leasure's partner at LAPD, Officer Ralph Gerard, also was charged with two counts of receiving stolen property and two counts of insurance fraud for the two motor yachts;[6] Smith was charged with receiving stolen property, the *Santine*.

That same day, Betsy Mogul was charged with a single count of felony perjury. The charge stemmed from the false tax information on her Mercedes—the form that stated she had acquired the car from a parent, when in fact she had bought it from Art Smith. As far as her colleagues could recall, the occasion marked the first time a Los Angeles city attorney had ever been charged with a felony. It was also the first and only time a false filing on car registration taxes was ever prosecuted as a crime, rather than simply generating a nasty letter from the state bureaucracy, as had happened in every other similar case. Positive that Betsy was "dirty," LAPD brass had pushed for prosecution of her on whatever they could find, and the false filing on the Mercedes was the best anyone could come up with. Under pressure from the police chief, Mogul's boss removed her from the high-visibility position prosecuting crimes that she had occupied at the City Attorney's Office, ordering her to ride a desk in the city's most massive bureaucracy, the Department of Water and Power. She filed a grievance over the demotion, then took a sick leave, and eventually filed a worker's compensation case, claiming that stress on the job created by the Leasure investigation had disabled her.

Police Chief Daryl F. Gates, at a press conference called to announce all of the new charges, provided little new insight into the case. "It's hard to really understand why a police officer would get involved in felony crimes," he opined, "but it would appear that greed is probably a basic reason."

Three months later, on May 22, 1987, the investigation of William Ernest Leasure reached its inevitable conclusion: Art Smith and Paulette de los Reyes were picked up and charged with one count of murder and one count of conspiracy to commit murder apiece. They had been forewarned by publicity over the Winebaugh arrest, and they had prepared themselves for this day. Both demanded attorneys and refused to make any statements, much to Arce's and Petroski's disappointment. All Paulette did was complain loudly to Detective Arce about his treatment of her. Before driving her to jail to be booked, photographed, and fingerprinted, he let her feed the dog, water the plants, and arrange for someone to take care of her son. Yet all she could do was complain about the handcuffs and how Arce had failed to buckle her seat belt after helping her into his unmarked police car. At that, he screeched to a halt and, with an air of exaggerated exasperation, buckled her in. She responded with a sigh. "I feel sorry for your wife for having to live with someone like you." Arce was bemused—this from a woman he had just busted for having her husband killed. "Well, Ms. de los Reyes," he said, dragging out each syllable, "I'm not married. So there!"[7]

There was no such scene for Bill Leasure. He received his new felony warrants that month in his jail cell, charged with two counts of murder and two of conspiracy for the killing of Anne Smith and Tony Reyes. Koller declined to charge him with the Cervantes killing for lack of evidence, though he planned to use information about that first killing when he brought Leasure to trial. Leasure had awaited this day, dreading it ever since he had seen that camera above Dennis France's head, and figured out the import of the questions his former friend had been asking. Leasure read the legal papers over carefully, twice, then placed them in one of the boxes under his bed.

Popular courthouse wisdom has it that the time between arrest and trial belongs to the defense, and that, constitutional guarantees of speedy trials aside, the longer this period can be elongated, the better it serves efforts to win an acquittal. More time means more chances for crucial witnesses to change their stories, to grow reluctant to testify, to suffer from faltering memories—or to disappear or die, for that matter. More time means better opportunities for private investigators to hunt down defense witnesses to counter the prosecution's case—people who can provide good character testimony or alibis. And, just as important, more time removes a sensational case from the public eye, eliminating political pressures that might influence judge, jurors, and prosecutors alike.

In most cases, this stereotype holds: Prosecutors push for trial as soon as possible (after all, their investigation is largely complete once the charges are filed); defense attorneys, meanwhile, petition for delays in order to prepare their cases (their work doesn't start until the prosecution's is done and charges are filed, an inherent disadvantage). In *People* v. *Leasure*, however, this pattern did not hold true. Both sides asked for repeated and lengthy delays.

In part, this was because of an agreement that Winebaugh, Smith, and de los Reyes would be tried first, separately. The prosecution hoped that convictions of these other players would lead them to cooperate with authorities, strengthening the case against the prime target, Leasure. At the same time, Leasure's defense team was perfectly happy to separate their responsible-seeming traffic officer from the more seamy lot of defendants he was charged with. Better to have Mild Bill alone and forlorn at the defense table than surrounded by that bunch. The less association visible between Leasure and the others, the better.

Another means of speeding the process along—plea bargaining—was rejected early on. Preliminary discussions of Koller's offer to settle for a sentence of twenty-five years to life, with parole possible, was short-circuited when Leasure said there was no way he'd plead guilty. He wanted a trial, he said. He wanted to prove his innocence.

There were other reasons for delay, other proceedings that had to be completed. The first was LAPD's move to fire Leasure, a bulky bureaucratic process that ended up helping its target as much as it hurt him.

Every cop the department wants to fire is entitled to an in-house hearing called a Board of Rights, presided over by three ranking officers, much like a military court-martial. Other police officers, called "advocates," assume the role of prosecutor and defense attorney. For simplicity's sake, the department chose not to make a complex case against Leasure, but settled on a single charge accusing him of knowingly possessing a stolen vehicle—the 1927 Studebaker roadster found in his garage. This would be more than sufficient to justify stripping him of badge and salary, and seemed like an easy enough case to prove. As with everything else in the Leasure case, complications arose. The supposedly simple hearing began in April 1987, but continued in fits and starts for more than a year before concluding in June 1988.

Most Board of Rights hearings are anonymous and ponderous, a bureaucratic exercise before an empty room. Leasure's hearing, however, sizzled within a highly charged atmosphere of publicity and paranoia, with guards posted at the door of the Parker Center hearing room and body searches of those in attendance. Based on preliminary—and, apparently, overinflated—reports from Internal Affairs, the LAPD brass feared that accomplices might try to spring Leasure, or kill him to avoid being exposed themselves. Leasure was kept shackled throughout the proceedings. Fears of a plot were based more on paranoia than fact, Arce and Petroski would later say. But at the time, the precautions seemed reasonable.

In comparison to these extraordinary security measures, the actual hearing was dull, at least at the outset. Leasure had hired an attorney to aid in his defense, but the lawyer was stuck in court elsewhere. The panel of police captains hearing Leasure's case refused to delay the proceedings to await the lawyer's arrival, and Leasure, objecting to this denial of legal representation, offered no defense at all.

Unchallenged, the evidence against Leasure seemed clearcut: Mickey J. Blowitz, who identified himself as a film writer and producer as well as a car buff, reported his vintage Studebaker stolen on February 11, 1984. He told police at the time that he had parked the car at a lot on the campus of California State University at Northridge, the site of an exotic car show that day (and close to the Leasure home). When he returned, his car was gone.

When police searched Leasure's house two years later, looking for evidence of stolen yachts, they discovered the Studebaker in his eight-car garage, covered over with a tarp and piled high with airplane parts and other Leasure treasures. Officer Jon Herrington, Leasure's friend and occasional partner at LAPD, testified he saw the car in the garage in 1984, that Leasure never, ever drove it, and that Leasure had told him he had bought the car at an auction in Reno, Nevada, an apparent lie.

Leasure's nemesis at Internal Affairs, Sergeant David Wiltrout, testified that he had found a computer printout in Leasure's briefcase that contained registration information on the Studebaker, and which showed the car to be stolen—proof that Leasure knew the car in his garage was hot. The printout was dated May 9, 1984—three months after the car was reported stolen—and was traced to a terminal at Central Traffic Division, where Leasure worked. There was no evidence that the car had ever been sold in Nevada.

The board quickly found Leasure guilty and ordered him fired, to no one's surprise. Such hearings are often little more than rubber stamps of the police chief's desires, and any other result would have been unthinkable. But, again to no one's surprise, at least outside LAPD, the department was forced on appeal to overturn the firing and to grant Leasure a new hearing, for the obvious reason that he had been denied legal representation the first time around. LAPD had to put the whole show on again.

But this time, the main investigator on the case, Sergeant Wiltrout, was mysteriously absent as a witness, and some messy conflicts between the Internal Affairs Division and the rest of LAPD spilled out into public view as a result, to the potential detriment of the case against Bill Leasure.

Between the first and second Board of Rights, it seemed, Sergeant Wiltrout had pressed a case against a friend of Leasure's and

Dennis France's, the ballistics expert Jimmy Trahin. The Trahin case was Wiltrout's undoing—during it, he was exposed for allegedly manipulating evidence and subjected to questioning so humiliating, he walked out of the hearing and never again worked as a police officer.

The odd thing about it all was that the stakes at the Trahin hearing had hardly been worth the trouble. Trahin was never accused of any serious criminal act—only administrative violations unlikely to produce harsh discipline. But, a lack of proof notwithstanding, Internal Affairs had suspected him of much worse, for a variety of reasons. Trahin had been close to the murderer Dennis France. He had sold him weapons. France had claimed to have inside information on ballistics tests in the Anne Smith murder (although he specifically said Trahin was an unwitting provider of this information). And Trahin had been the original ballistics examiner on the Tony Reyes case (again, there was no evidence of anything other than coincidence here; shotguns cannot be traced through ballistics tests, leaving no room for any malfeasance by Trahin, even if he were so inclined). When these suspicions failed to lead anywhere, Trahin was charged with five administrative offenses against department regulations, including falsely reporting his badge and police identification lost (they were found at his home); unlawful possession at home of a fully automatic rifle he used as a training aid at LAPD; and a charge that he knowingly bought a fraudulently obtained color television set from Dennis France for $230. France was the primary witness on this last charge, along with a copy of the canceled check written to him on Trahin's account.

By the time Trahin's hearing rolled around in January 1988, Sergeant Wiltrout had been on the Leasure case for nearly two years and had come under extreme stress. A few months before the Leasure case had begun in May 1986, Wiltrout, a former telephone installer with a master's degree in public administration, had been removed against his will from a position at LAPD's controversial Special Surveillance Unit. This was a team of officers that secretly tailed and videotaped policemen suspected of misconduct, in an attempt to catch them committing crimes. Although most officers in the department had nothing but contempt for SSU, Wiltrout wanted the job back, and he attempted to prove himself by working seventy hours a week on the Leasure investigation.

Wiltrout came to believe that a group of at least ten employees of LAPD were involved in contract murders, thefts, and illegal weapons sales, along with at least ten accomplices outside the department. France's statement that Leasure talked of setting up other murders—some of them on behalf of police officers—combined with longstanding rumors of a hit ring operating within the ranks of LAPD, convinced Wiltrout that Leasure was only the tip of a large and corrupt LAPD iceberg.[8] Furthermore, persistent allegations surfaced from within the department that members of the bomb squad and ballistics section had been misappropriating confiscated weapons parts and ammunition from LAPD evidence lockers, then reselling the material for profit—while LAPD brass ignored or covered up the violations.[9]

But others at LAPD began to see Wiltrout less as a dedicated investigator and more as a man obsessed. Detectives Arce and Petroski, as well as Wiltrout's own partner at the time, Tom King, were among them. They did not agree with Wiltrout's theories, finding no evidence to back such assertions. In particular, they believed Trahin was innocent of any serious misconduct. Wiltrout reacted by initiating an internal investigation of King, for supposedly not being aggressive enough when searching Trahin's house.[10] The investigation of King led nowhere, but Wiltrout's fears and suspicions continued.

Then something happened to escalate those fears. After murder charges were filed against Leasure and while the Trahin case was pending, a man broke into Wiltrout's home while he was away at work. The intruder held a small knife to Mrs. Wiltrout's throat, then asked where her husband was. Then he demanded she call Wiltrout at LAPD to ask him to come home, so he could stab him to death. The call was never made, however—the assailant was scared off when the Wiltrouts' teenage son overheard the intruder's threats, then crept downstairs with one of his father's guns.[11]

Detectives Arce and Petroski, summoned from a meeting at Jim Koller's office, quickly located a suspect in the Wiltrouts' neighborhood. He fit Mrs. Wiltrout's description—and he was a recently paroled rapist with a pattern of similar knife-to-throat assaults. But she couldn't make a positive identification, and they had to let him go. Nevertheless, Arce and Petroski were certain he was responsible for the break-in, and that it was a botched rape rather than an attempt on Wiltrout's life. Wiltrout, however, thought otherwise. Why would a rapist threaten to kill him instead of his wife? Just because the murder attempt was inept didn't make it any less real, he argued. Look at Dennis France. Wiltrout remained convinced that Leasure or his friends had put out a contract on him.

"Why, Dave?" Arce countered. "You just worked the boats, not the murders. They'd come after us, not you."[12]

But Wiltrout was adamant, insisting, "He was here to kill me." When they failed to agree, he became convinced that Arce, Petroski, and the rest of LAPD were not taking this event seriously enough. For the next month, at his insistence, police officers watched over his house around the clock to protect his family. Nevertheless, Wiltrout felt more stress than ever—he wanted to conclude the Leasure case as soon as possible in order to blunt the danger to his family. He began working even longer hours than before, intent on putting away everyone he could. At the same time, fearful and depressed, he began suffering chronic insomnia, shortness of breath, and constant headaches.[13]

Then came his testimony before Trahin's Board of Rights. During three days of brutal questioning by Trahin's attorney, Wiltrout grudgingly admitted that he had concealed evidence that tended to prove Trahin's innocence. It seemed Dennis France, in his original statement to the police, had said Trahin did not know the television he bought was stolen. Later, however, in a separate interview with Wiltrout, France said Trahin *did* know the TV was hot, and that it had been obtained through one of Jerry France's bad checks.

In compiling evidence for the department's charges against Trahin, Wiltrout passed on only France's incriminating statements about Trahin, and kept the original statement to himself—a violation of Trahin's rights and departmental rules. Trahin's commanding officer had suspended him on the basis of Wiltrout's one-sided report, pending the outcome of the Board of Rights hearing. Wiltrout also failed to pass on France's original statements to Trahin's lawyer until the Board of Rights hearing was already in progress, again a violation of legal disclosure rules. In short, Trahin's lawyer, Mike Stone, told the board, the star witness in the Leasure case had lied, and Wiltrout had kept silent about it, to Trahin's detriment.[14]

As Stone, a longtime defender of police officers in Los Angeles, hammered away at Wiltrout, the normally taciturn Internal Affairs sergeant suffered a breakdown on the witness stand. He left the room weeping, unable to continue testifying. Away from the hearing room, he told his captain that he had lied on the witness stand—a ploy, he would later say, to get himself fired so he would not have to go on. Instead, a friend and fellow officer brought him to a clinic for psychological counseling that day. He called in on sick leave a few days later, never to return.

Wiltrout, who had led the internal investigation of Bill Leasure and everyone else connected to him, was unable to return to work after that. He eventually retired for stress-related disorders that included depression, paranoia, obsessional thinking, feelings of hopelessness, loss of self-esteem, and gastrointestinal distress. The Leasure case, he would later say, "began the end of my life."[15]

The board of officers hearing the case found Trahin guilty of the charges related to his badge, ID, and the automatic weapon. But they exonerated him on the most serious charge against him—purchasing the stolen television. Though Dennis France had testified at the hearing against Trahin, the three LAPD officials on the board found the ballistics expert not guilty. Dennis France was too incredible to be believed, the board ruled—a stunning repudiation of the star witness in the Leasure case. Jimmy Trahin received a five-day suspension, then returned to duty.

When it came time for Leasure's second Board of Rights hearing, Wiltrout was unable to testify. His psychiatrist wrote a letter advising the city that Wiltrout could not testify in any hearings because it would bring on "severely disabling depressive symptomatology."

In Wiltrout's absence, Leasure's attorney in Los Angeles, Richard Lasting, argued that the Internal Affairs sergeant had performed the same "hiding of the ball" with Leasure as he had with Trahin. He suggested Wiltrout concealed or destroyed a receipt for the legitimate purchase of the Studebaker. Leasure claimed that receipt was in the briefcase Wiltrout had searched, but that the sergeant had disposed of it in order to build a case. Quoting Wiltrout's own partner, Detective Tom King, Lasting said, "Sergeant Wiltrout was out to get everybody involved in the investigation." He implied that the most incriminating evidence in the case—the stolen-car computer printout in Leasure's briefcase—could have been planted. None of these assertions could be proven, and Leasure offered no canceled check or other evidence that he had bought the Studebaker legitimately. But in Wiltrout's absence, none of Lasting's allegations could be rebutted, either.

"Wiltrout was vindictive and, in my opinion, he destroyed evidence or withheld evidence," Leasure's LAPD advocate, Officer Wallace Owens, added.

In Leasure's defense, his sister-in-law, Wendy Mogul, testified that she saw the Studebaker in the garage in late January 1984—the month *before* the owner, Mickey Blowitz, reported it stolen—and that she remembered the date because at that time she was having Leasure fix the carburetor in her Gremlin. She said she remembered it well because he had to finish it before Betsy's birthday on January 30. Betsy Mogul then testified that she had an invoice for a Gremlin carburetor Leasure had bought for Wendy, and that it

was dated January 30, 1984—again, before the Studebaker was stolen. (This would not be the first time Leasure used a receipt as a
key element in his defense—it would be a recurring theme later in
his murder case.)

Betsy Mogul also testified that Leasure told her he saw the
Studebaker at a swap meet and wanted a thousand dollars from her
to go toward buying it. "I said, as I said so many times, 'What do
we need another car for?' And I think he said something about,
well, this will be your birthday present. And I said, some birthday
present, if I give you the money."

Finally, Lasting pointed out that the Studebaker, at most, was
worth six thousand dollars, but that Mickey Blowitz had insured it
for—and collected—twenty thousand dollars after its theft. The
suggestion was that Blowitz had sold (or had someone else sell) the
car to Leasure, then reported it stolen. Leasure was a victim, not a
criminal, Lasting argued.

The board dismissed the Mogul sisters' testimony as uncon-
vincing or a fabrication, then found no evidence to support the defense contentions that Blowitz was lying. The car had been hidden
in Leasure's garage, he never drove it, and he never registered it or
obtained a license plate for it in the two years he owned it. All this
showed his consciousness of guilt, and the computer printout
showing it to be stolen eliminated any doubt, the board ruled. The
verdict: guilty as charged.

The board then reviewed his personnel record before passing
sentence. Though the first board, before his lawyer was on the case,
had interpreted his record as fairly good ("He's a competent officer
and does a quality job in the investigation of traffic accidents," one
board member stated), this new board found in his record "a pattern of petty misconduct consisting of neglect of duty." He had
shown a lack of initiative and a pattern of selective enforcement on
the job, the board members said. The pattern was capped by his
misconduct with the Studebaker, which was termed "totally inconsistent with his role as a police officer."

They fired him and stripped him of all pay, benefits, and pension. And yet, despite everything, Leasure saw in it a victory. He
had successfully attacked the hated Sergeant Wiltrout. He had begun to make LAPD a defendant, right along with him.

•   •   •

Wiltrout brought me back to jail during my first Board of Rights.
This was early on, before the murder charges were filed. He says, we're

*charging Gerard, and he's going to squeal. Maybe you could go home if
you talk first.*

*It was all bull, of course. He knew there was a bigger investigation,
that there was no way they would listen to anything I said. He just was
hoping I'd incriminate myself somehow. It was so obvious, so unsubtle. It
just shows you what a liar he was. . . . I know he destroyed that receipt.
I know it was in my briefcase before he opened it. Just like I'm sure he
fed Dennis France information. He wanted that job back spying on policemen so bad, he'd do anything. He thought I was the way he'd get
back in good with his bosses, so he'd get that job again.*

*On one ride back from jail, Wiltrout told me he suspected me in
a murder from 1968. He accused me of being involved in the deaths of
Ball and McCree* [two bomb squad co-workers of Trahin's who
were killed inexplicably while defusing a type of bomb they had
successfully dismantled many times before]. *And he accused me of
being Caspar the Northridge Burglar. That's ridiculous. Caspar hit
my house two times, but he was scared off by my alarm system.
Wiltrout was trying to get anything he could to stick on me. He was
just out to get me.*

*. . . They made a big deal at my Board of Rights about those
neglect of duty complaints in my package. They were all minor things,
paperwork. Most of it had to do with my not qualifying* [for marks-
manship] *on a certain date. One time I broke my glasses and had to
go to the eye doctor. . . . More important than the good things in my
record at LAPD is the absence of the bad things. You look at my package, and the worst thing you can say about me is I didn't write enough
traffic tickets. Big deal.*

• • •

Betsy Mogul's Mercedes provided another milestone after
Leasure's firing. LAPD wanted to prove she committed perjury
when she registered the car and paid no tax. In the end, the department couldn't do it.

A handwriting analysis confirmed that the signature on the
form, dated April 1, 1983, was hers, but the key marking on the
document—an "x" next to a multiple-choice box indicating the car
was a gift from a parent—could not be positively identified as hers
or anyone else's. She had bought the car from Art Smith, definitely
not a parent. But Betsy testified that she signed the form without
reading it after her husband gave it to her.

"I would never think that Bill would ask me to sign something
I shouldn't sign." Later, Betsy's normally rigid control evaporated

as she broke down on the stand and cried, saying she would lose her license to practice law if convicted.

Then Bill Leasure was brought in from jail to testify that he had filled in the form incorrectly, not Betsy. He swore that he had deceived his wife and committed perjury because he didn't want to pay six hundred dollars in state tax. Bob Horner, the former second-in-command at the City Attorney's Office who quit his job, then signed on as Betsy Mogul's defense attorney, told jurors, "On April Fool's Day 1983, Bill Leasure played a trick on his wife Betsy. Six and a half years later, nobody is laughing about that trick."

The jurors acquitted Betsy Mogul after just over three hours of deliberation. Mogul, no longer weepy, immediately attacked the police and prosecutors as "petty, corrupt and venal politicians," and she vowed to work toward proving her husband's innocence now that she was free from prosecution.

"This was a prosecution that was meant to destroy me . . . to teach me a lesson, and that's all," Mogul told a newspaper reporter. "They wanted to make me testify against my husband, and they held that over my head. . . . Now where do I get my reputation back? They just crush your life and walk away."

Betsy Mogul, acquittal notwithstanding, was fired from the City Attorney's Office, a move that had come long before the verdict was in, "for behavior that is unacceptable for any public employee, let alone an assistant city attorney," City Attorney James Hahn wrote in her termination letter.[16]

Mogul eventually received a $140,000 settlement for agreeing not to sue the city over the firing, and for dropping her worker's stress claim.[17]

The great irony in the case, however, persists to this day: Betsy Mogul still has not paid the six hundred dollars in taxes she owes the state on her Mercedes. The extraordinary decision to prosecute Betsy criminally circumvented the state's normal method of handling such offenses—a letter demanding the unpaid taxes. Betsy Mogul is still awaiting that letter; in three years, it has never come. The police, she observed, lost interest in the case.

The series of murder prosecutions triggered by the Leasure investigation began in January 1988, with Dennis Winebaugh's trial for the murder of Gilberto Cervantes—a kind of prologue to the main event of the Leasure trial. By then, interest in the case had waned so much that not a single Los Angeles newspaper or television station covered the trial or reported its outcome.

Just as every defendant would do in the case, Winebaugh's lawyer attacked Dennis France's credibility, pointing to the inconsistencies and changes in his story in the years since he first came forward. In particular, the defense lawyer hammered at the fact that France, in his meeting in Chinatown with a D.A. investigator shortly after the hit, had claimed he pulled the trigger on Gilberto, not Winebaugh.

Deputy District Attorney James Koller, concerned at the negative portrait being painted of France, went so far as to apologize for the grant of immunity to the welder, and even agreed with the defense attorney that France was "an animal." But freeing Winebaugh, who had admitted committing murder on tape, would only add to the injustice begun when France received legal immunity, Koller argued. "I'm not here to defend Mr. France. He'll have to answer to a higher court than this court. It's not a comfortable situation for anyone having to put a devil on the witness stand. . . . But we have to play with the cards we're dealt."

Winebaugh's attorney, Gerald Lenoir, laughed at this assertion. "Mr. Koller says that France will have to answer to a higher court. You think France is worried about that? . . . He smirked about it when he stands up there. He shows no remorse. He's not worried about a maker. France escaped the gas chamber, that's what he did. . . . Isn't it funny that everybody that he knows is in jail, except him?"

The jury certainly had its doubts about Dennis France. During their deliberations, they posed a question to the judge: Does it matter if they reject the prosecution's theory and believe France pulled the trigger, with Winebaugh as an accomplice? Clearly, the jurors had trouble believing the star prosecution witness's latest version of the crime. Were it not for the tape-recorded telephone call, Koller would later say, Winebaugh would have walked out of court a free man. The prosecutor's worries about convicting Leasure suddenly doubled.

As it was, the judge repeated his legal instructions to the jury, which, boiled down, said an accomplice shares equal responsibility for a crime. It didn't matter who pulled the trigger if the jury believed both men took part in the killing. The jury returned with a guilty verdict.

The police again attempted to work a deal with Winebaugh, but he maintained his innocence to the end. In a presentencing report, Winebaugh said his only knowledge of the murder was based on what France had told him over the years, and that he and France had played "role-playing games" over the phone in which

Winebaugh "pretended" to be a killer. "I was tricked into a tele-phoned taped conversation," Winebaugh insisted. "I am completely innocent." The probation officer who heard this story commented in his report, "The defendant's explanation . . . is beyond credibil-ity."

A month after his trial, Los Angeles County Superior Court Judge Michael Berg sentenced Winebaugh to life in prison—the maximum penalty in 1977, the year the crime was committed.

"This is admittedly an unusual case involving a very cold con-tract killing," Judge Berg said at the time, "and the prosecution wit-ness is a double or triple slayer who has avoided prosecution. All in a day's work for the witness and the defendant, it would appear."[18]

A year or so later, Detective Arce and Jim Koller drove to Cal-ifornia's infamous Folsom State Prison. They went to see Winebaugh hoping he might have changed his mind about testify-ing against Leasure. Though beyond the stage where he could make a plea bargain to reduce his sentence, cooperating with the police could still help him earn parole sooner or get him into a nicer prison, they suggested. Winebaugh shook his gray head and still said he was innocent.

"I've got nothing to live for, anyway," he told Arce and Koller. "My son ran off, my wife left me. I'm just going to keep appealing. Do you know how many guys have AIDS on the yard? I'll just keep appealing until I find something you guys did wrong." Then he ex-plained to his visitors how he kept two pictures hanging on his cell wall—one of a mountain, and one of a Honda motorcycle.

"I just stare at the pictures and imagine myself riding that bike on some wide-open road," he said. "I put myself in those pictures, and close my eyes, and I'm gone. That's all I have to live for."[19]

The trial of Arthur Gayle Smith for the murder of Anne Marie Smith came a few months after Winebaugh's conviction, in the fall of 1988. The laws under which Smith would be prosecuted were different, and the stakes were higher. By the time Anne Smith was killed, capital punishment had returned to California. If convicted, he faced a potential death sentence.

As in Winebaugh's trial, the defense targeted Dennis France as the weak link in the state's case. He was a killer and liar who could not be believed, Smith's defense team said. In this case, how-ever, Smith's attorneys claimed France had lied about being in-volved in the Smith murder—that, in reality, he had nothing to do with it. He had fabricated his role in the beauty shop slaying in order to incriminate Bill Leasure and earn his immunity deal, and poor Art Smith was dragged down in the process. In truth, the defense argument went, the heroin addict Charles Persico—who had since been acquitted and released on a motion from the District Attorney's Office—was the killer all along.

"The reason Art Smith is here is because of the obsession of the police and the District Attorney with William Leasure, a dirty cop in their view," Smith's co-counsel, Len Levine, told the jurors.

But Smith's principal attorney, Charles Weedman, made two grave errors. In his opening statement, he told the jurors he would prove Dennis France never owned a green Chevy Nova with the word "Rally" and white stripes that had later been painted red—the getaway car in both the Smith and Tony Reyes murders. And then he promised that Art Smith would testify before them, to explain his innocence firsthand.

Neither happened. A cardinal rule of courtroom practice dictates that a lawyer should never promise anything he or she can't deliver. All the evidence, including France's family photos, suggested he did own just such a car, sold years before the trial. A private investigator had tried to track down the car—or the junked remnants of it—to show it had never been repainted, but failed. And Smith changed his mind about testifying. He never took the stand in his own defense.

As with Dennis Winebaugh, jurors on the Smith case had many questions about France's credibility, but this time, they were resolved by relying on corroborating evidence. Smith's former employees and tennis partner testified that Art spoke of plans to kill his wife. Then there was the phone stiff with Dennis France, in which Smith responded to France's mention of "the beauty shop" by saying, "Don't say any more." After a month-long trial, Smith was convicted of first-degree murder, with a finding of "special circumstances." The special circumstance was that it had been a murder for financial gain. This finding made him eligible for the death penalty.[20]

In California, the law requires a separate, second hearing called the "penalty phase" whenever there is a conviction in a capital case. The jurors hear evidence to help them determine whether death or life in prison without possibility of parole should be the sentence. Art Smith, as convicted killers go, with no prior record and plenty of character witnesses, seemed an unlikely candidate for the gas chamber. But rather than risk it, a humbled Smith, who had always refused offers to negotiate a plea bargain, asked if the state might still be interested in his testimony about Bill Leasure. If he had made a deal before his conviction, Smith could have netted a reduced charge and a short sentence. Now his only reward would be to short-circuit the penalty phase and go right to life in prison, with no risk of the gas chamber, but no chance of parole. To do that, he had to be willing to nail Leasure.

"What's more important to your client, Bill Leasure or Art Smith?" Koller asked. Attorney Weedman did not hesitate. "What's more important is Art's life to him right now. . . . We come to you hat in hand."

Art Smith, in short, had to take whatever deal Koller was willing to give, or take his chances with a jury that just decided he had paid to have his wife murdered. Arce and Petroski were ecstatic. They detested Art, seeing in him an egotistical air of superiority that they were only too happy to see demolished by the guilty verdict.

Yet, as humble and seemingly cooperative as Smith became, the statement he gave that day was peculiar—on the one hand, offering a chilling new glimpse of Bill Leasure, while on the other becoming a source of frustration. Even when confessing, Art Smith couldn't bring himself to go all the way and admit he was at fault.

Instead, he shifted the blame for the plan, the killing, and the decision to go ahead with the murder to Bill Leasure, absolving himself of nearly all the responsibility. The tone of the statement, if not its content, was remarkably reminiscent of Dennis France's confession so many months earlier: Leasure manipulated me into this fix. I didn't want it to work out this way, Smith was saying, but Leasure insisted.

Speaking to Koller, Arce, and Petroski, seated in the empty jury chamber next to the courtroom where his penalty hearing was to have been heard, Smith recalled the events leading up to Anne's death. It started with his complaining to his friend Bill about how his marriage was crumbling.

"I was complaining to Bill, you know, I don't know what the heck's the matter, things just aren't going good, and one thing led to another, and he said, 'Do you want me to get rid of her?' I said, no, hell no. He said, 'Well, that can be taken care of.' I said, no, no, I couldn't do that.

"He then proceeded to tell me a story . . . that Big John's mother had married a younger man. This younger man was apparently spending a lot of her money. Big John wanted to get rid of the guy. Bill told me . . . we, meaning himself and somebody else, I think he maybe meant Big John, I don't know, but he said, we took this guy out, we had anal sex, well, he didn't call it anal sex, but that's what he meant . . ."

"What'd he say?" Petroski, always matter of fact, interjected.

" 'Fucked him in the ass.' And then shot him.

"And I says, you couldn't do that. He says, we did. He says, 'I just want you to know we can handle any situation.' I says, Bill, I don't believe that. He says, 'I'm telling you we did, and the police will never find out because they'll just think it was another homosexual killing.' "

Even Arce and Petroski, with all their suspicions about what lay beneath the surface of Mild Bill, were taken aback by this tale. They envisioned more investigation, more murder charges. But Smith was not through.

He told the prosecutor and detectives that he had loaned twenty-five hundred dollars to Bill so he could buy a Corvette, and that he had given him his company's telephone credit cards so Leasure could make phone calls his wife wouldn't know about. Smith also recalled the house trailer he let Leasure use for trysts. Leasure eventually agreed to buy the trailer for thirty-five hundred dollars, but never paid for it, Smith said. He also recounted how Leasure had tailed Anne for him after she broke into his insurance office and photocopied his ledger books. At this time, Smith recalled, Leasure again asked if Smith wanted "her taken care of." Again, Smith said, he declined.

Later, when Anne filed for divorce, Leasure renewed his offer. "I said, Bill, if anything happened to my wife now, the first one they're gonna come to is me. I said forget it. He said, 'It would be a hell of a lot easier. . . . I can take care of it, Art, you don't have to worry, your name will never come up.' "

After several more offers and refusals, Smith said he walked by Dee Ann's House of Beauty one morning and saw a sign in the window saying the shop was closed because of a death in the family. He didn't know it was Anne until he called to ask what had happened. Anne had been killed, and he had no idea it was coming, he claimed.

When Leasure came by to go to the funeral with Smith, "The first words he said to me was, 'How do you feel?' I said, Bill, there's a big void. I said, did you have anything to do with this? He smiled and said, 'They have a good I.D. on the guys that did it.' "

Smith said he had felt relieved then, taking Leasure's comment to mean he was not involved. After that, Leasure would periodically update him on the investigation, showing him the composite drawings, telling him when Persico was arrested, and when Delores Garofola, Anne's mother, identified Persico as the killer. "I said, Bill, I was always concerned that you may have been involved in it. He says, 'Well, I'll tell you, Art,' and he told me that he hired to have Anne killed." Then, according to Art's story, Leasure said Smith could forget the six thousand dollars he owed for the Corvette and the house trailer, and they'd be even.

At this point in Art's statement, the tape recorder was switched off, and both sides paused to "negotiate." When the recorder was switched back on an hour later, Smith changed his story somewhat, accepting a bit more responsibility than he had originally. "I was very angry and I may have said, I don't give a damn, or . . . kill 'em, or something, I don't know. . . . I did tell Bill it was okay to go ahead and proceed on eliminating Anne, and Bill used the word 'eliminate' a lot of times. But it was, I don't know, maybe a week or thereabouts, next time Bill came in, I said, Bill, I can't do it, I do not want you to go through with anything on Anne, forget it." But Bill must have gone ahead and killed her anyway, Smith said.

Over the years, Smith swore, he was never really sure Leasure did it. Sometimes Leasure would claim credit, sometimes he would say he had just been joking, that Persico really had done it as a robbery all on his own. "But I am convinced now, yes, there is no question in my mind that Bill was responsible for Anne's death."[21]

Koller, Arce, and Petroski were not completely satisfied with this statement of Art Smith's, but they decided they could live with it. They believed that other testimony, from the people who heard Smith threaten to kill Anne, showed he was a more active participant than he was willing to admit. They knew what he was trying to do by waffling on his statement—he avoided totally incriminating himself, in case an appeal of his conviction succeeded and he won a new trial. The statement wouldn't damage him as much as an outright confession (though it would appear to undermine the Charles-Persico-did-it defense), and in the meantime, it would keep him off death row.

Fine, Koller told the detectives. Just getting Smith to testify bolstered the case against Leasure. It didn't matter what he said, as long as he said something. Without Smith on the stand, John Doney, along with the others who had heard Smith threaten to have Anne killed by a policeman, would be barred from testifying at Leasure's trial. Their testimony against Smith was fine, but against Leasure, their stories became impermissible hearsay—unless Smith testified first. Then these witnesses could be brought in to rebut Smith's claim that he really didn't want Anne killed, while they simultaneously helped convict Leasure.

The victory in the Smith case had quashed any doubts aroused during the Winebaugh trial, the prosecutor and detectives decided. Or so they hoped. That night, Arce, Petroski, and Koller cracked a bottle of champagne and celebrated. They felt they had Bill Leasure right where they wanted him.

But in the next few days, when they tried to check out Smith's story, they came up dry. They learned Big John's mother had never married a younger man, nor could they find any unsolved murder like the one Smith had described. Yet, combined with John Doney's story of a double murder in Utah by Leasure,[22] and the body of Mark Schwartz found floating off Malibu with a bullet in his head, the detectives were more convinced than ever that there were other bodies out there. But that wasn't proof—and it made them wonder just how much they could rely on Art Smith when Leasure finally came to trial.

The final prelude to the Leasure trial came in December 1989, when Paulette de los Reyes, after spending two years in jail, negotiated a deal of her own—one that sounded almost as good as Dennis France's. One of her attorneys, Gigi Gordon, had been hinting that she would put LAPD on trial if the prosecution went forward. But unlike Leasure, who had attacked Sergeant Wiltrout as the source of a conspiracy to frame him, Gordon suggested that Wiltrout was the one investigator who had been on the right track in the case—that far more heinous crimes were being covered up, and that Leasure was merely an underling in some much larger murder-for-hire ring within the department. She even came up with another murder she would try to link to Leasure, which LAPD had not investigated: a taxi driver from Oakland who had sued Leasure's partner, Officer Ralph Gerard, for brutality. The man had been shot dead, once in the head, in 1980 on his way to a deposition in the case. The unsolved murder, Gordon argued, was yet another professional hit connected to Leasure and his friends.

Such a defense had some inherent problems with it—namely, a lack of substantial evidence to support the conspiracy theory, and the admitted emotional instability of its chief proponent, David Wiltrout. Gordon's attacking defense did not greatly trouble Jim Koller, but he foresaw other difficulties in convicting Paulette. The objectionable nature of the tapes with LAPD Detective Scroggins, the key evidence against her, might be too much for a jury to take, with their bullying, browbeating, and offer to assassinate Leasure. All Paulette had to do was sit demurely at the defense table and keep her mouth shut, and the jurors could easily sympathize with her enough to vote not guilty. If she testified, Koller was confident he could put her away, but he also knew Gordon, a seasoned criminal attorney, might never let the argumentative and unpredictable Paulette anywhere near the witness stand in her own trial. And so he offered a deal Paulette couldn't afford to refuse.

Paulette de los Reyes became, then, the state's final addition to its witness list against Bill Leasure. She agreed to testify at his trial in exchange for being allowed to plead guilty to the lesser offenses of second-degree murder and solicitation to commit murder. She would be freed on one hundred thousand dollars bail until Leasure's trial, with her sentencing held in abeyance. If she testified truthfully in the Leasure case, the murder charge would be eliminated. She would be sentenced solely for solicitation, which carried a potential prison term of two to six years in prison. She conceivably could receive a sentence of time served if she cooperated fully, and walk out of court free and clear.

There was a strange twist to the deal, however: For strategic reasons, Koller, Arce, and Petroski deliberately failed to ask Paulette what her "truthful" testimony would be. They gave her the deal blind. Whatever she ultimately decided to say, they were fairly certain it would consist largely of denials of any wrongdoing. Mostly, they just wanted to get her on the stand, so jurors could see and hear the sort of people Bill Leasure was close to—and so they would have a legal excuse to play the Scroggins tapes to rebut any denials of wrongdoing. Contrasted with Paulette live, Koller believed, the tapes wouldn't sound quite so bad. Furthermore, by not taking a statement from Paulette, they had no obligation to release it to the defense. Leasure and his lawyers would be in the dark, too.

Paulette would remain a wild card, right up to the moment of Bill Leasure's trial.

• • •

They didn't ask Paulette for a statement because they knew she would say I was innocent. And Art Smith's statement was all lies—he just said all that to avoid the death penalty. That's why he put so many obvious lies in there. That thing about Big John's mother is probably false. His mother never remarried. I think Art did that on purpose, to show that the whole statement was a lie. That's why he had me cursing in there, too. . . . You can go talk to anyone you want. I don't think you'll find a single person who's ever heard me use a bad word. I don't swear.

. . . I feel sorry for Art. He got a bad deal. But those things he said are lies. All lies.

CHAPTER 20

DELAYS IN THE TRIAL OF WIL-
liam Leasure exceeded all expectations. It got so bad Leasure himself began to complain loudly about his rights being violated,
though the delays were principally for his benefit.

First, the other defendants had to be tried. Then Leasure's
lawyers had to clear their busy calendars for the long and complex
case. In particular, one of Leasure's defense attorneys had two capital cases to deal with first, including another LAPD officer accused
of committing a murder for hire.

Orchestrating court time to accommodate a three-month trial
such as Leasure's is no easy matter, either, not even in L.A.'s
factory-like criminal courts building. Eighteen floors and more
than one hundred courtrooms cannot begin to contain the constant
flow of victims, perpetrators, and lawyers. The members of these
groups, each scrupulously avoiding the other and each with their
discreet uniforms and demeanor, stride, wander, and slouch across
the chipped linoleum of the courthouse, with its too-short supply
of hard, molded plastic seats and its graffiti-tagged bathrooms that
reek of a disinfectant chemically identical to the bouquet of Ba-
zooka bubble gum. If not for plea bargaining ending a majority of
cases before trial, critical mass would have been reached in the
courthouse long ago, and the Leasure trial would have been scheduled sometime in the year 2016. As it was, the original trial date in
1989 slipped into 1990, then 1991, and the case of *People* v. *Leasure*
faded into obscurity, with scarcely any publicity when his case
number finally returned to the docket. By the time the trial was fi-

nally set to begin, in late March 1991, the case had become old news. Which was just fine with Leasure and his attorneys.

Then the legal landscape in Los Angeles—particularly for policemen—underwent a drastic change just three weeks before Leasure's jury was supposed to be selected. A black motorist named Rodney King was stopped for speeding after a prolonged police chase. King had initially refused to pull over, and a fleet of squad cars had joined the pursuit. When he finally emerged unsteadily from his car, King was surrounded by at least a dozen white LAPD officers. With their suspect unarmed, prone on the ground, and defenseless, several of the policemen beat, kicked, and clubbed King with a machinelike viciousness that shocked the city, then the nation—not because the other policemen turned them in, but because, unbeknownst to the officers, a plumber who lived in the neighborhood happened to capture the beating on his new video camera. Batons rose and fell, rose and fell, with hammer-on-anvil impact on Rodney King's head, back, and shoulders, while an LAPD sergeant made sure his comrades did not become entangled in the lines from the electronic stun gun that had already delivered repeated powerful shocks to King. And if the beating had not been an awful enough sight, the sheer number of officers who just stood by and watched it unfold, doing nothing (and, later, reporting nothing), was even more disturbing. It suggested department-wide problems at LAPD of such grave proportions that the despotic and previously invincible chief of police suddenly looked like he would be dragged down by the scandal along with the officers responsible.

At first it was treated as a minor incident—the *Los Angeles Times* inexplicably buried its first story about the Rodney King beating on page A-28. It was the kind of hands-off media treatment LAPD had gotten used to. But outrage over the case quickly escalated as television stations began broadcasting the videotape over and over, coupled with the image of King's battered visage as he lay in his hospital bed, barely able to speak. The slow-motion replays of white officers beating a helpless black man were a staple of evening news shows, network newscasts, and CNN updates for weeks, becoming an icon for long-simmering, long-ignored allegations of police brutality and official racism in Los Angeles. Suddenly interested in the issue as never before, press accounts of other egregious police beatings began to appear—all because this time, for the first time, an amateur cameraman caught the moment on tape, with all its visceral horror. Federal and state grand juries launched investigations, the officers involved were prosecuted but were later acquitted, triggering three days of rioting, reforms were begun, and a special commission began to probe police abuses and to plot a new direction for LAPD. Polls showed that public confidence in the department, always an iffy proposition in Los Angeles, dove to new lows.

In short, it was just about the worst time possible to be a police officer in Los Angeles accused of misconduct and about to face a jury of his peers. The normal dose of credibility and respect that comes with the policeman's badge had been erased by a few seconds of videotape. And all the arguments in the world about not judging the entire department by a few bad apples—however valid—were not going to help Bill Leasure.

His case might no longer have been infamous, but his profession was. Any juror likely to serve on the Leasure case had to know about Rodney King, had to have heard or read about the scandal rocking LAPD. Any advantage of anonymity Leasure might have gained through his long wait in jail had evaporated, he lamented. In the midst of the most sensational police brutality case in the city's history, ex-Officer Bill Leasure was going to be tried for the ultimate brutality: murder.

• • •

That kind of thing at the termination of a pursuit is the rule, not the exception. That's the unwritten rule . . . beat the hell out of someone for running away. I'd never participate in anything like that, but I've seen it happen. . . . So I guess I'm guilty, too.

It happens. When you're a policeman, and you know your buddies are gonna lose their job, you keep quiet. . . . But several times in my career, I've stopped things like that. Now I have to worry about it hurting my chances for a fair trial. . . .

There are certain officers who behave that way. Too many. But I was never one of them. Never.

• • •

Leasure's attorneys, Richard Lasting and Michael White, at the height of their preparations for the case, were stunned by the timing of the Rodney King scandal. The obvious parallels between the two cases were glaring: LAPD officers caught brutalizing a suspect on video; and their Officer Leasure, caught on video making incriminating statements about committing murders. Much of their defense rested on their ability to balance a law-abiding policeman's character and career against the credibility of the murderous Dennis France. "Now, it really seems to me that it might be extremely difficult for a police officer to get a fair trial in Los Angeles," Lasting remarked as jury selection was about to begin. ". . . Bill could easily be lumped in with the prevailing attitude about LAPD. It couldn't have come at a worse time."

Richard Lasting is a soft-spoken and articulate ex-Virginian, with a bushy, graying mustache, old-world manners, and an unrelenting courtesy both outside and in the courtroom—even as he skewers witnesses on the stand. Though Leasure would later complain bitterly about his lead counsel for "not being aggressive enough," other courthouse observers of Lasting's style found him to be effective, even brilliant, particularly with complex cases such as Leasure's. Indeed, the reserved, martini-dry judge presiding over the case, Stanley Weisberg, was uncharacteristically effusive when introducing potential jurors to the case. The judge told them they were in for an unusual treat because of the high caliber of legal talent assembled before them.

Lasting had been hired years before by Leasure, when the only charges on the books in Los Angeles involved three stolen cars and his police Board of Rights hearing. After the new boat charges and the murder case were filed, Leasure was declared indigent—once he quit-claimed all his real estate to his wife and the IRS froze his assets for failure to pay taxes on income from stolen yachts. A capital case defense in Los Angeles can easily cost a half million dollars from start to finish. So Lasting was appointed by the court, his fees covered by the county's taxpayers.

Leasure originally had sought Lasting out at the suggestion of another police officer, Richard Ford, who had been a cellmate in the jail's 7,000 section. Leasure had asked Ford if he had a good lawyer. Ford, who with another police officer was accused of jewelry store robbery, attempted murder, and murder for hire, gave Lasting a glowing endorsement. Leasure took the advice.

Ford's was one of the two trials Lasting had to clear up before tackling Leasure's case. Found guilty of first-degree murder, Ford successfully fought off a death sentence the District Attorney had pushed hard to obtain. Lasting presented evidence that proved Ford, before committing any crimes, had gone repeatedly to LAPD supervisors and counselors for help, confessing he had violent, even homicidal urges—only to be rebuffed and told to get back to work. In the judgment of Ford's jurors, such psychological problems before the crimes, combined with his attempts to get help and the LAPD bureaucracy's poor response, warranted mercy in the case. They chose a life sentence instead of death for Ford.

The meticulous case presented during Ford's penalty phase

trial had been assembled by private investigator Casey Cohen, whose unique specialty is finding reasons for murderers to be spared the death penalty. His firm is the only one in Los Angeles that exists solely to examine the reasons men and women kill, finding explanations, though not excuses, for their crimes. Lasting was so impressed with Cohen's work in the Ford case, he persuaded the court to appoint the investigator, along with his associate, social worker turned investigator Sheryl Duvall, to undertake a similar investigation of Leasure's character, mind, and motivations.

If Leasure was acquitted, Cohen's and Duvall's findings would remain secret, a compilation of reports in a warehoused file. But Leasure's attorneys knew there could be no gambling on such an outcome—the defense had to be ready for a conviction. Even as they fought to free Leasure, they also had to prepare the somewhat contradictory argument that he deserved a life behind bars rather than the gas chamber. And so, before the question, Did he do it? was answered in court, Cohen and Duvall would tackle the legally irrelevant but endlessly fascinating question, *Why* would he do it? In many ways, this quest for the real Bill Leasure, though divorced from attempts to prove his guilt or innocence, would lead to the most intriguing findings in the case.

The decision of the District Attorney's Office to seek the death penalty not only dictated the need for such an investigation, it also entitled Leasure to a second court-appointed attorney. Lasting's partner, Michael V. White, joined the case.

Trim and athletic, with close-cropped, salt-and-pepper hair, White, like Lasting, was in his forties, a former public defender, a family man and transplant to Los Angeles—though his long years in California had erased any obvious signs of his midwestern heritage. Like his partner, White was also a veteran criminal defense attorney with numerous capital cases behind him. Witty and affable, his demeanor in the courtroom had a sharper edge to it than Lasting's, and some of the more pointed cross-examinations in the case would become White's chore. Together they posed a formidable team, a kind of defense attorney's version of "good cop/bad cop."

Their first priority in the case—and their first battle—had been to try to keep jurors from seeing the videotape of their client and Dennis France at the Los Angeles County Jail, the single most explosive piece of evidence in the case. They knew that without the videotape, and the earlier audiotape from the Contra Costa County lockup, a conviction would be less likely. Having the tape excluded would, in all probability, win the case for them.

Their attack was based on two legal points. First, it is unconstitutional for police to question a suspect once he has an attorney and has invoked his Fifth Amendment right against self-incrimination. Second, it is illegal to interrogate anyone against their will while in jail, a legal principle adopted because of past cases of police coercing confessions from people in their custody who, obviously, could not just get up and leave. Since Dennis France was acting as an agent for the police, the lawyers reasoned, his questioning of Leasure was no different from a cop in uniform marching up to Leasure and demanding answers.

Judge Weisberg ruled otherwise. First, he agreed with prosecutor Koller, who argued that Leasure had invoked his rights solely in connection with the stolen boat case. The police should not be stopped from investigating Leasure for murder simply because the former officer had hired a lawyer to defend him on theft charges, Weisberg ruled. (To which Lasting said, in vain, that the police weren't barred from investigating, they simply should not be allowed to send in undercover agents to wheedle confessions they cannot lawfully ask for directly.)

Furthermore, the judge decided, Leasure had not been coerced. Had he known Dennis France was working for the police, then the conversation would have been an illegal interrogation and the tape would have been illegal evidence. But Leasure clearly thought he was talking to a friend, freely and voluntarily, with whom he shared experiences and secrets, Weisberg said. As such, the judge ruled, there could be no coercion.

The tapes would come in. Jim Koller had dodged a bullet.

On the heels of that defeat, Leasure's defense was dealt another blow: Koller would be allowed to present evidence about the boat thefts and other crimes during the murder trial. This was a departure from standard courtroom procedure, and one that drove Leasure into a fit of fidgeting at his defense table during pretrial hearings.

In almost every case, judges bar evidence about crimes unrelated to those specifically on trial. Since this trial was for the murders only, Leasure's attorneys felt the boat theft evidence should be excluded, as should the stolen cars, the insurance frauds, and, most of all, the ominous black silencers seized at Leasure's house, which carried such heinous connotations, but which had nothing to do with any of the murders. Jim Koller planned to prominently display those silencers at the prosecution table, in plain view of jurors.

Koller said he needed to demonstrate the intimate relationships between Dennis France, Robert Kuns, and Bill Leasure, and to do that, he needed to be able to show how the three of them had been crime partners—stealing boats together, trafficking in illegal weapons together, laundering money together. Only by demonstrating this kind of close criminal relationship between the three men could he show how logical it was for Leasure to have told the Skipper about the murders, and to have actually committed them with France, the prosecutor argued.

Judge Weisberg agreed—an exception to the normal rules of evidence would be permitted, and limited references to the boat thefts and the silencers would be allowed. Koller, confident of winning that argument, already had his office staff produce enormous blowups of incriminating pages from Leasure's notebook on boat transactions.

Now Lasting and White were in a nearly inextricable bind. There were only two people who could explain the meaning of the videotape and the notes Leasure had written in his jail cell: Dennis France, the star witness, and Bill Leasure, who might not be a witness at all. The dangers of putting Leasure on the witness stand in his own defense were enormous, especially with Weisberg's ruling on the boat theft evidence. Koller made no secret of his desire to see Leasure up there, exposed for the first time, so he could grill the former policeman on yachts, cars, weapons, girlfriends, everything he could find to expose Leasure's character flaws and propensity to lie. Lasting and White knew their client would deny everything—the boats, the cars, and the frauds, as well as the murders. That was the greatest danger they could foresee. The jurors could easily look at the overwhelming evidence in the boat cases and lose sight of the fact that the evidence on the murders was far more ambiguous. They could just focus on Leasure and his credibility, decide he was lying, and convict him.

"We want the jury to focus on Dennis France and see *him* for a liar," Lasting told Leasure in explaining their trial strategy—and why it would be unwise for him to testify. "We don't want them to look at you and say the same thing."[1]

Still, the question of whether or not Bill Leasure would take the stand remained open—at his insistence. "We'll wait and see how it goes," he said at the start of the trial. "I really would like to tell my side of the story."[2]

It was something Lasting and White feared almost as much as the videotape.

Leasure had revealed a certain amount of unpredictability during court proceedings—and stark hatred for Koller—that worried the defense attorneys. During jury selection, Leasure had mentioned one prospective juror's name to a cellmate—by coincidence, both the cellmate and the juror had once worked in the same Immigration and Naturalization Service office. Then the cellmate telephoned the prospective juror, who complained to the court, raising the question of whether Leasure was trying to influence or intimidate jurors. Though the call sounded innocent enough, Koller complained that Leasure had a history of telephoning witnesses from the jail, intimidating them. Now, Koller suggested, it sounded like he was doing the same with jurors.

"That's wrong," exclaimed Leasure, his pale face turned crimson, his glare fixed on the prosecutor. His attorneys shushed him, and later, he apologized for the outburst. Then he told the court, "There was no attempt to influence or bribe. . . . I've never, ever called a witness and threatened them whatsoever. I resent the implication."

Judge Weisberg shrugged off the issue as unimportant. Look at it from the prosecutor's point of view, the judge counseled Leasure. The prosecution thinks you're a murderer. "Certainly there's nothing wrong with a healthy suspicion on their part."

Leasure shook his head, but remained silent. His face was red again.

"I hope he testifies," Koller remarked during a break. "God, I hope he gets up there. I know his attorneys don't want him to." And then, with a mischievous smile as the defense attorney strolled by, he added, "But they can't control him."

• • •

What did you think of my little outburst? I really got mad today. That's so out of character for me. I'm really usually so mild. I just really resent the implication that I'd threaten a juror or a witness—or anyone. . . .

It's really unfair, what Koller is doing. He's going to bring in the silencers and the boats, he's even got my girlfriend on the witness list, anything he can do to slime me, to make me look like a bad guy. This is supposed to be a murder case. Why shouldn't he just stick to the facts instead of trying to make me look like a bad guy? I didn't have those silencers until 1984. The last murder was in 1981. What do the silencers have to do with anything? They've never been used. They were just toys. But they look really, really bad sitting there on the table, and Koller knows it. He's playing dirty, and the judge is letting him.

. . . I can explain the boats. I never stole them, I never knew they were stolen. But my lawyers are afraid if I testify, and I say I didn't steal

boats, then the jury might not believe me and they'll convict me on the murders. It really stinks.

. . . But what really gets me is that the prosecutor is withholding evidence. Every day it comes up, there's tapes we know exist, but that they won't give us, that they say are lost. These are things we need to prove they're lying about me. It's not fair. My life is on the line.

I really would like to testify. I really would, but it's a hard choice to make. I'm still thinking about it. I just don't know.

• • •

Perhaps nothing that happens in a courthouse is more tedious, more time-consuming, or more ineffectual than the process of selecting a jury. In Leasure's trial, more than two hundred potential jurors were assembled to ensure a bias-free panel for the capital case. A courtroom crammed to overflowing had to be reduced to twelve men and women for the jury box, plus six alternates in case sickness, disaster, narcolepsy, or misconduct compelled the judge to remove a juror from service.

After jurors with hardship excuses were allowed to leave one by one, the prosecution and the defense began battling to select jurors from the remaining group who, during questioning, seemed most likely to side with their views on the case. The prosecutor wanted jurors willing to impose a death sentence, and who expressed a certain eagerness to convict and punish criminals. The defense wanted just the opposite: jurors who were reluctant to impose the ultimate sentence, not only so Leasure wouldn't die, but because people with reservations about the death penalty are also less likely to blindly buy a prosecutor's theories.

Inevitably, both sides compromised on the composition of the jury. Each side had a limited number of "peremptory challenges"— twenty apiece—with which they could reject, without explanation, any potential jurors they felt would be unsympathetic to their cause. But when the challenges were used up, the attorneys would be stuck with whatever jurors were left, except when questioning revealed a bias so profound that a juror could be stricken "for cause" by the judge. Lawyers on both sides dole out their challenges with miserly reluctance, for fear that a worse juror might replace the one they veto.

Gauging jurors' true feelings is about as exact a science as rain-dancing. Lawyers rely as much on gut instinct as on the content of jurors' answers. Leasure's defense team included Wendy Saxon, a consultant who specializes in using demographics and psychological profiles to size up the best possible jurors for a case, against which Lasting and White weighed their own perceptions of jurors' body language and demeanor. Koller sat alone at his table, piles of file cards spread out in front of him, looking outnumbered by the defense team, but intent on weeding out the most liberal potential jurors.

Throughout this tedious two-week process, Leasure sat at the defense table next to his two lawyers, an ill-fitting suit replacing his jail jumpsuit. He was pale and uneasy, trying mightily to look attentive, to meet the jurors' eyes, to look confident, and, most of all, to avoid yawning. Yawns are as inevitable as gravity during jury selection, but Leasure was anxious to avoid even the suggestion that he was bored or disinterested.

The only consistent observers during this process, day in and day out, were Leasure's gray-haired parents, Agnes and Ernest. They had arrived from Michigan to become a stoic and silent show of support in the front middle row of the gallery, looking for all the world like the couple in *American Gothic* stepped out of their painting and into their Sunday best. They never missed a day of trial, not a moment of testimony, even when the accusations—"the lies," as they called them—grew so horrendous they had to shut their eyes and shake their heads as if to drive away the words.

"We know he's innocent," Mrs. Leasure announced early in the case, her voice quavering but her stare firm and resolute.

Many people called to jury duty have never, in any context, been asked to articulate their views on the death penalty before, and they seem surprised when they are told to offer up their opinions publicly, stammers and all. The first round of questions focused exclusively on attitudes about capital punishment.

"I really haven't thought about it," one man, Jose Luna, candidly admitted. And so he sat there a moment in silence and pondered the question of capital punishment, apparently for the first time. Finally, he looked up and said, "I strongly believe individuals who have to spend the rest of their lives in jail would have a lot of time to think why they're there . . . and I really think that would be a more severe punishment than taking that individual's life."

Mr. Luna, the lawyers would decide, was a juror who would most likely be favorable to the defense—conviction minded, perhaps, but death penalty resistant. This one was such a close call, however, that the prosecutor said he probably would accept Luna, too. Each side made a notation on their jury list for later, when the time came to exercise their challenges. Then the next juror's turn came and the process began anew.

A few minutes later, a prospective juror who said, "I believe in an eye for an eye," earned a thumbs-up from the prosecution, but Lasting and White made a note to themselves: must go. Koller made a similar notation on the next juror, who said he didn't like the idea of the state killing people, and that the death penalty serves only one purpose: "It clears the decks."

And so it went, until finally a United Parcel Service warehouseman with crewcut gray hair by the name of Edgar Mito took the hot seat and said, "I'd hate to think Mr. Leasure would be charged without solid evidence. It's a terrible thing to go through unless there's solid evidence."

The defense lawyers interpreted this as a belief by Mr. Mito that no one was ever charged with a crime unless the evidence was overwhelming. Mito reinforced that impression by saying he believed that if a person was found guilty of two murders, he'd vote for a death sentence. "Isn't that what the law dictates?"

Koller happily put Mito on his "keeper" list. Lasting and White, concerned that the prospective juror seemed biased in favor of death, challenged Mito for cause, hoping the judge would remove him without using one of their precious twenty challenges. Judge Weisberg refused. Lasting, White, and Saxon unanimously decided to put Mito on the list of people who under no circumstances should be allowed to remain on Bill Leasure's jury.

When the death penalty questioning was complete, the final stage of jury selection began. Called *voir dire*, Old French for "to speak the truth," it was a more general questioning of jurors' attitudes. In Judge Weisberg's court, the clerk draws pieces of paper from a gray metal strongbox, picking potential jurors' names at random. The lawyers then question each member of the panel individually, and either accept the person as a juror or reject him or her by using a challenge. The process often takes all day or longer as the lawyers wrangle for the most theoretically favorable jury. But through a random quirk, a panel that pleased both sides, with a few exceptions, was assembled on the first draw. After exercising only a few strikes each (the defense used only three, nearly unheard of), Jim Koller and Richard Lasting found themselves, to their surprise, announcing that they accepted the jury. The judge asked these twelve men and women to stand and be sworn in. Bill Leasure had his jury.

His twelve peers, the women and men who would sift the years and theories and characters to decide his fate, consisted of a real-estate saleswoman and grandmother; a pharmacist; a federal health service representative who once was stopped at gunpoint by police without legal cause; an LAPD clerk-typist whose voir dire remarks included, "Some officers treat civilians like dirt" and "Police can also lie"; a telephone company clerk; a county probation department service manager; a chemical engineer whose personal hero was Louis Pasteur and who thought police officers appeared "callous"; a Board of Education office worker; three post office employees; and, in a last-minute decision by the defense, the UPS loading dock worker, Edgar Mito.

As the panel was assembled, Lasting and White had decided there were at least twenty potential jurors worse for the defense than Mito. His opinions bothered them, but because he seemed so happy-go-lucky and easygoing, they guessed he was the kind of juror who would give in to pressure from other, more acquittal-minded members of the jury. Rather than risk striking Mito and drawing a worse juror, the defense team, with Leasure's reluctant approval, opted to keep him.

This seemingly insignificant event would have far-reaching results before the case was over. For it seemed everyone involved in this uncertain process of jury selection was dead wrong about the surprising Mr. Mito.

Bill Leasure's wife, Betsy Mogul, had attended some sessions of the jury selection process, and she was there when the jury was finally sworn in. She sat primly in the gallery, scanning the faces of the jurors with the practiced eye of a seasoned trial attorney, as the new panel members filed out of the courtroom. When the bailiff gestured for Leasure to rise so he could be returned to his holding cell, Betsy stood up and blew a kiss to her husband.

"What d'you think of them?" Leasure asked quietly, canting his head in the direction the jurors had walked a moment before.

"They're not your peers," Betsy Mogul said. "I hate them all."

CHAPTER 21

I'm tired of waiting. I want to get it over with. It's been five years, and that's too long to have to wait for justice.

But there's always the dread of getting started, too. You don't want to hear people saying bad things about you. It's really hard to listen to that. And my parents are going to be there. I don't want them to hear that stuff. I know it won't be easy for them, but they want to be there for me. I've tried to prepare them, I explained that it's the prosecutor's job to make me sound evil. But I'm dreading them having to go through that.

And, of course, there's dread about the outcome. What if the jury doesn't see the truth? I know I'm innocent, but what if they can't see it? . . . Unless you've been through it, unless you've been here where I have been for the last five years, you can't even come close to imagining what it's like sitting here, accused of terrible things, and about to have twelve people decide your fate.

• • •

BEFORE THE TRIAL BEGAN, there was one other preliminary matter in Judge Weisberg's court: the matter of Bill Leasure's name.

Leasure and his wife let it be known through his attorneys that everyone involved in the case had been mispronouncing his last name, incorrectly rhyming it with the word "seizure." They had put up with it all these months, but finally, shortly before the trial, they had to say something. In fact, the court was informed, his name should be pronounced *Lezh-er*, to rhyme with "measure," a pronunciation he had always observed, but which few people got right. In such a formal setting as a murder trial—*his* murder trial—

Leasure thought the very least he could expect was to have his name spoken correctly. And from that day on, everyone involved in the case tried mightily to do so, though it was a practice observed more in the breach.

During a break after this request, Detective Bud Arce, who as investigating officer on the case sat with Koller at the prosecution table, griped about what he considered to be a petty complaint. "What, are there suddenly French people involved in the case? If he's all of a sudden *Lezh-er*, then I want everyone to call me *Ar-say*."

And with that issue resolved, on the morning of April 15, 1991, the long-awaited trial of *People* v. *William Leasure* finally began.

"This is a complicated case, ladies and gentlemen," a resolute but weary-sounding Deputy District Attorney James Koller began in his opening statement to the jury. ". . . This case is about ten years of crimes committed by a Los Angeles Police Department officer, a uniformed officer who took the oath, wore the badge and the gun, and for ten years, from 1976 to 1986, committed every crime from murder to fraud, from theft to perjury.

"The evidence in this case comes for the most part from Mr. Leasure's best friends, from the men he socialized with, the men he invited into his house, the men he traveled with, and the men he vacationed with. The friends of the defendant, Mr. Leasure, will tell you the dark side of Mr. Leasure that the Los Angeles Police Department didn't discover for seventeen years while he was on the job."

With those few sentences, Koller sought to undercut defense arguments he anticipated about the scumminess of the prosecution's key witnesses. By labeling them as Leasure's friends—which they were—he hoped to counter the inevitable character attacks that the defense lawyers would heap upon them. If these people were so terrible, Koller was suggesting, why was Officer Bill Leasure hanging out with them? At the same time, he clearly was trying to tap into any resentment jurors might feel about LAPD in the wake of the Rodney King beating, with his pointed mention of badge, gun, uniform, and dishonored oaths.

But from that promising start, with the jury leaning forward in their seats, anxious to hear more, Koller's opening statement bogged down. There were just too many players, too many loose ends. He told the jury that the case was complex and confusing, which it certainly was. But so were his three hours of opening remarks, as he described the mazelike jumble of names and relationships in the case in excruciating detail. Tony, Paulette, Gilberto, Art Smith, Dennis Winebaugh, and Dennis France: all got their due, along with tortillas and divorces, drive-by shootings and bullet types. Even his strongest evidence, the videotape, seemed confusing and out of context at this early juncture. Who could tell what it meant without being immersed in the case? And the subject at hand—Bill Leasure—seemed lost in the jumble of information Koller tried to cram into his opening remarks. Even at his own trial for murder, it seemed Bill Leasure had the ability to fade into the background.

Jim Koller had the air of an exhausted man, worn thin by the long case and by Judge Weisberg's infamous predilection for starting earlier and finishing later than any other jurist in the building. In contrast to the dramatic tale of murder, greed, and treachery Koller had spun in the earlier trials of Winebaugh and Smith, when it came time to go after his prime target, the prosecutor's depiction of "the dirtiest cop in L.A." sounded like a story he had told too many times.

When Richard Lasting's turn to stand at the podium came— the first time he had to argue the Leasure case before a jury—he did not try to weave together the complex web of events and people that Koller had addressed. One of the advantages the defense possesses lies in a simple rule of debate: Tearing apart a complex case by focusing on its weak points is far easier than building a case out of many disparate puzzle pieces. As expected, Lasting focused directly on Koller's weakest link.

"This case is based on the words of Dennis France. And the evidence will show you that his words are not true," Lasting announced. ". . . He knew that his only chance to avoid arrest, conviction and serious punishment for the crimes that he had committed was to direct the police investigation away from himself. . . .

"What kind of man would do this? . . . That kind of man is a liar, he's a thief. That kind of man is an extortionist. That kind of man is a schemer. That kind of man is a braggart. . . . That kind of man is the kind of man the prosecution relies on to prove the charges in this case. That kind of man is Dennis France.

". . . You will find that deals were made, plea bargains were given, immunity was granted, threats were made, phony reports and phony evidence cooked up. And this was the path that the Los Angeles Police Department chose to travel down to find the truth."

Then Lasting spelled out the heart of Leasure's defense. Paulette de los Reyes personally knew the killers Dennis

Winebaugh and Dennis France. They were all she needed to arrange the murders of her husband and her father-in-law. Why would she need Leasure as middleman?

As for Anne Smith's murder in the beauty shop, that was a more difficult question for the defense to resolve. Should they argue France was responsible for that killing, too, but without Leasure's knowledge—even though there seemed to be no connection between Art Smith and Dennis France until well after the murder? No, the defense team had considered such a defense early on, then rejected it. It had the advantage of explaining why France knew so much about Anne Smith's killing and why he apparently owned a vehicle identical to the getaway car, but it would be too dangerous a direction to take. They had no reasonable explanation for how France could have gotten involved in the killing without Leasure's participation. And so they went the same route as the unsuccessful defense in the Art Smith trial: They argued that the police had the right man all along in Charles Persico.

So anxious was LAPD to nail Bill Leasure, Lasting told the jury, the department was willing to set two murderers free—France and Persico. France had simply thrown the Smith killing into his initial recitation to the police to sweeten the pot, and because it created a trio of crimes in which Leasure was the only common element. France knew about the crime not as an accomplice, but simply because, as a police groupie, he had pumped Leasure for information on the case. Leasure told him all about it, even gave him composite photos of the killers, Lasting said. France would have gotten away with it, too, if not for one thing, the lawyer argued: The problem with lying is keeping all the phony facts straight. Telling the truth over and over is easy, but telling lies breeds inconsistencies, and France's story was rife with them. Every time he tells his story, it changes, the defense lawyer said. You'll see it happen, right before your eyes, Lasting promised the jury. And he would be proven right.

Only in the last ninety seconds of his arguments, right before he told the jurors how certain he was that they would find Leasure not guilty, did Lasting finally mention the one piece of evidence he didn't want them to focus on: the videotape. "When you hear the complete evidence that surrounds this tape," Lasting promised, "and you can put it in context, you will see that the videotape does not implicate Mr. Leasure in murders."

It was the one promise Lasting was not sure he could keep.

• • •

The jury would never hear about it, but Lasting and his partner Mike White knew that Leasure could not explain exactly what the videotape meant. "I know I wasn't talking about murders," Leasure said adamantly, but as far as what the notes he wrote to Dennis France actually did mean, he said too much time had passed for him to be sure what he had been referring to.[1] Bill Leasure was a man with an extraordinary memory for detail. He could still vividly recall and describe some minor slight he experienced during a high school play. He even boasted that he still remembered the phone number of his sixth-grade girlfriend. Yet he said of the visit with France—a visit during which he spotted a police camera spying on him—that he simply couldn't remember.[2]

For this reason, among others, Lasting and White knew their case probably would not be that rare sort where a client's innocence was proven outright. They would argue his innocence, of course, claiming France and Persico were the sole culprits. But they realized this was a case in which Leasure would be freed because enough doubt was raised to avoid a conviction, not because jurors were convinced he was totally clean.

Leasure did not see it this way, however. He tended not to look at the cumulative effect of the evidence against him, but focused on the myriad contradictions in Dennis France's story, each little point on which France was wrong or inconsistent, no matter how niggling. Then Leasure would say, "How can anyone believe anything he says? He lies so much, it proves I'm innocent."

As such, Leasure was a difficult, demanding, and often irritating client, regularly arguing with and instructing his lawyers on how best to conduct his defense (often with his attorney wife kibbitzing, until she was placed on the witness list and excluded from the courtroom). And yet, with it all, Leasure seemed to crave his lawyers' reassurance. Over the years, he had repeatedly asked them if they believed he was innocent, a delicate subject with any criminal defense attorneys because, as most will frankly admit, so few of their clients are innocent. Both Lasting and White generally shied away from this question—defense attorneys can't afford the emotional investment of such considerations, since both guilty and innocent men deserve the best possible representation. They concentrate on what the evidence shows and how best to present it to their client's benefit.

"It doesn't matter what we think," Mike White told him at one point. "It's what the evidence proves. . . . It's what the jury believes."

Still, Leasure would ask the question from time to time, just as he had with his attorney on the boat cases up north, William Gagen. He wanted to be believed. People had always believed in him. Why, he wondered, should this be any different? How could anyone believe a Dennis France over me?[3]

The remainder of the first day of trial, along with the next, was taken up by witnesses who, for the most part, provided prosecution "housekeeping" testimony—the ballistics experts, crime scene investigators, and others who offered small pieces of the overall puzzle, but whose information was more in the way of background than anything else. Mary Tritto, the elderly woman who walked her dog the day Gilberto Cervantes died, told the jury how she saw two men parked in a blue pickup truck outside the dead man's home. Lieutenant James Goodman of the San Gabriel Police Department recalled the letters from Tony Reyes, one of them posthumous, that accused Dennis Dean Winebaugh of killing Gilberto. Anne Smith's mother, Delores Garofola, recalled the terrible day she saw her daughter die—and how she had picked a heroin addict named Charles Persico from a police lineup. Dabbing at tears, she spoke haltingly of how the robber in the beauty shop had been shorter than Anne, and described his curious method of "robbery"—how he had taken Anne in back, then up front to the register, then to the back again, before finally shooting her in the back.

Each of these witnesses' observations would be retold later, from Dennis France's point of view. The similarities in their stories, Koller hoped, would bolster France's credibility.

Perhaps most important among these early witnesses—and the most dangerous for both sides—was Thomas Rumbaugh, the Toyota mechanic who worked next door to the beauty shop. In the matter-of-fact manner of someone who was doing his duty, but who had no emotional involvement in the case, Rumbaugh told jurors what he had seen the day Anne Smith died.

There was the suspicious-looking thin-faced man in a baseball cap who walked through the dealership toward the beauty shop, then later came back, Rumbaugh recalled. And there was the scruffy, Latin-looking man with a mustache and dark hair waiting in the car, which was a green Chevy Nova with white stripes and the word "Rally" on its side. He recalled working with a police artist to create composite drawings of the suspects.

Jim Koller, in questioning Rumbaugh, focused on the car, his strongest link to Dennis France. At the same time, Koller made sure jurors heard Rumbaugh say Charles Persico was *not* the man he had seen that day, notwithstanding the testimony of Anne Smith's mother.

Mike White, while avoiding the subject of the car, zeroed in on Rumbaugh's recollection of the getaway driver, who, by France's word and the prosecution's theory, was supposed to be Bill Leasure. But the man Rumbaugh described sounded nothing like the pale, balding defendant. In particular, the man Rumbaugh described wore no glasses, which Leasure did, and had about a week's growth of beard—something no working LAPD officer could possibly have.

White finished up with Rumbaugh, confident the jury understood that Leasure could not be the man Rumbaugh recalled driving the Nova. But at the defense table, an increasingly anxious Leasure whispered urgently to his lawyers to press further—to ask Rumbaugh straight out if he recognized Leasure. Lasting and White whispered back no, they couldn't ask that question. The risk was too high. Gambling was fine when Leasure was risking his forty-dollar wad at the blackjack table, but not in the courtroom. You never ask a question unless you already know the answer, the lawyers told him. Still Leasure insisted, but, much to his chagrin, the lawyers still refused. "I want to go for broke," he would say later. "I want to win this."[4]

Neither prosecutor nor defense lawyers were willing to ask that telling question for fear they would not like the answer. Rumbaugh had never seen Bill Leasure before in person, and no one really knew what his answer would be. Though he had seen a lineup of six photos in 1986 and had failed to pick out either Leasure or France, that did not necessarily predict his response in open court.

In the corridor, out of earshot of the jury, the lawyers got their answer. His testimony through, Rumbaugh talked with Detective Arce before he left. "You know, that guy, the defendant, didn't look like the driver, but he kind of looked like the guy who walked through the garage. In fact, I'm pretty sure it was him." In other words, Leasure looked like the man who was supposed to have been Dennis France—he looked like the shooter. And, in fact, Bill Leasure did look remarkably like that composite drawing. The wrong composite drawing.[5]

Neither side wanted the jury to hear such potentially confusing testimony, and neither side recalled Rumbaugh to the stand to ask him about it. From the prosecution's point of view—at least, at that point—such testimony would undermine both Rumbaugh's and France's credibility, even though, in the short term, it would seem to implicate Leasure in the murder. They knew Leasure had not walked by the mechanic and into the beauty shop that day. Jurors might hear that and decide to disregard everything Rumbaugh said, including the Chevy Nova testimony, Koller reasoned.

But Lasting and White didn't want the jurors to hear such testimony, either, no matter how contradictory of Dennis France it might be. You just don't court disaster by bringing in a witness to say, "Why yes, your client does look like one of the killers."

Had the defense attorneys acquiesced to Leasure's demands, they later concluded, their case could have been undone then and there.

After two full days of testimony from prosecution witnesses, the jurors had learned where the bodies of Anne Smith, Gilberto Cervantes, and Tony Reyes had been found, what sort of projectiles killed them, and what sort of wounds the victims received. They had times and places and dates. But they hadn't heard the name Bill Leasure mentioned once.

All they knew of the defendant at that point was what they had seen in the courtroom: the pasty, attentive man in his baggy bargain-basement suit, sitting to the right of his lawyer Richard Lasting, whispering comments and scrawling notes. They had heard about murders, but had seen no connection to the defendant. It was time, Jim Koller decided, to tell them exactly what kind of man Bill Leasure was.

On the afternoon of the third day of trial, Dennis Edward France took the stand. His brow deeply furrowed above small brown eyes, France glanced edgily at everything in the courtroom—everything except Bill Leasure. France appeared in court that first day wearing a shapeless wrinkled white T-shirt, untucked over blue jeans. Arce, who was shepherding France during the trial and had salted him away in a downtown hotel for the week, was caught off-guard by France's tattered appearance. France's forty-sixth birthday was a week away, but he looked a good ten years older. The jury eyed him curiously, and with evident surprise. He looked less like the professional killer they had been hearing so much about, and more like a member of the panhandlers' gauntlet outside the courts building, which the jurors passed through each day.

Leasure avoided looking at France during breaks, when the welder was standing around waiting or chatting with Koller or

Arce. But when France was on the stand, the former cop locked his stare on his ex-friend with the intensity of a sniper. Throughout the next four days of testimony, France never could manage to return that stare. When he entered the courtroom, Leasure's father would announce quietly, "Here comes the liar."

Dennis France appeared nervous and hesitant throughout his testimony. On the witness stand, he toyed constantly with the metal band on his Timex and a rubber band, occupying his hands to keep them from fluttering out of control. He stuttered and suffered memory lapses, even under Jim Koller's friendly direct examination. Leasure would later accuse him of staging a nefarious, brilliantly planned frame-up job against him, and (without discerning the apparent contradiction) of being coached relentlessly by the police and prosecution. Yet it was hard to listen to Dennis France speak so haltingly, and with such difficulty, and accept either contention as realistic. Though clearly he was strong on street smarts and low on morality, the Dennis France the jurors saw seemed neither rehearsed nor capable of hatching a complex plot. Yet Leasure's lawyers had to prove at least one of these was true if their strategy was to succeed.

In the first round of questioning, Koller patiently coaxed France through his story of three murders, trying to avoid confusing the prosecution's star witness. He didn't want to inject any more inconsistencies for the defense to exploit.

First came the account of how France drove Dennis Winebaugh to the scene of the first murder, the slaying of Gilberto Cervantes. As he had every other time he told the story, France tried to minimize his culpability by claiming that Winebaugh lured him into participating in a murder without his knowledge.

"He had told me that he wanted to go hit somebody. And by that I thought he meant beat them up, because he said that a police officer had asked him to do this, and had paid him to do this."

Still, even under Koller's gentle questioning, France revealed a certain callousness about violence, unsullied by conscience. He showed no remorse on the stand, only unease at being there. And when Koller asked him why he had agreed to take Winebaugh to a beating, France answered simply, "He wasn't beating me up. And I wasn't going to be beating up the guy. He was a friend. He asked me to do him a favor. So I drove him there."

Later, France said, Bill Leasure appeared at his apartment building in Paramount and visited with Winebaugh. France was told to leave. When Leasure had gone and France returned, Winebaugh was sitting at his kitchen table, counting one thousand dollars in cash from an envelope—partial payment for the hit. Later, France said, he drove Winebaugh to Paulette de los Reyes's house, where Forty-four was paid the balance of his five-thousand-dollar fee while France waited in the car. Eventually France got two thousand dollars for his share, he said.

After the killing and after Winebaugh moved back to Oklahoma, France got to know Leasure better. Leasure eventually admitted his role in the murder, France testified. He said Leasure often complained that Paulette hadn't come up with all the money she was supposed to have paid for the Cervantes hit.

Some of the most damaging testimony about Leasure's character came next, though it had nothing to do with the murders. France recalled, almost nostalgically, how he had gone on ride-alongs in Leasure's police car—a remark that had some jurors shaking their heads—and how they had traded pistols and rifles over the years. France described Leasure's ability to convert semiautomatic weapons into illegal machine guns, and he recalled Leasure owning illegal silencers. "I owned one, and Bill kept it for me," he said, almost proudly. Koller made a point of having France handle the silencers up on the stand, making sure the jurors had a good look at the assassin's devices.

France also retold for the jury his recollection of Leasure boasting about the bombing of Tony Reyes's car: "He had gone into the department the next day and listened to his sergeant say how the person that did this stuff was some kind of genius with explosives."

And, of course, France had to describe their career stealing boats together—the catalyst for his coming forward to the police. He also discussed his peculiar financial arrangements with Leasure. "I would get money . . . but I would give it to Bill to hold for me."

Jim Koller, who had Leasure's notebook to back up France's word on this point, asked, "He sort of acted like your banker?"

"Yes, sir."

"Why did you do that? Why didn't you just do it on your own?"

"Because I'd spend it. I'd blow it if it was easily gotten to."

The image of this confessed murderer hanging out with his pal Officer Leasure, trading in illegal weapons and using the policeman as a personal banker and financial conscience, was shocking enough. So was the image of Leasure taking adolescent glee in counting down a bomb blast, then showing up at roll call to hear his ingeniousness described. The testimony seemed all the more damning because of the blasé manner in which France delivered it, as if he was discussing a bowling date he and Leasure once had. Yeah, we stole boats together, he was saying. And it was fun.

With notebooks and silencers there in the courtroom corroborating France's story, his credibility was boosted—at least for the moment. As tough as things would get for France on other subjects once he was challenged by the defense, jurors would hear nothing to rebut this "bad character" testimony for the rest of the long trial. The first and most vivid image the jury heard of Bill Leasure, the man, was filtered through the eyes and words of Dennis France.

The next murder France described was Anne Smith's. Once again, he said he hadn't wanted to kill anybody else, but that Leasure had coerced him. Leasure's original plan, France testified, was for him to go to Anne Smith's home in Pasadena, where he would force his way in, then stage a fake rape or robbery before killing her. Later this plan was dropped, he said. (This story bore remarkable similarities to the tennis instructor Richard McDonough's statement to police, in which he recalled Art Smith threatening to hire two policemen to execute his wife while disguising it as a rape-kidnapping.)

France said he kept putting off the killing, but finally, because of an upcoming hearing in the Smith divorce case, Leasure said "it had to be done that day." Leasure came to his house, called in sick to LAPD from France's phone, told him to hide his gun in a sock, and drove him to the beauty shop in France's car. Then, France said, Leasure sent him in to kill.

Before going through with it, France claimed that he tried coming back to the car, telling Leasure that a mechanic had seen them. But Leasure insisted, and France had no choice but to obey. "He told me to shoot her twice, but I didn't. I only shot her once." It seems the hammer on his pistol kept getting snagged on the sock. He pulled the trigger as Anne Smith flinched, but nothing happened. Finally, he pulled the sock out of the way and fired a single deadly shot, then ran out into the parking lot, he said.

Tony Reyes's killing was outlined in much the same dispassionate way—a reluctant Dennis France stalked Tony for days, putting off the murder as long as he could. He said he deliberately missed him during a drive-by shooting with Leasure at the wheel. Then, only after Bill threatened him and drove him to the scene, France finally shotgunned the musician to death in a nightclub parking lot. France recalled that Leasure waited in the car, out of sight and with the motor running, while he stood behind the low wall of the parking lot and demanded Tony bring him his wallet. But Tony ignored him, France said.

"I took a couple of steps back where he couldn't see me and I told Bill that he wasn't bringing me the money. . . . Bill said, 'Shoot.' And I shot.

"I did not want to do the killing. . . . If Bill Leasure hadn't taken me there, I would never have killed him or anybody else."

On France's second day of testimony, he came to court remarkably cleaned up, in a crisp, button-up white shirt and blue slacks—Bud Arce's influence, and a quick trip to the nearest mall. He explained how the gun-in-sock plan had failed in the Anne Smith killing, because the casing had fallen out of the bullet hole in the sock as he got into his car. Because the murder weapon could be traced to that brass casing, Leasure demanded that France hand over his .45 automatic. France recalled that Leasure promised to destroy the gun by melting it.

After the killing, Leasure called France and told him there was a perfect description of his car, and that he should get the green Nova painted, France said. Then France identified for the jury two pictures, each about ten years old. The first was of the green Chevy Nova with its Rally stripes, his wife and three children posed in front of it, all obviously ten years younger than their current ages. The second picture showed the same car, repainted an orangy red, parked in Northern California beneath a giant Sequoia tree, which had been hollowed out as a roadway tunnel. "Our car in the tunnel log, Sequoia, January 1981," was written on the back of the photo by France's wife.

The first photo was a key piece of evidence in the trial. Lasting and White could claim all they wanted that France had fabricated his role in the Smith murder, Koller would later argue. But there was no way he could fabricate ten-year-old photographic proof that he owned a unique Chevy Nova identical to the getaway car in the murder.

"There's some facts we just can't explain," Mike White said later, during a break. "We just have to hope the jurors see him for what he really is—a liar."

At the end of direct examination of his star witness, Koller played the audio- and videotapes of France's two jailhouse visits with Leasure, with the confessed murderer providing commentary from the stand. As they watched the videotaped visit on a big-screen television monitor, Koller hoped the jury would find only one interpretation for Leasure's secretively written notes. What else could "Melted" mean, Koller would argue, other than Dennis France is telling the truth? What else could it mean, other than Bill Leasure is a murderer? And what innocent man would end his conversation with the demand, "Dump everything illegal?"

• • •

The task of cross-examining Dennis France—of destroying his credibility—fell to Richard Lasting. Before he was through, he would have the state's star witness on the stand for three days, reducing him to a hostile, tongue-tied, and truculent witness whose story was both confused and contradictory. France had started his testimony playing with his watchband in order to keep his hands busy. By the time the defense attorney was through, he had three or four rubber bands, several paper clips, and his by-then stretched and flaccid watchband, performing intricate little twists and turns with these toys, which he tried, not always successfully, to keep hidden from jurors' vision beneath the rostrum of the witness stand.

"He broke one of his rubber bands and I thought he was gonna die up there," Detective Arce muttered after the first day of cross-examination. One evening, after a brutal six hours on the stand, France had driven from his hotel thirty miles to Long Beach to get drunk. "I thought about just getting back in the car and keepin' goin'," a red-eyed France admitted to his handler, Detective Arce, the next day. "I'd have hunted you down, Dennis," Arce promised solemnly, "and put you away."[6]

Lasting, always the gentleman, was courteous, almost apologetic to France during breaks, offering to get him a glass of water or chatting amiably with him. But when court was in session, Lasting pressed France into a corner with brutal dispassion. His disgust at the man was clearly visible, even through the politeness.

"Have you ever bragged about killing people?" Lasting asked.

"Yes, sir, I, I have lied to a few people," France replied.

Lasting seemed surprised with the answer for a moment. France had just volunteered a key admission about himself, unsolicited. "I'm sorry?"

"I had lied to a few people."

"Well, let's start with bragging first," Lasting suggested. The lies would come later.

Lasting then forced France to retell his long line of false boasts about killing people—how he had once told the Skipper, Bob Kuns, that he had sliced up a doctor who mistreated his son, that he had killed "a man for a woman over insurance money," and that he had then killed the woman—Paulette de los Reyes—for failing to pay the bill on a contract murder.

"And had you killed a man for Paulette de los Reyes?" Lasting asked.

"I had killed Tony for Bill, because at that time I had not met Paulette de los Reyes," France countered.

"But what you told Bob Kuns was you had killed a man for a woman over insurance money," Lasting said, driving home his dual contention that the murder of Tony Reyes did not need to include Bill Leasure, and that Dennis France was a man who continually lied about committing murders. "Is that right?"

Reluctantly, France nodded. "Yes, sir." He had told Bob Kuns exactly that.

"Don't you like to portray yourself as a violent man, Mr. France?" Lasting asked.

"No, sir."

"Did you ever brag to Dennis Winebaugh about killing people?"

"I don't remember. . . . He was bragging to me . . . and he was telling me lies about he had said he had killed a police officer for another police officer."

France tried to fight back in this way at first, injecting such unsolicited accusations into his answers. This fencing with Lasting didn't last long, however. The defense attorney's attacks quickly beat the witness into submission.

"Did Mr. Winebaugh arrange for you to kill Tony de los Reyes?" Lasting asked at one point.

"No," France said, then smirked and laughed.

"Is that funny?" Lasting asked, rebuking France, whose laughter died in mid-guffaw.

"Huh?"

"Is that funny?"

"Yeah," France finally said, a half smile still on his lips. "That would be funny, if Forty-four had arranged that. No, sir, no way."

But France's reaction had been measured by every juror in the courtroom. It had been an unseemly display—a killer laughing derisively at the suggestion that he might need a fellow hit man's help in setting up a murder.

More dramatic still was the revelation, through Lasting's questions, that Dennis France still owned firearms—with the police department's blessing.

"I own a forty-five. A shotgun. A rifle. I own three rifles, I think it is, two handguns and a shotgun."

"What kind of shotgun do you own?" Lasting asked, knowing what the answer would be, setting France up.

"A Remington 870 pump."

"Is that the same kind of shotgun that you killed Tony de los Reyes with?" Lasting asked.

France hesitated, just a moment. "Yes, sir."

A juror gasped at this. Others shook their heads. The image of Dennis France still owning firearms was not a comforting one.

Then Lasting brought up France's story about going to meet a D.A. investigator in Chinatown to confess to killing Gilberto Cervantes and to beg for help.

"What was your motivation in going to meet with them?" the lawyer asked. "Why did you do that?"

In previous tellings, France had given two primary explanations: He wanted out of the "murder ring"; and he wanted to avoid having to kill Anne Smith. This latter explanation was impossible, a clumsy lie, since the meeting took place in 1978, and the Smith killing came two years later. The Smiths hadn't even begun divorcing at that point. Lasting had hoped to hear France repeat the same account, so he could tear it apart. But instead, at Leasure's trial, France offered yet another explanation.

"Bill was talking about a police officer's wife and child," France said. "This police officer, I think, wanted his wife and child killed because they were going to take his house and part of his pension or something. And he wanted me to do it. I didn't want to do it. And that's why I had gone [to the meeting in Chinatown]. . . . For some reason, it never came up after that."

Lasting was furious. France had told this story before to police, about the policeman who wanted his wife and child murdered, but always it had been described as occurring long after the Chinatown meeting. Just as Lasting had promised, France was changing his story, right before their eyes.

"Have you previously stated that the reason you went to see these two men . . . is because Mr. Leasure had asked you to kill Anne Smith?" he asked.

"I don't remember," France answered—a phrase he would begin to use with increasing frequency.

"Have you told so many stories about this that you can't remember which ones you told?" Lasting asked.

"Sir, I've told the same story, the best I could remember it, every time."

Yet, Lasting pointed out, you lied at the meeting and said you were the triggerman in the Cervantes killing, right? Now you say it was Winebaugh, and that you didn't even know a murder was about to happen. France conceded this was so. So you lied about committing a murder? Again, France conceded the point. And did you give the investigator Leasure's name? No, France said, I only knew him as "Bill" then. Yet, Lasting asked, you knew Leasure well enough for him to ask you to commit a murder?

The illogic of his statement suddenly hit home. France shrugged and mumbled, "That's what I said, yes, sir."

When France explained that he didn't know Leasure's last name for several years after meeting him because he was too illiterate to read the officer's LAPD name tag, Lasting got him to admit that, during that same time period, he had passed the written test for a California driver's license, and owned numerous books on how to avoid paying taxes.

Returning to the Chinatown meeting, Lasting said, "You lied to them . . . because you thought . . . they may give you a deal if you could nail a police officer?"

"No, sir."

Just as you lied at that meeting in Chinatown, Lasting continued, as if France's answer was too ridiculous to acknowledge, you lied years later, after Leasure was arrested, right? France shook his head. No way. But didn't you know the only way you could get a deal was if you gave them a cop?

"I was hoping," France conceded. "I figured the police department would want a police officer more than they would want me. . . . At that time, I don't know what I was thinking, sir."

"Well, let me see if it refreshes your memory to hear the statements you made on August 8, 1986." And then Lasting began the first of many dramatic readings of France's prior statements—the litany of inconsistencies Detectives Arce and Petroski had feared ever since they inherited the case. Lasting read:

DETECTIVE: Well, under the circumstances, Bill sure could have [cut a deal], but he never got the chance.
FRANCE: No, Bill couldn't because, you think about a police officer paying somebody to go shoot somebody. Now who's in more trouble? You're a police officer. I shot the person, but you paid me to do it.
DETECTIVE: Well . . .
FRANCE: Now who's Mr. Gates gonna want, you or me?
DETECTIVE: You got a point there. Mr. Gates would want me.
FRANCE: You betcha.

"All along your state of mind . . . was that if anything unraveled about your criminal conduct, you wanted to be in a position to blame it on a policeman, didn't you?" Lasting asked.

"No," France said. But the point had been made. France had known all along that he could trade a policeman for his own neck. He had known it when he went to the police after Leasure's arrest . . . and he had known it ten years before, in that meeting in Chinatown. And suddenly the notion of Dennis France scheming and plotting a frame job did not seem quite so outlandish as it had a few hours earlier.

In this way, throughout the day, Lasting kept hammering away at all the past and present inconsistencies in France's story. Every time France would score a point, Lasting would pull out a transcript and point out that France had said just the opposite during some interview or hearing in the past. Oh, now you claim you didn't know Cervantes was going to be killed. But didn't you tell Dennis Winebaugh that you were nervous on the day of the murder, because it was your first one? Now you say the brass casing in the Anne Smith murder rolled under a car, but didn't you always say before it was a Dumpster? And you only changed your story because, to your embarrassment, photos taken at the time show no Dumpster present? Then there was the matter of France's original statement to police that Tony Reyes's murder was the second. It supported the theory that France was lying—why else, Lasting asked, would he forget that Anne Smith's death came before Tony's? And so it went, with France gulping like a man drowning, his rubber bands and paper clips performing their absurd ballet as he retreated into a convenient, but utterly unbelievable, amnesia: "I don't remember. I don't remember."

As Lasting finished his first day with Dennis France, the witness had begun to answer "I don't remember" to virtually every question, even ones he had answered the day before for Koller. Perhaps his memory had degenerated somehow since the other day, Lasting suggested with mock concern. France didn't remember if it had or not. Battered and bewildered, France grew stubborn at that point. He wasn't going to answer anything now. He just stuck out his jaw and maintained the facade of memory lapse. The confessed hit man, who admitted murders without hesitation, was so worried about being made to look bad on the witness stand that he decided to answer nothing at all. "I just wanta get outta here," he muttered after the first day. "I don't want to be grilled."

When a few dozen fourth-graders entered the courtroom on a class field trip, one boy, listening to France testify, looked at the prosecution's star witness and mistook him for the accused. "He's guilty, all right," the boy whispered loud enough for half the courtroom to hear.

The next day, France only looked and sounded worse. Trying to raise doubts about the videotape, Leasure's attorney suggested France, not Leasure, had conceived of the idea of a melted gun. Lasting asked about a meeting France had with Betsy Mogul while he had been working undercover for LAPD with a body wire. According to Lasting, France had, among other things, asked Betsy about two .45-caliber handguns he had sold Leasure.

"Do you remember that you told Mrs. Leasure with regard to these two forty-fives, that Bill, her husband, was supposed to have melted one of them down?"

"I may have, yes, sir," France conceded.

"Do you recall that Mr. Leasure's wife told you that there were a lot of rumors flying around?"

"I don't remember what she said to me, no, sir."

". . . Do you remember that you told Mr. Leasure's wife that you were concerned about those forty-fives, and that she should ask her husband Bill about them?"

"I may have, sir."

"Do you remember saying to her, 'Ask Bill, ask Bill, and then I won't be worried, would you'?"

"I don't remember, sir."

". . . And that you said to her, 'Have Bill call me'?"

"I don't remember, sir. No, sir."

By that point, it didn't matter what France said. The questions, not the testimony, contained the information Lasting hoped to convey to jurors. He had established that Dennis France, not Bill Leasure, was the first person to have brought up the subject of a melted .45. Perhaps that explained the note "Melted" on the videotape. Maybe it wasn't a statement by Leasure to France.

Maybe, just maybe, it was a question.

Lasting also played portions of the audiotape of France's first jail visit, then questioned France's oblique method of trying to incriminate Leasure—by hinting at the subject of murders, without ever mentioning them outright. "Right off the bat," Lasting asked, "why don't you ask him if he has the forty-five that you shot and killed Anne Smith with?"

"I don't know," France replied. ". . . I don't remember."

When a portion of the tape recording revealed France commiserating with Leasure over the "lies" charged against him, Lasting stopped the machine and asked, "At this point, why don't you bring up the murder of Anne Smith instead of telling Mr. Leasure, 'You haven't done nothing'?"

"I have no idea why I didn't." France, so rattled at this point, didn't think to mention Leasure's nervousness during the meeting, or the jailed policeman's repeated warnings to France to avoid speaking about anything incriminating. Nor did France mention his instructions from police—his script—that dictated he should avoid making Leasure suspicious by being too overt. Such explanations would have blunted this attack, but France was too flustered or too angry to make them. All he could say was, I don't remember, hoping his ordeal would soon end.

Strangely, when his turn for redirect examination came a few minutes later, prosecutor Koller did not clear up this misimpression. He moved on to other areas, and France's inability to ask Bill Leasure a direct question about murders would be left unexplained—a point Lasting and White would return to for the rest of their trial.

France couldn't ask about the murders directly, they would argue, because he knew Bill Leasure to be an innocent man. He knew Leasure would say, "I don't know what you're talking about." And the case would be blown.

A few anticlimactic minutes later, Dennis France's testimony concluded after four and a half days on the stand. He shuffled out of the courtroom, shoulders hunched, a man who had been shown to be a murderer and a liar and a man who couldn't be believed. His credibility was nil, just as Detectives Arce and Petroski had feared so long ago. And just as defense attorneys Lasting and White had hoped.

• • •

I really wanted them to ask the mechanic right out—did he recognize me or not? But they wouldn't do it. They were afraid because he was hostile, he wouldn't talk to them in the hallway. So probably they were right. But this is life or death. I know I wasn't there. I say, go for all the marbles. Be bold!

. . . Dennis France refines his testimony every time. He adds things. He's coached. The first time he told the story about why Anne Smith had to be killed, it was because she was running up high medical bills. Now he says it's a marriage counselor, which he could only get from the police. First he says, Bill hired me to kill her for the boyfriend. Then it became a divorce. He's been so coached and rehearsed. It really bothers me to sit there and hear it and have to take the lies.

. . . I really don't remember what I was talking about in those notes in the video. It's been so long. I don't know why I wrote "melted."

Maybe he mouthed the word, and I wrote it down. I just don't know. All I know is, I wasn't talking about murders. And neither was he.

• • •

While the lawyers vied with witnesses and one another, criminal justice consultant Sheryl Duvall was still conducting her penalty phase investigation, focusing on very different questions from the ones unfolding in Judge Weisberg's courtroom. And the portrait of Bill Leasure she had assembled differed so starkly from Dennis France's and LAPD's as to sound like an entirely different person. In years of death penalty investigations, Duvall had never seen a defendant whose background seemed so unlikely. Or, rather, a man who seemed so unlikely a defendant in a murder case.

Duvall would later say she'd go to her grave without understanding Bill Leasure. "I'd be willing to swear he hasn't changed since he was four years old."

She had spent long hours with Leasure, studying his pale bland face as they sat and talked in the jail's attorney conference room, a long corral of a room filled with rows of metal stools, narrow counters, and the soft hum of furtive conversation. Even with his ghostly jailhouse pallor, Bill Leasure looked harmless, inoffensive, incapable of the acts he was charged with. For the past four years, Duvall had made a career of finding shreds of decency within the most heinous murderers, stubbornly assembling reasons to spare the lives of serial killers and sociopaths. She redeemed the unredeemable, crawling inside their lives and minds and, almost without fail, uncovering pasts haunted by abuse or incest or drug-addicted parents—lives that had taken shape without kindness or love. This didn't mean they deserved freedom, Duvall believed. Sometimes, though, it earned them mercy.

But Leasure was different. The social worker turned death penalty investigator had searched his past and found no reason for him to kill—no horrors, no excuses, just a nice man with nice parents. Just an ordinary man, accused of extraordinary evil.

"I can't find out anything bad about you, Bill," she had reported to him shortly before the trial began. "Everyone I talk to says you're a quiet, mild guy."

"That's because I am. Tell the jury that!" Leasure had answered. "You can't explain why I'd be a killer, because I'm innocent. It's that simple."[7]

Duvall had traveled east to Wayne, Michigan, seeking out friends, family, neighbors. She looked for one of two things: a nightmare childhood, so common in murderers; or some trauma that altered Leasure's life, a hidden pain so terrible that he was twisted and changed by it. She found neither.

He was the same shy, nonassertive person in grade school and in the Marines as at LAPD. He suffered no terrible loss in Wayne, no battle trauma in Vietnam, no upheaval at LAPD. His life before Bob Kuns and Dennis France was baby food—bland and homogeneous. Finally, Duvall had to give up on explaining why Leasure might kill. She came to believe he was quite probably innocent—not based on the facts of the case, with which she had only passing familiarity, but based on her evaluation of Leasure's psychology and background. He had none of the scars borne by every other murderer she had known, none of the sociopathy. She saw no killer within him. Most of her other clients were quite credible as murderers, but Leasure was not. She asked him a dozen times if he had done it, and always he would look her in the eye and say, absolutely not. No. Never.[8]

Yet her job was to assume Leasure would be found guilty. And if she couldn't provide jurors with a sympathetic explanation for that guilt, then she had to be able to do the next best thing—prove Leasure had too much good in him to be executed, despite his actions. Essentially, she fell back on finding witnesses to attest to Leasure's good character.

Such witnesses could be used in either the guilt-innocence phase of the trial or the subsequent penalty phase—the lawyers would decide that. Duvall found no shortage of character witnesses. Her intelligent, soothing manner put even suspicious LAPD officers at ease, and she soon found dozens of witnesses who felt Leasure was incapable of violence despite the charges against him—sergeants, former partners, and street cops among them. This was an extraordinary occurrence. Testifying for an accused "dirty" cop never earned plaudits at the department. Quite the opposite. And yet there was a long list of officers ready to take the stand.

Virtually everyone Duvall talked to who knew Bill had similar things to say. She soon had a procession of good character witnesses to describe Leasure's gentle, helpful, peaceable character. Yet Duvall also knew, from the LAPD investigation, that Leasure had cheated on his wife, deceived and manipulated his mistress, hung out with disreputable and murderous characters, obtained stolen vessels, and lived a strangely separate, disconnected life from his wife. A quiet and passive man, he had used quiet, passive means of getting his way—secrecy, lying, silence. And the fact that many of his friends were as shocked at the news of his mistress as they were of him being arrested raised the obvious question: How well did these character witnesses really know Bill Leasure?

In all, Leasure was a puzzle to Duvall, unlike any murder defendant she had ever encountered.

Psychologists hired by his lawyers had found Leasure to be normal, for the most part. But on one battery of tests, with questions designed to show whether or not he was answering honestly—questions like, "Have you ever told a lie?"—Leasure answered, no, I have never lied.

After several similar answers, the psychologist administering the test had called him on it, and said, "If these answers are true, then you must be a perfect person."

Instead of being prodded by this comment into making less perfect answers, as the psychologist had expected, Leasure had answered simply, "Yes, you're right. I am."

• • •

My investigator went back to Michigan to see what kind of secrets I had in my background. There aren't any. I gave her a list of everyone I knew. She talked to just about everybody, people I haven't seen since high school, or earlier. She said what she found was unusual, she had never seen it before. I was basically the same type of person that I am now—Mr. Nice Guy, basically.

Her job is to find flaws, something to blame my behavior on. But there wasn't anything. She couldn't find anything bad because there's nothing bad to find. There's no explanation because I'm innocent. I'm so squeaky clean, it's unusual.

. . . I'm the nicest, quietest, mildest guy you'll ever want to meet. I've never killed anyone. I'd never hurt a fly.

CHAPTER 22

"THE MAALOX BOTTLE'S been getting a real workout," Jim Koller admitted the day after Dennis France's testimony concluded. "You never know what's going to happen until you get 'em in here."

His carefully planned presentation of evidence and witnesses had suddenly begun to unravel. It wasn't Koller's fault—the prosecutor had recovered from his problematic opening statement and had been pressing witnesses with incisive questions as he wove together the dozens of separate accounts he needed to prove his case. But on April 24, 1991, the eighth day of trial, events beyond his control had sliced a huge chunk of evidence from his case.

Arthur Gayle Smith had decided to renege on his deal.

There had been warning signs. Shortly before trial, Koller and Detective Arce had gone to the state prison at Tehachapi to meet with Art and discuss his statement. Smith had said everything he told them before was a lie. He refused to discuss the facts of the case with them. Instead, all he would talk about was how lousy prison life was, and how his cellmate stole the freeze-dried soup Smith hoarded in his cell, then passed gas from the top bunk. Other than those two subjects, Smith would say no more. Delays in the trial had worked to Leasure's advantage: Smith had an appeal pending by then, and he said he would refuse to testify. Later, though, after the visit to Tehachapi, Smith had second thoughts, and his lawyer told Koller that no firm decision had been made on testifying. They would have to call him to the witness stand to see what happened.

So Koller subpoenaed Smith as a witness, and had him hauled

down from the relatively expansive Tehachapi state prison to the dismal confines of L.A. County Jail. The prosecutor knew Smith would stew there for at least a week before he was called into court. Detective Arce was gloating at the prospect, but as soon as he saw Smith walk into the courtroom in his blue jail coveralls, he could see by the look on his face that he was going to refuse to testify.

"I wish to institute my Fifth Amendment rights," Smith announced, with jurors removed from the courtroom and waiting in their deliberation room. "I'll take the Fifth."

Judge Weisberg ordered Koller to question Smith, making a record to show that the witness understood the potentially dire consequences of his decision. Glaring angrily at Koller, whom he clearly despised, the reluctant witness answered tersely, often through gritted teeth, pale and overweight but still holding the erect bearing of a former Marine.

Smith said he didn't want to endanger his appeal. Yes, he realized his original statement to the police could be used against him if he did win a new trial on appeal—a virtual assurance that he would be reconvicted. He also understood that he faced a potential death sentence if he refused to testify. Judge Weisberg, taking over the questioning, spelled it out for Smith.

"I understand, sir," the former insurance adjustor said bitterly. "And I will say this at this point. It really doesn't matter. Life imprisonment without the possibility of parole is worse than the death penalty."

Smith then launched into an angry tirade against Koller, returning to the position he maintained before his trial—that officials had framed him in their lust to convict Leasure. "Anything I say will obviously be twisted not to my benefit. . . . The District Attorney and his staff has lied about me in the past and they will continue lying. . . . They manufactured stuff, they lied. And I can't help it, I am bitter about the way I was treated. . . . I do not trust the District Attorney and his staff. And I don't feel free to say anything."

And with that, Smith was led from the courtroom back to his holding cell. As he passed, he tried to say hello to Leasure, but the defendant sat silently, pleased at the outcome, but wary about even appearing to communicate with Smith. He didn't want anyone to accuse him later of coaxing Smith into silence. Leasure's lawyers were jubilant.

"We really didn't know what he was going to say," Lasting confided after the hearing. "It changes things."

That it did. The loss of Smith as a witness eliminated more

than just his personal testimony. His recorded statement to the police after his guilty verdict two years earlier, so damaging to Leasure's defense, also was rendered inadmissible by Smith's decision. With that, any evidence that Smith had paid Leasure for murder evaporated. Now the defense lawyers would get up and say, see, the prosecution promised to show you how Leasure profited from the murders. And he was wrong.

Worst still, Smith's change of heart meant Koller most likely had lost two of his most prized witnesses, John Doney and Richard McDonough—the two men who swore that Smith had talked of hiring policemen to kill his wife. If Smith had testified—and repeated his story that he really never believed Leasure would kill his wife—Koller could have called the two men to "impeach" Smith with contradictory testimony. They would show that Smith had indeed intended to kill his wife. But without Smith on the stand first, their testimony became inadmissible hearsay, just like the taped statement. Unless Koller could find some other legal basis to get the testimony in—and none seemed apparent—potentially devastating evidence against Leasure had suddenly been rendered worthless.

And the case was up for grabs.

Another near disaster for Koller's case was barely averted that same day when Sandra Zysman, Tony Reyes's girlfriend, was called to testify. Zysman provided some crucial corroboration of France's story. The problem was, when she saw round-shouldered, middle-aged, balding Dennis France in the hallway of the courthouse, she grabbed Detective Arce and said in a panic, "You've got the wrong guy. There's no way he's the man who shot Tony."

But then Arce and Koller showed Sandra a ten-year-old picture of a slimmer, darker, hairier France, an old Polaroid shot he had dug up of himself in a welder's outfit. When Zysman saw it, she relaxed. Yes, that could be the man I saw shoot Tony. She couldn't be sure, but it could be him. And she confirmed that on the witness stand.

The outspoken Zysman had also berated Koller before appearing in court. She was livid when she heard Paulette de los Reyes had gotten a lenient plea bargain. "I wanted her to fry," Zysman said simply, expressionlessly. "That woman deserves to die."

As a witness, Sandra Zysman, a short, stout, youthful woman with curly dark hair, was straightforward, clear, and well-spoken—a refreshing change after more than four days of Dennis France, both prosecutor and defense attorneys agreed. The Tony Reyes she described was "very, very caring. . . . His son, in my eyes, adored him. He followed him around like a trained puppy." She clutched a ragged Kleenex and broke into tears midway through her testimony. "I still miss him so much," she said during a recess as she tried to calm herself. "It's been ten years, and I'm still mourning him. I still have his picture on my bureau. He's still the love of my life."

Her composure recovered after a short break, Zysman's testimony corroborated key elements of France's account. She recalled the drive-by shooting in the months before the killing, and how an angry Tony had pursued the car from which the shots were fired. He pulled over only because Sandra begged him to stop. France had described the encounter in similar terms for the jury.

But Zysman could not say if there was one or two men in the car, leaving room for defense arguments that France acted alone. Zysman did say the car passed by with its passenger side closest to Tony's car, creating a rather difficult shot for the driver, but an easy one for a passenger. And the car was orange-red, she said—the color Dennis France had painted the green Chevy Nova after the Anne Smith killing. Tony had never called the police, she concluded—just as France had testified earlier.

Her description of the murder was also quite similar to France's—the demand for money from a shadowy figure, Tony's and her decision to ignore the man, and the sudden, fatal shot. These were the areas Koller focused on.

But defense attorney Mike White found ample—and significant—contradictions. France had said he stepped back, out of sight, to consult with Leasure when Tony had refused to cough up the wallet. That was when Leasure supposedly gave the order to shoot. But Zysman recalled it differently.

"I kept watching because I was afraid he would come—I thought he was going to rob us at first. But he never left that corner. . . .

"My eyes weren't off this man but maybe for a split second. . . ."

She heard nobody else but the man and his demand for money. She neither saw nor heard a getaway car leave. All she saw was Tony crumple to the ground after the sound of a shot. She was aware of little else after that.

"I started to yell help. . . . Nobody would come. Nobody came. I grabbed Tony, I saw the blood everywhere."

White had gotten just what he wanted from Zysman—a witness who put Dennis France at the murder scene, but who disputed him on every detail that suggested a second person was involved. The defense could say, sure, everything France said about killing Tony was true—except for the parts that put Leasure at the scene. The parts he made up.

Finally, to draw focus away from Leasure and toward another culprit, White asked, "Did you tell Paulette de los Reyes of Tony's death?"

"Yes," Zysman recalled bitterly. "She laughed in my face."

The trial, after that day, became a roller coaster. The defense lawyers, pessimistic about their chances at the outset, suddenly saw a case that looked winnable. They had destroyed France on the witness stand, Lasting and White decided, and now Smith had backed out on his deal with the prosecutor. They left the courtroom that afternoon buoyant. Koller stopped at the drugstore for another bottle of antacid.

But the pendulum swung in the other direction on the ninth day of trial, when Robert Kuns was called as the next prosecution witness. Lasting and White argued, once again, that testimony about boat thefts should be barred. It was unfair to tar Leasure with those unresolved charges, which everyone agreed had nothing to do with the murder case.

Once again, Judge Weisberg sided with the prosecution. Koller had to be able to show the close relationship between Kuns and Leasure, and that would be impossible without getting into the boat thefts, Weisberg ruled. Koller relaxed. "Finally," he said, "something is going my way."

Lasting promptly announced that the defense would not even try to contest the boat theft allegations during the trial. They would focus solely on the murders. Judge Weisberg, commenting on this strategy from the bench, observed, "It certainly will give credibility to the defense to concede certain matters and go on."[1]

Surrounded by lawyers in tailored suits, Robert Kuns, fresh off his sailboat, appeared in court in a bright Hawaiian shirt and chino pants, sandals on his feet, no socks. His once-shaven scalp was covered over with thick, curly reddish-brown hair, and he had trimmed his weirdly long, medieval beard, making him look far younger than he had five years earlier in the Contra Costa County lockup.

Since striking his deal with Koller, he had left jail, remarried, and was living in Newport Beach aboard a used sailboat he was refurbishing. Still pursuing his dream of retiring to the Caribbean, Kuns vowed that, this time, he would make it on the earnings from legitimate charter business, rather than booty from stolen yachts. Still, his presence in Newport Beach, where more than a few yachts had vanished with the Skipper at the helm, was a cause for consternation among the monied local yachtsmen. Koller got a few calls from Kuns's victims, suspicious of the Skipper's new boat. The prosecutor tried to soothe them, but he avoided making any official inquiries about Kuns's vessel. He really didn't want to know how Kuns had managed to buy it.

Kuns was an amiable, relaxed witness, never flustered or defensive. He sat with his legs crossed at the stand and refused to be drawn in by hostile questioning from the defense. He was a good storyteller, vividly re-creating his initial meeting with Leasure, his decision to begin stealing boats, and his eventual partnership with Leasure.

"I would describe him as the closest friend I had," Kuns said at one point in his testimony.

"Well," Koller asked, "how did it come about that you would tell a policeman that you . . . had a stolen boat?"

"I was over at his house. And he inquired about the boat. . . . I was real reluctant to say anything, for fear it was a setup. But the conversation went such, and he said a few little things about it, he's done a few little things himself, and this and that. And I just got the feeling that he was okay, I could talk to him.

"He was interested in where I got the money to get such a boat. I said I didn't get the money to do it, I just took the boat."

"And how did he respond?" Koller asked.

Kuns smiled, sitting back to deliver the punch line. "That if I did any more of it, he would like to crew with me."

Kuns then gave the jurors an overview of the boat business, how they would steal a yacht, alter it, resell it. At various stages in "the business," Leasure was part of the hired crew, then a full partner, then back to a mere salaried crewman again. The customers included Art Smith, Kuns testified, and the crew of thieves eventually came to include Dennis France, on Leasure's recommendation.

"Bill said that he would be a good employee," Kuns recalled. "Said he had done some rather heavy work for him. And that I could trust him and depend on him."

Kuns said they recruited France to act as a straw man in a

boat insurance fraud. Leasure didn't want to do it himself, Kuns said, "because he didn't want to have to explain to his wife why he had a boat." Once again, an unflattering side of Leasure's character had surfaced—his propensity for deceiving loved ones. It was the sort of detail the lawyers barely heeded at the time, but which they would later learn had left a deep impression on jurors.

When Koller went to the easel at the front of the courtroom and began showing Kuns pages from Leasure's notebook, each entry, in the policeman's own handwriting, seemed to confirm everything Kuns had just testified to—the first stolen-boat trip to Colombia, Smith's boat, the Canadian trip, Leasure's *Thunderbolt*, and the arrest up in Richmond aboard a yacht they had taken from San Diego. He concluded that they had stolen about two million dollars' worth of yachts, from which he had made about a half million, while Leasure made about fifty thousand dollars.

Kuns made it clear that, in his opinion, he had been the ringleader, he had assumed most of the risks, and, therefore, he had deserved the lion's share of the profits. However, these earnings estimates did not include Leasure's ownership of the one-hundred-thousand-dollar *Thunderbolt*, the seventeen thousand dollars he charged his fellow officer Ralph Gerard for a share of that boat, or the ten thousand extra he charged Art Smith for the *Santine*, Kuns said later, outside of court. Adding in those sums raised Leasure's earnings to nearly two hundred thousand.

On the stand, Kuns said Leasure had sold him illegal machine guns and a silencer. He said they shared many secrets: He knew Leasure had a bank account in the Cayman Islands he kept hidden from his wife. He knew about Leasure's extramarital affairs, he knew about Leasure's silencers and automatic weapons. And then there was the matter of Paulette de los Reyes.

Sticking to his original statement to Arce and Petroski, Kuns testified that Leasure had spoken of an unnamed woman who had asked him to arrange for the murder of her husband. Leasure had hired Dennis France to take care of the job, Kuns said. "I was told it was for the insurance money."

Years later, in the holding cell during the boat case, Leasure had told him the woman's name was Paulette. This was long before murder charges were filed, but Leasure already had been worried about a murder investigation getting underway in Los Angeles, Kuns said.

Kuns also retold his story about Leasure and the Anne Smith killing. This time, however, the story seemed slightly embellished from his police statements.

Leasure, when introducing Smith to Kuns, had told the Skipper that Anne Smith had been killed in a robbery. She had been taking her husband "to the cleaners in a divorce action," Kuns said, quoting Leasure.

"Later on, down the line, he told me that it had been a staged robbery. . . . I was always curious, but I never asked much of anything because it is just not something that you did. But it came up occasionally. And he would let out a little bit more like the robbery wasn't the real intent of the action, the killing was the intent. And that his expressions and body language said that he knew more than he was telling me.

"And down the line one day, I asked him, I said, 'I know what happened,' I said, 'Dennis did the shooting and you did the driving.'

"And he just kind of looked at me with an expression on his face like a kid getting caught with his hands in the cookie jar. He didn't say yes. He just said, 'I'm a good driver.' "

This was a departure from Kuns's original statement to police years earlier, when he merely said Leasure gave him a look "as if to say" he was a good driver. Now he had Leasure saying it aloud. It was no longer his interpretation. It was a direct admission by Leasure.

When his initial round of questioning by Koller ended and a recess was called, Kuns approached Leasure's parents, who sat stiffly in the front row, the suffering obvious on their careworn faces. Kuns sighed deeply, his hands thrust deeply into his pockets. "I'm really sorry you have to go through this," he said.

Agnes Leasure stared straight ahead. Ernest Leasure nodded and mumbled something in reply. The Leasures were not interested in the Skipper's apologies.

Outside the courtroom, Kuns stood in the crowded hallway near the elevators and pay phones and said he had no doubts that Leasure had done contract murders. "He's a mercenary," Kuns said. "For him, it's strictly business."

Kuns said this not to condemn his former friend, but in praise of him. Clearly, he admired Leasure. And there was no mistaking the nostalgic, fond way he recalled their days on the high seas together. He missed the life, the wad of bills in his pocket, the thrill and the danger. He still hoped to write a book someday based on their adventures—the hero would be a sort of "bad good guy or a good bad guy." The title, he said, would still be *Fun and Games*. He said he thought Leasure would appreciate that.

"I don't like many people. I really liked Bill. I still do. I know that sounds funny, but it's true. There's very few people I'd want to live next to. Bill's one.

"Bill did these things, sure, and murder is terrible and all that, but it was business. Outside his 'business' life, he was never one to hurt someone out on the street. He was always a very nice man, very gentle. Some people are able to separate that one portion of their lives from the rest. Bill could do that."

In his own way, even Bob Kuns was a character witness for Bill Leasure. "He's the nicest man I've ever met." And unlike so many others who spoke of Leasure, Kuns did not use the past tense.[2]

When Mike White cross-examined Kuns, there was no repeat of Dennis France's retreat into memory lapse. Kuns maintained his composure and good humor, even when White accused him of being a liar. Kuns quite cheerfully admitted the boat theft business depended upon his ability to lie to people.

"So would it be fair to say, Mr. Kuns, that you are a very good liar?" White asked, a friendly smile masking the biting question.

"I guess so," Kuns said agreeably.

"You are a world-class liar, is that right?"

"Sounds pretty bad," Kuns smiled, "but I guess you would say that."

"Sounds pretty true, though, doesn't it?" White asked.

"Yeah."

Kuns admitted he had been willing to lie under oath early in the boat case so that Leasure would go free. "In my way of thinking, it is noble to lie to get a fellow businessman off, very unnoble to lie to convict him."

White elicited some crucial testimony from Kuns about a conversation he and Leasure had while sitting in a holding cell in Contra Costa County.

"Did he tell you that he was concerned about two forty-fives that had been taken from Mr. Leasure's house?"

"Yes."

"Did he tell you that he was concerned about those weapons, because he was afraid they may have been used in a crime by Mr. France and given to Mr. Leasure?"

"Yes."

"Did he also tell you that he was worried about some brass that had been found in Mr. France's house?"

"Yes."

"And that he was worried that that brass could be matched up to a gun, one of those forty-fives?"

"Yes."

"And by the way," White asked, "didn't France tell you he always cut up his guns with a welding torch? That he melted them?"

"Yes."

With that series of questions, White had laid the groundwork for explaining the videotape with Dennis France. The notes about guns and brass and "melted" pertained to those two weapons Leasure had bought from France, not to the Anne Smith murder, the defense would argue.

And Kuns had given it to them without hesitation. Leasure had described the conversation to his lawyers long before, and now Kuns had confirmed it, word for word. It was something they really hadn't expected: Kuns telling the truth. Their truth.

In a way, it created a problem for them, for now they had to tell jurors to believe Kuns's testimony, at least in part. At the same time, they were also trying to prove Kuns a liar when it came to the "I am a good driver" testimony and his statements about Paulette. Those parts, Lasting and White wanted to argue, had been fabricated so Kuns, the ex-bank robber and world-class liar, could get a deal and get out of jail.

But now the jurors could rightly ask, if he's a liar, why would he not lie about the .45s? If his true motive was to get Bill, he could have just said no, Bill never mentioned any .45s, and that aspect of the defense would have been obliterated. Yet he didn't.

"Kuns could have really shafted Bill, but he didn't," Lasting later said. "He's just a more polished liar. He knows how to do it."

But Koller would later suggest that Leasure's supposed worries about those .45s were simple prudence on his part. After all, he knew France was a killer: Those guns could have been used by France for any number of crimes. But that didn't mean Leasure wasn't guilty himself—it merely meant he was concerned about a lot of things when he was busted. Those concerns included the murders of Tony Reyes and Anne Smith, as well as a couple of unrelated guns he had bought from his friendly neighborhood hit man.

As far as the prosecutor was concerned, Kuns told the truth about the .45s, because he was telling the truth about everything. Or as Kuns would put it when his testimony was over, "If I wanted to make up a story to get Bill, I could have made up one a lot better than this."

• • •

White's final attack on Kuns was the suggestion that the Skipper based his original story to the police by culling information from newspaper stories. A month after Dennis Winebaugh had been arrested in Oklahoma, a newspaper there had broken the story about a local security guard busted for contract murder. The Los Angeles papers picked up the story next, and they outlined the facts of the three murders—Smith, Reyes, and Cervantes. The stories appeared in Los Angeles on December 6 and 7, 1986. Kuns's meeting with Koller, Arce, and Petroski came two days later, on December 9. Kuns could not have seen the L.A. papers while jailed five hundred miles north, but he admitted his family, in phone calls from Los Angeles, had mentioned the articles.

"You now had enough information to go to the police and get your deal, is that correct?" White asked.

"I had no more information than I had before," Kuns said. His family had not provided any details from the articles, he said.

"Oftentimes snitches are lying in order to get out of jail, isn't that right?" White asked.

"Yes."

"And, Mr. Kuns, isn't that what you were doing on December 9? . . . Isn't that what you're doing today?"

"No."

The timing of the articles' publication and Kuns's abrupt decision to talk to LAPD seemed too great to be coincidental, White suggested. And Kuns already had admitted that the only reason he rolled over on Leasure was so he could get out of jail—an ideal motive to lie.

But just when the defense was certain they had scored, Detective Arce took the stand. His chronological record of the case, yanked out of the voluminous Leasure "Murder Book," showed he had met with Koller on December 2, 1986, to discuss a call the prosecutor had received from Kuns's lawyer. The Skipper was ready to talk to the homicide detectives, Koller reported at that meeting.

Arce and Petroski had put in for travel vouchers from LAPD on December 4, according to another record Arce pulled from his notebook. The only reason the meeting with Kuns was on December 9 was because LAPD bureaucrats didn't come with travel money until the day before.

Kuns hadn't offered to deal because of what he read or heard about from the news, Arce testified. He had been ready to talk four days before those articles appeared.

• • •

Everything is moving too fast. It makes me nervous. I thought there would be more time, but here we are, almost halfway through the trial. So far, it's not so bad, I think. I was really depressed after day two, but things are getting better.

Kuns is a unique individual. I really liked him at one time. And at least he had the guts to come out and say the only reason he was testifying was to get out of jail.

Now I think things are looking pretty good. Kuns's testimony wasn't too bad for us. He could have hurt us, but he didn't. He had to say what he did to keep his deal. Before he left court, he tried to talk to me, but Arce wouldn't let him. I think he feels bad about lying about me, maybe. I don't know.

'Course, that doesn't mean I'll ever forgive him. We could never be friends again. He's potentially sending me to the gas chamber to take two and a half years off his sentence. Would you forgive him?

• • •

After the trial was recessed for the day, an ebullient Lasting and White spoke of their interview with Dennis Winebaugh a few days before, at the conclusion of the first week of trial. Forty-four had been brought down from prison to the county jail, ostensibly a prosecution witness. Jim Koller had planned to call him, expecting Winebaugh to deny being involved in murder, as he always had before. Then Koller could play the incriminating tape recording with Dennis France in order to rebut Winebaugh's testimony. But Koller had backed off from that plan after Lasting and White repeatedly announced that they liked the tape—that they thought it helped Leasure rather than hurt him. On that tape, the defense lawyers pointed out, Winebaugh said Leasure knew about the murders, but knew nothing for certain and could "prove nothing." Although the prosecutor had initially interpreted these statements as meaning Leasure was involved, but not present during the killing, the defense lawyers said they would argue that Winebaugh meant Leasure had learned of the killing after the fact, and therefore could prove nothing. In truth, since either interpretation was valid, they hoped their comments might persuade Koller into withdrawing the tape from evidence, which he did. Then he decided not to call Winebaugh at all.

But now, after talking to Winebaugh, Lasting and White had decided he would be a good *defense* witness. Likable, direct, with those bird-of-prey eyes, Winebaugh had told them France was a violent killer, who had willingly and knowingly taken part in the Cervantes murder. Furthermore, contrary to France's testimony, Winebaugh said the welder had known Leasure's last name all along.

Finally, Winebaugh said flat out that Leasure had nothing to do with the murder of Gilberto Cervantes. Paulette had set it up, and Leasure "might have put two and two together," but he was not part of the contract, Winebaugh told them. The reason he knew, he admitted for the first time ever, was because he really had pulled the trigger on Cervantes.

"I'm telling you guys this because you were straight with me," Winebaugh said. "But I'll never testify to it. I don't want my family to know I killed anyone. If you put me up on the stand, I'll say I didn't do it."

But Winebaugh said he would testify about everything else, including his belief that Leasure had nothing to do with the murder of Gilberto. As for Tony Reyes and Anne Smith, Winebaugh couldn't help them. He was in Oklahoma by then and had nothing to do with those killings. But he could help further destroy France's credibility—and he would do so happily.

His one complaint to the lawyers concerned his health. At the state prison, he received medication for his heart condition, but the jail wasn't giving it to him, Winebaugh complained. "I told them if they brought me down here, I'd never make it back alive," Winebaugh said morosely.

Lasting took a liking to Winebaugh during the visit. The man had a certain good-ol'-boy charm about him. He was a good talker, an engaging spinner of tall tales.

"Were you really that good a shot?" Lasting asked him.

"Best shot you'll ever see."[3]

The defense team's plan to turn Winebaugh into a witness for Leasure quickly ended, however. The following week, when the lawyers assembled in court for a full day of trial, Koller said he had an announcement.

"I've got news," he said simply. "Winebaugh's dead." Heart failure had killed him in his cell, Koller explained.

Lasting and White looked stricken. Leasure hung his head and stared at the table before him. "You're joking, right?" Lasting finally asked. Koller shook his head and said, "The witness pool is dwindling."

"He said if they bring him down here, 'I'll never make it.' That's what he said. He was right," a morose Mike White said.

The roller coaster had crested another hill. Winebaugh's testi-

mony was history, and so was the tape of his conversation with
Dennis France, except for a few minor snippets already played to
the jury. Another chunk of evidence, this time nominally in
Leasure's favor, had been rendered useless by outside events.

On the eleventh day of trial, Paulette de los Reyes made her
entrance, the wounded widow who swore she had done no wrong.
Her auburn hair done up with a large black bow, she was clad in
a low-cut black and white polka-dot dress, wide-brimmed straw
hat, and tinted glasses. She had arrived at the courthouse wearing
a dark wig, but it was so outlandish, her lawyer made her take it
off. Koller immediately labeled her Rebecca of Sunnybrook Farm.
Her new husband sat in the gallery listening steadfastly, his face
flushed throughout her prolonged testimony which, including inter-
ruptions and days off, spanned two weeks.

Sighing frequently and exclaiming "Heavens!" whenever she
was asked something unpleasant, Paulette de los Reyes—as Koller
expected—denied being a party to murder. In her first official ac-
counting since her arrest, she denied asking Leasure to kill Tony,
and denied hearing him agree to do it. And she said her guilty plea
did not mean she was guilty. She just wanted out of jail, and the offer had been too good to refuse. She even named the appellate
court decision, *People* v. *West*, that validated the concept of pleading
guilty in one's own best interest rather than from a consciousness
of guilt.

Paulette was a difficult, combative witness. She boasted during
one recess that, "I'm going to say what I want to say, no matter
what they ask me." And, in fact, her answers were long, meandering, and often unresponsive to the questions put to her. A question
about the tortilla factory prompted her to launch into a long, apocryphal account of how she built the business from scratch, driving
a truck herself for two years. A question about whether she ever
thought of killing Tony led to a monologue on how deeply she
loved her ex-husband, his hideous faults notwithstanding. The normally impassive Judge Weisberg grew increasingly irritated with
her, and finally warned Paulette to answer the questions without
elaborating. The warning did not seem to help much. Her six days
on the stand left everyone in the courtroom drained and cranky.

During questioning by Koller, Paulette conceded that her
marriage and divorce had been ugly, and that Tony had been cruel
to her. She agreed that there was supposed to have been a will that
would have passed on the family fortune and business to Aaron,

with her in control as the boy's guardian. And yes, she might have told Leasure she would get two million dollars when Tony died. But she would never have hurt "her Tony."

"Sometimes love is very strange," she said mournfully.

Paulette said she had been cheated out of her rightful inheritance. The will had been consumed in a fire, Paulette said, and Tony Jr. had claimed the entire estate (which was substantial, but considerably less than two million dollars) with a mysterious handwritten will even the victim's lawyers hadn't known about. Paulette and Aaron got nothing from Tony's death, though she had expected they would get everything.

"I had been told that," she agreed. This was the motive for murder Koller sought to demonstrate. As long as Paulette and Leasure believed there were two million reasons to kill Tony, it didn't matter whether they were right or not.

Later, Paulette recalled how Tony had hired Dennis Winebaugh in 1977 to kill her for five thousand dollars. The first and only time she had met Winebaugh, Paulette swore, was over the course of three nights, when he told her he wouldn't kill her, and instead gave her tapes of Tony hiring him. She repeated the same account she had given over the years—that the hardened hit man Forty-four Magnum had spared her life because he fell in love while tailing her in preparation for murder. She swore she never met him before or after he turned over those tapes. Of course, this was contradicted by both France and Winebaugh, who had said Paulette knew Forty-four intimately. Jurors would never hear from the late Forty-four, but White and Lasting had other ideas for proving Paulette a liar.

She also swore that she never identified a picture of Winebaugh for police when she reported the murder plot to LAPD—a lie, according to police reports on the incident. He gave me my life, Paulette testified in 1991, and I promised to protect him. Yet she pointed his photo out to LAPD officers in 1977. If it was a lie, it was a curious one. Her latest testimony—that she did not identify Winebaugh—made her look more, not less, conspiratorial. Which was fine with Leasure and his lawyers.

Although Paulette had presented herself as weak and fearful, forever victimized by those around her, jurors heard a different Paulette on a tape she had made in 1977. They heard a forceful, taunting Paulette confronting Tony about his hiring Forty-four to kill her—and holding the tapes Winebaugh had given her over Tony's head.

"My problem?" she had said to Tony, mockingly, liltingly. "I don't think I have a problem in the world. My problem is I don't know what to do with five little tapes." And then, on the tape she had made herself, she threatened to report Tony to the police.

Tony replied, "Well, if you do that, I'll just say that you engineered the first one, dear."

"Uh-huh. Me? Well, I'll tell you, on your tapes, Tony, it says a whole lot different."

This was an unmistakable reference to the first murder, the killing of Gilberto Cervantes—even Paulette agreed to that when questioned by Michael White.

Still more damaging to the image she was trying to project from the witness stand was the revelation that she had held onto those tapes without contacting the police for five months, as she wrangled with Tony over tortillas and divorce. Both prosecution and defense had achieved their shared goal with this testimony: a portrait of Paulette de los Reyes as a person who would use any means she could to achieve her goals, even knowledge of murder and attempted murder.

On her second day of testimony, Paulette came to court in a sailor suit, a jarring contrast to the conservative gray suits of the lawyers. Koller began playing the awful tapes of Paulette's sessions with Detective David Scroggins, alternately numbing and shocking the jurors with their contents. He wanted to play only the brief incriminating parts of the tapes, but the defense attorneys objected. There were more than seven hours of tapes, and most of that time consisted of Paulette denying her and Leasure's involvement. To play only the incriminating minutes would distort their context, Lasting and White argued, saying the jurors should hear it all, no matter how painful. The judge agreed, and the jury had to hear all seven terrible hours of Paulette de los Reyes and Detective David Scroggins. The twelve men and women strained to hear the tinny recordings, flipping through transcripts and watching Paulette's reaction as she listened to Scroggins yell and herself sob five years earlier.

On the stand, Paulette de los Reyes disavowed everything on the tapes, claiming she had said only what Scroggins had wanted to hear. She testified that she had been desperate for his help and afraid he might kill her. She stuck to this story even after the tapes revealed her affectionate conversations with Scroggins, her insistence that he help her, and her agreement with him that Leasure should die.

Whenever Paulette heard herself say something incriminating on the tape—such as she knew Leasure had bombed Tony's car, or she had asked Leasure to do away with her ex-husband—she would put her glasses on with a pained expression, peer intently at her transcript, shake her head, and deny all. She either swore she did not recall saying such a thing to Scroggins or, if she remembered it, that she made it all up to get his help.

The tape finally rolled up to Scroggins's "sermon," where he urged her to trust him, and she said yes, I asked Bill Leasure to kill Tony. When Koller demanded she explain such a remark, she said, "I just told David that . . . to keep him pacified."

During cross-examination, Mike White questioned Paulette gently at first, reassuring her like an old ally, leading her along the path the defense wanted her to take.

"The only way he [Scroggins] would help you is if you told him what he wanted to hear?" White asked.

"Yes," she replied.

"And he made it very clear to you that what he wanted to hear was that Bill Leasure was involved in the murder of Tony de los Reyes, is that right?"

"Oh, yes."

"And he told you that the only way that you could avoid the gas chamber is if he would help you, and the only way he would help you is if you told him that Bill Leasure was involved in the murder of Tony de los Reyes?"

"Yes."

"Did you ask Bill Leasure to kill Tony de los Reyes?"

"No."

Finally, with that testimony established—and after hours more of the Scroggins tapes—the defense attorney went on the attack.

"Mrs. de los Reyes, after you found out that Tony had changed his will [to benefit Aaron], did you go back to a man that you had had an affair with in 1976 and 1977, Number Forty-four?" This was the heart of the defense contention on Tony Reyes's killing—that Paulette and Winebaugh, not Leasure, conspired with France to kill Tony.

Paulette seemed stunned at the question. She looked at White as if he had slapped her. "No," she said finally. "I never had. I would have to come from another planet to have an affair with this man."

Mike White, who had just come from visiting Dennis Winebaugh, who had described at length his liaisons with Paulette de los Reyes, asked, "Did you go back to the man that you had hired to kill Gilberto Cervantes?"

"No."

"Did you go back to Dennis Winebaugh, Number Forty-four, and ask him if he could kill your husband, Tony de los Reyes?"

"Surely you jest, Mr. White," Paulette huffed.

White was through, though. He was confident the jurors would conclude that Paulette had lied about her relationship with Dennis Winebaugh—to the police in 1977, to David Scroggins in 1986, and on the witness stand in 1991. And why would she deny knowing Dennis Winebaugh each time she told her story? Because, White would argue, she had hired him to kill.

• • •

I like what Paulette's saying. She's telling the truth about me. They fed her those phony reports, she was pressured by Scroggins, and she wanted help, she was scared. She never really said on those tapes, "I did it." She was just throwing him a few bones so he'd help her. There's no way anyone can believe those tapes.

And I think she's taking a big chance by testifying for me. She maybe could lose her deal for being honest. But I think she wants to help me.

I feel bad that my lawyers are going to beat her up. I really don't see it that way, but that's what's going to happen. They think she's involved with the murders. I think she probably was, but I don't know.

• • •

The prosecution called the other witnesses needed to buttress Dennis France's story, most of them mercifully brief after the long days of Paulette de los Reyes and her tapes. Anne Smith's divorce attorney attested to the viciousness of Smith versus Smith, the violence and the allegations of financial improprieties—Art's alleged motive for murder. Tony Reyes's lawyer talked about wills, and how Tony had died the day before he was supposed to bequeath his inheritance to Aaron and Paulette.

John Doney, Art's former employee, was barred from mentioning Art Smith's threat to hire Bill Leasure to kill his wife. Judge Weisberg deemed that testimony inadmissible hearsay once Smith invoked his Fifth Amendment rights and refused to testify. He did repeat his story for the judge—with the jury excused—and Weisberg nearly allowed the testimony as a demonstration of Smith's state of mind during the murder conspiracy, much to Leasure's discomfort. But in the end, Weisberg ruled that the testimony was improper, and Doney was ordered to remain silent about it once the jury returned. However, he was allowed to testify

358 MURDERER WITH A BADGE

that Leasure was a regular visitor to Smith's insurance office. Leasure would appear in uniform, in his police car, as often as several times a week in the months before Anne Smith was killed, Doney testified.

It was during that period, Doney testified, that Art Smith said of his wife and his pending divorce, "She came into the marriage with nothing, and she would leave the marriage with nothing."

Koller concluded his case with the same powerful evidence with which he had begun it—the videotape. An FBI agent who had enhanced the blurry, poor-quality video at the FBI's laboratories in Quantico, Virginia, walked the jury through the images of Leasure writing notes to Dennis France. Now, Koller believed, the jury had enough information to fully understand what was going on in that videotaped meeting.

Once again, jurors saw, more clearly than on the original tape, Leasure's written greeting to France: "Don't say anything."

Then, a few minutes later, "Did you have any brass from that one?" And, "Your phone is tapped. Mine too."

After crossing out and erasing these messages, Leasure's next note, in reply to France's question about the gun from Avenue 60, was, "Melted."

When France asked why Leasure questioned him about the brass, Leasure wrote, "They have the one."

And that final, damning message, the words of an accomplice, not an innocent man: "Dump everything illegal."

The tape was hard for Leasure to watch, hard for his lawyers to watch, hard for his parents to watch. For all their efforts to undermine the word of Dennis France, that tape seemed to back up everything he had said—unless they could provide a better explanation.

With the tape finished and the television monitors switched off, Jim Koller rested his case.

H IS ATTORNEYS HADN'T tipped their hand in their opening arguments, but Bill Leasure's defense would rest on more than just slashing at Dennis France. And after a few preliminary witnesses for the defense, a new assault on the prosecution case began.

They brought in Leasure's alibi.

Charles Sondergaard, a Los Angeles building inspector and an old friend of Leasure's, took the witness stand to testify about a day in 1980—he couldn't be sure of the exact date—when he helped Leasure build a new eight-car garage at the house in Northridge. This was the garage whose contents would so fascinate LAPD Internal Affairs years later, and cinch the yacht case in Contra Costa County as well. But at the time, it was just a set of plans and a few holes in the ground, Sondergaard recalled.

The building inspector said he remembered taking time out from work to help Leasure that day. Between taking a breakfast break and driving to a construction site he was supposed to inspect that morning, he testified, he stopped by Leasure's house to make sure anchor bolts for the garage foundation were correctly set in preparation for a concrete pour. He remembered being there at around 9:00 A.M. Later that same afternoon, he recalled, he returned to oversee the delivery and pouring of the concrete on top of those anchor bolts, sometime around 3:00 P.M. Both visits were definitely on the same day, Sondergaard swore, ten years after the events he was describing.

Lasting and White then produced receipts from the Leasure family records, issued by the Bonanza concrete company and the

Aloha concrete pumping company. The name William Leasure was signed at the bottom of the receipts. Authenticated by witnesses and records from the two companies, the receipts proved that concrete for a garage foundation had been delivered and poured at the Leasure residence on May 29, 1980, at about 3:00 in the afternoon.

Two other things of note had happened that same day: Leasure had called in sick that morning with a "severe case of diarrhea," according to LAPD records. May 29, 1980, also happened to be the day Anne Smith was murdered.

The receipts, by themselves, did nothing to support Leasure's innocence. He easily could have taken part in the murder of Anne Smith, who was gunned down shortly after 9:00 A.M., and still arrived back home hours before the 3:00 P.M. delivery of the concrete. The key was Sondergaard's recollection of being with Leasure at 9:00 A.M. that same day, helping him prepare for the concrete delivery. He was only there five or ten minutes, he said, but that was more than enough. The Leasure home and the beauty shop where Anne Smith died were separated by a minimum forty-five-minute drive. If Sondergaard was to be believed, Leasure could not have been out murdering Anne Smith that day. He was home, building a garage.

The jury wouldn't hear about it, but this was the second time that receipts had been unearthed from the Leasure household archives to help defend him against criminal charges. A few years earlier, at Leasure's police Board of Rights hearing, a receipt for a new carburetor had been used to bolster the recollections of Wendy Mogul, Leasure's sister-in-law. She testified about a stolen vintage Studebaker found in the Leasure garage, and the receipt—from repairs Leasure had performed on Wendy Mogul's car—helped her place the stolen Studebaker in the garage on a date that would help Leasure's case.[1] As with the concrete receipts, the carburetor sales slip proved nothing directly itself—but in both cases, the receipts seemed to legitimize testimony about remote events from people close to Bill Leasure. With the receipts in hand, the witnesses did not have to remember exact dates—the precise sort of recollections that, to most jurors, would sound suspicious and fabricated. Instead, they only had to remember general occurrences. The receipts—firm, unambiguous, objective—filled in the key dates and times.

If Sondergaard had walked into court on May 14, 1991, and said, I remember exactly what I was doing on the morning of May 29, 1980, he would have been laughed out of the courtroom. In-

stead, with his more vague and natural-sounding recollections and
the receipts to back him up, Sondergaard's story sounded believable . . . and unshakable.

Jim Koller knew he was in trouble as he tried, during lengthy
cross-examination, to undermine Sondergaard's stolid testimony.
But the large, pleasant, bearded inspector with the ruddy complex-
ion would not be shaken. When Koller asked Sondergaard if he
could be mistaken, if he might have come by earlier in the week to
prepare for the concrete, Sondergaard said flatly, no. He was sure:
It had been the morning of the day on which concrete was poured.

But the prosecutor did score a couple of points. First, he established that Sondergaard had helped with a variety of chores with
the garage construction over a period of months—in fact, he had
done the bulk of the work. Sometimes Leasure was there helping,
sometimes he wasn't, Sondergaard testified. When asked about different jobs—putting on the roof, framing the walls—Sondergaard
could not say at which times Leasure was present and at which
times Sondergaard did the work solo. "I can't remember," he said
simply.

Yet, Koller asked, you can remember that Leasure was there
that one particular, oh-so-important morning? Yes, Sondergaard
insisted, I remember that one. He did not explain why.

The other point Koller scored on was unintentional. He asked
Sondergaard who else was at the house the morning he claimed to
be preparing for the concrete pour. Sondergaard swore there was
no one else there.

Lasting and White had been prepared to call another friend,
Terry Staley, the trucker who had known Leasure since childhood.
Staley had been prepared to testify that he was there that same
morning, too. But to bring him to the stand now would create a
glaring contradiction. It might even add weight to the argument
Koller inevitably would make: That the alibi was cooked up. Staley
was already an iffy witness for the defense—he had been a paid
crewman aboard two stolen yachts, and had been given stolen
property by Leasure. Though he was not a suspect in the boat
thefts, and his presence on stolen yachts may have been completely
innocent, the prospect of having him on the stand, with Koller eagerly questioning him about Leasure's sea-going escapades, was not
a welcome one. Lasting and White decided to tell Staley, who was
waiting in the hallway during Sondergaard's testimony, to go home.
They wouldn't call him to testify after all. Sondergaard would have
to stand alone as Leasure's alibi for the Anne Smith murder.

For similar reasons, another childhood friend of Leasure's,

Gary, was not called by the defense, though he provided something close to an alibi for Leasure on the night of Tony Reyes's murder. Gary was staying with the Leasures for several weeks, including the night preceding Tony's September 10, 1981, shooting. He was prepared to testify that Leasure was home that night and, as far as he knew, had not left the house after nightfall. There was a problem, though: Gary went to bed at around 11:00 that night. The murder was several hours later in the early morning. He could not account for Leasure's whereabouts at the critical time, and the defense lawyers feared Koller could use his testimony to raise more questions than it answered. With Leasure's reluctant okay, they chose not to present an alibi for the Tony Reyes slaying at all.

The main advantage the defense has at trial is their ability to surprise the state. Through the process of discovery, the prosecution has to show all its cards to the defense long before the trial begins, but the reverse is not generally true. Koller had never heard of Charles Sondergaard until that day. At the prosecutor's request, Detective Tom King had come to court to see the defense's star witness on the stand. Now Koller gave King a mission: go out and find some way to disprove or discredit the alibi. The prosecution inevitably has to scramble this way to rebut defense evidence, a frantic search for some contradiction or motive to lie that would upset a carefully crafted defense. The detective left, looking for—there's no other way to put it—dirt on Charles Sondergaard.

Meanwhile, the defense buttressed the alibi Sondergaard provided with testimony that tarred Charles Persico, the addict originally convicted of killing Anne Smith. Detective Nelson Crowe, the original detective on the case, testified that he had interviewed Persico's wife, Elvia, and that she told him Persico had confessed to killing a woman in a beauty shop. A reluctant Elvia, hauled to court by sheriff's deputies, contradicted this testimony, denying telling Crowe anything about her husband. But she still helped the defense—by swearing that Persico's friend, Arturo "Tutti" Gomez, had owned a green Chevy Nova with Rally stripes, a duplicate of the getaway car.

Once again, though, Koller attacked this defense testimony with some success. First, he got Crowe to admit that Art Smith had been their original prime suspect. Crowe recalled that Smith had refused to talk to detectives on the day after his wife's death (or at any other time), and that Anne's daughter, Christine, had answered their knock on her door by asking, "Are you here to arrest me?"

Then Koller sought to show Crowe's investigation had been botched—either by carelessness, or worse. Crowe's log on the case showed the mechanic, Thomas Rumbaugh, had picked Persico out of a photo lineup. Later, Rumbaugh would look at Persico in person and tell the police they had the wrong man. But his initial identification of the photo was the main reason Persico became a suspect, Crowe testified.

Koller then produced a handwritten note from Crowe's old LAPD case file on the murder investigation. The note had been written after Crowe showed the mechanic two photo lineups—one with Persico, and another with Tutti Gomez. The note read, "He looks like the driver, definitely not the man who was walking through the garage." In other words, the note suggested that the man Rumbaugh saw walking through his garage—the killer—had not been identified after all when the mechanic looked at the photo lineup. Crowe's logs and testimony were wrong, the note seemed to suggest. Persico had never been identified at all before he had been arrested, Koller suggested.

The detective's logbooks reinforced Koller's theory. Immediately after Rumbaugh looked at those pictures, the log entries virtually stopped. Nothing happened on the case for nine months. If Rumbaugh had truly identified Persico, why didn't they go out and arrest him? Crowe said he didn't recall—it had been so long. Wasn't it more likely, Koller suggested, that the case stalled because Rumbaugh had *not* identified Persico? Crowe said no, he was sure the mechanic had identified Persico from the photo and that the note the prosecutor had seized upon was being taken out of context—it probably applied to Tutti, not Persico. But Koller had already made his point. The case had stalled because Persico was not the right man, the prosecutor was suggesting. Then, nine months later, after Persico was picked up for another robbery he did not commit, Anne Smith's mother was dragged into a lineup where she finally pointed the finger at the heroin addict.

It was strange to hear. The prosecution and the defense had switched roles, with the defense lawyers trying to convict Persico of murder, and the D.A. suggesting, without coming out and saying it directly, that the police had framed an innocent man.

The next crucial defense witness was William Jennings. The former neighbor of Dennis Winebaugh and Dennis France, Jennings had been living in rural Arkansas, driving a truck and living a relatively quiet life, when one of Leasure's private investigators tracked him down. A towering man of substantial girth, like an offensive lineman gone to seed, Jennings was an amiable but reluctant witness, fearful about decade-old threats from both Dennis Winebaugh and Dennis France.

Although he had originally been listed as a prosecution witness, Koller had decided against calling him. But Lasting and White wanted—and needed—some of the things he would say. At the same time, they desperately wanted to keep the jury from hearing portions of his testimony that might be damaging to Leasure. And, for the most part, they got their wish.

Jennings's full story, told with the jury cleared from the courtroom, contained considerably more detail than his original account to Detectives Arce and Petroski in 1986. "I racked my brain," he said, and remembered more.

He recalled, first of all, that Winebaugh and Paulette de los Reyes had a romantic relationship, that Winebaugh had been a frequent visitor to the tortilla factory after Gilberto Cervantes was killed, and that Winebaugh had even persuaded Paulette to hire Jennings as a delivery man at the factory. "She would go through me to get in contact with Mr. Winebaugh when she couldn't contact him herself," Jennings added.

All of this flatly contradicted Paulette's sworn testimony that she didn't have a personal relationship with the hit man Winebaugh. Jennings also testified that he recalled seeing France with Winebaugh during one visit to the factory. The two of them had a closed-door meeting with Paulette, Jennings swore.

This was exactly what the defense needed to show—a connection between Paulette and the killers, making Leasure's role as middleman unnecessary for two of the three killings. Judge Weisberg ruled that all this testimony was admissible, and Jennings subsequently repeated it for the jury.

But Koller was not so fortunate. On cross-examination—without the jurors in the room—Jennings recalled both Winebaugh and France bragging about killing a man. From hearing scuttlebutt among the other workers at the tortilla factory, Jennings eventually realized the man the two Dennises had been speaking about was Paulette's murdered father-in-law, Gilberto Cervantes. He also said France and Winebaugh threatened him if he blabbed about their role in the murder.

"I was told the Mafia was involved. I was told officers were involved. . . . He said Bill was one [of the officers].

". . . I was told that if Mr. Leasure ever heard or knew of me or my wife knowing anything, that's it. We were history." Out in the hallway, during a break, Jennings put it even more graphically. "They said, if Leasure finds out I know anything, 'He'll waste ya.' "

Jennings, referring to Dennis France as "what you would call a crazy person," also remembered that France, in saying Leasure was "involved," only used his first name, "Bill."

If the jury had heard this round of testimony, it would have confirmed much of France's story. First, Jennings proved France had talked of Leasure's complicity in murder long before the welder was in danger of being arrested—and, therefore, long before he had a motive to lie about Leasure in order to earn legal immunity. Furthermore, Jennings supported France's story on another key point: that he apparently didn't know Leasure's last name. He just called him Bill. After hearing Jennings, the I-couldn't-read-Bill's-nametag explanation that Lasting had so ridiculed didn't seem so outlandish after all.

But the jury would not hear any of this damning portion of Jennings's testimony. After initially leaning toward allowing it, Judge Weisberg determined that these subjects were impermissible "double hearsay." Jennings was repeating the words of Dennis France, who, in turn, had been parroting only what Winebaugh had told him. (Dennis France had testified earlier that at first his only knowledge of Leasure's involvement in the Cervantes homicide was through the words of Dennis Winebaugh.) Such testimony was inherently unreliable—like the schoolchild's game in which one child whispers something to another, who then whispers to another schoolmate and so on, until, at the end of the line, the final whisper inevitably bears no similarity to the first. If Winebaugh had lived and had testified, then Jennings could have told the full story as an impeachment witness. But just as the Art Smith witnesses had been thrown out of court, so was Jennings's testimony about Leasure limited.

Lasting and White were spared the ignominy of destroying their defense with their own witness. They hadn't known everything the hastily located Jennings would say until he walked into the courtroom. "We really dodged a bullet on that one," a relieved Mike White said later.

Koller did manage to get two additional observations of Jennings's in front of the jury. He had seen Leasure visit Winebaugh twice at the apartment complex in which he, France, and Forty-four had lived in 1977. One time, Jennings said, Leasure arrived in plain clothes, and Jennings was asked to leave so France, Leasure, and Winebaugh could speak alone. Another time, Leasure drove up in a Corvette wearing his LAPD uniform, and walked to Winebaugh's apartment carrying something he had wrapped inside a jacket.

It didn't seem like much at the time, but upon reflection, Koller realized Jennings was the only witness, other than Dennis France, who proved there had been a close relationship between Bill Leasure and Forty-four Magnum. The defense lawyers believed they had scored a victory with William Jennings, but, in the days and weeks to come, they would be forced to decide otherwise.

• • •

It was a good day—with a nasty surprise at the end. But you know, I think Bill Jennings is telling the truth. My interpretation, when he says they told him, don't let Bill know you know anything, is that, hey, Bill's a cop. He'll bust you. Of course, I'm looking at things differently than anyone else. It could be pretty damaging. I'm glad the judge is honest and has the guts to keep that testimony out.

I was pretty mad at my lawyers—we didn't know any of that was coming. I was sitting there turning red. They didn't interrogate him. They just put him up on the stand. . . .

Everything is really going well, though. Now you see why I've been so confident all along. I knew where I was the day Anne Smith was killed. Now I've proven it. How can Dennis France be believed over Charlie Sondergaard? Charlie has no motive to lie. He's a friend, but he'd never go in there and lie for me.

. . . We showed they didn't need me to hire for Gilberto's murder. Jennings proved that. So the next logical question is, why would they need me to hire for Tony? Obviously, the jury has to find me innocent.

But I'm still scared to death. I think it's going well, but everything's going so fast. . . . I've talked to a lot of judges and lawyers who've watched some of the trial, actually, Betsy's talked to them, and they say there's no way I can be convicted. No way. I can't imagine the jury coming back guilty, even if we rested now. And I really can't imagine getting convicted, because there's more to come. . . .

I really want to testify. I think somebody ought to explain a lot of this stuff. I really think I should. It remains to be seen if I will. But it looks like I'm going to.

. . . With any luck, I'll be home for Memorial Day.

• • •

The only questions that remained after Bill Jennings testified were whether the defense should mount a "good character" defense, whether Betsy Mogul should take the stand, and, most important of all, whether Bill Leasure should testify.

Lasting and White's instinct had been to say no to all three, but their client felt otherwise. At the defense table, Leasure had continually urged them throughout the trial to object to prosecution tactics more, to ask more questions (even when the answers might hurt him), to "Be bold!"

His hatred for Koller grew more intense with each passing day, and it had rubbed off on Leasure's relatives. At one point, a member of the family approached Lasting and castigated him for being "too friendly" with the prosecutor during recesses. Lasting shrugged off the criticism. They were professionals. He and Koller would never be best buddies, but they had mutual respect for one another. There was no animosity. They were just doing their jobs. Why make it harder by being rude and unprofessional?

Leasure, however, was convinced that the prosecutor was holding back evidence that would exonerate him. Lasting did not believe this. Yes, Internal Affairs had allegedly "lost" several dozen tape-recorded interviews of people, and Leasure felt, correctly, that he was entitled to have those tapes. But most of it was useless talk with people who had worked with Leasure, or who were involved somehow with the boat case—the missing tapes, however suspicious, apparently had little or nothing to do with the murders. Lasting had talked Leasure out of basing his defense on attacking LAPD and his nemesis, Sergeant Wiltrout. A private investigator had tried to find something on the Internal Affairs sergeant to suggest he might have conspired against Leasure, hiding or destroying evidence, but there had been nothing there. Other than his run-in over the Jimmy Trahin case, Wiltrout was clean, Lasting said.

Now Leasure had transferred his venom to Koller, and Lasting and White were afraid that if he testified, Leasure would lose control on the stand and convict himself with angry, hostile answers. There was also the fear that Leasure's blanket denials of any wrongdoing in the boat and car theft cases would seem incredible to jurors, leaving his claims of innocence in the murder case unbelievable as well.[2]

As for Betsy Mogul, the problem did not lay in what she would say on the witness stand—she would say her husband was honest, gentle, incapable of violence. The problem lay in what Jim Koller would ask. Every day, before court convened, he would wheel a creaking, bent, gray metal busboy's cart into the courtroom, piled high with notebooks and transcripts, most of it pertaining to boat thefts, stolen cars, and Leasure's other nonviolent criminal cases. If Betsy got on the stand, Koller would wade through notebook after notebook, asking how the husband she claimed she knew so well could be stealing boats and cars and fill-

368 MURDERER WITH A BADGE

ing her house with stolen property without her getting the least bit suspicious. The pictures of their home and the garages crammed with stolen property would be passed about for ogling by the jurors. Betsy Mogul's trial for perjury would be fodder for a good hour of cross-examination alone if Koller had his way. And then there was Irene Wong, the angry mistress, whose testimony could become relevant once the door on Leasure's character and relationships was opened by the defense. Koller would try to show how Leasure had totally deceived both Irene and his wife with false promises of fidelity if Betsy Mogul took the stand. And Leasure would come out looking far worse than before his wife walked into the courtroom.

No, Betsy was out as a witness, as far as the defense lawyers were concerned.

As for the impressive array of character witnesses that investigator Sheryl Duvall had assembled, the same problems existed. The only image jurors had of Leasure so far was what Dennis France and Robert Kuns had provided. All they had heard about was just one more dirty cop, even worse than the bunch that surrounded and beat Rodney King. The defense really wanted to counter that, and Duvall's witnesses would accomplish the task. But Koller would—if the judge let him—attack the character witnesses' belief that Leasure was a good man by asking if they knew he stole boats, or if they knew he stole cars, or if they knew he owned silencers. And if they said no, as Koller knew they would, then he could ask, "Well, I guess you didn't really know Leasure so well after all?" Such witnesses could end up making Leasure look worse, not better.

Lasting's one hope for putting on such a defense was if he could persuade Judge Weisberg to limit Koller's cross-examination. He proposed limiting his character witnesses to commenting on whether or not Leasure showed violent tendencies. They would all say no. Lasting said he would steer clear of any questions about Leasure's integrity or honesty, avoiding "opening the door" to questions about the thefts, or adultery or other "bad character" testimony.

But Weisberg declined to make any rulings in advance. He had to hear each witness testify for the defense; then he would rule on the extent of Koller's cross-examination. "You will have to take your chances," the judge advised.

More than anything else, the defense lawyers would later recall, Judge Weisberg's remarks helped them convince Leasure that silence might be the best defense—in terms of character witnesses, and of taking the stand himself. They told him things were going well, that they were farther along at this point than they thought they would be, with Art Smith and other damaging testimony kept from the jury. They told him that his best chance of winning was to not take the witness stand.[3]

When the other defense witnesses were through, Judge Weisberg asked Leasure if he had decided to testify or not. Since testifying in one's own behalf is a fundamental constitutional right, the judge had to make a formal record of Leasure's decision to waive that right. His lawyers had already said their client would not be testifying, but the judge wanted to hear Leasure say it himself. To the defense lawyers' alarm, Leasure hesitated when he should have been saying no.

"I had always intended to," Leasure said finally, quietly. "But at this point I think it's in my best interests not to."

And with that, to Jim Koller's great disappointment and mild surprise, the defense rested its case on May 15, exactly one month after testimony began.

"The decision was made more than a week ago that he wouldn't testify. Why do you think we've been so calm?" Mike White said after court was recessed for the day. "Who was the worst witness to testify in the case? Dennis France, right? Everyone can agree to that. That's the way we wanted it. That's the way we wanted to leave it."[4]

• • •

They're getting conservative, conservative. I want bold, bold, bold! They decided not to put Gary [the Tony Reyes alibi witness] on, because it's going so well, they say we have it won, why take the chance. They're afraid the prosecutor might trip him up, that Koller could say, hey, Bill could have slipped out at midnight to go kill Tony. . . . But as far as I'm concerned, I've got two alibis. He would have known if I left in the middle of the night. I was home in bed when Tony got killed.

I wanted character witnesses, I wanted to testify, I want to explain the video. They told me we're winning, and that we better leave well enough alone. . . . I decided not to testify that moment, when the judge asked—and I'm still not convinced.

. . . If I was on the jury, I'd want to hear me testify. But my lawyers say the bad would outweigh the good. They say, well, we don't want the girlfriend thing to come up, and the thing with the taxes on my wife's car. But when it comes right down to it, who doesn't cheat on their taxes? That doesn't make me a murderer. If it did, I'd have a lot of company.

. . . It's true I don't like Koller—he's slimy, he's misleading about

the evidence. A prosecutor ought to be out to find the truth, not to win. I never thought about it when I was a cop. I always thought people I arrested were guilty. But now I understand the system. . . . That doesn't mean I'd lose it or anything on the stand with him. I'd never do that. I've testified many times. I don't lose my temper. I know better than that.

They're being conservative. I hope it works. But if there's a mistrial or something, next time, I'm going to testify.

• • •

While the defense presented its case, a friend of Leasure's stopped by the courtroom, fellow traffic officer and flying buddy John Balicki. Balicki had been lined up as a character witness until Lasting and White decided to abandon that defense. He was still on the list for testifying during the penalty phase—if there was one.

Balicki had stood by Leasure throughout his long travail. He thought Mild Bill was a wonderful friend, a fine, honest man. "He'd give you the shirt off his back. . . . He'd never hurt anyone. Just the opposite."

His high opinion of Leasure aside, though, he was a perfect illustration of why Leasure's lawyers opted against presenting character testimony.

Balicki, although he had known Leasure for twenty years, never knew Leasure owned a yacht. He never knew Leasure had a longstanding extramarital relationship with another woman, not to mention the fact that Leasure had been engaged to marry Irene Wong for years, even while he was married to Betsy Mogul. "I just can't believe it," Balicki said when he learned of the secrets Leasure had kept from him. He had always considered Leasure a dreamer, someone who hatched get-rich schemes and other wild fantasies, but who would never have the gumption to go through with those plans.

"I was confused before," he said. "Now I'm even more confused. None of it makes sense. That's not the Bill I know."

It was the last sort of testimony the defense team would want the jury to hear.

Detective Tom King had, indeed, found some unflattering information about Charles Sondergaard. In the fifth week of testimony, after the defense rested, Koller was permitted to present this new evidence in this stage of trial reserved for "rebuttal" testimony.

Despite the detective's digging, he couldn't actually disprove Sondergaard's story. King had come up empty looking for

work records or inspection reports that might have put Sondergaard somewhere other than Bill Leasure's house on the morning
Anne Smith died. But King did find numerous co-workers of Sondergaard's who characterized him as a man of dubious character.

His work record included numerous, mostly unsubstantiated,
complaints from the public, including allegations that he made un-
wanted sexual advances and exposed himself to a citizen whose
property he was inspecting; that he had been abusive and profane
to another citizen while on the job; and that he had used his position as an inspector to make real estate deals on the property he
was inspecting. A representative for the inspection department testified that Sondergaard was untruthful at a hearing concerning one
of these complaints. He had been suspended briefly after one complaint.

Perhaps more significantly, a co-worker, Arky Miller, recalled
that Sondergaard told him Leasure was paying him for the garage
construction job with a refurbished Corvette. Miller claimed to
have later seen Sondergaard driving the car to work. The testimony
directly contradicted Sondergaard, who had said he did the work as
a favor for a friend, without any compensation.

Koller also presented hours of testimony on the proper manner of installing anchor bolts and concrete for foundations—the job
Sondergaard said he was helping Leasure with that day. According
to building experts Koller brought in, there was no reason for
Sondergaard to have been there that morning. The metal anchor
bolts should have been added after the concrete was poured, not
before, as Sondergaard said he did. Koller wanted jurors to conclude that Sondergaard fabricated an extra step in the process so as
to be able to claim, falsely, that he was there that morning. Other
witnesses, however, under questioning from the defense, sided with
the technique Sondergaard described—either was acceptable, they
said. An afternoon of eye-glazingly boring testimony about anchor
bolts ended up a draw.

Another rebuttal witness, brought in from Oklahoma, dis-
pelled the defense suggestion that Dennis Winebaugh might have
been in on the Tony Reyes murder. Brandishing a sheaf of employment records, Grady Ash swore that the late Dennis Winebaugh
had been in Moore, Oklahoma, the day Tony died, working as a supervisor in a machine shop. He had been there all week without a
day off, Ash said.

Finally, Charles Persico testified. The man once imprisoned
for Anne Smith's death said he was innocent of the murder, though

he freely admitted doing time in almost every prison in the state, spending twenty-four of his forty-eight years behind bars, starting at age thirteen. But all of his other convictions were for narcotics use. He never did a violent crime, he said, and his lengthy record bore that out.

A mixture of sincerity and street-smart wiseguy banter, Persico shuffled into court having been off heroin for more than a year, although he had not shed the gangbanger persona of a lifetime. "I was frequently being rousted by black and whites," he said, referring to the two-tone LAPD patrol cars. ". . . We used to play cops and robbers."

Persico explained that he copped to manslaughter in the Smith killing because he knew he would be out on the street in a few years if he accepted the deal. He pleaded guilty not because he was guilty, but because the risk of awaiting a verdict was too great with a life sentence on the line. Although the judge had ordered the subject off-limits, Persico also managed to sneak in the fact that he had volunteered for a lie-detector test shortly after his arrest, but that LAPD had never taken him up on the offer.

Uncharacteristically hostile and rude in his cross-examination—the lie-detector remark had really aggravated him—Richard Lasting's first question to Persico concerned a lawsuit Persico had filed for false arrest. Persico was trying to cash in on the Leasure case, Lasting charged. And just how much money was he trying to get by suing LAPD, Leasure, and others? "It was eighty-five million dollars, I believe," Persico replied glibly. (The suit was later settled for $150,000.)

Persico then conceded that in 1980 he had resembled the composite drawing from the Anne Smith killing. Later, Lasting produced records from Persico's methadone clinic that showed he had not been there on the morning of Anne Smith's murder, as he had once claimed. Persico's alibi from his trial years before had been a lie.

These recently discovered clinic records had been subpoenaed for the first time during the course of the Leasure trial, and they were brought into court by the defense blind—neither side knew what was in them until the day they were presented to the jury. Because of the uncertainty, Lasting and White had wanted to forget about them. For all they knew, Persico's alibi could have been proven. But Leasure insisted on having them. And while Persico's alibi proved false, the same records showed he had been in for methadone treatments in the weeks before and after the killing. To Lasting's dismay, the records suggested that Persico's alibi could have been an honest mistake made years after the fact—there had been so many visits to the clinic, he could easily have mixed up the days, especially since he was arrested nine months after the day in question.

With that, both sides rested their cases for good on May 21, 1991, the trial ending on the same note of ambiguity with which the case had begun. Not a single bit of evidence in the case seemed completely straightforward, other than the irrefutable fact that people had died and someone was responsible.

Dennis France was a murderer and a liar, that was obvious—yet much of his story checked out. He had the car, he knew details of the murders, he had been Leasure's friend. On the other side, Leasure had an alibi that had sounded unshakable at first, and yet that, too, had been tainted. Paulette was a liar, all the lawyers seemed to agree—but was she a liar on the witness stand, or on the tapes with Scroggins, or a mixture of both? One interpretation convicted Leasure. One set him free.

Even the videotape, the one piece of evidence that seemed concrete, graspable, which told the same story every time it was presented to the jury, unlike so many other elements in the case—even that tape was, in the end, subject to human interpretation. What did Bill Leasure really mean when he wrote those notes to Dennis France? Was he afraid of being framed? Was he afraid of being revealed to be a murderer? Or could it have been just one more act by a habitually secretive man—someone who had never fully revealed himself to anyone—simply doing what came naturally? A passive man uses passive means to fight back. Could he have been writing notes, not out of guilt, but because that's the way he was: a man with secrets? A man who, bottom line, believed that, whatever he had to say to his good friend Dennis France, it was nobody's business but his own?

• • •

I was feeling so confident. Now I'm not so sure. Koller's trying to confuse them. I still can't imagine being convicted, but I feel like the jurors have got to be confused by now. He's not interested in finding the truth. He just wants to get me. He'll do anything, say anything, slime anyone.

I feel pretty good about things. But now I have some doubts. I don't know what's going to happen.

CHAPTER 24

"LADIES AND GENTLEMEN
. . . it will be your job to determine whether or not the defendant
in this case, William Leasure, is the most corrupt policeman in the
City of Los Angeles in its history.

"It is your job to determine whether or not this man was a cop
and a criminal with a dual life, a man bored with writing traffic
tickets, a man who needed some excitement in his life, a man that
turned to crime for that excitement—whether or not he is a man
who needed risks, who needed to commit crime to fill some inner
need."

Gone was the tired, sighing prosecutor who began the case of
People v. *Leasure*. Jim Koller, at last, had found his outrage. The
jury listened attentively, an apparently receptive audience.

Koller launched his closing argument to the jury with a re-
vamped theory of Leasure's motives for committing crime—that he
was a thrill-seeker. Later, upon reflection and over a few stiff drinks,
Koller would concede that Bill Leasure seemed more grandmoth-
erly than a thrill killer. But at the time, standing at the podium before attentive jurors, most of whom were scrawling notes as Koller
spoke, the prosecutor felt he had to suggest a motive for why a traffic cop would go bad. With the loss of Art Smith as a witness, any
hint of the financial gain Koller had described in his opening remarks had evaporated. So why not suggest thrill killing? The limited view jurors had of Leasure seemed to confirm it: They had
seen the ex-traffic cop solely through the eyes of gun-toting murderer Dennis France, thieving buccaneer and mercenary Robert
Kuns, and a video minicam that caught Bill Leasure at his worst.

The jurors had never seen pictures of Leasure playing with Spot the Bunny or Spot the Goat, they had never heard an LAPD partner recall Bill Leasure coming to the aid of drunks in alleyways, they didn't know the Leasure who had spent his youth working on a farm and being nice to handicapped kids. And, to be fair, neither had Koller when he advanced this new theory. The defense had presented no such evidence. And so committing crimes for the thrill of it was an explanation that fit the limited facts before the jury, if not a full picture of Bill Leasure. The prosecutor's job, Koller would later say, is to argue the available facts to his advantage—to focus on the "best facts." And to win.

"These are conscious decisions of a seventeen-year veteran of the Los Angeles Police Department. These aren't accidental. . . . These aren't flukes. . . . These are planned, premeditated murders by a man who liked to risk things, risk his life, risk his family, risk his career—a man who would make a conscious decision to possess silencers, knowing that the possession of one of these items would put him in prison. Just the mere possession of this item would risk his family, his job, and going to jail—just to possess a silencer."

As Koller spoke, Leasure focused on the prosecutor, staring at the side of his head with a blank intensity. Sometimes he would jot notes, or whisper agitatedly to his lawyers. But mostly he just stared. Leasure would later say this was one of the moments in the trial he hated most—hearing this stranger paint a scalding portrait of him, knowing his parents were sitting there, suffering through "the lies." When Koller spoke, Ernest and Agnes Leasure just sat silently, as they had for the entire trial, waiting stoically for the defense lawyers to set the record straight, to tell the truth about their boy.

Also sitting in the gallery, freed at last from the rule excluding witnesses from the courtroom, Betsy Mogul fumed and made an occasional whispered comment about the hated Koller. She said she was frustrated by not being able to testify, by the lopsided picture the prosecutor was painting of her husband, and by the unfairness of the judge's rulings that allowed Koller to "smear" Leasure with allegations about silencers and stolen yachts. Even if, for argument's sake, he did steal a boat or possessed a silencer, that did not prove he was a killer. It only prejudiced the jury, Mogul complained.

"Is this the personality of a thrill killer?" she asked at a pause in the proceedings. "A mild-mannered traffic officer? Why not go for the SWAT team? Where he could be crazy legally for thrills? Bill's mellowness and the fact that he's nonjudgmental got him in trouble. It let him be friends with Kuns and Dennis France. Does that make him a criminal?"

But the decision had been made to keep Betsy Mogul off the stand. Her complaints would not be heard by the jury, and there was little she could do but listen to Koller describe a double life she claimed didn't exist. Later, during another break, she blew Leasure a kiss, then, in an aside, said, "Is that the face of a thrill killer? I can beat him up, that's how aggressive he is. It's so ridiculous!"

The prosecutor, however, continued hammering out a very different portrait of Leasure. "The defendant led a dual life, essentially beginning . . . with the ultimate crimes of murder, planned murders. And not so much for anything that would motivate someone, but almost for a thrill, for being able to get away with it, to help somebody out. To be somebody important."

And as if answering Mogul's complaint, Koller said, "Mr. Leasure is not charged in this case with all of the crimes that you have heard about, but you have heard about them because those are the same people . . . that have knowledge of Mr. Leasure's life. They know what he did. They know how he lived his life for the last ten years. . . . The evidence came from the defendant's best friends."

Then Koller turned to his best evidence, the videotape, playing it once again for the jurors. But this time, he suggested, don't strain so much to see the notes Leasure wrote, or to interpret their meaning. Just watch the way the two friends communicate.

Koller had stayed up late many nights watching that tape on his home VCR, long, numbing hours following that disembodied hand writing its cryptic notes. And finally, one night in the midst of the trial, something had clicked, something he had missed all those other times he had watched the tape. Once he saw it, it seemed so obvious, a demonstration of the close bond between Dennis France and Bill Leasure: that adolescent, boyish quality to their friendship, the very same mentality that had them stealing and giggling in Leasure's patrol car.

"Think to yourself how little is said and how much communication is really taking place," Koller suggested. "I'm sure all of us have done something in our life with a friend, or you have a secret with someone that nobody else knows about, maybe some prank. Maybe you let the air out of the coach's tires. And he comes out and all his tires are flat, and it is just you and your buddy.

"And nobody would know about that but you and your buddy. No one would know that you were the two guys that let the air out of the coach's tires. . . .

"Then you see your friend, and you haven't seen him in a while. You go, 'The coach. The coach.'

"He would be the only one that would know. If you walked up to somebody else, they would think you are nuts, wonder what is going on. Only one person would know what you are talking about.

"That is the communication going on here between two murderers. There is only one person that would know what they are talking about. That is the person that they committed the crime with, like letting the air out of the coach's tire. . . . Just one word kicks them into what happened and what took place."

And on the video screen, Bill Leasure wrote one word on his little square of paper: "Melted."

Bill Leasure was fuming during the recess that followed Koller's argument. "He's lying and he knows it," he railed to his lawyers. They calmed their client, then exchanged a few words of support with Leasure's quiet, cordial parents. "I guess you know, me and the wife believe in our son's innocence," Ernest Leasure remarked casually to an observer in the gallery, as if anyone watching them day after day in the front row of that courtroom could have any doubt about their position.

Richard Lasting rose first to attack the prosecution case. He would be followed by Michael White, who would comment on the defense witnesses. Both had to try to anticipate Koller, who, in deference to the state's burden of proof, would get to speak last, just before the jury retired to deliberate.

"The prosecution's case is really based on five things," Lasting began. "In addition to the numerous efforts to smear Mr. Leasure by showing you that he had these silencers, and he had a girlfriend, and these allegations about the boats, the prosecution's case is based on three people and their honesty. They were described to you as Mr. Leasure's friends. And if he were on trial for picking his friends real poorly, you wouldn't have to deliberate long, would you?

"But that's not the charge here. They were described to you as thieves, murderers, and cheaters. That's the District Attorney's characterization of them. But they are the people he asked you to believe to establish that Bill Leasure is guilty of murder and conspiracy to commit murder.

"He left out a very important characteristic of those people. They are not just thieves, which Mr. Kuns is, and murderers, which

Mr. France and Ms. de los Reyes are, and cheaters, which undoubtedly they all are.

"They are also liars.

"And one thing about a liar is, you never know when they're telling the truth. Liars don't lie about everything. . . . They lie when it's to their advantage."

The police department's methods were appalling in this case, Lasting said. And to illustrate his point, he described at length the procession of deals the state made with the three main witnesses against Bill Leasure—France, who received legal immunity; Paulette de los Reyes, who served two years in jail for murder; and Robert Kuns, who served two years in jail for a dozen boat thefts. Not often does a defense attorney get to stoke jurors' outrage at the coddling of criminals—usually it's the prosecution making that appeal—but this was a special case, Lasting knew. All the criminals in the case got off—as long as they turned on Bill Leasure. If that wasn't motive for them to lie, Lasting asked, what was?

The defense version of the murders was intricate. Lasting had to argue first that Dennis France had told the truth, for the most part, about two of the three murders. He told the truth when he said he drove for the killer of Gilberto Cervantes, and when he swore he pulled the trigger on Tony Reyes (the defense had abandoned an earlier theory that France, not Winebaugh, pulled the trigger on Cervantes). The only part France lied about regarding these two murders, Lasting said, was when he injected Bill Leasure into the mix.

Yes, France was right about his description of the Tony Reyes killing in almost every detail—except for the parts of his story that allowed for Leasure being present. Sandra Zysman saw no one else there, heard no one else. She said she never took her eyes off Dennis France, and that he never spoke to anyone else, as he had claimed. Yet on every other detail, Zysman and France were in agreement.

"What is the evidence to establish that Bill Leasure drove the car that night? The evidence is that Dennis France told you he did. And there is nothing else to establish that.

"When you really boil it down and look at the evidence to implicate Bill Leasure in the murder of Tony de los Reyes and in the murder of Anne Smith, what you have is Dennis France's word for it. And how much is that worth?

". . . If Bill is the big risk-taker, has to be there when it happens, Mr. France doesn't even support that. Bill Leasure, according to Mr. France's lies, Bill Leasure is sending him out alone to commit the murders."

France's account of the Anne Smith killing, however, could not be presented as partial truth. It had to be a complete lie, according to the defense theory. This had to be a killing France falsely threw into his confession because he knew it would bolster his story by creating a series of murders with Leasure as the only common link. Sure, France got some details right, Lasting said. He got a lot of them wrong, too. Don't believe him, the defense argued. Charles Persico is the real killer.

"There is not a single witness who has ever identified Dennis France or Bill Leasure as the people that were at the beauty shop that morning. Not a single witness."

As for Paulette de los Reyes, Lasting urged jurors not to follow Koller's advice, which was to believe the tape recordings of her speaking to Detective Scroggins rather than her testimony in court.

"In order to get the truth out of somebody, this is what you do," Lasting sneered in describing the genesis of those tapes. "You deliver some phony documents to them. You lie to them about evidence in which you say somebody is implicating them. . . . You threaten them. You tell them they will go to the gas chamber, their son will be an orphan. You scream at them. You do this over and over again. A good idea to have some drinks while you are doing this. Let's be drinking while we are having this discussion, because alcohol is a noted truth serum. You use abusive and profane language. You tell them that the person you want them to implicate has implicated them, so that they can get a little payback by saying, wait a second. He is implicating me, all right. I will implicate him. And then you take all the statements out of context.

"That is the path to truth for Paulette de los Reyes."

And yet, Lasting pointed out, with all the pressure Scroggins applied before Paulette finally accused Bill Leasure, she still lied on those tapes about one thing. She still claimed she didn't know Dennis Winebaugh. Why deny that relationship, Lasting asked, unless he was the real killer of Tony Reyes? France said Paulette knew Forty-four. So did Bill Jennings. Even the taped meeting between France and Paulette made it clear she cared about the man: Oh, she had asked, how is he? So why deny it? Because, Lasting said, Dennis Winebaugh was the real mastermind of the Tony Reyes murder, just like he killed Gilberto Cervantes years before. And the last thing she wanted to tell David Scroggins, or anyone else, was the truth about who committed the murders, Lasting suggested. So she gave him what he wanted instead. She gave him Bill Leasure.

"I don't know where to start in describing her," Mike White said of Paulette de los Reyes when his turn came later that afternoon. "I think it is fair to say that she is the kind of character that you may read about or that you see on television in a series like 'Dynasty' or some of these kinds of other shows. But seldom do you really come face-to-face with a person like that.

"But we saw her face-to-face for a number of days during this trial. Conniving, self-centered, greedy, immoral, lying, manipulative. You name it. I mean, the string is as long as your arm. I think there is no doubt in anybody's mind that she was involved."

As for Charles Persico, another liar, White said, the evidence against him was overwhelming, enough to persuade Persico to plead guilty to a killing he now claimed he didn't commit. Surely that alone should create reasonable doubt about Leasure's guilt, the lawyer said. Add to that the alibi provided by the building inspector Charlie Sondergaard, and, clearly, Bill Leasure was innocent.

In the gallery, though, Detective Tom King was thinking that, contrary to Mike White's assertions, he was sure Sondergaard was wrong. Scanning the stony faces and crossed arms of the jurors, he concluded that most of them agreed. King believed Bill Leasure to be just diabolical enough to have ordered a concrete delivery on the very afternoon he committed murder, just so he could cook up an alibi someday—just in case, somehow, he was caught. The defense wants everyone to think Dennis France is that Machiavellian, King later said with a laugh, "but you take one look at him, and you know he's incapable of that kind of planning. All you have to do is listen to him. He's a follower, not a planner. But Bill is capable of it. He's proven that. I know he wasn't building a garage that day. He was out killing Anne Smith. If I thought otherwise, I would be up there testifying for the defense."[1]

There was one other crucial subject that had to be addressed by the defense: the videotape. That job fell to Lasting.

His goal was to provide an alternative interpretation to Koller's, one that, even if it didn't fit perfectly, would give receptive members of the jury an excuse to set Bill Leasure free. So he described the series of events leading up to the France visit, providing the "context" for the video. He recalled that shortly after his arrest, Bill Leasure had learned of the allegations that Jerry France had fabricated against him, the outrageous claims of piracy and murder on the high seas. Leasure received a copy of the search warrant for his home, and inside he read those false charges from Jerry France with alarm. He saw that the police seemed to believe them, too, and that they had searched his home for murder weapons based on Jerry France's dubious word.

And on those same search warrant documents, Leasure saw how the police had ignored a room full of guns in the Leasure house, and, at least at first, seized only two weapons—a pair of .45-caliber automatics Leasure had acquired from Jerry's brother, Dennis France. Only later did the police come back and seize all of Leasure's other weapons, enraging him by scratching evidence numbers into his prized toys, and test-firing mint-condition guns, ruining their collector's value. But at first, only those two guns previously owned by Dennis France were seized. That scared Leasure. And that, according to Lasting, is what Leasure was worried about when he wrote those notes to Dennis France.

"He becomes concerned that Dennis France has given him, without his knowledge, a forty-five . . . used in some kind of crime. . . . Mr. Leasure is concerned about brass from these guns that he has."

Assume for a moment that Dennis France has told you the truth, Lasting suggested to the jury. That means Leasure had reduced the murder weapon to a puddle of molten metal. If that were true, then Leasure couldn't possibly be concerned about it, as the prosecutor would have you believe. Why would Leasure write notes about a weapon he destroyed, that was forever beyond the ability of the police to seize and examine? He wouldn't, Lasting said. And that meant the conversation in the jail, at least Leasure's end of it, must refer to some other weapon Leasure was worried about—namely, the two guns France had sold him. He wrote rather than spoke aloud because, as a policeman, he knew jails are often bugged. He knew innocent words could be twisted later and used against him. And he was right, the defense attorney suggested.

Richard Lasting is a convincing man, a lawyer well known for his sincerity and integrity, and his explanation for the video seemed, at first blush, to make as much sense as the prosecution's interpretation.

The problem with this theory, however, lay in the fact that on the videotape it was France, not Leasure, who was pretending to be worried about the gun that was supposed to have been melted. France asked about it and Leasure answered, not the reverse. But Lasting was right about one aspect of the conversation: It was Leasure, not France, who brought up the subject of "brass." Leasure wrote: *Did you have any brass from that one?*

And that begs the question: Why would Leasure be concerned about the police finding France's used brass bullet casings? Leasure knew the economically minded welder held onto his used casings, reloading them with bullets and powder because it was cheaper than throwing away the brass and buying new cartridges. A "reload freak," Bob Kuns had called him. But so what? Leasure was a gun collector and self-styled expert on firearms. He had to know that once the police seized those two .45s from his house, they could test-fire them, then attempt to match the slugs and brass to ballistics evidence from any crime they wanted. The police didn't need France's spent casings to do that. They had the guns in hand. And, in fact, the police did test-fire Leasure's guns, including the two he had bought from France, and they came up clean. Lasting, then, was mistaken: Leasure's question about brass could not possibly apply to those two .45s.

The question about brass does make sense, however, if it pertains to a weapon that has been destroyed—the murder weapon in the Anne Smith case. *Do you have any brass from that one?* In this scenario, France's used brass casings, which he had accumulated over the years by scooping them from the ground after target practice, would bear the firing-pin marks from the weapon that had shot them. A used casing fired earlier from the murder weapon theoretically could be matched to the casing found at the beauty shop, even if the gun itself no longer existed. It would be like comparing one fingerprint to another without ever seeing the hand that left the prints. If that happened, the police would have known that France had, at one time, possessed the murder weapon. He wouldn't have had the chance to cut a deal for immunity; he would have been arrested on the spot. And, undoubtedly, Leasure would have been next. Such a fear would be more than enough reason for Leasure to ask his friend if he had any brass. And to tell him, "Dump everything illegal."

If such fears did lay at the root of Leasure's notes, they were unfounded: The police never thought to make such a comparison of brass casings, although they had found boxes of old brass at the France house. And even if they had thought of it, the brass casing found at the Anne Smith murder scene had been destroyed years earlier, standard procedure for a closed case, since Charles Persico had already been convicted. Only photographs remained; a successful comparison was unlikely.

But at the time he wrote his notes to Dennis France, Bill Leasure couldn't have known that.

Such arguments aside, there was another big problem with Lasting's explanation for the video: It was strictly a defense lawyer's speculation. Only one person had gone to the witness stand to testify about the meaning behind Bill Leasure's scribbling: Dennis

France. The only other person who could do that, Bill Leasure, chose to keep silent. That was his right, as the defense lawyers and judge repeatedly reminded the jury. The jury was forbidden to hold that against him. But his explanation for the video, for better or worse, would remain unknown to the jury. As would the fact that, in the end, he really had no explanation at all.

The next day, on the morning of May 30, 1991, five years and one day after Bill Leasure was arrested, Deputy District Attorney James Koller made his final remarks in the case, a final pitch to the jurors. With that, he hoped, a long, difficult case would finally grind to an end. His wife and children were virtual strangers to him now. After eight weeks of trial, he couldn't remember the last time he had seen the kids awake. He left for the courthouse before dawn to beat the traffic and arrived home well after dark, a pile of transcripts in hand, still waiting to be read. It was the same story with the defense team—at night, a few muttered words to the loved ones, go to court early, back to the office to work until midnight, go home and fall into bed, then start the cycle again. There was none of the usual retiring to the nearest tavern after court to discuss the testimony of the day. There was no relaxing and unwinding. This was a capital case, a career case. After this day, the deaths of Anne Smith, Tony Reyes, and Gilberto Cervantes would be avenged. Or the reputation of William Leasure would be restored.

Koller addressed each of the defense contentions in his final remarks, but he made three main points that stood out—two that enraged Leasure, who called them "a dirty, gutless trick," and a third that earned even the defense lawyers' grudging admiration.

The prosecutor talked for a while about the dangers of eyewitness identification, how easy it was to confuse one person with another. It had happened to Anne Smith's mother when she mistakenly pointed to Charles Persico as a killer, he said. And maybe it happened when the mechanic Thomas Rumbaugh described the two men he saw that day—men who didn't really look like France or Leasure.

Koller went to an easel at the front of the courtroom. The ten-year-old picture of Dennis France, his face dark and scruffy, his hair and mustache shaggy, hung there. Next to it was an old LAPD portrait of Bill Leasure, his face looking young and thin, his eyeglasses off. And below both these pictures were the composite drawings from the Anne Smith killing, drawings based upon the mechanic Rumbaugh's recollection.

France didn't much look like the composite drawing of the shooter—the thin-faced man in a cap whom Rumbaugh remembered walking through his garage toward the beauty shop. And the composite of the unshaven, dark-haired Latino man Rumbaugh put behind the wheel of the green Nova looked nothing like the balding, clean-shaven Officer Leasure. These drawings constituted an apparent repudiation of Dennis France's story and the prosecution's case. Acknowledging this, Koller previously had argued that Rumbaugh was just wrong about the men. He was a mechanic. He focused on the car, not the people, and his descriptions, therefore, were off.

But Koller had pondered those photos for enough years to formulate an alternative explanation, one he had never mentioned until that moment. He had noted Rumbaugh's parting comment to Detective Arce: Leasure sure looks like the guy I saw walk through the garage. And going back to one of his earliest statements to the police, Dennis France had said he originally thought the composite drawings really did resemble him and Leasure. Impossible, unless . . .

As the jury watched, Koller reversed the order of the composites, putting the scruffy one under France's picture and the thin-faced man with the hat under Leasure's. Look at them this way, he said. The transformation was startling: The drawing of the supposed driver, the unshaven dark-haired one, looked remarkably like the younger, unkempt Dennis France. The other composite drawing, the thin, clean-shaven man with the hat, whom Rumbaugh remembered striding through the garage, "bears a striking resemblance" to Leasure, Koller said. And he was right. It did—at least, as much as the cartoonlike sketch could look like any three-dimensional human being.

Perhaps, Koller said, in the days that passed between the time Thomas Rumbaugh saw the two men in the green Nova and when the police came to question him, his memory had played a trick on him. He got the descriptions right, Koller suggested, but he just confused the two. The scruffy man had been the one to walk through the garage and shoot Anne Smith. The thin-faced man waited in the car. "It is another possible explanation," Koller said. "They could easily be reversed."

Leasure looked like he was about to go ballistic at this point. He was red-faced and whispering vehemently to Lasting to object. But the defense lawyers were helpless. Koller was legally entitled to get the last word in—he had the burden of proof. Leasure's attorneys had tried to anticipate what the prosecutor would say and to address those points in their own closing statement, but they had not imagined such a novel, if speculative, argument. There was no evidence to support it, no testimony to back it. They could shred it in a moment—if they could address the jury again. But they could not. They could only sit and watch.

The next point Koller made outraged Leasure even more—an attack on the alibi witness, Charles Sondergaard.

"Mr. Sondergaard has not made a statement in this case for eleven years. He makes a statement this month, eleven years later, that Bill Leasure was at the house pouring concrete, getting ready for concrete in the morning. What's the first thing that makes you a little suspicious about that?

"If you were the person in jail for four years, and you knew you were home pouring concrete, you knew there was a witness to it, would you wait until 1991 to tell people about it? Would you sit there in jail for four years, five years, waiting? If you had someone to say where you really were, that you couldn't have done it? If you were that person in custody, is that what you would want your friend to do? Just sit tight, wait for 1991 to roll around?"

With that, Koller branded the alibi a fake, a story concocted at the last minute. Obviously, an innocent man would have presented this information immediately and proved his innocence, Koller argued.

Like Lasting's argument about the videotape, it seemed to make sense. But it really didn't—which is what enraged Leasure so. The system just doesn't work that way. Leasure could have known for years that Sondergaard would be a witness, but he never would have told the authorities. The police had already decided he was guilty. He had been charged. Giving them Sondergaard before trial would simply have given them more time to undermine his testimony, to disprove his account, to find more dirt. They would do everything they could to crush his alibi, so why give them more time to do it than necessary? Of course, that left him open to Koller's charge that he concocted a defense at the last moment. Either way, it was a no-win situation for Leasure.

The final point Koller made, more than anything else, struck at the heart of the defense, for it shattered their explanation of the video. Strangely, Koller accomplished this not with the videotape, but with the tape of the first jail visit between Dennis France and Bill Leasure—the one that was audio-recorded only. During the trial, almost all attention had focused on the more dramatic videotaped meeting. The first tape had been virtually ignored. Koller, it seemed, had been saving it, hoping the defense would leave it alone—and leave him an avenue to exploit. They did.

As a repudiation of the defense theory of the videotape, it was devastating. On the audiotape, the first thing France says is that the police have been by to see him. They ran down his car and they have the composite, France says, and he is worried.

"You are innocent, right," Koller said, asking jurors to put themselves in Leasure's place—the Leasure the defense had portrayed. "You don't know anything about the murder. You are in jail on boats. What would you say? 'What are you talking about, Dennis? What composites? What do you mean, run down your car?' What would a normal person say?"

But Leasure said none of these things on the tape. Instead, he did this, Koller said, and picked up a piece of paper, rustling it, as if he was writing—the same sound the jury heard a moment later, when Koller switched on the tape. These sounds were followed by Leasure's spoken comment, "No big deal."

Then, on the tape, France asks Leasure about Avenue 60 and "What about the mechanic?" Koller switched off the tape and asked: What could those two things refer to other than the murder of Anne Smith? And who could understand what they meant, other than someone who was involved?

"What's Mr. Leasure's response?" Koller again asked. "Panicked writing. More shuffling and paper flying all around."

Koller turned on the tape again. The sound of writing ends, and France responds, "Yeah, but why are they looking at it? If he confessed to it? That's what I'm wondering, why are they, you know, if somebody confessed to it, why are they looking at us?"

"What do you think Mr. Leasure wrote in that panicked shuffling of papers?" Koller asked. The prosecutor supplied his own answer: Leasure wrote a note about Persico taking the rap for the Anne Smith murder. They were in the clear because, Leasure wrote, "Someone confessed." And that had generated France's question, Koller said.

"This is what Mr. Leasure has to say about his crime. This is the man who swore to protect and serve the citizens of Los Angeles," Koller said.

The crowning blow to Lasting's argument came as the tape spun on, to a portion of the conversation in which France and Leasure switched topics. They spoke, out loud, about the two guns the police had removed from Leasure's house—the guns that once belonged to France, and which the defense lawyer had argued were the real subject of Leasure's note-writing. Except, on this tape, the two men were speaking aloud about those guns. Without notes.

"And the reason he's comfortable to speak is because what he's speaking about is not a crime. He's talking about some guns that were exchanged between himself and Mr. France that aren't murder weapons. He's not worried about anybody hearing it."

Only when the subject is brass or mechanics or Avenue 60—things related to murder—only then are notes written. And only then, Koller said, is Leasure concerned.

"What he said then . . . those are the words of a man who drove the getaway car in two murders."

With that, the case of the *People* v. *William Ernest Leasure* was entrusted to the jury.

• • •

I've been waiting a long time for Charlie to testify. It was no last-minute story. Koller really outdid himself with that one. I felt pretty comfortable, until he started talking about us paying off Charlie. That thing about me giving him a Corvette is a lot of bull. It's not true.

And that switching the photos, that was ridiculous. I wore glasses then. The man the mechanic saw didn't. I always have worn them, except for a short time when I had contacts, after the Anne Smith murder. That's the one picture they could find where I wasn't wearing my glasses. And what really steams me is, I wanted to bring my eye doctor in here to say I wore glasses then. I knew they had that old photo of me for some reason. But Lasting said no, it's not necessary. It's not fair. Koller didn't have the guts to say any of that before, when we could have responded to it. He just springs it when he knows we can't say anything.

The tape of the jail visit in Martinez, Koller managed to twist that pretty good, too. Dennis France mentioned the composites, but that didn't mean I was talking about murders. I had given the composites to him—not just for the Anne Smith murder, but the Night Stalker, the Hillside Strangler, I don't remember what all I gave him. But I knew it was nothing. He had mentioned it before, in that telephone call he didn't tape-record—that they say he didn't tape-record, but I don't believe that. So when he mentioned it again, I just said, "So what?" I had heard it all before.

Not everything on that tape that Koller said was the sound of paper crumpling really was. Some of it was the sound of the aluminum chair scraping on the floor, the way the microphone picked it up. Obviously I did write some notes, though. But a lot of the time I really didn't know what France was talking about. . . .

If I could have testified, I could have been convincing. But the jury didn't hear anything about me. These people don't know who I am, what kind of person I am. . . . I would never kill a person. I would never hurt anyone. Somebody should have told them that.

CHAPTER 25

I think they'll just look at each other and say, "He's innocent, right?" That's my fantasy. That they won't even have to deliberate. That they'll just say not guilty, and I can go home.

. . . The popular wisdom is, the longer it takes, the better the chance for a not guilty verdict. But I see things differently than most people do. There's more than enough reasonable doubt. I think they've proved I'm innocent beyond a reasonable doubt. It shouldn't take very long.

• • •

THE JURY DELIBERATED FOR four weeks. They began considering the evidence at five minutes after three in the afternoon on May 30, 1991. They kept on going until late in the morning of June 28, despite predictions by both sides that the verdict probably would come quicker, a week at the most.

The trial had been long and complex, and there was much for the jury to haggle over. Fifty-one witnesses had taken the stand. One hundred and seventy-seven exhibits were filed by both sides—boxes filled with documents, photos, charts, transcripts, and reports for the jury to peruse. And, of course, there were some twelve to fifteen hours of tape-recorded conversations, plus a video, for the jury to wade through. The tape player, television, and VCR were set up in the jury room, and the sound of tapes playing—Dennis France's ghoulish laughter, or Bill Leasure complaining about the police ruining his guns—could occasionally be heard drifting out.

At the outset of the deliberations, both defense and prosecution expressed cautious confidence. Koller still said, "You never know what a jury will do," but he also believed he had made his case. He couldn't see how a jury could conclude otherwise. The police investigators who had lived with the Leasure case for so long also expressed optimism about the jury "reaching the right conclusion." "I'd be heartbroken if they didn't do the right thing and convict him," Detective Tom King said. "I really would."

The defense team, Lasting and White, felt the same way. They candidly admitted that coming into court on the first day of trial, they had been pessimistic. The state's evidence had looked overwhelming. "Now," Mike White said, "we really think we might be able to win this thing. We definitely have a shot at it. We're way ahead of where we thought we would be."

And their client, Bill Leasure, more than anyone involved in the case, seemed to exude confidence at this juncture. Over and over, he said, "I can't imagine being convicted."

In phone calls from the jail, he said he was nervous, yet he sounded almost jolly. "I know I'm innocent, and I think the jury can't help but know it, too," he said during that first week of deliberations. As the days passed, he imagined a single juror holding out for conviction, with everyone else clamoring, Set Bill free! "If that happens, the judge will dismiss the case," Leasure predicted assuredly. "There's no way I should have to go back to trial if eleven people out of twelve decide I'm innocent."

He also began to sound like a man about to go home. "I've been trying to remember," he said early in the deliberations, "the last time I petted my cat."[1]

But as the days wore into weeks and still the jurors remained sequestered in their room six hours a day, confidence waned and nerves frayed. The mindless bureaucracy of the jail was so grounded in its system of transporting inmates that Leasure was still brought to court every morning, as if the trial remained in progress. But the courtroom was dark and locked, and Leasure could only wait in cramped and lonely misery, stuck in a cold, uncomfortable holding cell. They left him there all day, handcuffed much of the time, with no place to sit or lay down but a narrow and hard metal bench. There was no way to get comfortable, especially shackled. At lunchtime, a guard tossed him a brown bag with a mystery meat sandwich inside, his only relief from the nail-biting monotony of waiting. Lunch was always the same: a reddish-gray disc that resembled baloney, riding between two slices of nearly fresh white bread. Then, at the end of the day, he would be hauled back on the bus to the jail, where the waiting was slightly more comfortable, but no less maddening.

Gradually his confidence began to slip. He tried to concentrate on reading or watching television or imagining walking out of jail a free man, but he couldn't. He could only think that questions of his liberty, life, and death were now in the hands of twelve strangers—twelve people beyond his ability to affect or touch or control.[2]

• • •

I really think twelve people can do anything. I may spend the rest of my life in jail—and it may not be a very long one. You try to be prepared, but I don't think you really can be. . . . I mean, that's why I have an investigator doing nothing but talking to my friends—so they can come in here and say I don't deserve the death penalty, just in case I'm convicted. I don't expect that to happen, but you have to be prepared. And so you steel yourself, but it's hard. . . . It wouldn't be so bad if I were guilty. Then I could say, you dumb shit, what'd you do that for? But I'm not guilty.

. . . It's been so long now, and I'm getting scared. What can they be talking about all this time?

• • •

Over the next four weeks, a deputy occasionally would appear at the door to Leasure's cell and say, "Time to go to court." Leasure had no way of knowing if a verdict had come in or not, and so, each time, his heart would begin to pound as he prepared to meet his fate. Torture, he would call it later on: "Not knowing is the worst thing of all." But each time he was summoned during those four weeks, it was only because the jurors had a question, and all parties had to be present before the judge could deal with it.

He would walk into the courtroom, led by the bailiff, and ask his lawyers, "Is this it?" They would shake their heads and say no, and he wouldn't know whether to be disappointed or relieved as he collapsed into his chair. At least these moments relieved the tension for a time and got him out of the handcuffs. And his parents, who still came to court every day through the long month of deliberation, lived for those fleeting glimpses of their son. The rest of the time, they sat in the hallway outside the locked courtroom, watching the ebb and flow of defendants and lawyers, braving the bubble-gum odor of the restrooms, subsisting on cafeteria coffee and hope.

On the second day of deliberations, the jury sent out its first request. They wanted the court reporter to read back the testimony of three witnesses, all of them concerning Tony Reyes's murder.

The defense took this as a bad sign. They assumed the jury would choose to deal with the murders chronologically, beginning with Anne Smith. And the Smith killing was the strongest case for the prosecution, since the videotape applied to it alone. The request suggested that the jury had resolved the Smith charges already, then moved on to Reyes.

"We thought that sounded pretty bad for us," Richard Lasting said afterwards. "If they decided anything quickly, we were pretty sure that meant a guilty verdict."

But eight days later, another set of requests came out. The jurors wanted more testimony read back—all of it pertaining to the Anne Smith murder. Nothing, apparently, had been resolved after all. And at that, the lawyers gave up making predictions and confessed to having no idea what was going to happen.

Early in the case, Judge Weisberg's staff had dubbed the Leasure jury "the Wild Bunch." Some juries, intimidated by courtroom decorum and three-piece-suited authority, tend to look cowed and submissive, like subjects petitioning the king. Not this group. Every now and then, during breaks in the testimony, raucous laughter had spilled out of the jury room. One day, during a hearing outside the presence of the jury, the strains of "Happy Birthday" could be heard drifting into the court from the jury room, followed by wild applause. Someone had brought a birthday cake for a fellow juror—the clapping came when he blew out the candles.

Often, jurors come to resent the time they are shut in their little room while lawyers and witnesses discuss the evidence without them. In murder trials, especially, hearings outside the presence of the jury are common, as the judge and the lawyers wrangle with legal issues or discuss evidence the jury is barred from hearing. Leasure's case was no exception—there were hours of such hearings during which the jury sat idle, and even more bench conferences, pauses in the proceedings when the lawyers and the judge huddled and whispered at the front of the courtroom, out of earshot of the jurors. Judge Weisberg even cautioned the jury to try not to resent being excluded at such moments. It was a necessary evil, he said.

But he needn't have bothered—this group didn't seem to mind. The breaks in the action were enjoyable to them. They had their room with its pleasant view of Los Angeles's Little Tokyo and, just a few blocks over, the odd granite tomb that houses the *Los Angeles Times*. They had their group lunches and their after-hours cocktails. On breaks, the jurors could be seen in the snack room together, gulping coffee and pastries. The Wild Bunch liked one another's company. There was stress and an awesome responsibility, but for them, *People* v. *Leasure* was a pretty good time.

On the first day of deliberations, the boisterous group elected its quietest member, pharmacist Tom Maldonado, to be foreman. Then they took a vote. Five jurors favored conviction on all counts. Four favored acquittal. Three said they needed to talk about the evidence before they could decide. And the tension in that small jury room at last began to rise.[3]

Still, as the jurors each took turns speaking, a few areas of agreement became clear. Everyone wanted to know where Art Smith was. Why hadn't they heard from him? Or at least, why hadn't they heard more about him? (The jurors were not told he had been convicted or that he claimed his Fifth Amendment right to remain silent. Such information could tend to prejudice their opinions on the case, since it meant that another jury had decided Smith hired Leasure to kill.)

Second, everyone agreed that Paulette de los Reyes was a liar. "We all thought her testimony was worthless," foreman Maldonado would later recall. "If she had been on trial, she would have been convicted by all of us. The first day."

"She was a character on stage," juror Terri Villanueva, a telephone company employee, told her fellow jurors. "She just isn't a real person. . . . She basically convicted herself."

And, finally, though it was based on scanty information at best, the jury created for itself a detailed portrait of Bill Leasure, the man. Given the dearth of testimony about his character, some of their observations seem uncannily insightful.

"I know it sounds funny, but I never think of him as a policeman," real estate saleswoman Emma Rodriguez told her fellow jurors, echoing the sentiments of most of Leasure's colleagues— people the defense had opted not to bring to court. "I heard all the testimony, and he just didn't fit the image of a policeman."

"He's kind of a mysterious person," Villanueva suggested, again a common theme among the people who know Leasure. "He's kind of deceitful. He had a kind of double life. He's a very quiet man, obsessively so, but maybe he knew a lot. He was probably very smart."

"He was a genius," Karen Hawkins, a schoolboard office

worker, said. "But he was burning the candle at both ends. If only he had devoted his intelligence to police work, he could have gone far."

Maldonado summed Leasure up this way for his fellow jurors: "Silent waters run deep."

The jurors agreed that yes, he probably had broken the law. He had silencers, he stole boats. To their credit—and contrary to White's and Lasting's fears—the jurors quickly agreed that those other crimes did not mean Leasure was a murderer. There was no evidence that he profited from the killings. They laughed at Koller's "thrill killer" argument. If he was so bent on thrills, they agreed, Leasure would have done the shooting himself.

If anything, Leasure was the planner, the manipulator, the man who pulled the strings from behind the scenes, then sat back and watched it happen. Maldonado figured he did the killings for favors, "to be collected later." But for thrills? Not Mild Bill, Maldonado said.

With the jury divided, the foreman suggested they begin to sort through their differences by attacking the case chronologically—not with Anne Smith's murder, as the lawyers had assumed, but with Gilberto Cervantes, the very first murder. Even though it wasn't charged in this case, they felt the Cervantes hit had been the precursor for everything that followed. After a day, they remained divided on the question of Leasure's involvement in that killing. From there, they moved to Tony Reyes, since his murder seemed linked to Cervantes. At the end of a week, they voted again. They remained virtually split down the middle between guilty and not guilty verdicts, with two undecided.

Debate on the case had crystallized into a single question: Could Dennis France be believed? It was exactly the question Leasure and the defense lawyers wanted them to focus on. Let them put Dennis France on trial instead of Leasure. The more they considered France, the better the defense's chances.

After a week of haggling, half the jury said France seemed too unsophisticated to frame anyone, much less a clever fellow like Bill Leasure. The others said he was a clear liar. If you discarded his testimony, there was no evidence to put Leasure at the scene of any murder, these jurors said.

"I just don't believe Dennis France," Edgar Mito, the UPS loading-dock worker, announced early in the deliberations. "I think he's been coached. Look at all the inconsistencies. He lied to get a deal."

The soft-spoken, crewcut Edgar Mito had been the juror the

defense wanted removed during jury selection. Only at the last moment, and with great reluctance, had Leasure, Lasting, and White decided to keep him. Of all the jurors on the panel, he was the only one who had eschewed taking notes during the trial. He had sat attentively, often with a small smile on his face throughout the long proceedings, and the lawyers on both sides had pegged him as a get-along, go-along sort of fellow who would bow to the will of the majority.

The defense couldn't have been more wrong about Edgar Mito. Nor, for that matter, could the prosecution, which had considered Mito an ideological ally. As it turned out, Mito was Leasure's staunchest advocate on the jury.

"You can talk all you want," Mito said after the second day in the jury room. "I'm not going to change my mind. I'm not convinced. I'm not going to vote guilty."

After that first futile week, with the jury split on the Tony Reyes murder, the foreman suggested they move to the Anne Smith murder. Again, their first vote was nearly fifty-fifty. But then they played the videotape—four times over the course of the next week. And they listened to the audiotape of France's first visit with Leasure in jail. With that done, they all agreed, even Edgar Mito, that the defense explanation for Leasure's secretive notes did not hold up to scrutiny. Clearly, the jurors agreed, the two men were discussing the weapon that killed Anne Smith. On that matter, Dennis France had been corroborated.

As for Leasure's alibi, the jury unanimously rejected it as a phony. Koller's argument that Charles Sondergaard would have come forward much sooner if the alibi was genuine scored big with the jury. And no one except Edgar Mito believed that the heroin addict Charles Persico could be the real killer.

Once they had eliminated the alibi and decided the videotape backed up Dennis France's assertions, there was a shake-up in the jurors' opinions. A majority decided that on key points about both killings, France had been proven accurate after all. He knew too much, he had the right car. The testimony by the defense witness Bill Jennings was deemed to be favorable to the prosecution. The jury focused on Jennings's recollection of Leasure giving Dennis Winebaugh something wrapped in a jacket—corroborating, most jurors decided, France's testimony about a payoff in the Cervantes hit. The defense attorney's reason for calling Jennings—to suggest that Paulette hired Winebaugh, not Leasure, to kill Tony Reyes—was never seriously considered by the jury.

After two weeks, Maldonado called another vote. It was ten

for conviction on all counts, two for acquittal. Leasure was two votes away from a potential death sentence.

But while one of those two votes wavered—at one point, it was eleven to one on the charge of conspiracy to kill Anne Smith—Edgar Mito would not back down. The deliberations descended into angry shouting and wild charges—"Did you get a Corvette, too, Edgar?" one juror asked acidly at one point.

"They said, it has to be Bill," Mito recalled later. "I said, where's the evidence? And then we would go through it all over again. . . . I would just sit back and listen, but they didn't change my mind.

"I suppose he's probably guilty. But that's not conclusive. That's not enough to convict. I think everybody had doubts, but the videotape overpowered them. I conceded Bill was guilty of obstruction of justice or aiding and abetting. I think the tape shows he melted a gun from a murder. But that could just as easily have been after the fact. That doesn't mean he did the murder."

"I'm quite sure Bill's not a decent person," Mito later told his fellow jurors as they tried to shake him from his position. "But I have to be objective."

Toward the end of the fourth week, Mito admitted to his companions that he had violated the judge's instructions and read a newspaper article about the case. He had read a story on Art Smith's refusal to testify. The story had quoted Smith at length on his belief that the police and prosecutor had lied throughout the case. Some of Mito's fellow jurors thought this suspicious, since he had made similar arguments throughout the deliberations, suggesting that the police had coached witnesses into lying about Leasure.

"You think every police officer in the case was lying except the one on trial," Karen Hawkins complained at one point in the deliberations. Mito just smiled his placid little smile and shook his head.

In the end, foreman Maldonado decided the article hadn't really affected Mito's judgment in the case. He declined to report it to Judge Weisberg. Instead, the twelve jurors marched into court on June 28 with a different announcement.

The crucible of witness stand and cross-examination had failed to answer the questions and resolve the ambiguities in the case of *People* v. *William Leasure*. The foreman said the jury was hopelessly deadlocked. They could not reach a unanimous verdict. They were hung.

The final vote remained at ten to two on all counts, in favor of conviction. The result was as ambiguous as Bill Leasure himself. Ten ordinary citizens had looked at him and said, murderer. Two others had said he should go free.

Judge Weisberg declared a mistrial. There would be no verdict that day. They would have to do it all over again.

Deputy District Attorney Jim Koller was devastated. Several jurors would later say they felt sorry for him, that he was wearing his heart on his sleeve, that his rumpled, exhausted appearance showed just how hard this case had been on him. In truth, he would later say, what bothered him most was not so much the failure to reach a verdict as the prospect of having to go through it all once more.

Richard Lasting and Michael White were no less stunned. The lopsided vote told them they had badly misread their chances for success. And after they had talked to a few of the jurors in the hallway, they left the courthouse dispirited. They had given it their best, and had still come perilously close to a guilty verdict.

Ernest and Agnes Leasure, stoic as always, took the news with quiet despair. Their son, the man they believed in totally and without question, had almost been taken from them for good. Several of the jurors glanced at the elder Leasures sympathetically as they filed out of the courtroom, but none said a word.

"Psychologically, I'm sure they were put there for our benefit," Terri Villanueva said later. "And it did soften your heart a little. I felt sorry for them. But only over the fact that their son would do this to them."

No one seemed more stunned at the result than Bill Leasure. In the courtroom, he was his usual mild self, still and unmoving as the announcement was made, showing little emotion—far less, for instance, than he showed during his occasional bouts of red-faced anger at Jim Koller during the trial. Later, though, his anger bubbled to the surface. The fact that ten out of twelve people considered him guilty of murder beyond a reasonable doubt left him shocked and fuming—and ready to lay blame.

And Bill Leasure's blame list was a long one. He blamed the jurors for being too dense to see the truth. He blamed his lawyers for blowing the case. He railed against Koller for "slimeball tactics." He accused LAPD, once again, of framing him. He blamed the media for its negative take on the trial.[4] He blamed the judge for unfair rulings, and public sentiment about the Rodney King police brutality case for making a fair trial of an ex-cop impossible in Los Angeles.

Leasure lashed out at individual jurors, too—in the process, showing his peculiar habit for rewriting history to his own benefit.

Early in the case, he had called one juror—a woman employed as an LAPD office worker—"my favorite juror." He had even commented that he had noticed this juror doing "a double take" when Dennis France told the court that he still owned guns. "I think that's a good sign," he said during the trial. But after the verdict, suddenly this same juror should never have been seated in the first place, according to Leasure. It was "crazy" to have an LAPD employee on the jury. "I never wanted her in the first place," he railed. "They wouldn't listen to me. I had bad vibrations about her all along."

Everyone, it seemed, deserved a share of the blame, in Bill Leasure's eyes. Everyone but himself. If only his lawyers had listened to him, he said, things might have come out better.

"Next time," Leasure vowed, "things will be different."

The one bright spot he noted after the hung jury announcement was the expression on Jim Koller's face. "He was really upset. I heard him say all the liquor was gone at home, that his wife said, don't come home if Leasure's acquitted. He really took it personal." Leasure had to pause to chuckle at the memory of the moment. "I would have loved to have had a camera."[5]

• • •

They think the end justifies the means. That's how innocent people go to prison. . . . I know if I wasn't a policeman, none of this would have happened.

Dennis France made up all kinds of wild accusations, about me, about Jimmy Trahin, about armored car robberies and LAWS rockets. . . . The police and prosecutors know Dennis France made all this crap up, but they still believe him on the murders. It doesn't make sense to me.

This next time is going to be different. We're going to pull out all the stops. More witnesses, character witnesses, my other alibi witnesses. I'd like to testify, and I think I'm going to this time. I think the jury should hear what kind of person I really am. . . .

You know, Koller suggested a twenty-five-years-to-life plea—if LAPD cleared it. That was a long time ago, way before the trial. But I'd never do it. No way. I wouldn't even take a second-degree murder plea. And that would make me eligible for parole in six or seven years.

The ten to two vote scared the hell out of me, but I'm not going to cut a deal. I'm going for broke. I didn't kill anybody. I've saved lives. I've even brought lives into the world, delivering babies. . . . I think, this time, things will go my way.

• • •

Four months passed before the second trial of *People* v. *Leasure* would return to the docket in Judge Weisberg's court. In that time, the Rodney King case would fade from the headlines, to be replaced by an unprecedented series of new revelations about brutality, corruption, and crime within Los Angeles law enforcement. The city learned it had narcotics investigators caught dealing drugs, federal agents who laundered money, sheriff's deputies who formed a white supremacist gang called the Vikings, a rash of brutality cases that included what appeared to be an execution-style shooting of a suspect by an officer. LAPD, thanks to the Rodney King videotape, was subjected to one hundred days of scrutiny from a special commission headed by Warren Christopher, an esteemed former Deputy Attorney General and Deputy Secretary of State. The scathing report produced by the Christopher Commission excoriated the department. The chief, Daryl Gates, refused calls for him to resign, then promised he would depart, then backed off his promise—politics as usual in Los Angeles, the only major city in America where no one is empowered to fire the police chief. It was, in short, still a bad time to be a cop accused of crimes in L.A.

Leasure worked constantly on his case during those four months, reading files for hours each day (the eight boxes under his bed had expanded to ten with the addition of the transcript of his trial). His "theory book" bulged with new questions and approaches for his lawyers. Over the summer, he had considered replacing his attorneys outright. He went so far as to speak to a particularly high-profile Los Angeles criminal defense lawyer, well known for her aggressive courtroom tactics and frequent success, but she asked a fee of several hundred thousand dollars, too high a price tag for the loose change left to Leasure by the IRS. His court-appointed lawyers were free, but if he wanted new ones, he would have to pick up the tab. And that he was not prepared to do.

He also talked to his wife about representing him at the second trial, but this plan, too, was eventually rejected. "She's a really good attorney, much better than the ones I have," Leasure said at one point. He was irritated, still, at what he considered to be Lasting's and White's failure to listen to him during the trial. Betsy and he saw eye to eye on the important points of the case, he said.

But there are credibility problems with having your wife as your lawyer, he acknowledged. Or, as Mogul put it, "I have complete confidence in his innocence. But then, I'm just the lying wife."

So, in time, after discussing his case with Lasting and White, he decided to keep his defense team intact. "They're seeing things more my way," he reported. "We're going to do some things differently this time around. I want them to object more. And I want to bring in more witnesses. It's going to be different this time."

With that decided, jury selection for "Leasure II" began on October 31, 1991. Mogul was in court, huddling with her husband during breaks, as the lawyers flipped through juror questionnaires and prepared to pick a new group to decide the case. But then the proceedings were interrupted by an unusual, lengthy conference in the judge's chambers—just Leasure, his lawyers, Jim Koller, and Detective Arce, marching off to discuss something in secret with Judge Weisberg. Arce's presence seemed to upset Betsy Mogul for some reason. "What's he doing in there?" she asked bitterly. "He's got no business being in there." She refused to say what the meeting in chambers was about, or why she cared if the detective was present or not, other than to carp about his tax-paid salary going to waste when he should be out fighting crime.

But the reason for her concern became clear later, when court was recessed for the day. Before Leasure was removed by the bailiff, Betsy stood behind her husband, leaning over the wooden rail that separates the defense table from the gallery. Before parting, she said, "I want you to think about taking it. For me."

Leasure looked at her, mild as always, and said simply, "It depends on what they offer."

The import of their exchange was unmistakable. Bill Leasure was doing something he had vowed he would never do, and Betsy had been worried that Detective Arce would somehow interfere.

Leasure was trying to cut a deal. They had been discussing it in chambers, even as they prepared to go to trial: They were negotiating a plea bargain to end the case.

The next day, though, nothing had been resolved. Judge Weisberg issued an ultimatum. They would begin seating a jury that day. After that, they would go to trial, all the way. No deals from then on. So decide now.

Leasure asked to be alone in the courtroom with his lawyers, then his wife. The judge permitted it. After a half hour, Detective Tom King peeked in, thinking it was time to get started again. The courtroom held only two people in a silent tableau, looking small and forlorn amid the echoes and high walls of dark wood. Betsy was standing behind Leasure, her hand on his back, rubbing in slow circles. Leasure sat, his head bowed so low it almost touched the table.

Jim Koller had offered him the chance to plead to two counts of second-degree murder. Each count carried a mandatory fifteen-years-to-life sentence. It was the same sort of plea Leasure had said, only a few months earlier, that he would never, ever take. But if he did accept the plea, there would be no life sentence without parole, and no death penalty—the only two options left if a jury convicted him of first-degree murder with special circumstances.

And then there was Betsy, rubbing his back and saying, "I want you to come home some day."[6]

Koller made the offer because of the uncertainties the hung jury had created in his mind, and the fear that Dennis France and other witnesses might suffer even greater "memory problems" than before when it came time to testify again. He couldn't—and wouldn't—reduce the charges further, but in his conversations with jurors since the trial, only a few said they would consider a death penalty for Leasure anyway. With a forty-five-year-old defendant, fifteen years to life was not that much different from life without parole. So, Koller said to his boss, why not?

Lasting and White were surprised to get the offer—not that Koller would make it, but that the higher-ups at LAPD and the D.A.'s office would go along with it. Politically, it was not so wise these days to give a police officer a plea bargain, and the D.A., Ira Reiner, was up for reelection. (Indeed, the very next day, a campaign-sensitized Reiner would announce a no-more-plea-bargains policy in major criminal cases.) But once they had the offer, the defense lawyers were faced with a difficult choice. They thought they had a good case, but the ten to two vote was a sobering wake-up call. In the end, Lasting told Leasure, "It's your decision. I'm not going to tell you what to do. But I have to tell you, there's a real substantial likelihood that you could be convicted."[7]

Still, nobody thought Leasure would take the deal—not the prosecutor, not his lawyers, not the police. He had always said he was innocent. He had always said no deals. But by all accounts, even Leasure's, his wife talked him into it during that half hour alone in the courtroom.

Finally, Leasure turned to his lawyers and said yes, he would take the deal. There was only one condition. "It has to be a no contest plea. I'm not going to say I did it. It's no contest or we go to trial."[8]

Koller and Arce had filed back into the courtroom by then. The prosecutor said he didn't care if Leasure wanted to plead no contest or not guilty—the legal effect would be the same. He would still be pronounced guilty by the judge, and he would still go to prison for just as long. If Leasure thought saying he no longer contested the charges, rather than admitting guilt, somehow saved face, fine, the prosecutor said.

"I couldn't care less. This way he can keep saying he's innocent," Koller said. "There are a lot of innocent guys in prison. Especially murderers. They're always innocent. Winebaugh was the same way. It's their last hope. People need hope. Even murderers."

And with that, on November 1, 1991, Bill Leasure entered his official change of plea, replacing "not guilty" with "no contest."

"It's a bitter pill to plead to something you didn't do," Leasure told his lawyers. "But on the other hand, my wife wants me to get out some day."[9]

Judge Weisberg accepted the plea and pronounced Leasure guilty of murdering Anne Smith and Tony Reyes. Only the lawyers, the court staff, Detectives King and Arce, Betsy Mogul, and Leasure's parents were on hand to witness it, an anticlimactic ending to a perplexing case. But perhaps the no contest plea, Leasure's final refusal to admit doing anything wrong, was a fittingly ambiguous end to an ambiguous case.

"You got to understand his personality," Detective King said afterwards. "He cannot say he did it. He can't accept what he did. He's like a little kid, saying over and over, I didn't do it."

• • •

I didn't want to do it. I maintain my innocence. But Betsy said she'd rather have me back in a couple years than not at all. It was in my best interest. I figure I'll do ten to fifteen years actual time. And then I get to go home.

CHAPTER 26

I still believe I could have won. I am innocent. Innocent of boat thefts. Innocent of car thefts. Innocent of murder. But the first trial was . . . sobering.

• • •

BECAUSE BILL LEASURE agreed to a plea bargain, there would be no penalty phase in his case, no decision to make about whether he deserved to be executed for his crimes. His sentence was programmed by statute, with no option left to judge or jury. Fifteen years to life. Under complex state guidelines and with credit for jail time served, Leasure would be eligible for parole no sooner than 2004. The rest was up to the parole board.

The witnesses and evidence gathered by his private investigator, Sheryl Duvall, would not be presented in court. And the prosecution and defense would not battle to define the true nature of Leasure's character—to debate if he should live or die.

Still, the information they would have used in that debate remains available. The witnesses are there. Conclusions are possible. What explanation, if any, might the defense have offered for Bill Leasure's conduct if he had been convicted in that first trial and a penalty hearing had been convened? The defense lawyers have said their penalty defense would have centered on Leasure's good character, but the same witnesses could have been used to tackle another question: What would make Bill Leasure kill?

The first thing that would have been proven in a penalty phase, conceded even by the police and prosecution, is that Bill

Leasure is not a cruel person. He never displayed the personality of a thrill killer—or any other kind of killer. He never liked to hurt anyone or anything, not people or animals. He didn't even hunt.

There is nothing vicious about a person who, as a youth, protected a disabled child from the cruel mockery of other kids. He was the beat cop who didn't just run the drunk on the street into jail—he called the ambulance and had him checked out. He was the traffic officer who hated to write tickets. Witness after witness would have entered the courtroom to say so.

His boredom with the job hadn't driven him to commit crimes, as the prosecutor argued. On the contrary, Bill Leasure loved his job, the more monotonous the better. He was the CPA who wandered into the squad room. Not much of a cop, perhaps. But he wanted nothing more from LAPD than to put in his eight hours a day—less when he could manage it—with plenty of time left over for his extracurricular activities: his cars, his boats, and, yes, his girls. His secrets.

Here was a fellow who grew up in a family that lived payday to payday, strong on traditional values, not so strong on communication—a shy father and a Sunday school teacher mother. Bill was shy, too, preferring to spend his summers on his cousin's farm, mingling with the animals instead of hanging out with friends. If not animals, he preferred surrounding himself with cars, tractors, machines of any kind—anything but people. Secretly, he felt unappreciated, even put upon by some of his teachers. But even when he was angry, he submitted to authority. When he didn't like being disciplined unjustly by a teacher, or if he hated his assignment in the class play, he either took it in silence or quit and walked out. He seemed always to choose silence over protest, to bury his feelings, to be the blank wall.

From school, Leasure went to work briefly on the General Motors assembly line, impersonal machines his daily companion. From there, he joined the Marine Corps, another authoritarian, dehumanized environment for him to submit to. He did his time in Vietnam, but his commanders found him an indifferent Marine, doing just enough to get by.

After the Marines, he chose a career with another quasi-military organization—LAPD. It was yet another institution he could submit to, another job in which he did just enough to get by. And then he chose a wife, Betsy Mogul, who was the assertive, outgoing partner in their marriage. The pattern is unmistakable: Bill Leasure spent most of his life submitting to others, taking whatever was thrown to him, complying silently, even seeking it out. It was his role in life, the quiet man, the silent waters.

But then, his lawyers might have argued, sometime in the mid-70s, something happened that jogged Leasure into a new pattern. Somehow, he saw new possibilities for himself. Perhaps it was getting a rogue cop for a partner by the name of Big John. Perhaps it was falling in with a charismatic hit man by the name of Dennis Winebaugh, or an unscrupulous, manipulative woman named Paulette. Perhaps it was finding a groupie like Dennis France, who would do anything Leasure wanted, a taste of absolute power. Whatever happened, something during that time frame triggered a change. And Bill Leasure began a secret, separate life, one in which he didn't have to submit to anyone.

It was a life in which he could plant a bomb to scare a friend's abusive husband and then laugh silently in the police station the next day as his colleagues tried in vain to find the culprit. It was a life in which he could introduce his hit man friend to Paulette and Tony de los Reyes—and a seventy-six-year-old tortilla magnate could end up dead as a result. It was a life in which the knowledge Leasure had gained working auto-repair fraud cases at LAPD could be put to work on his own auto frauds—earning him a passel of stolen Corvettes in the process. And, later, after he met and fell in with Skipper Bob Kuns, he could really cut loose: He could acquire yachts, he could work insurance scams, he could lay plans to traffic in stolen airplanes. His good friend Officer John Balicki recalled Leasure as a dreamer. But somewhere along the line, Leasure realized those dreams could come true.

Just as suddenly, in the latter part of the 70s, the shy, mild Bill Leasure who was always so afraid of women had girlfriends, lovers, a fiancée—all in addition to his wife. And none of them knew about the others. Irene Wong was in the dark. She was going to marry Bill, she wanted his child, she had his engagement ring on her finger. Betsy Mogul was in the dark. Her friends remember her complaining about Bill's secretive ways, his refusal to reveal his work roster or his days off. "I think that these two people had totally separate existences," Betsy's good friend Kay Kuns had told the police. He wouldn't even let Betsy see the inside of his briefcase, one friend remembered. He always kept it locked.

Yet, even as he divided his time into separate, secret lives, Bill Leasure still maintained his old image, the mild, easygoing, nonaggressive cop, the guy who took pride in knowing he's the one a friend will call when the car breaks down or you're a few bucks short on the bills that month. "I'm the nicest, mildest guy you'll ever want to meet," Leasure says of himself. And when he did do something less than admirable—deceiving Irene Wong, for instance—he would invariably put a gloss on it. He would make himself the hero. He wasn't just an adulterer shacking up with a woman fifteen years his junior. No, Bill Leasure was saving Irene from abusive parents. He was showing her the world that had always been denied her. He was doing her the favor, just like he always did. He was helping Irene Wong.

And maybe, when his good friend Big John was in trouble, Leasure arranged for a perjured witness to bail him out, with the able assistance of Dennis France. And when his confidante, friend, and lover Paulette de los Reyes needed help, when she said her drunken, raging ex-husband had beat her, threatened her, tried to kill her—maybe Leasure decided to help her, too. He wouldn't do anything violent himself, that wasn't his way. Even as a cop, he rarely, if ever, used force. But he had Dennis France, the guy he toted around in his patrol car, the groupie who stole with him, like a giddy adolescent, thumbing his nose at the police department that had never properly appreciated Bill Leasure. France would do whatever Leasure said. And when things got so bad for Paulette that he couldn't bear it anymore, Leasure could have said to France, let's take care of Tony. Paulette needs help. She's my friend, he's slime. Let's do it, Dennis. I'll drive. You take care of business.

He would have been helping a friend with an intractable problem. It wasn't mean. It was necessary. It was justifiable, self-defense, really. Just like he helped Art Smith. The divorce was ruining poor Art, his wife was taking him for everything he was worth. He and Art would lose the island, the resort, the *Santine,* everything, if she wasn't stopped. And there was Dennis France again, waiting for his orders. It would have been easy, like punching in the codes on a nuclear missile. You didn't have to see the people die. You just pushed the button.

The motive wasn't money, or thrills, or viciousness. If Bill Leasure killed, it was because he was doing a favor for a friend.

He was a man who had buried himself in silence all his life. Yet he desperately wanted to be the man people turned to for help. He was the perfect person, just as he had told the psychologist who came to jail to test him. Bill Leasure was the nicest guy you'd ever want to meet—that's how he spoke about himself. He'd always help a friend. He'd give you the shirt off his back. He'd be there for you, always.

He might have been Code 1 when his LAPD sergeants were looking for him, but if you were Mild Bill Leasure's friend, he'd just about kill for you.

There is another scenario, too, just as plausible, just as consistent with the facts—but that suggests Leasure might be innocent of murder.

From the start, the police theory of the case was that, if you believe Dennis France killed Anne Smith, then Bill Leasure had to be involved in the murder, too. According to this construction of the facts, there was no connection between France and Art Smith until years later, when the boat thefts began. Therefore, the theory goes, Leasure had to be on hand to act as the middleman—he had to be the one who set it all up. That's why Leasure's lawyers tried so hard to prove Charles Persico really killed Anne Smith. That's why they tried—and failed—to blunt the undeniably compelling evidence that Dennis France was the killer in the beauty shop.

But does conceding that Dennis France really was the killer truly mean Leasure had to be his accomplice? The defense argued, plausibly, that Leasure was an unnecessary cog in the Tony Reyes murder, because Paulette de los Reyes had met the hit men, France and Winebaugh, years before. She could have cut a deal with the killers herself, without Leasure. Indeed, half the jurors in the Leasure case, at least initially, considered this a valid argument.

Why couldn't this have happened with Art Smith and Dennis France as well? After all, there is only one source to tell us Smith and France didn't know each other until after the murder: Dennis France himself. And to paraphrase Richard Lasting's closing arguments, just what is Dennis France's word worth?

In the months before the killing, Art Smith was embroiled in a vicious divorce. Anne was trying to ruin him, he believed. He told everybody he knew all about it, in cutting, violent, angry words. He discussed it with his friend Bill many times. And maybe, just maybe, Bill Leasure, the man who loved to come to the rescue, the perfect friend, finally said, Art, I can help. How about I follow your wife, find out who she's having an affair with, how she's trying to hurt you. And I've got a friend, Dennis France, who would love to help, too. He can follow Anne while I'm working.

So both Leasure and France might have begun tailing Anne Smith, then reporting back to Art. Except, perhaps, after a few tail jobs, Dennis France suggested to Art Smith, Hell, buddy, why divorce her? I'll waste her for ya. And Art's response was not, forget it. Instead, he asked, how much?

In this scenario, Bill Leasure is out of the loop until after the murder. Only then does Dennis France go to his good friend, Officer Bill Leasure, to say, hey, I'm in trouble. I need help. I did Anne Smith, and now I'm afraid both me and Art are gonna get caught.

What would the man who is always there for his friends do then? Might he help cover up the crime? Would he pump his friend Jimmy Trahin at ballistics for information on the case? He called the original detectives on the Smith case and kept track of the investigation—Leasure admits that much. And perhaps he would even melt down a murder weapon when he found out it could be traced to the bullet that killed Anne Smith.

Edgar Mito saw it that way. Of all the jurors, he looked at the incriminating videotape and asked, what does it really prove, literally? Arguably, that videotape shows three things: Leasure knew Dennis France killed Anne Smith. It shows Leasure is familiar with the evidence in the case (the composite, the mechanic, the green Nova, the one brass casing). And it shows he melted a gun—after the murder.

The videotape, in short, shows fairly conclusively that Bill Leasure covered the tracks of a murderer. You can infer, then, that he also participated in the killing—a reasonable conclusion. But it doesn't actually *say* that. Nowhere on the tape does he admit planning, paying for, or committing murder.

One of the greatest problems with Leasure's defense strategy was that it required his lawyers to challenge France's account of how he killed Anne Smith. They could not do that easily. France was too accurate, too clear on too many significant details. He knew the gunman at first forgot the cash register. He knew the gun was in a sock. He knew.

But if the defense could have conceded that France was the killer of Anne Smith and that Leasure merely covered up the crime, then all of France's inconsistencies make sense—because they concern Leasure's role in the murders, not his own. It explains why France was so confused about the amount of money Leasure paid him, and when, and where. If you're telling the truth, your story stays the same. If you're lying, it changes with each telling, unless you're very, very good. Could that be why France got so many details right when he was talking ammunition, gun types, and the locations of all three murders, while telling contradictory stories about how Leasure first offered him a contract to kill and how much he was paid? Certainly, it explains why Sandra Zysman saw and heard only one person at the Tony Reyes murder scene, though France claims to have been talking to Leasure, asking for instructions. And it explains why Leasure was so secretive on that videotape—a man who covered up for murder wants to protect himself as much as the murderer does.

It is not a perfect theory. It doesn't explain why Art Smith would tell friends and employees—months before Anne Smith died—that a policeman was going to kill his wife. It requires a belief that Art Smith's post-trial confession was a lie. It doesn't explain Leasure's peculiar question to his "second mother," Flo Ong: "What would you say if I told you I had killed someone?" It doesn't explain why both Dennis France and Robert Kuns would say Leasure, not Paulette, paid for the hit on Tony Reyes. Nor does it explain why Leasure would brag—falsely—that he persuaded Charles Persico to confess to the Smith murder, something France, Kuns, and Art Smith all recall him doing. Unless it was all intended to enhance Leasure's image as savior, the man who could, literally, fix anything.

That image lies at the crux of this theory—it fits Leasure's personality as much as anything the prosecution has advanced, if not more. He would want to help his friends Art, Paulette, and Dennis. More than that, he would want them to conclude that he was the man who could take care of things. "Piece of cake," Paulette remembers him saying. Mild Bill, unappreciated in school, by the Marines, by LAPD—he'd show them all. He was a man willing to possess illegal silencers and machine guns, no matter what the risk. He possessed stolen boats and cars, he committed fraud and perjury. Adding a little obstruction of justice to the mix wouldn't be much of a stretch. Why not aid and abet a few misguided friends who had decided to dispense justice with a gun? Turning them in for murder, after all, wouldn't bring anyone back to life. But melting a gun and slipping a little cash to a hit man would sure help his good friends. Would a Los Angeles cop turn his head the other way to murder? Would Bill Leasure?

He's not a decent person, Edgar Mito had said. But that doesn't make him a killer.

The maximum prison sentence in California for aiding and abetting a murder is three years. That's less time than Leasure spent in jail waiting to go to trial.

"It would have been an interesting defense to present in court—because it really fits all the facts," Richard Lasting said a few weeks after his client had pleaded no contest to two counts of murder. "There was only one problem with it: Bill."

This scenario is no fantasy. Lasting had tried to broach elements of it with Leasure long before the trial began. Isn't it possible, Lasting had inquired, that you might have asked France to follow Anne Smith, just to report on her movements? Just to help Art on his divorce case? Dennis France, the would-be cop, the police groupie, would have loved to do something like that, Lasting had suggested to Leasure. And from that seed, a murder plot could have grown—without Leasure being a part of it.

But Leasure shot Lasting's idea down. No way. It didn't happen. I would never do that. I had nothing to do with following Anne Smith. It wouldn't be right.

And that was that. Such an explanation—that Leasure covered up the crime after the fact—could only work in the courtroom if Leasure were willing to admit it. He would have to concede, finally, that he did something wrong. And that Bill Leasure just would not do.

He took the same position on the boats and the cars and everything else: I did nothing wrong. I never stole a boat, I never stole a car, I've never done anything to deserve what's happened to me. Even when the evidence against him was overwhelming, Leasure denied everything. Even a tawdry extramarital affair becomes a noble thing when Leasure describes it. That's the reason he couldn't testify in his own behalf. That's the reason his potentially best defense could not be used. That's the reason he has no credibility. Who can believe the perfect man?

Whichever scenario fits, guilty or innocent, is irrelevant now as far as the justice system is concerned. The Superior Court for the great state of California has passed judgment, and William Ernest Leasure is guilty of murder. And because his conviction comes from a plea, not a verdict, there can be no appeal. His case is over.

The great irony in the case is this: Leasure's inability to admit wrongdoing of any kind could doom him to spend the rest of his life in prison. Even though his sentence makes him theoretically eligible for parole within twelve years or so, Leasure's insistence on innocence means he might never get out.

"I'll tell you why I really didn't mind offering him the plea," prosecutor Jim Koller said after the case had ended, Leasure was headed for the penitentiary, and Koller was contemplating an unexpectedly relaxed Christmas. "The parole board, before it will let anybody go, wants to hear the defendant accept responsibility for his crimes. Just because he's eligible for parole doesn't mean he'll get it. The sentence is fifteen years to *life*, and if the parole board sees fit, they can keep him there for the rest of his life."

It's like this for Bill Leasure: sometime in his late fifties, early sixties, if he wants to get paroled out of prison, he will have to admit, finally, that he committed murder.

"I don't think he can do that," Koller said. "They may never let him go."

The prospect seemed to cheer the prosecutor immensely.

• • •

I figure I'll have to do fifteen years until I can get out. I still maintain my innocence—it was the toughest decision I ever made. My plea is not an admission of guilt—it's strictly . . . in my best interest not to go to trial.

But I understand the realities of the parole board, too. I know what they'll expect to hear before they'll let me go. I don't know what'll happen. . . .

I'll just have to cross that bridge when I get to it.

EPILOGUE

Bill said shoot. I shot.
—Dennis France

CHAPTER 27

THE FILES AND PHOTOS, THE
spent bullets and silencers, and the long tape recordings of Dennis
France luring his fellow conspirators to their doom are in storage
now, safely inside the vaultlike clerk's exhibit room in the cool gray
basement of the Los Angeles County Courthouse. *People* v. *Leasure*
has been reduced to a small pile of boxes, tucked in a maze of
seized drug bundles and stolen television sets and endless court
files—artifacts that briefly served the vital causes of liberty and justice, only to be entombed by the county like a pharaoh's possessions.

The Leasure case had once generated sensational publicity,
along with grave—and legitimate—concerns about police corruption within LAPD. Yet the case drifted to an end with scarcely a
ripple of attention, in spite of the many unanswered questions at its
heart.

In 1986, the notion of a policeman committing unchecked
thefts, frauds, bombings, and contract murders for the better part
of a decade seemed frightening enough. But when evidence surfaced that one of Leasure's fellow policemen was involved in a
bombing, that another took part in the thefts and frauds, and that
still more policemen had sought Leasure's services in either the stolen yacht trade or the murder-for-hire trade, then LAPD brass had
good reason to fear a department-rending scandal.

But the fears were never realized. The outside scrutiny of the
press soon ended, as it nearly always does when complicated cases
drag on too long. Concern within LAPD faded as well, once investigators failed to link more murders to Leasure, and failed to find

a larger web of cop corruption within the department. LAPD has not disproved the existence of more murders and a wider conspiracy—indeed, the common sentiment among investigators involved in the Leasure case is that there are more undiscovered bodies and crimes out there. Dennis France's recollections of several different policemen wanting to hire Leasure to kill and Robert Kuns's tale of two or three other cops seeking stolen vessels remain uncontroverted.

Eventually, though, other, more explicable scandals took precedence. Brutality, not corruption, became the bane of the department by the time Leasure's case was resolved, thanks to the riveting videotape of motorist Rodney King's beating by LAPD officers. And while that tape has brought the promise of real reforms to LAPD, the sudden and unsurprising "discovery" that racism and brutality were problems in big-city law enforcement has drawn attention away from the smaller, but more pernicious, area of police corruption.

In the wake of Rodney King, the department's commanders have shown little interest in the startling questions posed by the Leasure case: How could LAPD, which has prided itself on making policing a science, which inspired "Dragnet" and Joe Friday and just the facts, ma'am—how could the vaunted LAPD have a Bill Leasure in its midst and not know it? How could an officer who stole, defrauded, bombed, and killed for a decade, who owned too many cars and homes and yachts for any honest cop, go undetected? How could the department fail to note Leasure's connection to the victims and suspects in three, if not more, murders—going so far as to drop an investigation of one of his best friends, Art Smith, in order to arrest and convict an innocent man? How could LAPD fail to realize that one of its own officers recruited other policemen to break the law, and used department computers, radios, and training in the process? Didn't anyone even notice his long disappearances during his shifts, his unauthorized ride-alongs with Dennis France? And, finally, shouldn't someone be asking just how William Leasure managed to fool his instructors, the LAPD psychologists, and his sergeants all those years, becoming and staying a cop?

Good questions, Detective Bud Arce concedes, but far beyond the bailiwick of his now-closed homicide investigation. And there is no other investigation any longer—with the stress-induced departure of Sergeant David Wiltrout, the massive Internal Affairs probe quickly wound down, the Leasure team was disbanded, the Leasure room was given over to other uses, the mountainous files were boxed and forgotten. When the murder case was concluded against Bill Leasure, LAPD closed the books on him for good.

There is one more irony in the case. As LAPD pursues post–Rodney King reforms and increases efforts to screen out the type of officer candidates who might have brutal tendencies, it is seeking a calmer prototype for its street cops. LAPD wants the sort of officer who is not too aggressive, who has good relations with the community, who exerts a pacifying influence, strong on negotiation rather than confrontation.

In other words, before it came to the decision that he was a murderer, LAPD would have been looking for new cops a lot like Bill Leasure.

With the investigation closed at last, Detective Addison "Bud" Arce has moved on to other murder cases, an endless landscape of drug-dealer assassinations and gang-banger drive-bys. When the Leasure case concluded, he was assigned as a principal investigator on the Rodney King brutality case. He will be eligible for retirement soon, but says he has no plans to leave the department he loves.

Detective Henry Petroski has retired from LAPD, and supplements his police pension by doing insurance investigations and putting together sport-fishing charter trips.

Deputy District Attorney James Koller has transferred from the Special Investigations Division at his office, ending his career pursuing rogue cops in favor of prosecuting more typical felons.

Richard Lasting and Michael White remain law partners with offices in Santa Monica, California. Their representation of William Leasure ended with his sentencing.

Sheryl Duvall continues to perform death penalty investigations, and continues to make sense of her clients' crimes—except Bill Leasure's.

Irene Wong has a successful career and marriage, but remains extremely bitter over Leasure's deceptions, and had hoped he would receive a far harsher sentence. She says now that what she had believed to be a second pregnancy with Leasure at the time of his arrest turned out to be a false pregnancy. "I never told him. I wanted him to feel bad."

Arthur Gayle Smith lost his appeal to the California Court of Appeals, and continues to serve a life sentence without possibility of parole for the murder of his wife, Anne Smith.

Dennis Dean Winebaugh's sentence for the murder of Gilberto Cervantes ended with his burial in June 1991.

Betsy Mogul has a private law practice and, according to a letter to the court, is awaiting her husband's return from prison.

Robert Kuns and his wife are planning to finish restoring their sailboat, then move to Hawaii, the Skipper's legal troubles behind him. He noted before his departure that his and Leasure's long career as yacht thieves has not led to any reforms in the registration of vessels. Anyone with a phony letterhead and a little nerve can still steal all the yachts he or she wishes, Kuns warns. The Skipper vows he has gone straight, however, despite missing the thrill of crimes undetected and the comfortable feel of a large roll of cash in his pocket. He is still working on his unpublished novel, *Fun and Games,* about a "good bad guy" with ninja moves and a private code that transcends morality. A character modeled on Bill Leasure will play a principal role in it.

Dennis France, who has never served a day in jail for three murders and an array of other crimes, is living with his wife and children in Southern California, driving a passenger bus for a living. He owns numerous guns and still has his beloved hunting license. After Leasure's conviction, he remarked, "It wasn't all killing people. We had some good times, too. Like the time we busted into that bank. Me and Bill."[1]

The police have never investigated Leasure or France in connection with any bank break-ins.

Paulette de los Reyes appeared in court for her long-delayed sentencing on January 6, 1992, with diamonds glittering on her fingers and a cylindrical fur hat canted above her brow, shaped roughly like a mink roll of toilet paper. Clearly, she expected to walk out of court on her new husband's arm—and on probation. "This has been a nightmare," she wept to the judge.

Paulette's grasp on reality was tenuous at best. Just before the hearing began, she announced that a probation department report written to aid Judge Weisberg in determining her sentence was "very favorable." But the report was anything but favorable: The probation officer pronounced her "an impulsive, self-oriented and manipulative individual," and opined that her "removal from the community is deemed imperative."

Judge Weisberg agreed. "In my view, you are not a truthful person," he said, dismissing her rambling assertions of innocence and finding overwhelming evidence that her crime showed a "high degree of cruelty, viciousness, and callousness." Though the charges of murder and conspiracy against her had to be dismissed in accordance with her plea bargain and agreement to testify, the judge imposed the stiffest sentence he could on the remaining charge of solicitation to commit murder. As Paulette sobbed and repeatedly tried to interrupt, Weisberg sentenced her to six years in state prison.[2]

Shunted along by the judge's linebacker-sized bailiff, Paulette de los Reyes left the courtroom wailing, begging in vain to be allowed to leave her watch and jewelry with her husband. Her muted cries drifted into the courtroom long after the lockup door slammed shut.

Her son, Aaron, was away in military service at the time. In 1989, a lawsuit was filed on his behalf accusing his mother of defrauding him of the $75,000 awarded him in the settlement of his father's estate. Aaron won his suit, and a bonding company that insured Paulette's performance as his legal guardian was required to repay him the money she had bilked, plus interest.

In contrast, William Leasure's sentencing was a muted affair. There was no testimony or debate—the penalty for the crime he was convicted of, second-degree murder, left Judge Weisberg with no options. Once he pronounced Leasure guilty, the only sentence allowed by law was fifteen years to life.

Still, the defense submitted a lengthy sentencing report by investigator Sheryl Duvall, along with a pile of letters written in behalf of Leasure. The thirty-four letters were addressed to Weisberg, but they really were intended for consideration by the state parole board ten or fifteen years down the line.

All the character witnesses Leasure did not dare present during his trial, for fear they would be battered on the witness stand, were now being used to bolster Leasure's chances for parole. Letters, unlike witnesses, cannot be cross-examined. The people signing testimonials for him would never be asked how they could claim to know Bill Leasure so well, yet know nothing of his stolen yachts, stolen cars, illegal silencers, and adulterous relationships. They knew nothing of Irene Wong's feelings about Bill Leasure, and never had to hear that young woman saying through gritted teeth that she would have gladly volunteered to "pull the switch" if Leasure could only be sentenced to death.[3]

And so Leasure's friends, relatives, and fellow officers filed an impressive array of letters attesting to his good qualities, his gentleness, his peaceful, kindly nature. Even his old Sunday School teacher wrote in his behalf, remembering him as "a pleasant, quiet boy, in control of himself." He didn't roughhouse like the other boys, the teacher told the judge, as if this proved Bill Leasure could not kill four decades later. Most of the authors of these letters knew little or nothing of the facts of the case—they had not attended the trial, saw little or no news coverage, and only knew what Leasure, his wife, or his parents had told them, if that. All they knew for certain was that the allegations against Bill Leasure must be "lies." Sisters wrote of what a wonderful brother he was, friends said he was incapable of committing murder, businessmen offered him employment after he left prison, his parents said they were contemplating moving from Michigan to whatever city was nearest the state prison in which Leasure ended up. "Surely there has got to be someone who will take the time to find the outstanding merits, the fine qualities and gentle nature so characteristic of this man," one life-long friend of Leasure's wrote, asking Judge Weisberg for leniency he could not—and would not—give.

"Bill is a man who always looks for the good in others and simply does not see the bad, no matter how obvious it may be to others," Betsy Mogul wrote—echoing Leasure's own oft-repeated comments about himself. All his troubles came down to running with the wrong people, people who betrayed him and lied about him. "I believe that is why we are in the situation we are in now. Bill unwisely chose to associate with some people whom it would have been better to avoid. . . .

"Now we are looking toward the future. Bill has many good things inside of him. . . . I certainly intend to stand by him and to build a future that he can come home to. . . . His sweetness of character and his compassionate nature will make him once again a productive, contributing member of our community." (At a subsequent hearing, however, in which Mogul tried to fight a court order seizing some of her and Leasure's property to cover the cost of his legal defense, Mogul seemed to back off her vow to stand by her man: She said she intended to seek a divorce.)[4]

Investigator Sheryl Duvall concluded her report on a hopeful note, careful not to assert the innocence of a man convicted of murder, but equally careful to avoid mentioning anything negative about Leasure. "Bill has much to offer society. . . . Bill is remorseful and ashamed that his conduct has reflected poorly on his family and on the police department he had served so well. Given his many positive qualities and the extent and depth of support for him in the community I have no doubt that his prognosis for successful re-entry into the community is excellent."

At the sentencing hearing, Judge Weisberg said the letters

were fine but, basically, beside the point. The testimonials in them notwithstanding, there was substantial evidence that Leasure was a murderer. And with that, he passed sentence.

As part of Leasure's plea bargain, the boat theft, car theft, and insurance fraud cases in Los Angeles and Contra Costa County were dismissed. Leasure had already spent more time in jail awaiting trial than he could have served in prison if convicted in the theft cases, so the dismissals had no real impact. The Internal Revenue Service obtained a legal settlement for back taxes, placing a lien on several of his properties and his police pension fund. The stolen yachts had been seized and auctioned off. His garage had been swept clean by the police. Leasure had lost everything he had gained from the yacht business.

In addition, federal prosecutors agreed that whatever sentence he received for possessing silencers would be made concurrent, rather than added to, his fifteen-years-to-life sentence for murder.

Finally, based on his finding that Leasure owned a fifty-thousand-dollar airplane, a pension fund, and rental property, Judge Weisberg ordered him to repay Los Angeles County a portion of his $423,000 legal defense bill. Leasure attempted to prove he was virtually penniless—he had transferred ownership of his property to Betsy Mogul soon after his arrest, attempting to elude paying such a bill. But Judge Weisberg ruled otherwise, and ordered Leasure to pay the county ninety-three thousand dollars.

There was one other postscript. Bill Leasure also wrote a letter, addressed to the court but aimed at the parole board. In it, he apologized for the disgrace his case brought to LAPD, and expressed sorrow for the loss suffered by the families of the murder victims in his case. More important, Leasure's carefully crafted letter tries mightily to fulfill the parole board's desire to hear him accept responsibility, though he does it without actually admitting guilt.

"I take full responsibility for the situation that I am in now," he wrote. "There is no one else to blame. I know that I am here because of bad choices which I made. Bad choices in who I associated with. Bad choices in my own conduct. Therefore, I accept whatever punishment I receive and I intend to demonstrate by my conduct in prison that I can once again be trusted to abide by society's rules."

In other words, just as Betsy Mogul wrote, Leasure blames his downfall on his decision to befriend Robert Kuns and Dennis France. This is no admission of guilt. This is no acceptance of responsibility for the deaths of Anne Smith and Tony Reyes. It is an excuse, designed to read like an admission. In truth, though the letter doesn't say so, Bill Leasure still asserts his innocence, still blames his imprisonment on lying witnesses and unfair authorities. But Bill Leasure also knows what the parole board wants to hear.

The letter is just a start. He has a decade or more to practice, to refine the formula, to find the explanation that will free him. In the meantime, he will be a model prisoner, conforming, quiet, always submitting to authority—the type of inmate who needs the least security and earns the most trust. He will move through prison like he moved through the Marines, and LAPD, and life itself: mild and passive, keeping his peace. Keeping his secrets.

• • •

Dennis France was a fairly casual acquaintance, actually. He was a pest. He's a real nobody. I couldn't have cared less about him. . . . It's his fault I'm here. . . . This never would have happened if I wasn't a police officer. . . .

I've never stolen a boat. I've never stolen a car. I've never killed anyone. . . .

I maintain my innocence. . . .

But I want to go home.

NOTES

PROLOGUE

1. From the author's interviews with William Leasure and investigator Sheryl Duvall.

CHAPTER 1

1. From the author's interview with William Leasure and several of his colleagues at LAPD.

2. The account of the Kuns-Leasure relationship is based primarily on the author's interview with Robert Denzil Kuns, although, without admitting any criminal conduct, William Leasure confirmed the basic facts as Kuns presented them.

3. This account of Gray's May 29, 1986, encounter with Leasure and Kuns is drawn from Mervin Gray's testimony in Contra Costa County Municipal Court Case No. 604305-3, *People* v. *Kuns and Leasure;* from the LAPD interview report, dated June 10, 1986, of Gray; and from the testimony and the author's interview of Robert Kuns.

4. In March 1986, Gray had purchased the *Coruba* from Kuns for $65,000. Gray and his wife began living on the sleek forty-footer while they made some repairs. On May 22, they moved the boat to a customizing shop next to the Park Street Bridge on the busy Oakland Estuary, a tiny finger of smooth gray water off the San Francisco Bay. The boat was there only for a few hours, but that was enough time for yacht broker Laurence Lister to spot it while driving across the bridge on his way to the bank. Sandwiched between a concrete plant and a row of towering grain silos, the yacht caught Lister's eye because his company just happened to

be the sole importer for that type of boat—a twin-engine Nova Sundeck trawler made in Taiwan. Of all the people who might have crossed that bridge and gazed at the yacht below in the three hours it was moored there, only Lister knew those $150,000 vessels inside out. When he parked and walked by for a closer inspection, he saw the hull numbers were in the wrong place and did not match the manufacturer's code. And, more to the point, his company had not sold this boat, which was virtually impossible, since he had sold almost all of them.

5. From records and testimony in Contra Costa County Municipal Court Case No. 604305-3, and the author's interview with Detective Sergeant William Godwin, Oakland Police Department (retired).

6. According to Detective Godwin, in testimony, police reports, and an interview with the author.

7. This italicized passage is a direct quote from the author's series of face-to-face and telephone interviews with William Leasure over a period of ten months in 1991, before, during, and after his trial and the resolution of his case. Similar passages, in the voice of Bill Leasure, will appear in this form elsewhere in the book, without further footnotes.

8. Detective Godwin, in testimony and police reports, recalls that Leasure admitted owning the gun and the green athletic bag. Kuns, in an interview with the author, conceded the gun and bag actually were his, but that he had asked Leasure "to take the gun rap, which he did." Leasure, in an interview with the author, admits that the gun was originally his, but claimed Kuns must have stolen it from him. He says he never agreed to lie for Kuns, and that Godwin perjured himself in his police reports and testimony about the gun. The question is a crucial one, because the presence aboard the stolen boat of a gun that appeared to belong to Leasure became significant evidence, cited in order to obtain search warrants, and supporting investigators' contention that Leasure was involved with the boat thefts. Why else would his gun be on board, they argued? Leasure claims he had no idea it was on board the *La Vita* until *after* his arrest. Kuns says Leasure was well aware the gun was stowed on the boat, and that they had brought it because of their premonition that something might go wrong on this trip. It is also true that Leasure had added incentive to claim the gun was his: Having his own firearm with him during a boat trip was perfectly legal; supplying it to a convicted felon, however, could create serious problems for a policeman who should have known better.

9. This account is drawn from Godwin's sworn testimony and an interview with the author. Leasure agrees with it except for his admission about the gun, which he adamantly denies making.

10. From an LAPD report, dated May 29, 1986, on an interview with Oakland Police Detective Arthur Roth.

11. From a six-page written statement made to the Oakland Police by William Leasure on the night of his arrest.

12. According to Robert Kuns, in an interview with the author.

13. Ibid.

CHAPTER 2

1. From the author's interview with retired LAPD Sergeant James Berg and several other of Leasure's fellow officers.

2. From *Report on the Independent Commission on the Los Angeles Police Department,* the 1991 investigation of LAPD launched after an amateur video cameraman recorded the beating of a black motorist by four Los Angeles officers while many others looked on.

3. From the author's interview with Barbara Sanchez.

4. From the tape-recorded LAPD interview of Sergeant Richard Litsinger, on July 22, 1986, LAPD Tape #106930-A.

5. From the author's interview with Officer John Balicki.

6. From the report on the interview of retired LAPD Detective Philip Anninos by private investigator Sheryl Duvall.

7. From a report on interviews conducted by private investigator Sheryl Duvall, supplied by Leasure's attorney, Richard Lasting. A summary of Duvall's reports was filed in Los Angeles County Superior Court Criminal Case A-951256.

8. From the author's interview with retired Sergeant Jim Berg. Leasure confirms that he looked into buying planes from Saudi Arabia, but said he never had the chance to carry out the plan.

9. The information that Leasure's fellow officers had on his life-style and possessions is based on their recollections of what he told them over a period of years. The account here is drawn from a series of interviews of virtually all Central Traffic Division officers who knew Leasure, performed by LAPD internal investigators, and supplemented by the author's interviews with several of these officers. In most instances, their recollections proved accurate, though some of the claims appear exaggerated (i.e., Leasure planned to buy an island in Belize, but apparently never did). Whether the exaggeration was due to Leasure's false claims or the other officers' faulty memories is a matter of conjecture.

10. Jerry France's tale is detailed in search warrant affidavits filed by LAPD Sgt. David Wiltrout and Detective Tom King, a series of LAPD interviews with Jerry France, a videotaped conversation between William Leasure and Dennis France in which they discuss Jerry France's allegations, and a memorandum of facts filed in Los Angeles County Superior Court Criminal Case A-951256, *People* v. *Leasure, et al.* Jerry France's record as a bank robber is detailed in files in U.S. District Court in Los Angeles.

11. "Irene Wong" is a pseudonym, used at her request and for her protection. She was never charged or accused of any wrongdoing, and was characterized by herself, her friends, and the police as a victim. She believes public identification would endanger her new job and marriage.

12. The account of Leasure and Wong's first meeting is contained in police and FBI reports detailing official interviews with Wong. In an interview with the author, she provided additional details. Leasure, in an interview with the author, confirmed the basic facts of their introduction.

13. As told by both Leasure and Wong, as well as mutual friend Ted Moore.

14. From police interviews with Wong. Leasure admits the relationship, but denies making marriage plans with her. His friend Robert Kuns, however, supports Wong's version. He says Bill spoke often of running away with Wong.

15. According to Irene Wong's account to the police and the FBI, and in an interview with the author. Leasure does not dispute the basic facts of her account, although he insists he never deceived her about his marital status, that he never manipulated her, and that he never planned to leave his wife for her.

16. From Wong's statements to the police and her sworn testimony in Contra Costa County Municipal Court Case 604305, *People* v. *Kuns and Leasure*. Leasure, in an interview with the author, maintains that Wong knew he was married to Betsy throughout their affair. Leasure's friends Robert Kuns and Ted Moore, however, say Wong did not appear to know.

17. From Wong's testimony in Contra Costa County Municipal Court Case 604305.

18. Ibid.

CHAPTER 3

1. This account is drawn from the testimony and statements of Dennis France, the testimony of Detective Gilbert Hetrick, and from interviews

with Deputy District Attorney James Koller and Detectives Henry Petroski, Addison "Bud" Arce, and Tom King.

2. This account was related by Detective Tom King and confirmed by Detective Addison Arce. Sergeant David Wiltrout, who has since retired from LAPD, declined repeated requests for an interview.

3. From interviews with Detectives Tom King and Addison Arce, and from the testimony and statements of Dennis France.

CHAPTER 4

1. Account provided by Barbara Sanchez, in an interview with the author. Leasure confirmed that such an incident occurred, but said he did not recall his wife asking him to get a gun or to shoot the transient if necessary. He also said he did not recall Betsy making critical remarks to him then or ever. Betsy Mogul, however, who also confirmed the occurrence, said if she had mentioned getting a gun, it would have been more joking than serious. She said people frequently misunderstand her sense of humor.

2. Barbara Sanchez, in an interview with the author, related this incident, which occurred during a two-week visit to the Leasure home in 1979.

3. Information supplied by William Leasure, in an interview with the author.

4. From the LAPD Internal Affairs interview of Assistant City Attorney Christine Patterson, dated January 6, 1987, on LAPD Tape #107755.

5. From the author's interview with Barbara Sanchez.

6. Information on Leasure's good behavior and the lone spanking is drawn from reports on interviews of Leasure's parents performed by private investigators Casey Cohen and Sheryl Duvall, provided to the author by Leasure's attorney, Richard Lasting, with Leasure's approval. His parents declined requests from the author for interviews.

7. From the author's interview with Bill Leasure.

8. The name "Joan" is a pseudonym. Leasure's former wife declined to be interviewed by the author.

9. From the author's interview with Bill Leasure.

10. Ibid.

11. From the LAPD Internal Affairs report on an interview with John J. Wieland, dated December 4, 1986.

12. From the author's interview of retired LAPD Detective Philip Anninos, a former partner of Leasure's.

13. Information drawn from Orange County Superior Court marriage dissolution file D-72391, *Leasure* v. *Leasure.*

14. There is a dispute as to whether or not Leasure and Mogul earned enough money after taxes to make payments on their real estate and still afford Leasure's yachts, planes, automobiles, and travel. Leasure and Mogul are adamant in insisting they had more than enough legal income to account for all their purchases. Police, prosecutors, and the Internal Revenue Service, however, have accused Leasure of earning tens of thousands in undeclared income from various thefts and other crimes. The couple has settled a claim with the IRS, which seized much of the Leasures' cars and property.

15. Descriptions provided by Barbara Sanchez, Irene Wong, and Flo Ong, a friend of Leasure's he described as his "second mother."

16. From the LAPD Internal Affairs interview with former Assistant City Attorney Kay Kuns, dated January 21, 1987, LAPD Tape #109291. Kay Kuns is the younger sister of Robert Kuns, the yachtsman with whom Leasure was arrested.

17. Ibid.

18. From LAPD Internal Affairs interview reports with Officer Jon Herrington.

19. According to Arthur Gayle Smith, in a November 14, 1988, statement to the Los Angeles County District Attorney's Office and the Los Angeles Police Department. Smith also described how Leasure would use Smith's company telephone credit card, "because he said he didn't have one and if he got one Betsy would see it and would question a lot of times what his phone calls were." Leasure's friend and LAPD sergeant, Jim Berg, recalled Leasure told him how he concealed assets from Betsy.

20. From the November 14, 1988, Smith statement.

21. From an interview with Barbara Sanchez, by the author.

CHAPTER 5

1. This dialogue is constructed from the recollections of Paulette de los Reyes, captured in a series of three lengthy, secretly taped conversations with an undercover police informant in 1987. The tapes and related transcripts were filed as exhibits in the case of *People* v. *Leasure, Smith and de los Reyes,* Los Angeles County Superior Court Criminal Case A-951256.

In the tapes, Paulette described numerous occasions when she discussed Tony's murder with Leasure, all similar in tone and content. In subsequent court testimony, Paulette insisted she was never serious when making such remarks. In an interview with the author, Leasure denied having such conversations with Paulette.

2. From Paulette's taped statements and court testimony.

3. From the testimony, taped statements, and statements to police of Paulette de los Reyes.

4. From Paulette's taped statements.

5. If Leasure made this claim, as Paulette says, it was a lie. His Marine Corps record revealed no demolition training.

6. This account of the bombing is contained in Paulette de los Reyes's tape-recorded statements, and is also recounted in a criminal complaint filed against Leasure, part of conspiracy to commit murder charges against him. Dennis France also testified that Leasure and Big John took part in the bombing of Tony's car. Neither was ever charged with that specific crime, however.

7. From the statements of Paulette de los Reyes.

8. From the author's interviews with Gilberto's nephews, John, Alex, and Alfonso Cervantes; and interviews with San Gabriel Police Lieutenant James Goodman.

9. According to Paulette de los Reyes and Gilberto Cervantes's nephews.

10. Although Paulette denies being introduced to Winebaugh or employing him, Leasure provided an account of this introduction. Several independent witnesses, including two former tortilla factory employees, attest to Winebaugh working at the plant and visiting Paulette there.

CHAPTER 6

1. This section combines accounts from LAPD interviews with John Wieland and Dennis Winebaugh, and from the author's interviews with LAPD Detective Addison "Bud" Arce and William Leasure. Leasure is in general agreement with this account of his meeting Wieland and Winebaugh, except on the matter of the silencers. Leasure denies building or working on silencer parts at Wieland's shop—he says the devices came in prefabricated kits that he assembled at home without welding or machine tools. However, he says he did work on a shotgun at Wieland's, welding a swivel for a rifle sling onto the barrel, and that the shop owner might have misinterpreted the purpose of the job. However, the Decem-

ber 4, 1986, LAPD interview report on Wieland's statement portrays the man as unequivocal: "Wieland was asked by Leasure to weld pins on a portion of the silencers with silver solder. Wieland opined the pins were used to attach bayonets, or to lock the silencers onto the weapons. Leasure provided commercial schematics to show the placement of the pins. The silencers were fully assembled at the time Leasure brought them to Wieland's shop. . . . Leasure also showed Wieland a collection of weapons kept in a front bedroom of the [Leasure] residence. The weapons included automatic weapons and silencers." The dispute is critical not so much to prove Leasure owned the illegal weapons, but to show the time frame in which he owned them. Leasure's version has him buying silencers long after any murders took place. Wieland's account, however, has them in Leasure's home *during* the time of the murders. Even though they weren't used in any crimes, possession of the silencers shows Leasure's state of mind, prosecutors would later argue. The sole purpose for silencers is shooting people quietly.

2. According to the testimony and statements of Dennis France, Robert Kuns, and Paulette de los Reyes, Leasure expressed the attitude in many conversations over the years that his police officer status granted him the ability to violate the department's policies and the law with impunity. In particular, he described for Dennis France how he liked to sit and listen to unsolved crimes described during roll call at his police division, silently laughing to himself, knowing that he was responsible for those crimes.

3. This assessment of Winebaugh and Leasure's relationship is based on statements by Dennis France, William Jennings, and Dennis Winebaugh—neighbors and friends during this period—and on the theories of prosecutors, police, and Leasure's defense attorneys. Leasure, however, adamantly denies knowing anything about Winebaugh's criminal behavior during their relationship. "I always tend to see the good in people, and ignore the bad. . . . It's gotten me in trouble, obviously." But even if he conceded knowing Winebaugh was a crook, Leasure and his attorneys rightly contend, such knowledge does not make Leasure himself guilty of anything. The argument that Leasure had knowledge of crimes without actual participation in them could have become a key element of his defense.

4. From the LAPD interview of Tammy Winebaugh.

5. Information on Carlos Sepulveda was provided by Leasure, in an interview with the author.

6. In her interview with the police, Tammy Winebaugh recounts how Leasure asked her husband to "scare some Mexican who assaulted his wife." Dennis France also recalled that Winebaugh was supposed to assault the man. Leasure denies ever asking or hiring Winebaugh to do any-

thing to Carlos, although in an interview with the author, he described Carlos's harassment of Betsy Mogul, and admitted preparing the mug shot and description of Carlos. This paper and photo were found in Winebaugh's possession, something Leasure said he could not explain.

7. Paulette de los Reyes has consistently denied knowing Winebaugh or meeting him at the factory, saying her only contact with him was when he was hired by Tony Reyes to kill her, but spared her life instead, giving her incriminating tape recordings of Tony. She had clung to this position in interviews with police, during surreptitiously recorded conversations in which she admitted other criminal conduct, and in sworn court testimony. However, several other witnesses—a former tortilla factory worker, Dennis France, Leasure, and Winebaugh himself—attest to the existence of a long-standing relationship between Winebaugh and Paulette that began with Leasure's introduction.

8. Account based on the recollections of William Jennings, in testimony and an interview with the author, and Dennis France, in testimony and extensive interviews with the police.

9. According to the testimony of William Jennings. Both Paulette and France denied any such meeting took place.

CHAPTER 7

1. Art Smith describes this incident in a lengthy statement given to the Los Angeles County District Attorney's Office (Tape #117277) on November 14, 1988. A transcript of the taped interview with Smith, kept confidential by police and prosecutors, became public record when it was filed in U.S. District Court in Los Angeles, attached to a deposition in Civil Case 87-08416, *Persico* v. *Los Angeles, et al.*

2. Anne Smith's best friend, Donna Bennett, her sister-in-law, Nicki Pontrelli, and her mother, Delores Garofola, each recalled in separate interviews with the author this threat to Anne. Anne had described it to them, however; they did not witness it directly. Independently, in interviews with the police and in sworn testimony, Art Smith's employee John Doney recalled Smith telling him that his wife came into the marriage with nothing, and would leave with nothing—virtually identical wording.

3. Anne's brother and sister-in-law, Vito and Nicki Pontrelli, recalled Anne worrying about being followed by Art or men working for Art. Dovie Gordon, Art's former secretary and a friend of Anne's, told the police she recalled Anne specifically complaining that she was afraid of Leasure and that the policeman had been following her. Art Smith, in a posttrial statement to the authorities, confirmed that Leasure had fol-

lowed his wife for him, trying to determine her activities prior to their divorce filing.

4. From the author's interviews with Delores Garofola and Donna Bennett.

5. Information provided by Vito and Nicki Pontrelli, Anne Smith's brother and sister-in-law; Delores Garofola, Anne's mother; and Donna Bennett, her best friend.

6. As recounted by Florine Ong, in an interview with the author. Dennis France corroborates this impression, testifying that Leasure spoke several times about Anne Smith spending too much of Art's money. Leasure, however, in an interview with the author, said he liked Anne Smith and never spoke ill of her.

7. As recounted by two of Art's employees, Dovie Gordon and John Doney, in interviews with LAPD and in court testimony.

8. Flo Ong, Barbara Sanchez, and several police colleagues of Leasure's recalled him boasting of his partnership with Art in owning an island in Belize. Smith, however, claims sole ownership of the island, and Leasure said in an interview with the author he was only *planning* to buy into an island with Art, without ever going through with the plan. He said he probably did speak more definitely about the project than he should have, giving friends the wrong impression. The issue became important later, when the police tried to show a financial relationship between Art and Bill in the wake of Anne's murder.

9. From the November 4, 1988, statement of Arthur Gayle Smith to the Los Angeles County District Attorney's Office.

10. From the testimony and police interviews given by Richard McDonough.

11. Ibid. It should be noted that Bill Leasure was not a plainclothes detective at this time or ever, although he did on occasion come by Art Smith's office in civilian clothes.

12. From the testimony and police interviews given by Richard McDonough. At times inconsistent in his recollections, McDonough testified at one point that he never told Anne about this threat. However, Donna Bennett, Delores Garofola, and Nicki Pontrelli all recalled Anne telling them about Art "putting out a contract" on her, and that her friend Rich was the source of the information.

13. According to Art Smith's November 14, 1988, interview with the District Attorney's Office.

14. From the testimony and police interviews of Richard McDonough. McDonough did not recognize the two officers and could not say if one

of them was Leasure or not. Leasure denies being present at the wedding; Smith said Leasure was there, but he identified another friend of the family who was an LAPD officer as the person who ousted McDonough.

15. From Smith's November 14, 1988, statement to the District Attorney's Office.

16. Ibid. Leasure denied ever following Anne Smith.

17. As told by Dennis France. Leasure denies asking France to follow Anne Smith. However, France was able to bring police to a medical building in Orange County, south of Los Angeles. Inside was a family counselor who had treated both Anne and her son.

18. From Smith's November 14, 1988, statement to the District Attorney.

19. From police interviews with Richard McDonough and Art Smith, and from filings by Smith in Los Angeles Superior Court Civil Case D-020447 (*Smith* v. *Smith*).

20. From the testimony and police interviews of Dovie Gordon.

21. From police interviews of John Doney, and from his sworn testimony at the trial of Arthur Smith in 1988. His story obviously bears a striking resemblance to Richard McDonough's. The two men do not know one another.

22. Doney testified at a hearing during Leasure's trial in 1991 that Art Smith said he wanted to have his wife killed by Leasure, but then later, in the same conversation, he said he couldn't go through with it.

23. Information on the judge's comments and the angry tenor of the divorce were provided by Anne Smith's divorce lawyer, Martin Shucart. Art's statement, "This isn't over," was recounted by Nicki Pontrelli, based on her conversation with Anne Smith that night.

24. Descriptions of Anne Smith, her marriage and divorce, her relationship with her husband Art, and the events leading up to her death were assembled from the following sources: Los Angeles Superior Court Civil Case D-020447 (*Smith* v. *Smith*); the transcript of a November 14, 1988, D.A. interview with Arthur Gayle Smith, filed in case 87-08416-PAR in U.S. District Court in Los Angeles; the testimony of Delores Garofola and Eleanor Trethaway in Los Angeles County Superior Court criminal cases A-366405 (*State* v. *Persico*) and A-951256 (*State* v. *Smith, et al.*); the testimony of Dennis France in A-951256; the chronological record, witness interviews, and other reports filed by Detectives Westbrook and Crowe in Los Angeles Police Department File No. DR-80577969 (the original investigation of the Anne Smith murder); and the author's inter-

views with Delores Garofola, Nicolette Pontrelli, and Vito Pontrelli, Anne Smith's brother.

All sources agreed that relations between the Smiths had deteriorated, but while most of the family placed the blame on Art's coldness, philandering, and preoccupation with money, Anne's daughter, Christine, sided with her stepfather. Her testimony in the divorce proceedings contradicted Anne's account of an attack by Art, placing blame for the incident on a hysterical and assaultive Anne. She also said the marriage deteriorated because of Anne's disinterest and unpleasantness, not Art's.

25. The detectives' initial focus on Art Smith as a suspect was related in Los Angeles Police Department File No. DR-80577969 (the original Anne Smith murder investigation) and in the sworn deposition of retired Detective Nelson R. Crowe, filed in case 87-08416-PAR, *Persico v. The City of Los Angeles*, in U.S. District Court in Los Angeles. Nicolette Pontrelli's statement to detectives asserted flatly that the murder was a contract hit by Art Smith. The detectives made repeated attempts to question Art, and went so far as to determine what sort of firearms he had registered in his name. (He had a .38-caliber handgun; Anne was killed with a .45.)

26. Dennis France testified to owning such a car, and produced a photo of it with his family posing in front of it as proof. The age of his children in the photo dated it in the approximately correct time frame.

CHAPTER 8

1. From the police interviews of Irene Wong (as noted previously, a pseudonym).

2. As recalled by William Leasure. The point in time is key, since the introduction apparently occurred before the death of Gilberto Cervantes (Winebaugh left town shortly after the killing). In his initial statements to the police, France puts their first meeting even earlier, in 1974 or 1975, then, at Leasure's preliminary hearing, estimated it was as early as 1973.

3. From the police interviews and testimony of Dennis France.

4. Leasure confirms making such record checks, but says they had nothing to do with inquiring about possible murder charges or other violent crimes. Leasure said France explained the need for a records check by saying he only wanted to know if there were any outstanding traffic-offense warrants that might make returning to Los Angeles risky for either of them.

5. France has told a variety of stories about these sales—that he didn't know the items were stolen; that he did know, but that he didn't tell

Leasure or Trahin; and that they knowingly bought stolen property. Leasure and Trahin denied knowing. Leasure has never been charged in the matter; Trahin faced administrative charges within LAPD but was subsequently cleared when a board of senior LAPD officers found the state's key witness in a massive police corruption scandal, Dennis France, was not credible.

6. France related this story to the police. He did not know the woman's name, but said she was from Pasadena and was heavy-set. Flo Ong, at the time, was both heavy and living in Pasadena. Furthermore, she had made Leasure executor of her estate, although he was not in line to inherit any of her property or savings.

7. From the testimony, police statements, and the author's interview of Robert Kuns, corroborated by Dennis France in police statements and testimony. Police never investigated Kuns's claims about molestation, and there is no evidence that it ever actually occurred.

8. From the author's interview with Robert Kuns.

9. As recalled by William Jennings, in an interview with the author.

10. From the testimony of Tammy Winebaugh, during the murder trial of Dennis Winebaugh. In his testimony at that same trial, France recalled the incident, but said the boy had pointed a BB gun at the dog. He denied pointing his own gun at the boy.

11. As recalled by Dale Lloyd Boyce, from his testimony in the murder trial of Arthur Gayle Smith and from his statements to the police and to Smith's private investigator. France described the conversation in similar detail. It is important to note that Boyce has no independent knowledge of Leasure being involved with France and a "hit ring"—he only knows what France told him. Furthermore, Boyce's credibility as a witness was challenged on two grounds: He was an alcoholic who suffers periodic memory lapses; and he was convicted of child molestation and sentenced to prison in 1985.

12. From the testimony of Alan Tomich, in both the Smith and Winebaugh trials.

13. According to France's testimony about the Little Joe's meeting, he gave Tomich the name "Bill." He swears he did not know Leasure's last name at the time, because Forty-four just called him Bill, and because he was still too illiterate at the time to read Leasure's LAPD name tag (notwithstanding the fact that he was literate enough at the time to pass a driver's test). When he testified years later about the 1978 meeting, Tomich said he did not recall the name, but that it was "a common one, like Jones." France was of course wrong about Leasure's wife—she was a

prosecutor for the city of Los Angeles, a separate agency from the county-run District Attorney's Office. The confusion is a common one, however.

14. France insists he made this offer. Tomich testified he does not recall if France made it or not, but that if he had, he would have declined to go. At the time, Tomich said, he felt France had given him enough information to go on.

15. Boyce testified that France admitted lying about several key facts of the murder, for fear he would be killed as an informer by Leasure or other members of the hit ring. He had intended to tell all, but he lost his nerve, Boyce recalled. But when it came time to tell his own version in court, France said the only point he was untruthful about to Tomich was saying he shot Cervantes, rather than Winebaugh. France's explanation for omitting Winebaugh's role and admitting a murder he didn't commit was that he had wanted to avoid implicating someone else until he was sure he could get help—and protection—from Tomich. He said his decision to be dishonest was the correct one, since Tomich "wouldn't help me."

CHAPTER 9

1. According to Sandra Zysman, from police statements, court testimony, and an interview with the author.

2. Ibid.

3. According to Paulette de los Reyes. The marriage lasted less than a year.

4. From the testimony and author's interview of Sandra Zysman.

5. From a document entitled "Last Will of Antonio Reyes," dated April 1981, and from the testimony of Andrew Evangelatos, the Los Angeles attorney who prepared the will for Tony.

6. From the testimony and secretly recorded statements of Paulette de los Reyes.

7. This is drawn from Paulette's uncorroborated (and undisputed) account of Tony's abuses, as related in court testimony and in the secret police tapes of her conversations.

8. From the police interviews of Dennis France.

9. From the September 25, 1981, LAPD interview of Addie Gomez of Palm Springs, California, who said she had known Tony Reyes since 1947. Gomez also told police that Tony had said Paulette was responsible for arranging Gilberto Cervantes's murder. Police reports (San Gabriel Police Case File No. 77191-17, the homicide investigation of Gilberto

Cervantes) and the author's interviews with Cervantes's nephews revealed that both Gilberto and Natalia had made allegations that Paulette was involved in the occult. Part of this was their abhorrence of Paulette's Jewishness; Cervantes's favorite nickname for her was *la judia*, The Jew, and he apparently equated her Jewish heritage with dabbling in the occult. Both Gilberto and Natalia had accused Paulette of placing curses on them. He and Natalia told relatives that Paulette had stalked them one night, sneaking into their bedroom while they slept, straddling the old man's chest and making several incisions over Gilberto's heart—an attempt to snatch his will through black magic. A deputy coroner would later find the shallow scars, but Paulette laughed it off when San Gabriel police detectives questioned her about the tale. Yes, I sold occult supplies once, but it was just a business, nothing more—a way to make money, she said. "I'm not into anything like that. Tony and his family are the superstitious ones. Natalia used to go to the factory every day and bless it."

10. According to Addie Gomez's LAPD interview.

11. The account of Tony's murder is based on LAPD File No. DR-81-705359, the original investigation report on the murder of Tony Reyes; and the eyewitness statements taken by LAPD of Sandra Zysman, Lisa Davido (the waitress), and Carl Triola (the singer), as well as the court testimony of Sandra Zysman.

12. From the testimony of Sandra Zysman.

13. From the tape-recorded conversations of Paulette de los Reyes.

14. From the author's interview with Sandra Zysman.

15. Ibid.

16. From San Gabriel Police File No. 77181-17, the murder investigation of Gilberto Cervantes, reopened in February 1982 after new evidence was received from LAPD investigators assigned to the Tony Reyes killing: "The prime suspect in both cases is Paulette . . . —who is Tony de los Reyes's ex-wife twice over. Her motive in both murders was the inheritance of the property of Gilberto Cervantes."

17. According to Lt. James Goodman of the San Gabriel Police Department, the lead detective on the original investigation of the Gilberto Cervantes murder.

18. According to the August 17, 1987, report of an interview with Ron Schines by LAPD Detective Addison Arce.

19. From the sworn testimony of Robert Denzil Kuns, Kuns's statement to the police, and his interview with the author.

CHAPTER 10

1. This discussion was related by Robert Denzil Kuns, in sworn testimony at Leasure's trial and in several other court proceedings, in statements to the Los Angeles Police Department, and in an interview with the author. Leasure, in an interview with the author, denied that this conversation ever took place, and he denied taking part in boat thefts or knowing about Kuns's involvement in boat thefts. However, a large body of evidence exists to support Kuns's version of events and to contradict Leasure's protestations of innocence in the boat thefts. Another witness—Dennis France—attests to Leasure's knowing involvement in stealing boats with Kuns. Evidence seized at Leasure's house after his arrest also supports Kuns's story: Personal property from five different stolen yachts was recovered from Leasure's garage; notebooks that detail earnings from several of the yacht thefts and insurance frauds were found in Leasure's briefcase, written in Leasure's hand; and several phony boat registration documents were filed by Leasure with the state of Oregon. Leasure's own attorney in the primary boat theft case in Contra Costa County, William Gagen, said in an interview with the author that the evidence of Leasure's guilt is overwhelming, and that there is no plausible defense to be offered.

2. From Kuns's testimony and an interview with the author. Leasure confirmed that such a trip took place.

3. According to both Kuns and Leasure.

4. Police have been unable to identify this accomplice of Kuns's. He said he never knew John from Boston's full name.

5. From the author's interview with Robert Kuns. Leasure does not dispute making the trip to Colombia with Kuns, but he denies knowing the yacht was stolen.

6. Account provided by Kuns.

7. From the testimony and police interviews of Robert Kuns.

8. Ibid.

9. From a statement to LAPD by Irene Wong. Both Leasure and Smith denied that Leasure owned a portion of the *Santine,* although several of Leasure's friends and colleagues recalled him claiming the sailboat was his or partly his.

10. From the author's interview with Robert Kuns.

11. This particular form was filed with the Oregon State Marine Board for the yacht *Deliverance.*

12. According to Kuns and to Leasure's notebook.

13. From the testimony of Dennis France and Robert Kuns. Additionally, records show France lacked sufficient funds or credit to make such a purchase. Leasure and Kuns paid for the rental of a boat slip and for insurance on the boat.

14. According to Kuns and Leasure's notebook, seized by the police. The notebook includes a section on boat deals, one page of which is labeled "Profits," with this list displayed beneath:

    "Columbia (sic)................2,000
    "Art & Me 10,000
    "Canada..........................4,000
    "Dennis..........................10,000"

This list corresponds to the first four boat thefts and the amounts Kuns testified that he paid Leasure for each.

15. Printouts of such vehicle registration searches were found in Leasure's LAPD locker and at his house. He conceded in an interview with the author that he performed the computer searches for Kuns, but that his intent was innocent. Kuns, according to Leasure, told him he wanted to know who the registered owner was so he could be assured that the title was clear before completing a sale. Even so, such an unauthorized use of LAPD computers would be a violation of department regulations.

16. Again, this account is based largely on Robert Kuns's sworn testimony and interviews, corroborated by evidence seized from Leasure's house and police locker. While Leasure does not deny making these boat trips with Kuns, he does deny being a knowing participant in thefts.

CHAPTER 11

1. From the police statements and testimony of Dennis France and Officer Jon Herrington.

2. From Florine Ong, in her police statements and an interview with the author.

3. From the police statements and court testimony of Irene Wong.

4. Records filed in Los Angeles County Superior Court Criminal Case A-797022, *People* v. *Gerard,* show that the loan was approved and a check issued on November 15, 1984. Kuns testified that he kept about sixteen thousand dollars from that check, to cover his fee for the theft and the cost of the identity-masking alterations. Leasure got the other nine thou-

sand, according to Kuns. Supporting Kuns's story, Leasure's notebooks show he earned $9430 from the sale of the *Deliverance*. Bank records seized by the police also seem to confirm his testimony in part—Irene Wong's account shows the deposit of a four-thousand-dollar check from Kuns written to Leasure the next day, November 16, 1984.

5. From the police statement of Officer Jon Herrington.

6. From a search warrant affidavit dated June 17, 1986, by LAPD Detective Donald C. Cheatham and Sgt. David D. Wiltrout (filed in Los Angeles County Superior Court under Master Search Warrant Number 26322, and signed by Judge Glenette Blackwell).

7. Ibid.

8. According to Florine Ong, in statements to LAPD and in an interview with the author.

9. From an interview with Florine Ong.

10. From an interview with Robert Kuns.

11. From testimony in Los Angeles County Superior Court Criminal Case A-797022, *People* v. *Gerard.* Leasure agrees with this account, with the caveat that he did not know the yacht was the stolen *Billy G.*

12. This conversation was recounted by Robert Kuns, in an interview with the author.

13. As told by Robert Kuns, in an interview with the author.

14. This is Robert Kuns's account. The information about Leasure laying plans for acquiring a Sabre Jet and other military aircraft, as well as his talk of finding a hangar in Mojave, is corroborated by others who knew Leasure at LAPD. However, Leasure denies any criminal motive and denies any one-year retirement plan with Kuns.

CHAPTER 12

1. This account is based on the recollections of Detectives Addison Arce and Henry Petroski, in interviews with the author.

2. According to Detectives Tom King, Addison Arce, and Henry Petroski, in interviews with the author.

3. According to Detectives Arce and Petroski, in interviews with the author.

4. This quote, and those that follow, are verbatim transcriptions of the taped interrogation of Dennis France at the District Attorney's Office on

August 8, 1986, commencing at 10:47 A.M., and filed as an exhibit in Los Angeles County Superior Court Criminal Case A-951256, *People* v. *William Leasure, et al.*

5. From the August 18, 1986, interview of France by Detective Jerry Stephens. France was the only source to suggest Big John participated in paying off Winebaugh. No other evidence surfaced to corroborate this claim, and France himself contradicted it later as he struggled to recall who paid whom, how much, and when. Big John was never charged with any crimes related to Leasure, Winebaugh, or France.

6. From the handwritten notes taken by LAPD Homicide Detective Jerry Stephens at the August 8, 1986, Internal Affairs briefing. Anne Smith was killed in her mother's beauty shop on May 29, 1980. Tony Reyes died on September 10, 1981.

7. In interviews with LAPD investigators, Jimmy Trahin denied ever sharing information on murder cases with Leasure. In an interview with the author, Leasure said he did not specifically remember asking Trahin about the Smith case, but suggested he might have, simply because the Smiths were his friends and he was curious about the status of the investigation.

8. Pseudonym used. France recalled her true first name.

9. The source for this is Deputy District Attorney James Koller and court files on the Sandidge case. Defense attorney Barry Levin, a former policeman who had partnered with both Leasure and Big John years before, represented both Big John and Sandidge. In an interview with the author, Levin said he was so dubious of Terry France's testimony that he took the extraordinary precaution of giving him a lie-detector test before going further. Terry passed the polygraph test, and Levin reluctantly listed him as a witness. Internal Affairs investigators took Terry France's statement, and what had been a straightforward case of deliberate murder became muddled by Terry's contradictory testimony that Big John and Sandidge did little more than escort Chavez from the market's premises. Neither LAPD nor Levin ever knew Terry France had a connection to Bill Leasure and Big John—everyone involved in the case thought the witness was just a disinterested observer, Levin said. In an interview with the author, Leasure denied any role in setting up the testimony of Terry France, although he said he was at a loss to explain how Dennis France's brother would turn up as a witness on behalf of Big John. Neither Terry France nor Big John could be located for comment. Terry France is listed as a defense witness in the criminal case filed against Sandidge (Los Angeles County Superior Court Case A-371012). Levin said he now believes he was duped by Leasure and Big John. "Those bastards set me up," a

chagrined Levin said. Neither Leasure, Big John, nor Terry France were ever charged in connection with the witness-creation incident.

10. This quote and the ones that follow are from the transcript of the interview of Dennis France by Detectives Arce and Petroski, on August 8, 1986, commencing at 8:49 P.M.

11. According to Detectives Arce and Petroski, in interviews with the author.

CHAPTER 13

1. Seven years later, after Persico sued the city for false arrest, Detective Crowe would say he did show photos of Persico to the women, but that they had been unable to identify him. Later, he recanted, saying he had been mistaken in his recollection—only one other witness, a mechanic, Thomas Rumbaugh, had been shown a photo lineup. But the uncertainty would lead to suspicions that the women might indeed have been shown a photograph, perhaps in a way that improperly prompted them to identify Persico as the killer later on. This hypothesis formed the heart of Persico's lawsuit, and Crowe's contradictory statements kept a federal judge from dismissing the suit. However, Anne Smith's mother, Delores Garofola, has testified consistently that the detectives never showed her a photo of Persico.

2. The information on the Persico investigation is culled from police reports and logbooks from the original murder case; testimony in Los Angeles County Superior Court Criminal Case A-366405 (*People* v. *Persico*); the deposition of Elvia Persico in U.S. District Court Civil Case 87-08416(*Persico* v. *Los Angeles, et al.*); and transcripts of an interview of Elvia Persico by Persico's court-appointed private investigator, Doug Payne. Information on Detectives Arce's and Petroski's review of this information and comparison to Dennis France's statements is culled from police reports and logbooks compiled by Arce and Petroski, and from the author's interviews with the detectives.

3. From the statement of Sandra Helene Zysman, taken by Detectives Arce and Petroski on August 19, 1986, and from Zysman's testimony at Leasure's trial. In the statement, Zysman estimated the time of the drive-by as two years before Tony's murder; in subsequent testimony, she said the incident may have occurred as soon as a few months before. France described it as occurring a few weeks before, although he, too, expressed uncertainty about the timing.

4. From the statement of Dale Lloyd Boyce, taken by Detectives Arce and Petroski on August 18, 1986.

5. From the statement of Alan Tomich, taken by Detectives Arce and Petroski on August 22, 1986.

CHAPTER 14

1. From the July 29, 1987, testimony of Dennis France at a preliminary hearing for William Leasure, Arthur Smith, and Paulette de los Reyes, before Judge David M. Horwitz, in Los Angeles County Municipal Court Criminal Case A-951256.

2. From the tape-recorded LAPD interview of Dennis France on August 8, 1986.

3. This conversation was related by Detectives Arce and Petroski, in an interview with the author.

4. Ibid.

5. From the LAPD report on an interview with Officer Jon Herrington on June 11, 1986, by Detectives R. Kautz and W. Szymanski, and a "reinterview" on July 8, 1986, by Detectives G. Hetrick and Szymanski.

6. From the July 8, 1986, LAPD interview of Herrington.

7. From the twenty-five search warrant affidavits and returns of search warrants filed in Los Angeles Superior Court under Master Search Warrant Number 26322, and from the report on the LAPD "property show-up" conducted at Parker Center on June 21, 1986.

8. From France's statements to LAPD and the author's interview with William Leasure.

9. From the FBI FD-302 interview report of a June 2, 1986, interview by Special Agent Keith Clark, for FBI Los Angeles File 45B-1383.

10. From the author's interview with Irene Wong.

11. From the June 4, 1984, interview with Detectives King and Syzmanski.

12. From the *Los Angeles Daily News*, March 22, 1987, "Hahn ignored warning on assistant."

13. From the author's interview with Leasure, and from his statements during secretly tape-recorded sessions with Dennis France. Also, a deed filed by Betsy Mogul with the Los Angeles County Recorder's Office, which deeded Leasure's ownership interest in his home to his wife after he was arrested, cites "dissolution of marriage" as the reason for the ownership change, allowing them to forego paying a property transfer tax. According to Deputy District Attorney James Koller, Mogul testified in a

1992 hearing that she and Leasure drew up a separation agreement in 1986 after she learned of his extramarital affairs. No divorce papers were filed as of March, 1992, six years later; however, Mogul testified that she still intended to divorce Leasure, according to Koller.

14. Quotes of Kay Kuns, Catherine Vale, Bob Vale, and Christine Patterson are drawn from interviews by LAPD Sergeant L. Hinrichs and Detective A. Brethour, recorded on LAPD Tapes #109291 and 107754.

CHAPTER 15

1. This account is based on interviews with Deputy District Attorney James Koller and Detectives Arce and Petroski.

2. The conversation between Dennis France and Arthur Smith was recorded on LAPD Tape #108374, entered as an exhibit in Los Angeles County Superior Court Criminal Case A-951256, *People* v. *Leasure, Smith, and de los Reyes*. The circumstances of the call were described by Detectives Arce and Petroski, and Deputy District Attorney James E. Koller, in interviews with the author.

3. From LAPD Tape #108374, filed as an exhibit in Los Angeles County Superior Court Criminal Case A-951256, *People* v. *Leasure, et al.*, phone call from Dennis France to Dennis Winebaugh, September 10, 1986.

CHAPTER 16

1. Excerpts from the Leasure-France telephone conversations are from the transcript of District Attorney Tape #86-603, filed as an exhibit in Los Angeles County Superior Court Criminal Case A-951256, *People* v. *Leasure, et al.*

2. The conversation between France and Leasure is drawn from LAPD Tape #108203, recorded September 18, 1986, at the Contra Costa County Jail in Martinez, California, and filed as an exhibit in Los Angeles County Superior Court Criminal Case A-951256, *People* v. *Leasure, et al.* Information on the alleged contents of the notes Leasure wrote during the conversation was drawn from two sources: a taped interview of France by Detective Arce following the visit; and from an October 17, 1986, handwritten report by Detectives Arce and Petroski, captioned "Discussion with Dennis France of interview between Dennis and Wm. Leasure."

3. Conversation and the contents of the notes are drawn from LAPD Tape #108433, the video and audio recording of the October 14, 1986, meeting of Dennis France and William Leasure at the Los Angeles

County Jail. The tapes were an exhibit in Leasure's trial. A portion of the videotape was enhanced by an FBI laboratory to render Leasure's notes easier to read.

CHAPTER 17

1. Conversation recalled by Robert Kuns, in his sworn testimony at the preliminary hearing for William Leasure, Art Smith, and Paulette de los Reyes on July 27, 1987, in Los Angeles Municipal Court Criminal Case A-951256.

2. Ibid.

3. From the transcript of the preliminary hearing in *People* v. *Kuns and Leasure*, Contra Costa County Municipal Court Case No. 604305-3 (Superior Court Criminal Case No. 33219). At the hearing, twelve victims of the yacht thefts testified, along with nine police officers from Oakland, Los Angeles, and San Diego. Sessions were held for ten days, spread over a period of more than two months, with more than 127 exhibits entered into evidence. The preliminary hearing was longer and more complex than most full-blown criminal trials.

4. According to Robert Kuns, in an interview with the author.

5. The term "confidential reliable informant," or CRI, has a strict legal definition, and is applicable only to people who have provided information to the police in the past, usually for pay, that has proven true and led to arrests and prosecutions. By attaching this label to informants, police are permitted to omit their identity from search warrants for the express purpose of protecting them from the criminals they have implicated. Since warrants are part of the public record, identifying snitches can lead to their death. But because not even the judge who signs a search warrant knows the identity of a CRI, police representations about informant reliability are crucial. If, after a search is made, it is learned that the CRI's reliability was fabricated, evidence discovered in the search, and sometimes entire criminal cases, can be thrown out of court.

6. From the preliminary hearing transcript in Contra Costa County Municipal Court Case No. 604305-3.

7. From the six-page statement of William Leasure on May 29, 1986, taken by Oakland Police Sergeant William Godwin, Oakland Police Department Report R.D. No. 86-56414. Leasure would later take issue with the accuracy of this statement, penned by Godwin as Leasure spoke during a fifty-eight-minute interview. Leasure said in an interview with the author that he had told Godwin he had never crewed a boat as a favor for Kuns in the past. He simply didn't mention other occasions when he

crewed for pay. Godwin, however, testified that he read the statement
aloud, sentence by sentence, as he wrote it down, then read it aloud again
in its entirety at the conclusion of the interview. Leasure then signed it
and initialed each page—and, the document shows, even made correc-
tions at some points, initialing each correction. He did not correct that
statement where he is quoted as saying he never crewed with Kuns before
the trip that led to their arrest. The interview was not tape-recorded, according to Godwin and other Oakland Police officials. Leasure has said he
believes that the conversation was recorded, but that the tape is being
withheld because it would prove his innocence. To buttress this claim, he
points to a taped interview of Robert Kuns by Oakland authorities—made
many months after their arrest—whose existence the police previously denied. Leasure's attorneys received the tape, apparently by mistake, with
some other files handed over by prosecutors. In any case, it is
uncontroverted that Leasure crewed with Kuns on numerous occasions;
the statement, as Leasure signed it, is inaccurate, and this inconsistency
was cited as part of the justification for holding him accountable for the
yacht thefts.

8. From the author's interview with attorney William Gagen.

9. From the testimony of Irene Wong (a pseudonym), as recorded in the
preliminary hearing transcript for Contra Costa County Municipal Court
Case No. 604305-3.

10. From the testimony of LAPD Detective Gilbert Hetrick, as recorded
in the preliminary hearing transcript.

11. From the testimony of LAPD Internal Affairs Division Sergeant Roy
Michael Kautz, as recorded in the preliminary hearing transcript.

12. Leasure's notebook was People's Exhibit 77 in the preliminary hearing
in Contra Costa County Municipal Court Case No. 604305-3.

13. The reference to "Mike's Boat" appears to refer to the yacht *Morlov,*
reported stolen from Marina del Rey in Los Angeles in December 1985
and sold in San Diego to Michael Maseline as the yacht *New Directions.*
When Kuns and Leasure were arrested, several sets of keys were on board
their boat. One set of keys was labeled "Mike's Boat" and fit the *New Directions.* The other set of keys included one that opened the gate to the Island Harbor Marina in San Diego, where the *Holiday/La Vita* was stolen.
That key had been reported lost by Maseline earlier; however, it had been
passed on to Kuns, allowing him easy access to the docks. The "Mike's
Boat" notebook reference, according to the police, reflects a $3,000 pay-
ment due Leasure from Kuns for participating in that theft. Maseline was
eventually charged and convicted in the case in San Diego. He was a
friend of Kuns's.

14. From the author's interview with Robert Kuns.

15. Ibid.

16. From the author's interview with William Gagen.

17. As Kuns tells it, this means he was going to lie on Leasure's behalf. As Leasure tells it, it meant Kuns was planning to tell the truth.

18. From the December 9, 1986, police interview of Robert Kuns by Detectives Arce and Petroski and Deputy District Attorney Koller.

19. To this extent, Kuns and Leasure agree on what was said in the holding cell. Kuns maintains that Leasure went on to incriminate himself; Leasure denies this vehemently.

20. From the author's interview with Robert Kuns.

21. The date of this call, December 2, 1986, is according to the sworn testimony of Detective Addison Arce during Leasure's trial in Los Angeles County Superior Court Criminal Case A-951256. The timing of the call is important because of subsequent allegations by Leasure and his attorneys that Kuns derived his information about homicides related to Leasure from newspaper articles published on December 6 and 7. The fact that he had his attorney call before that was cited by Arce to blunt those assertions.

22. From the April 25, 1991, testimony of Robert Kuns in the trial of *People* v. *Leasure*.

23. From the author's interview with Robert Kuns, and from the transcript of LAPD Tape #109076, the December 9, 1986, interview of Kuns by Detectives Arce and Petroski and Deputy District Attorney Koller.

24. From the author's interview with Assistant Public Defender Terri Mockler.

25. From a letter from Deputy District Attorney James Koller to Assistant Public Defender Terri Mockler, dated March 5, 1987, and filed as an exhibit in Los Angeles County Superior Court Criminal Case A-951256, *People* v. *Leasure, et al.*

26. From the transcript of the December 9, 1986, police interview of Robert Kuns by Detectives Arce and Petroski and Deputy District Attorney Koller.

27. From the written report by Detectives Arce and Petroski on their December 9, 1986, interview with Kuns.

CHAPTER 18

1. From LAPD Tape #108268, a recording of the September 25, 1986, telephone conversation between Dennis France and Paulette de los Reyes.

2. From LAPD Tape #108421, a recording of the September 29, 1986, meeting between Dennis France and Paulette de los Reyes.

3. From the author's interview with Detectives Arce and Petroski.

4. From the preliminary hearing testimony of Detective David Scroggins, in Los Angeles Superior Court Criminal Case A-951256, *People* v. *Leasure, et al.*

5. Paulette would later testify at Leasure's trial that she only received a single page. Dennis France and the detectives, however, say the entire packet of phony reports was delivered, and that Paulette simply chose not to show them to Scroggins so as to avoid making him doubt her innocence.

6. From Scroggins's preliminary hearing testimony.

7. The account of the first meeting between Scroggins and Paulette is drawn from LAPD Tape #108891, the November 19, 1986 meeting, and corresponding transcripts.

8. The accounts of the second and third meetings between Scroggins and Paulette are drawn from LAPD Tape #108951, the November 25, 1986, meeting, and Tape #108993, the December 7, 1987, meeting, as well as from corresponding transcripts filed in Los Angeles Superior Court Criminal Case A-951256, *People* v. *Leasure. Note:* The author discovered numerous discrepancies between the audiotape recordings and the official transcripts of those tapes. In such cases, the author's own transcription of the original tapes was used rather than the material contained in the printed transcripts prepared by the D.A. and defense attorney staffs. This choice was made in the interest of accuracy, and is consistent with standard courtroom practice, where the actual tape recordings are the evidence, while transcripts are merely visual aides for jurors as they listen to the tapes.

9. From the author's interview with Nicolette and Vito Pontrelli, confirmed by Detectives Arce and Petroski.

10. From the March 3, 1987, LAPD report on the interview of John Lynn Doney, by Detectives Arce and Petroski.

11. From the March 16, 1987, LAPD report on the interview with Richard McDonough, by Detective Arce.

12. From the August 2, 1988, and September 7, 1988, LAPD reports on interviews with Dovie Gordon, by Detectives Arce and Petroski.

13. Both Art Smith and John Doney related similar accounts of Mark Schwartz's tenure in Belize, in interviews with LAPD.

14. From the September 12, 1986, LAPD report on the interview with William Jennings, by Detectives Arce and Petroski.

CHAPTER 19

1. The preceding section and quotes are drawn from information supplied through the author's interviews with William Leasure. Basic information on jail conditions facing Leasure were corroborated through court records and officials of the Los Angeles County Sheriff's Department.

2. From an interview with San Gabriel Police Detective Mike Hudson.

3. From the November 14, 1986, LAPD report on the interview of Tammy Randel by Detectives Petroski and Smith.

4. From the November 13, 1986, LAPD report on the interview of Dennis Dean Winebaugh by Detectives Arce, Petroski, and Hudson.

5. From the author's interview with Detective Mike Hudson.

6. Ralph Gerard was convicted by a jury on two counts of presenting a fraudulent insurance claim, but acquitted on the receiving stolen property counts. He was fired from LAPD and sentenced to five years probation.

7. As told by Detective Bud Arce, in an interview with the author.

8. From LAPD records, the author's interviews with Wiltrout's former partner, Detective Tom King, and reports from Wiltrout's Workers Compensation file, California State Department of Industrial Relations, Division of Industrial Accidents File #88-VN-183299. Wiltrout declined requests for interviews with the author.

9. From *Ross* v. *Los Angeles*, U.S. District Court Civil Case (L.A.) CV-89-5277, in particular, the deposition of former LAPD Lieutenant Jimmie Finn. While internal LAPD probes showed some weapons and ammunition slated for disposal had been removed by officers, the department found no wrongdoing and took no action against members of ballistics and the bomb squad. Finn, however, who had pressed for disciplinary action against the officers, including Jimmy Trahin, soon fell from grace at LAPD.

10. From the author's interviews with Detectives Arce, Petroski, and King, and LAPD records.

11. From the Wiltrout Workers Compensation file, #88-VN-183299, and the author's interviews with Detectives Arce and Petroski.

12. From the author's interviews with Detectives Arce and Petroski.

13. From the Wiltrout Workers Compensation file.

14. From the declarations of Michael P. Stone, and attached transcript excerpts, filed in California State Court of Appeals Case #BO-37138, *Gerard* v. *Gates, et al.*

15. From the Wiltrout Workers Compensation file.

16. Quotes from the trial testimony and arguments, as well as Betsy Mogul's comments afterward, are drawn from coverage in the *Los Angeles Daily News*, from three articles by staff writer Dawn Webber: "Ex-L.A. aide testifies on document," August 2, 1989; "Prosecutor says Mogul lied on form," August 3, 1989; and "Mogul found not guilty of perjury," August 4, 1989.

17. The settlement Mogul reached with the city was, by agreement, to be kept secret. However, during testimony over William Leasure's extensive county-paid legal fees, Superior Court Judge Stanley Weisberg ordered Mogul to reveal the $140,000 figure, which she did. This account of Mogul's testimony is based on the recollection of Deputy District Attorney James Koller, who attended the hearing.

18. Trial excerpts are drawn from the record of *People* v. *Winebaugh*, contained in California State Court of Appeals file #BO-33100. (Winebaugh's appeal was denied and his conviction and sentence affirmed by the Court of Appeals. Appeals to the State Supreme Court and to federal courts also failed.)

19. From the author's interviews with Detectives Arce and Petroski.

20. Trial excerpts are drawn from the record of *People* v. *Smith*, California State Court of Appeals File #BO-44768. (Smith's appeal was denied and his conviction and sentence affirmed by the Court of Appeals in 1991.)

21. From the transcript of LAPD Tape #117277, an interview of Arthur Gayle Smith, on November 14, 1988, filed as an attachment to the deposition of James Koller in U.S. District Court (Los Angeles) Civil Case 87-08416, *Persico* v. *Los Angeles, et al.*

22. Arce and Petroski searched for unsolved murder cases in Utah that fit Doney's description, and found none.

CHAPTER 20

1. The author was not present during conversations between Leasure and his attorneys. These quotes, like others elsewhere that recount communications between Leasure, Richard Lasting, and Michael White, are reconstructions based upon the recollections of Leasure, corroborated by his attorneys, through interviews with the author before, during, and after the trial. Statements regarding trial strategy are also based upon the author's interviews with Leasure, Lasting, and White. In this particular reference, as in most similar instances, Leasure provided the information, which the author then corroborated with the defense attorneys.

2. From the author's interviews with William Leasure.

CHAPTER 21

1. From the author's interviews with William Leasure.

2. Ibid. Leasure explained that he did not realize immediately after the taped jail visit that the import of his notes to Dennis France would be crucial to his life and liberty. Murder charges were not filed until the following year, and the existence of the videotape was not disclosed until months after that, Leasure said. By then, he said, he no longer remembered what the notes he wrote to France meant. The explanation only makes sense, however, if Leasure did not realize he was being taped at the time. But Leasure conceded to the author that he did see the camera in the jail visiting area that day, and therefore knew about the probable existence of a videotape and of a homicide investigation long before formal charges were filed. The importance of remembering the details of such an encounter should have been apparent to any criminal defendant, but especially to a police officer. Leasure insisted, however, that there were several weeks of lag time between the visit and his eventual realization that France had sold him out—enough time to impair his memory about the notes. "I don't know what I meant when I wrote, 'Melted,' " he said.

3. From the author's interviews with William Leasure, Richard Lasting, and Michael White.

4. From the author's interviews with William Leasure, corroborated by his attorneys Lasting and White.

5. According to Detective Bud Arce. Richard Lasting reported having a similar conversation with Rumbaugh in the hallway.

6. According to Detective Arce.

7. From the author's interview with Bill Leasure, who reconstructed the conversation. In a separate interview, investigator Sheryl Duvall agreed with Leasure's representations on the subject—that she found no abuse or other trauma in Leasure's background to explain why he might have committed murder. She said she could not reconstruct exact conversations.

8. From the author's interview with Sheryl Duvall.

CHAPTER 22

1. In an interview with the author, Lasting explained he was not as upset as his client over the judge's decision to admit the yacht theft evidence. Leasure saw that ruling as just one more element of the conspiracy against him, an attempt to prejudice the jury by introducing irrelevant allegations. Lasting saw it differently. He planned to tell the jurors simply that Leasure would have his day in court to face those boat charges, but that they should focus on murders for now.

"On the one hand, the D.A. wants this in to show Bill's a bad guy," Lasting said. "So that's why we objected. It would be incompetent not to. . . . But I won't mind having the jury hear some of the boat testimony. Let the jury see what a real case looks like—and why the police were so inclined to believe the worst about him once Dennis France came along. Let them compare the evidence in the boat case to the sketchy evidence in the murders. The jury will think he must have done something to be brought in here—let them think it's boats. . . .

"I think the video proves Bill and France were involved in criminal activity together. The question is, what?"

2. From the author's interview with Robert Kuns.

3. From the author's interviews with Richard Lasting and Michael White. Winebaugh died before he could be interviewed by the author.

CHAPTER 23

1. Wendy Mogul testified at Leasure's Board of Rights hearing that she remembered seeing the Studebaker when Leasure was repairing her car at the Leasure home. The receipt for the carburetor bought by Leasure for those repairs showed a purchase date well before the day on which the Studebaker's owner reported his vintage car stolen. Her testimony enabled Leasure's attorney to argue that Leasure could have obtained the Studebaker legitimately, and that later, the previous owner fraudulently reported it stolen in order to collect on an insurance policy. The LAPD

board hearing the case rejected these contentions, finding that they were contradicted by the bulk of the evidence in the case.

2. From the author's interviews with William Leasure, and corroborated by his attorneys.

3. From the author's interviews with Michael White and Richard Lasting.

4. From interviews with Lasting and White.

CHAPTER 24

1. From the author's interview with Detective Tom King.

CHAPTER 25

1. From the author's interviews with Bill Leasure.

2. Ibid.

3. Jury deliberations are secret. The course of the deliberations in the Leasure case, re-created here and in the passages that follow, are based upon the author's interviews with jurors Emma Rodriguez, Terri Villaneuva, Edgar Mito, Thomas Maldonado, and Karen Hawkins. Quotations are drawn from the words of the juror quoted.

4. It was true that what little news coverage there had been during the first trial had focused exclusively on the prosecution's case. But this seemed to be a function of reporters being preoccupied with the simultaneous and vastly more sensational Rodney King police beating case. Pretrial hearings in the King case, in which four police officers were charged with assault, were in progress during the Leasure trial.

5. From the author's interviews with Bill Leasure.

6. According to Bill Leasure. Betsy Mogul would not comment on the decision to accept the plea agreement.

7. From the author's interviews with Bill Leasure and Richard Lasting.

8. Ibid.

9. Ibid.

EPILOGUE

1. From the author's telephone interview with Dennis France.

2. With credit for over two years in jail before reaching her plea bargain, plus another fifteen months "good time credit," Paulette de los Reyes will be eligible for parole in one to two years.

3. From the author's interview with Irene Wong.

4. According to Deputy District Attorney James Koller.